The DAY the REVOLUTION ENDED

19 October 1781

WILLIAM H. HALLAHAN

CASTLE BOOKS

This edition published in 2006 by
CASTLE BOOKS ®
A division of Book Sales, Inc.
114 Northfield Avenue
Edison, NJ 08837

This edition published by arrangement with and permission of
John Wiley & Sons, Inc.
111 River Street
Hoboken, New Jersey 07030

Originally published by John Wiley and Sons, Inc., Hoboken, New Jersey
Published simultaneously in Canada

Illustration credits: page xi: National Park Service; page 2: Courtesy of the R.W. Norton Art Gallery, Shreveport, LA; pages 78, 93, 106, 117, 130, 197: By permission of the Independence National Historical Park.

Library of Congress Cataloging-in-Publication Data:

Hallahan, William H., date.
    The day the Revolution ended / William H. Hallahan
            p.   cm.
    Includes bibliographical references and index.
    1.   United States—History--Revolution, 1775-1783--Campaigns.
    2.   United States—History--Revolution, 1775-1983-Peaces. 3. Generals--United States--History--18th century. I. Title.
    E230.H35   2003
    973.3'37--dc21   2003005317

ISBN-13: 978-0-7858-2260-8
ISBN-10: 0-7858-2260-7

Printed in the United States of America

For Janet, Rick, and Katie

Can We Gain Independency?

A Continent of 1000 miles Sea Coast defending themselves without one Ship of War against 300 Battle Ships completely manned and fitted—a Country that can pay but 30 thousand men, at War with a Nation that has paid, and can pay 150 Thousand—A Country of three millions of inhabitants, fighting with a Nation of 15 million—A Country that can raise but 1 Mil. of Money at War with a Nation who can raise 20 Mil. in specie. A Country without Arms, without Ammunition, without Trade, contending with a Nation that enjoys the whole in the fullest Latitude.

—New Hampshire *Gazette,* January 1776

You cannot conquer a map.

—William Pitt to the House of Commons

Contents

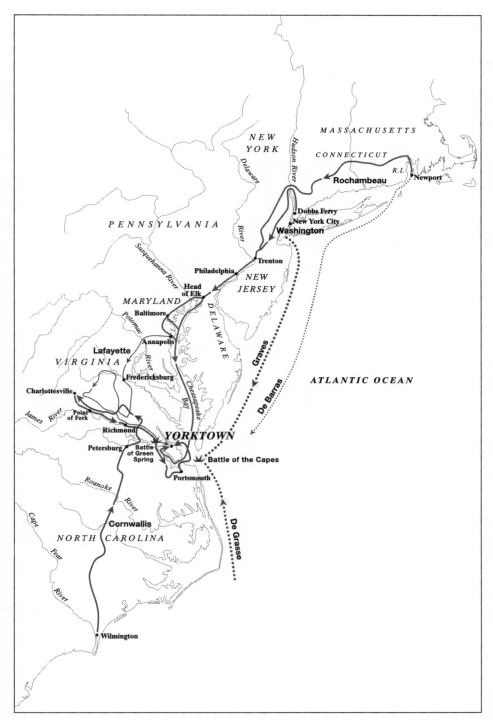

The Battle of Yorktown

One

Adversaries in a Cauldron

On Broadway across from Bowling Green in New York City, Benedict Arnold, American turncoat and now a brigadier general in His Majesty's Royal British Army, limped into British army headquarters. It was late November 1780.

Arnold had been summoned by Sir Henry Clinton, fifty, commanding general of the British forces in North America, to get his marching orders for a new attack on the rebels. This was to be Arnold's first action against his former compatriots, and he had been urging Clinton to let him attack Philadelphia, a storehouse for vast quantities of military supplies and also the seat of the Continental Congress—those dozens of gallows-bait revolutionists whom Arnold hated so passionately. Such a military strike could entomb the revolution. Clinton had declined. Arnold then urged an attack in one of the southern states. Clinton had taken time to think it over.

General Clinton was squirming in a military and political cauldron. Nearly six years after the American Revolution had begun, the British army seemed no closer to defeating the rebels. In fact, for two and a half years, since the Battle of Monmouth in New Jersey, George Washington and his ragged band of starvelings had been waiting a few miles north on the Hudson highlands for Sir Henry to come out of his New York fortress to challenge them again on the battlefield.

The two men sitting here across from each other were the very yin and yang of personalities: phlegmatic Sir Henry, the ever-planning, cautious, slow-to-move British career soldier; and mercurial Arnold, the ever-dangerous, explosive, militarily gifted Connecticut soldier, a legend even among British officers.

As a gifted military strategist and a very reluctant campaigner, Sir Henry—Harry to his friends—was searching desperately for the single masterstroke—entailing very little risk—that would bag that wily American fox, Washington, and ship him to the gallows in London—the stroke that would win the war, shower him with glory, and earn him a statue in St. Paul's Cathedral.

1

Sir Henry Clinton in 1787. A miniature by Thomas Day.
(Courtesy of the R. W. Norton Art Gallery, Shreveport, LA)

And here sitting across from him was the very paladin he needed—this ambulating maelstrom, this brilliant battlefield berserker. In his spanking-new British general's uniform, thirty-nine-year-old Benedict Arnold had one thing on his volcanically erupting mind: revenge. Revenge on the pack of politicians in the Continental Congress who, he believed, had ganged up on him and driven him into his new red coat.

From his first meeting with Sir Henry Clinton, Arnold had talked obsessively about his master plan for personally finishing the revolution. By pouncing on Philadelphia with a cadre of redcoats, he would destroy the vitally important manufacturing infrastructure and supply nexus of the Continental Army there, make an inferno of the supply ships and docks, then, surrounding the State House, pluck from it all his enemies in both the Continental Congress and the Pennsylvania Assembly to haul them in chains across the ocean and fling them at the feet of George III, the whole rotten pack of them, a noose around each neck.

Pennsylvanian Joseph Reed; that New England gang—especially the Adams cousins, Sam and John; Horatio Gates; James Wilkinson; Thomas Conway; and many more. That one stroke could destroy the core of the revolution and bring the resistance to a sudden end.

And toward that end, with Clinton's encouragement, he was busy forming a new, fast-moving, hard-hitting military legion to be composed of the very men who would be most highly motivated to attack—American deserters, each with his personal score to settle.

But as the two talked now, Arnold realized that Sir Harry, while talking about an attack in the South, was issuing some very strange orders.

"You will be pleased to proceed with the troops which are embarked under your command to Chesapeake Bay," Sir Henry told him. And with those 1,600 lightly armed and mobile troops, he was to set up a base of operations there at Portsmouth, strategically situated on the Elizabeth River, right in the comforting shadow of the masts and rigging of British warships—his built-in naval escape hatch in the event of major attack by land or sea.[1]

This was to be a temporary naval and raiding base, not a permanent major military installation. From there he was to mount a series of punishing raids on the Tidewater region. Destroy the rebels' military storehouses, particularly in Richmond and Petersburg. Stop the flow of troop reinforcements and supplies to General Greene in the Carolinas and cause his army in the South to wither and die. Ruin the Virginia economy, which was helping to finance the rebel cause. Most of all, snap the spine of the colonial snake, thereby separating the North from the South, for piecemeal conquest.

Sir Henry also specified certain other activities in those marching orders: Arnold was to issue a call to the Virginia Loyalists, those "well affected to His Majesty's government," then arm and train them—a whole army of them. Arnold was also to build a number of boats and assemble a naval force in Albemarle Sound "for the purpose of annoying the enemy's communications and trade and securing means of intelligence or even of a retreat for his detachment in case a superior French fleet should take a temporary possession of the Chesapeake."[2]

That single thrust into Virginia offered other benefits. It could distract Washington from his plans to invade New York City. It would smooth the royal brow in London. Most important, it could regain the initiative for that fizzling Carolinas campaign from which Clinton had promised London so much.

And always that timid stipulation: Do this only if it can be done "without much risk." Sir Henry wanted daringly safe warfare.

Then Clinton stunned Arnold, must have made him regret turning his coat. Arnold was not getting an unfettered command. He was part of a troika. Going with Arnold were lieutenant colonels Dundas and Simcoe—"officers of great experience and much in my confidence." Further, "I am to desire that you will always consult those gentlemen previous to your undertaking any operation of consequence."[3]

In short, Clinton was putting Arnold on a leash—two leashes. Arnold's actions could be vetoed by the other two lesser officers. In effect, the timorous Clinton was sending his prized new champion into battle handcuffed. Then he weakened his own orders to the level of request. Lord Cornwallis, in the South, would also be able to veto any of Arnold's moves.

Clinton's orders were explicit: "You are directed to obey His Lordship's commands."[4]

This was a typical Clinton move, cautious, equivocal, with built-in escape hatches, creating a self-canceling troika to fight a risk-free battle.

Yet taking risks—audacious, breathtaking risks—was the one feature that had made Arnold such a ferocious, brilliant, and victorious general. One need not guess at Arnold's opinion of Clinton.

No other British general knew the Americans better than Sir Henry. Born in New Brunswick, Canada, he spent many of his boyhood years in New York City while his father, Admiral George Clinton, was royal governor of the Colony of New York. He had gone to school with colonists' sons, and at fourteen received his first military commission, as captain-lieutenant of the New York militia.

Few in the British army had spent more time fighting the rebels. Arriving in Boston right after the Battle of Lexington-Concord, he was present at the Battle of Bunker Hill, which the British, suffering an unimaginable slaughter, won only after the embattled farmers had run out of ammunition and left the field. The slaughter of redcoats on that hill on that day was so great (44 percent casualties—1,154 men and officers killed and wounded) that even the Americans were awed.

Sir Henry had warned General Thomas Gage that the frontal attack uphill against an entrenched enemy was suicidal. He recommended instead that British troops outflank the Americans and cut off their escape route from Bunker Hill. General Gage ignored him.

In the five intervening years, Sir Henry had fought many battles against the American army.

The pivotal moment came on June 28, 1778, a brutally hot day at Monmouth, New Jersey, in a stand-up, head-on, thumb-in-your-eye battle. Clinton had been moving his army from Philadelphia to New York and was caught with a seventeen-mile wagon train behind him. The Americans took on the redcoats in classic European style, musket against musket, bayonet against bayonet. This time, the Americans didn't run out of ammunition, didn't break and run from the deadly British bayonets. Using the British army's own tactics, they were winning when darkness descended. Historians still disagree over who might have won if the light had not failed. It is possible that dusk saved Clinton from the most disastrous British defeat of the war.

The next morning the Americans found that, on the plea of getting his army into camp in New York City, Clinton and his army had slipped away during the night, leaving Washington in possession of an empty battlefield. The Americans claimed victory.

Clinton also claimed victory, but it did not really sit right. He knew the American army had finally gelled. From that moment on it was every bit a match for his own. Since that day, Sir Henry had seemed reluctant to face his adversary again.

Unlike his high-born, aristocratic second in command, Lord Cornwallis, Sir Harry didn't act like the aggressive general he should have been, heavily bemedaled and battle-eager, nor, also unlike Lord Cornwallis, did he look the part. At age fifty, his baggy body had gone soft, his face so coarse-featured he looked more like a publican in a rough neighborhood than a member of the British peerage.

When confronted with the need for action, Sir Henry delayed. He hesitated. He planned to excess, loved to spin out one scheme after another without end, many of them brilliant. But then, unable to settle on one, he settled on none.

One of his major failings was the inability to communicate clearly. He hated to argue with people who disagreed with him, so he came to regard opposition to his ideas as disloyalty to him personally. Yet his subordinates often couldn't figure out what he wanted. In truth, he himself often seemed not to know. Like his handwriting, his orders were undecipherable. Often running for pages, they contradicted themselves. The puzzled readers did what seemed best. Then Sir Harry would complain that they had not carried out his orders.

When confusion brought on failure, Sir Henry would shift blame onto others. He would invent orders from his superiors in London, or single out a subordinate, confront him with previous conversations that never took place, then extract from him abject apologies. He kept notes, listing the errors, failures, and even scraps of conversation of others. As a result, Sir Henry believed himself surrounded by conspiracy.

This neurotic, indecisive, often paranoid manner cost him the friendship of most of his colleagues in America. Few people liked him; fewer trusted him. He was isolated.

Thomas Jones, justice of the Supreme Court of the Province of New York, dismissed Sir Harry in one sentence: "Clinton was one of the most irresolute, timid, stupid and ignorant animals in the world."[5]

Old Major General James Robertson, governor of New York, had observed many times the endless bickering between Sir Harry and the aged, feeble Admiral Arbuthnot, who was so lost in his dementia he often could not remember five minutes later any promises he had made. Robertson described them as "birds of a feather" and opined that "it was hard to tell which was the greater fool."[6]

Admiral Rodney, after his latest visit to New York, let his assessment of Clinton be known all over London: "Nature has not given him an enterprising and active spirit, capable of pushing the advantages he may have gained in battle. But when success has crowned his arms, an immediate relaxation takes place; and his affection for New York (in which island he has four different houses) induces him to retire to that place, where without any settled plan he idles his time and . . . suffers himself to be cooped up by Washington with an inferior army, without making any attempt to dislodge him." Rodney condemned Clinton's officers for putting on plays instead of chasing rebels.[7]

Like most loners, Clinton had few friends in London to speak up for him because he had few friends—which meant that in Whitehall, to counter growing criticism, he had no advocates, while the winsome Cornwallis had many. In a military beauty contest, Clinton would never claim the crown.

Sir Henry also knew that almost every man who served him, down to the lowest stable boy, disliked him—many detested him. Here was a shy man, a diffident man, insecure and deeply tinged with paranoia, who had surrounded himself with a collection of second-raters, smiling incompetents ever ready with gushing praises for their leader. Sir Henry was a passive man in an action job.

He lived in fear that Washington's men, in a reprise of their haunting Christmas night attack at Trenton in 1776, would attack him in his fortress city. On some dark, bitter night in the coming winter, after the Hudson had frozen to five or six feet, the ragamuffin army on bleeding bare feet would come bursting out of a blinding snowstorm across the ice and onto the streets of Manhattan to take him in his bed.

But he was also ever aware that among British generals America was known as the "grave of reputations." And that made him very careful.

On Friday, October 20, 1780, George Washington summoned the twenty-three-year-old commandant of his Virginia light horse legion, Major Henry (Light-Horse Harry) Lee, to his headquarters at Tappan on the Hudson and gave him a stunning mission: Kidnap Benedict Arnold.

Washington had come to rely increasingly on this very young officer who was already an army legend. A passionate Virginian to his bootsoles, Henry Lee was graduated from Princeton at seventeen in 1773 and, several years later, was just about to board ship for law school at London's Middle Temple when the war broke out. Barely twenty, as a newly minted captain of a Virginia cavalry outfit, he rode off to war and fame, which quickly came—particularly after his excellent defense of Eagle Tavern and his raid on Paulus Hook in August 1779. Washington elevated Lee and his cavalry to a key part of his army.

That evening, by the time that he had cantered the twenty miles or so back into his camp in Totowa, New Jersey, Major Lee was very conscious that he had been given one of the strangest assignments any cavalryman had ever received. So serious was this mission that Washington had assured Lee that the man who kidnapped Arnold will "lay me under great obligations personally, and in behalf of the United States I will reward him amply."[8]

Lee had already picked the man to do the job, a battle-seasoned fellow Virginian from Loudoun County, his own highly prized sergeant major, John Champe, twenty-four, who had enlisted in 1776, a trooper "rather above the common size—full of bone and muscle—of tried courage and inflexible perseverance." Major Lee, from a noted Virginia family and the future father of Robert E. Lee, was about to be promoted to lieutenant colonel under a newly formed corps, Lee's Legion. Giving up Champe meant giving up his hard-to-replace top noncom at a crucial time in the legion—that is, of course, if he could convince Champe to take the assignment. When he dismounted, Lee issued a call to Champe to come to his quarters.

Champe refused the job. And for one obvious reason: Champe had to become a deserter. He had to cross the Hudson River into British-held New York City, join a hated turncoat's legion, put on that hated redcoat, then at the right moment enter Arnold's house late at night and with the aid of one other man—one of Washington's spies named Baldwin—drag Arnold down to the river, row him across the Hudson, and turn him over to Major Lee, who would be waiting for him at Hoboken with a party of dragoons.

Champe, a passionate patriot devoted to both his new country and his Virginia legion, had fought valiantly for both during the war. To take Washington's assignment would mean that his fellow troopers would regard him as a traitor. Hanging would be too good for him. His reputation would be ruined for the rest of his life.

Lee countered by saying he had Washington's promise that Champe would be fully restored to his legion, his singular service to his nation extolled with proper citations as well as promotion—which meant a commission, probably as a lieutenant. Major Lee emphasized the glory to be lost to the legion if Washington would turn his quest over to another unit in his army. Someone else would win glory for some other outfit. Champe's comrades would be disappointed with him.

Champe's resistance faded. He agreed, and Lee read him his written instructions.

Champe now turned to the practical problem of deserting. Between the legion camp in Totowa and the Paulus Hook crossing of the Hudson River lay nearly twenty miles of heavily patrolled terrain, which would force him to take a zigzag course around the many checkpoints and ambling night patrols. Lee assured him he would personally delay a pursuing party as long as possible.

Abruptly Champe was gone. It was nearly eleven at night. Major Lee was not sure that Champe would make it as far as the river.

Just before eleven thirty P.M. Captain Carnes, officer of the day, hurried into Major Lee's quarters and reported that a cavalryman had just galloped out of camp. When the mounted night patrol had challenged him, the trooper evaded them and raced off into the darkness. Carnes wanted to raise a party for hot pursuit.

Lee, fighting to give Champe as much lead time as possible, insisted on knowing who the trooper was. Camp personnel spent some time checking. The answer astonished everyone. It was none other than the twenty-four-year-old sergeant major, the legion's top-ranking noncom and one of the legion's heroes, who had gone off "with his horse, baggage, arms and orderly book," obviously not planning to come back. When last seen, he was heading east directly for the Hudson River.[9]

Benedict Arnold had defected to the British weeks before and was calling loudly for American deserters to join him in New York City to form a new American Legion. Washington and the Continental Army were holding their breaths for fear that the new low in morale that Arnold's defection had caused would lead to massive desertions of whole army units. So the flight of a sergeant major from one of Washington's few crack outfits would be sobering news to the Continental soldiers.

Lee spent more time selecting the posse to pursue the defector. Then he pondered the choice of leader, changing his mind several times before he settled on Coronet Middleton, whose youth and inexperience, Lee thought, made him least likely to catch up with Champe.

By the time the pursuers got on the road, Champe's lead was nearly an hour. On and off throughout the night, showers fell. Following Champe's rain-wet sandy tracks, identifiable by the cavalry farrier's mark on the horseshoes, the pursuing party rode eastward. Just past dawn, the dogged Middleton saw Champe in the distance and picked up the pace. The party pursued Champe through the town of Bergen and down to the point at Paulus Hook.[10]

With his pursuers only some 200 yards behind him, Champe dismounted at river's edge, tied his valise onto his back, drew his sword, and dove into the water, swimming toward two British patrol galleys offshore, shouting to them as he swam. The captain of the galleys, sensing Champe was an American deserter, covered his escape with some scattering fire to drive the horsemen off the beach, then lowered a boat to pull Champe onboard.

Lee had been wrong about Coronet Middleton: He had almost nabbed Champe.

Sergeant Major Champe was carried across the Hudson River to New York, where he was held in the provost jail over the weekend to await interrogation. A clerk in the office of the adjutant general's office made an entry in the journal book, *Information of Deserters and Others:* "John Champe, sergeant major in Major Lee's corps, deserted from Passaic Falls last Thursday night."[11]

The following Monday morning, Champe was questioned for two hours, a full hour personally by the commanding general of the British forces in America, Sir Henry Clinton, who was interested in the morale of American troops, hoping that Champe was the beginning of mass American desertions. The sergeant major told him what Lee had coached him to say, opining, among other things, "the soldiery are much dissatisfied with the French." Champe seemed to tell him what he wanted to hear, for at the end of the interrogation, Sir Henry personally tipped Champe two gold guineas, the standard reward for American deserters, and then tried to sign him up for the British army. Champe declined, saying he wanted to find a civilian job. With that he was released and stepped into the streets of New York City.

Within the hour, Champe managed to catch the eye of Benedict Arnold, resplendent in his new, red, custom-fitted British general's uniform. Arnold recognized Champe's green-jacketed dragoon's uniform and hailed him. He told Champe that he was forming a unit to be composed of American deserters, called appropriately enough the American Legion. The unit would have the standard legion mix of cavalrymen and mounted infantry. So far, he claimed, he had signed up more than 200 American deserters and was actively advertising for more in New York newspapers, through his "Address to the Inhabitants."

A sergeant major with years of battle experience, Champe was a catch in any cavalry outfit, but for Arnold Champe was as good as a veteran commissioned officer. In fact, if he'd held out, Champe might have wangled a commission from Arnold because so far Arnold had signed up "8 officers, three sergeants, 28 common soldiers and one drummer."[12]

Recruiting enough officers was Arnold's greatest concern. He had boasted to General Clinton that a large part of the American army would desert after he did. So far it had not happened. Arnold hadn't signed up a single American deserter with an officer's commission, for not one had heeded Arnold's call to cross over. So far. The only officers he had collared were all foreigners.

Nor was Arnold getting any officers from British ranks—and for an obvious reason: When Washington had hanged as a spy the very popular and charming young British officer John André, who had negotiated Arnold's defection, a period of deep mourning settled over the British military establishment. His close friend Lieutenant Colonel Banastre Tarleton ordered his British Legion to wear black on their sleeves. His other close friend, Lieutenant Colonel John Simcoe, attached black and white feathers to the bridles of his Queen's Rangers. Most of the subaltern British officers in particular felt strongly that Arnold should have saved André by surrendering himself to Washington, that André's noose should have been around Arnold's neck. And they were refusing all enticements to serve under him.

Arnold was all alone, a pariah to both sides, in command of a legion of largely stacked muskets and empty tents. If Champe had his way, Arnold would not have even that command for long.

Major Henry Lee now sent a written report to his commanding officer on the progress of the kidnapping plot.

> I have engaged two persons to undertake the accomplishment of your Excellency's wishes. . . . The chief of the two persons is a sergeant in my cavalry. To him I have promised promotion, the other is an inhabitant of Newark; I have had experience of his fidelity, and his connexions with the enemy render him, with his personal qualifications very fit for the business. To this man I have engaged one hund. Guineas, five hundd. acres of land and three negroes. . . . The outlines of the scheme . . . are the Sergeant should join Gen. Arnold as a deserter from us, should engage in his corps now raising, and should contrive to insinuate himself into some menial or military birth about the Genls. person. That a correspondence should be kept up with the man in Newark, by the latter's visiting the former every two days. When the favorable moment arrives they should seize the prize in the night, gag him, and bring him across to Bergen woods. . . . The Sergeant is a very promising youth of uncommon taciturnity, and invincible perseverance. . . . I have instructed him not to return till he receives direction from me, but to continue his attempts, however unfavorable the prospects may appear at first. I have excited his thirst for fame by impressing on his mind the virtue and glory of the act.[13]

Washington replied in a note filled with encouragement, alarm, and careful warnings:

> To Major Henry Lee
> Hd. Qrs. October 20, 1780
>
> Dr. Sir: The plan proposd for taking A——, the out lines of which are communicated in your letter which was this moment put into my hands without a date, has every mark of a good one, I therefore agree to the promised rewards, and have such entire confidence in your management of the business as to give it my fullest approbation; and leave the whole to the guidance of your own judgment, with this express stipulation and pointed injunction, that he A——d is brought to me. No circumstances whatever shall obtain my consent to his being put to death. The idea which would accompany such an event, would be that ruffians had been hired to assassinate him. My aim is to make a public example of him: and this should be strongly impressed upon those who are employed to bring him off.[14]

At Continental Army headquarters in Tappan on the Hudson River, 20 miles north of New York City, and some 400 miles north of an end-of-the-road village named Yorktown, Commanding General George Washington, forty-eight, was battling his biggest enemy—despair. With the onset of another winter, he was thinking seriously of disbanding his army and sending them off to find food for themselves.

His army was completely, irrevocably bankrupt. As another Christmas loomed—his sixth away from home—Washington's war chest was so empty that he had to discontinue the courier service between his headquarters and French general Rochambeau in Newport because, he wrote, "There not being so much money in the hands of the Quarter-Master General as would bear the expense of an Express to Rhode Island." He couldn't afford to feed the courier's horse. In the past two months, he hadn't received a penny to feed his table. "We have," he wrote, "neither money nor credit adequate to the purchase of a few boards for doors to our log huts."[15]

Washington wrote urgently to his aide-de-camp in Paris, John Laurens, for immediate help. "If France delays a timely and powerful aid . . . it will avail us nothing should she attempt it hereafter. We are at the end of our tether."[16]

The arrival of French forces, which had raised hopes so high, proved to be another disappointment. Louis XVI had sent far too few troops, far fewer than he had promised. Worse, he had sent no navy of consequence. Yet on the French navy depended everything—a navy capable of breaking the British blockade that was strangling the American economy, capable of forcing ports open, capable of moving American troops about swiftly over water. More than any other single factor, the British navy had enabled Britain to dominate the war. Washington knew that without a naval force to counter England's, the Americans would ultimately be defeated. Louis understood this. Until he sent a navy, the French king could only dream of revenge on England.

Washington also felt that the dominance of this reborn French navy would be short-lived. After the French and Indian War, England had let much of its navy rot at the piers while France rebuilt hers. But soon enough the British would have the most powerful navy in the world once again; it was the essential factor in their worldwide trade.

Washington could have had no illusions about France's relationship with America. Louis XVI could have no more love for American democracy than did his hated rival, George III. Altruism wasn't Louis's guide; doing George III in the eye was. If in the process America's new kingless republic rotted into the ground, Louis could not have cared less.

Nor did Washington have any illusions about how much command he had over those French troops now bedding down for the winter in Rhode Island. After conferring with Washington about a siege against New York, General Rochambeau had equivocated. Their meeting—their first—ended as nothing more than an icebreaker. Both went back to their camps discouraged, with nothing decided.

Washington by himself did not have the resources to make even a fake attack on New York, which would require some 8,000 barrels of gunpowder.[17] And he did not believe he could rely on the continued presence of those French forces now camped in Rhode Island. Capricious Louis could whistle up those troops to go elsewhere in an instant. In fact, the two allies, France and Spain, both with very weak economies, could sign a separate peace treaty with England at any time. And that would insure the total collapse of the revolution in America.

Washington also had other reasons to despair. The previous spring, Clinton had dealt a staggering blow to the American cause when he sailed out of New York with a large army and captured Charleston, South Carolina. That was almost enough by itself to rend the last tissues of rebel resistance. But with the loss of Charleston came the loss of an entire irreplaceable American army under General Benjamin Lincoln, foolishly trapped inside that city. Then, at Camden, South Carolina, just weeks later, Lord Cornwallis faced a second American army, under command of General Horatio Gates, and utterly crushed it. Those two forces, which might have stopped Cornwallis, were now dying by the thousands on fever-ridden British prisoner-of-war hulks in Charleston Harbor. Few were ever to come home.

At least the worst hadn't happened. Benedict Arnold failed to put Washington, his entire command staff, as well as the plans to West Point into Sir Henry Clinton's hands.

General Cornwallis could now look all the way from South Carolina to Washington's Continental Army camp on the Hudson without seeing any serious military opposition in between.

Washington then put his last cartridge in the chamber. He sent not another army—there was none—but one man, Gen. Nathanael Greene, probably his best general. Resourceful, dogged, endlessly optimistic, Greene had gone galloping down to the Carolinas to take command of the bits and pieces of the American military presence there. Realistically, Greene's troops, outnumbered two to one, demoralized and sick, raw and ill equipped, peppered heavily with unreliable short-term militia, could hardly be expected to stop Cornwallis's battle-toughened redcoat regulars who had the smell of final victory in their nostrils.

But perhaps—somehow—Greene could slow the earl down, perhaps buy time. Perhaps Washington and Congress, with enough breathing space, could scrape together one more effort, one more do-or-die battle, throw a winning haymaker before going down and out. On such improbable dreams had Washington sustained himself for six years. Every once in a while one of them had come true.

Most of the remains of Washington's army were camped around him on the Hudson highlands. Few would call it an army. Barely armed with muskets, many without shoes, lacking blankets and adequate ammunition, on starvation rations, not paid in months, having mutinied repeatedly, his army now faced the most implacable of enemies—winter. Unless help came soon, cold and starvation could do what Clinton couldn't—kill them off in their huts. Disaster like that had happened before: during that winter in Valley Forge, 2,500 men had died of fever, famine, and frost.

But from whence would come any help? The Congress was bankrupt. Reduced to a debating society, all they could do was talk about removing him from command. And that was grimmest humor of all: only a fool would want his job—any successor would likely arrive just in time to sign the instruments of surrender.

The states were in no better condition. Lacking the courage to impose taxes on an increasingly disaffected population, they had printed paper money as fast as the presses could operate until the inevitable happened: They, too, were about to collapse financially.

In that light, Washington had to wonder if his troops had even one more battle left in them. Desperation impelled him to cast about for some way to boost their morale, a morsel of hope that could carry them through gaunt winter's terrible hug—something equal to a major military victory. Something impossible that would lift the spirits of every patriot in all thirteen colonies.

And he felt he might have found it. He would kidnap Benedict Arnold. Now that would be a holiday present for his army: hanging high the Christmas goose in a red coat.

In the French army camp in Newport, Rhode Island, 180 miles from Clinton's headquarters in New York City and nearly 600 miles north of Yorktown, Jean-Baptiste-Donatien de Vimeur, Comte de Rochambeau, commander of the French army in America, sat and fretted.

The count bore a very great burden: On his shoulders rested the honor of France. He had been sent to America at the head of a French army bent on redeeming the humiliation it had suffered in the Seven Years' War against Britain (in America, known as the French and Indian War). The count was driven night and day by the haunting dream—and need—of capturing the battle banners of the British army in a glorious victory, and dropping them at the feet of a purring Louis XVI and a cheering France.

Also, to make up for the loss of Canada and France's other American territories to England eighteen years before, Rochambeau was equally determined to pry loose from George III's stubborn fist his prized American territory—those thirteen priceless colonies.

The count was admirably suited for his assignment. A career soldier with more than thirty-five years in uniform and a master of siege warfare, General Rochambeau, at fifty-five, was appropriately built like a short, stocky battering ram. His face proclaimed the man: unblinking measuring eyes that saw everything—particularly the truth—and a skeptical expression put there by long experience. The scar on the side of his face and his slight limp were his ample battlefield credentials. Capable of great charm and warmth, right now everything about him was buttoned up, reserved, solitary. He oozed no friendliness or warmth, presented a manner that was barely cordial. A man difficult to know, more difficult to impress—a man who well knew that on the battlefield there were no fairy godmothers.

Rochambeau had every reason to pace with frustration. He was in a dangerous position. He had arrived in Newport in July, five months before, with a very inadequate 4,000 troops, and there encountered disaster. The second French squadron bearing the additional troops he had been promised had gotten as far as the seaport of Brest when someone somewhere in the French bureaucracy—someone who did not wish him to find glory—had shunted them elsewhere. He was informed that there would be no more troops for him. His king, Louis XVI, had sent just enough troops and ships to be maddeningly, tantalizingly inadequate. Scraping the bottom of his exchequer, Louis XVI was hoping to buy an enormous victory over England on the cheap.

Then the small French naval force that had carried his half-an-army to America had been promptly bottled up by the British navy, which even now was restlessly pacing outside Narragansett Bay, liable at any time to rush in with a huge British army.

Desperate as he was for more men, Rochambeau's main goal was summed up in his insistent cry: "We must have naval superiority—that is indispensable for the success of the campaign."[18]

Also, he regarded Washington as a huge problem. On paper, the count's French army unit had been sent to serve in the American army under the command of George Washington. Yet while General Rochambeau had to find a way to appear to obey orders, to maintain the most cordial relations and to materially help defeat the British, he would not—could not—follow the orders of a soldier "whose judgment he come to doubt."[19]

For the count was thoroughly unimpressed with this revered American leader, who had tried to conceal from him the weakness of his American army. In addition, Washington's plan to take New York by siege was an absurdity. Although he had brought siege guns with him, the count did not think for a minute that a siege against New York City was the right place to attack the British. Sieges consume vast amounts of time and money. And he was not sure that the American army could last much longer. Besides, he did not have the fleet he would need for such a siege.

There seemed to be no good news anywhere he looked. On his arrival, the general had discovered that the American army he had come to fight beside was almost nonexistent. Further, it was composed in part of ninety-day militia who were little better than goose feathers blowing in the wind, notorious for running off the battlefield at the first shot. Worse, the American Congress was bankrupt and, by its own Articles of Confederation, lacked the power to raise money or to compel the states to raise money. Congress was little more than a convocation of squabbling beggars trying to wheedle from the states what they could not—or dared not—command.

Then there was Lafayette. Comte Rochambeau had just barely been wellborn and disliked the ebullience of this irritating young aristocrat with one of the largest fortunes in France. Indeed, he regarded with contempt this twenty-four-year-old American general, a mere boy who was nothing more than a jumped-up reserve lieutenant from the French army. Also he distrusted his own liaison officer, Major General Chastellux, whom he believed was mocking him behind his back.

In the midst of all this he had been deeply disappointed to learn that his king had passed him over for the key position he desired—that of France's secretary of war. His king had sent him to America, then refused to give him the post because he was out of the country.

In addition, Rochambeau was receiving reports from France that his officers' letters home complained about him for treating them like "rascals or idiots." So his officers' morale was obviously as low as his.[20]

All these facts told General Rochambeau two things: With a punishing New England winter coming rapidly, his position was extremely vulnerable. Clinton, a short sail away in New York, had the troops and the navy to smother the French encampment anytime. So Rochambeau had to conjure up a plan that could take him on the offensive against that old woman Clinton now. Otherwise he would perish.

On December 12, in Philadelphia, 299 miles north of Yorktown, Virginia, the gentlemen of the Congress, greatly agitated, met in their chamber on the second floor of the Pennsylvania State House, directly above the chamber where the Declaration of Independence had been signed and dispatched to George III five years before. They were embroiled in an uproar that was threatening to tear that body to pieces.

As the two fireplaces of the room flamed against the damp chill that was settling in for the winter, the Congress, gripped by the same despair that dogged Washington, sat at their thirteen green baize tables, thinking about the unthinkable: to use the Continental Army to collect the desperately needed, long-overdue fifty million dollars owed by the states.

With that money, Congress could put military shoes on bare feet, fill empty bellies, whistle up smart new uniforms, load up the ammunition wagons—in short, could conjure up a spanking-new army ready to batter down the walls of New York City to crush that insolent British army inside. Could seize victory. Could become an independent nation in full control of its own territory, its own destiny.

Without that money, the Continental cause would become a historical footnote.

Everyone knew that the only way Congress could collect that money from the states was by dunning them—by bringing in an army to kick open the legislative doors, hold the members upside down, and shake the money out of their pockets.

Just weeks before, on October 10, 1780, the New York state legislature declared by resolution that the New York delegates in Congress should introduce the motion "that . . . whenever it shall appear . . . that any State is deficient in furnishing its Quota of Men, Money, and provisions or other Supplies required of such State, that Congress direct the Commander-in-Chief, without delay, to march the Army, or such Part of it as may be requisite, into such State; and by a Military Force, compel it to furnish its deficiency."[21] Less than a month later, on November 8, 1780, at the regional Hartford Convention, delegates from all four New England states clutched the New York resolution to their collective bosom and ordered it be introduced to Congress forthwith—the following month. The bill even earned the endorsement of General Washington: "We can never manage the publick Interests with Success till this Disposition [to collect funds by way of military arms] becomes general."[22]

Now, on December 12, the proposal had arrived at Congress's doorsill.

No one was more aware than the members of Congress that the United States was neither united nor a country. No one was more aware that the Congress was powerless. It had no executive except in name only—President—had no court system, had no powers of consequence, certainly no power to tax anything. All bills had to be passed by unanimous vote. A single negative, out of thirteen, could kill a proposal.

Money was raised by passing the hat among the states, which like as not ignored it. Deliberately made harmless, the Congress was a confederation of thirteen independent countries, all deeply distrustful of and hostile toward each other, forced together to make common cause. A Delian League, a League of Nations, a NATO agglomeration, a UN, the Congress was little more than any of those. It was expected to deal only with the army and with foreign affairs, leaving the rest to the states. Most states behaved as though the Congress was a temporary arrangement that would be folded up and put in a closet when—and if—ever peace came.

Two intractable problems prevented Congress from collecting money by force. First were the Articles of Confederation themselves. These had never been ratified. Maryland, nagged by a border dispute with Virginia, still held back its ratifying vote. So in effect, Congress was not even a legal body. Further, the Articles, once approved, still did not specifically delegate powers of taxation—Sam Adams bellowed that the Articles specifically forbade such acts. Many congressmen had wanted for years to impanel a committee of skilled lawyers to study the wording of the Articles of Confederation to seek for any implied powers to tax, but this had always encountered stiff opposition.

One fact seemed to be clear to everyone except Samuel Adams and Richard Henry Lee of Virginia: A government that does not have the authority to raise money is no government at all. No tax, no army. No army, no liberty. No liberty, British gallows.

It wasn't as though the individual states didn't know this, didn't understand. A committee of the Congress had recently sent to the states the latest in a series of solemn warnings: "There is no money in the treasury, and scarce any provision in the public magazines. The states are greatly deficient in the quotas of money, they have been called on for. More than fifty millions of dollars, of the quotas that have come due to this time, remain unpaid. . . . In consequence of which the army begin again to be in want, and without immediate and decisive exertions for their relief they must disband or provide for themselves."[23]

The time was past when states could try to outwait each other. All of them wanted freedom, yet most of them were waiting for the other states to pay for it. Now they had to send in the lucre—not those worthless fire-starters, but real money, specie—or become once more low-rung colonies fettered to the British Empire. If that happened, the money-starved debt-ridden George III would teach them how to use an army to collect taxes—taxes to pay for the war he had conducted against them.

Yet Congress might have been trying to shake leaves from a tree in winter. The states, barely five years old, were also on the verge of financial collapse themselves. The British navy was strangling the American economy.

The circumstances confronting the Congress were nothing short of terrifying. In retrospect, 1780 had been one of the worst years of the revolution: the fall of Charleston, the loss of Lincoln's army, the loss of Gates's army, the betrayal of Benedict Arnold, the sweeping success of Cornwallis in the Carolinas. Every observant person knew wherein lay the problem. The Continental Congress had been crafted by courageous, intelligent leaders—statesmen—who then went home. They sent back politicians.

Washington pointed at "the fatal policy too prevalent in most of the states, of employing their ablest Men at home." He said bluntly,

"Congress is rent by party. Much business of a trifling nature and personal concernment withdraws their attention from matters of great national moment. . . . Do not . . . let our hitherto noble struggle end in ignominy."[24]

Bleak-eyed Congressman Ezekiel Cornell wrote to his fellow Rhode Islander, General Nathanael Greene, with consternation:

> We have not one farthing of Money in the Treasury. And I know of no Quarter, from which we have a right to expect any. Yet we go on Contented, pleasing ourselves with the sanguine hopes of reducing New York. I have seen many new sceens, before I came to this place. But what I have experienced since exceeds anything I have ever seen before. I never before se[e] a set of men that could quietly submit to every kind of difficulty that tended to the ruin of their Country, without endeavouring to make one effort to remove the obstruction. I beleive they wish their Country well, but suffer their time almost wholly to be taken up in business of no Consequence.[25]

People were now openly saying that Congress couldn't get the job done. And everyone knew what that meant—a man on a white horse was needed. Indeed, the idea of handing the government over to Washington rippled constantly through the minds of the desperate congressmen. No secret this. Congressman Cornell wrote to General Greene that the need to make Washington dictator was discussed "as the only means under God by which we can be saved from destruction." "Saved from ourselves," he should have said.[26]

Waiting at the doorway, eager to confront the new bill—to smother it—waited Mr. Liberty himself, Samuel Adams of Massachusetts, and his "Yankee phalanx."

Still bitterly remembering colonial life under an arbitrary, unjust king, Sam Adams feared the idea of a powerful Congress more than he feared the waiting king's noose. Everyone saw that time had passed him by. In his out-of-date-clothing, ill-fitting wig, and palsied hand, the man who had brilliantly ignited the revolution was now out of step, out of touch, and very much in the way. He wanted history to be fixed forever on April 19, 1775, his moment of victory. When the clock of history refused to be stopped, he tried to hang onto the pendulum. But instead of stopping the clock, he had caused one near disaster after another.

He rose up now in the Congress to vehemently assert that the idea of Congress voting itself authority over the states was nothing short of "tyranny." Every congressman there knew what that meant. This noted master of parliamentary legerdemain was going to bottle up the bill in committee to prevent a full debate on the floor, where it might, just might, someday, stand a chance of passage.

The proponents of the Hartford bill tried one other tactic. They moved—once more—to have a committee appointed to study the Articles for a source of "implied powers." And they watched—once more—as it was tabled.

Politically paralyzed, the most pessimistic members had to wonder if the rebellion would even last the next few weeks to Christmas.

In London, King George III felt his throne rocking. The year 1780, which had started out oh so splendidly, had metamorphosed into a baggywrinkled horror. England was already struggling under a national debt of 200 million pounds sterling, much of it going back to the Seven Years' War. The American war alone had so far cost seventy million pounds, with no victory in sight. Agents of the crown were shopping for new loans in Europe and finding very high interest rates. Worse still, the American war had done ferocious damage to the British economy: Unemployment was high, and the West Indies trade was in ruins, while other businesses that had traded with the colonies in peacetime had either gone bankrupt or had suffered along for years while waiting for the war to end and the trade to resume. The founder of Methodism, John Wesley, traveling throughout England, warned Lord Dartmouth that working men were starving to death and rebellion was in the minds of the masses.[27]

John Adams, watching from Paris, informed Congress that during the winter of 1780 some twenty-five English counties passed resolutions hostile to the crown, mainly for wasting public funds but also for the crown's undue interference in public matters and, as always, the nose-holding corruption of Parliament. On March 28 the county of York declared that the cause of all England's troubles was the American war. Two weeks later, the Freeholders of Surrey declared unanimously that "the corrupt influence of the crown" and "the ill-founded assertions . . . in Parliament" had caused the American war, and that the American war was the cause of "the present calamitous situation of the country."[28]

That 1775 "minor" riot in Boston had blown into a full-scale revolution and then, ever expanding, evolved into world war with France, Holland, and Spain. Now, while everything was deadlocked, terrifying sums of money were draining out of the king's exchequer, a dangerously weakened economy was threatening to collapse, and a growing caterwaul of critics—many in high places—wanted him to end the war on any terms. The king was running out of time, out of money, out of support—out of options. If only he could win in America. If only that General Clinton would bestir himself anew.

The worst time had come six months earlier, during the week of June 2–9. The mentally unstable Lord George Gordon had stirred up cataclysmic mob riots that had rocked England and ruined George III's national birthday celebration on June 4. The effects were to be felt for years.

It all began when Lord Gordon, an unhinged Protestant fanatic, a nephew of the Duke of Atholl and godson of George II, brooding over the minor concessions Parliament had granted Catholics two years before, set out to erase them. His self-proclaimed Protestant Association was nothing more than a collection of motley mobs from the smoldering underclasses, wildly drunk on Gordon's gin, freely given and seemingly endless, and whipped into a destructive orgy by Gordon's frenzied orations. London watched, immobilized by fear, as mobs destroyed Roman Catholic churches and torched many businesses. The worst London fire since the Great Fire of 1666 quickly burned out of control. The mobs had paralyzed London. Gordon warned the first minister, Lord North, that he would turn his mob loose on the cabinet itself if those concessions to Catholics were not rescinded.

In the House of Lords the lord chancellor sat clutching his seat in terror. The magistrates were so frightened that they abandoned their duty to put down the rioters. Not one of them dared to raise a hand. Finally, George III himself grasped the nettle. He assembled his Privy Council, from whom, with the help of the attorney general, he had coaxed a ruling to suspend the Riot Act, which was required to be read aloud before attacking the drunken, looting mobs. The king prepared to personally lead his Guards into the London streets to scatter the riots. "I lament," he said, "the conduct of the magistrates, but I can answer for *one* who will do his duty."[29]

When the last rioter had been chased off the streets, more than 300 people were dead. The mobs had not gone quietly; in Fleet Street they had wildly attacked armed soldiers. Many credited George III's stern moves with stopping even greater bloodshed.

London—England—worn down by the ever-growing war, was close to despair. Many believed the riots had gone far beyond anti-Catholicism and had begun to smack of the revolution in America. Only the greatest of military victories could have raised British hearts, and that's what they got—from America an awesome joyous victory, the taking of Charleston and the capture of an entire American army.

The storming of Charleston by itself was a major American defeat. It had been an economic beehive in banking and insurance and a thriving port for South Carolinian merchants who, through blockade runners, had supplemented lost trade with England with more profitable trade with European countries, three of which were at war with England: France, Spain, and the Netherlands.

Charleston had also been an auction port for teeming privateers whose captures of British shipping were punishing the British economy.[30] For years, the Carolinas and Georgia had been peaceful backwaters of the revolution where roaring economies had made fortunes for many and given vital financial and military support to the revolutionists up north. The capture of that city changed all that.

London became hysterical. General Clinton was a national hero, toasted in every home and tavern. Self-confidence returned briefly. The king informed Clinton that he had saved the country from civil war.

Two months later, England had another heady victory and another hero to toast when Lord Cornwallis destroyed a second American army under former British officer General Horatio Gates, who fled the battlefield. He followed that up with a series of sharp skirmishes and barn burnings that brought about the complete collapse of resistance in South Carolina.

Surely now peace was at hand; even the most stubborn Americans must see the folly of further resistance. But in October, instead of a third victory, London was fed the crushing news of Kings Mountain, where Tennessee mountain men armed with rifles had snuffed out Cornwallis's entire left wing to a man, hanging a number they hadn't managed to kill on the battlefield.

King George III had pressured the Secretary of State for American Colonies, Lord George Germain, and General Clinton to defeat the damned rebels and ship their leaders to London to be hanged. It was small consolation to know that Louis XVI's exchequer was weaker; that Spain's was the weakest of all; that the colonists' economies were all about to collapse. George's own royal exchequer was still draining at a mind-numbing rate. Financiers warned that England's economy could collapse. Time was running out.

Frosty, imperious, widely disliked because of his unpleasant personality, considered contemptible by many, Lord George had responded to the king's pressure with his current war policy, a brilliant conception. Everyone had said so, at least until recently.

Lord George, at sixty-five, was literally in a crucible. Appointed in November 1775, months after the Battle of Lexington/Concord, he had from the beginning tried to quarterback a very fluid war situation from London, 3,000 miles away, often with dismal consequences. He quarreled with Howe, with Carleton, with Clinton. A large share of the disaster at Saratoga, among others, rested on his shoulders. And now he was interfering in the relationship between Clinton and Cornwallis.

Germain was no fool. He had his administrative virtues. He also had had a brilliant military career, showing great courage in battle—at Fontenoy his attack was so violent he drove through the French lines and into the tent of the king of France, where he was stopped only by severe wounds. By 1755 he had been elevated to brigadier general, only to suffer a great fall. At the Battle of Minden, he questioned an order that would have led his group into a victorious final charge. Obeying the order too late, he was court-martialed on orders of the furious King George II for cowardice. Although the court found him guilty only of disobedience of orders, it also deemed him unfit to serve in any way in the army. His name was struck from the list of the king's Privy Councillors. Many considered his punishment unjustified.

Entering Parliament, he soon launched a second career in politics. In time, with persistence, he wiggled his way into the cabinet of the young King George III where, unfit to serve in the army, he was appointed head of it.

Lord George, never in America, knew the nature of his colonial enemy only through hearsay and gossip—which is to say, he understood the American not at all.

In his new policy of 1780, Germain had envisioned a swift, two-part plan of conquest. First the British army, in splendid array with banners flying, brass band blaring, would recruit legions of young American Loyalists, putting them in red coats under British officers. Lord George had been assured that there were literally multitudes—armies—of such Loyalists in the Carolinas, sons of the enormously rich planters of rice and indigo, all eager to be brought under British war banners. No one, Lord George had been assured, hated the rebels more than these young American Loyalists. They would fight like tigers.

The British army would create a series of forts in a strategic arc throughout South Carolina. When the Carolina Loyalists had volunteered in sufficient numbers, after proper British army training they would take over control of those forts under a cadre of British officers. The ideal loyalist unit would be mounted—dragoons who could fight from the saddle with their sabers, and mounted infantry who could rush to a battle site, dismount, and function like classic infantry with musket and bayonet.

The second part of his plan was equally brilliant. So they said. These young Loyalist tigers would range out from their forts to attack rebels everywhere—terrorize them; subject them to shooting, hanging, imprisonment, barn burnings; break their will with a brutal, unforgiving scorched-earth program, and thereby keep them scattered and unorganized, disarmed and harmless, until they submitted on their knees once more to royal control.

After the pacification of South Carolina, Lord Cornwallis would then march up into North Carolina and repeat the process: Subdue it, leave it in the hands of newly recruited North Carolinian Loyalists inside a string of forts there, then continue the rollup through Virginia all the way to New York.

"Brilliant" was the word used around Whitehall and Parliament. Lord Germain was literally changing the nature of the colonial war—from a revolution fought between Americans and British redcoats to a civil war fought between rebel Americans and loyalist Americans. The new warfare would save the king the need of an entire British army in America, freeing those troops to fight elsewhere. George III would tuck a handsome saving into his scarred and dented exchequer. The British army could then function much like a coat holder. And in time, the colonists would be groveling at the royal feet.

Lord George's new policy, pleasing to the king himself, had been promptly endorsed by General Clinton in New York. In fact, Sir Henry had just the man for that job—his prickly second in command, General Lord Charles Cornwallis, Germain's favorite.

At first everything had gone very well indeed: the fall of Charleston, the destruction of Gates's army. Then came the reverses that quickly led to the crushing disaster of Kings Mountain. Now the crown was frowning again. Morale in London was sagging badly once more. Protesting voices, at first murmuring, were now becoming strident.

Lord George fired off letter after letter to America, demanding action—demanding success. With all eyes on him, he fumed in his cabinet offices and angrily awaited the next and ultimate victory.

In Versailles, the twenty-seven-year-old king of France, Louis XVI, having seized the British lion by the tail and twisted it with great gusto, now found himself in a quandary: After four years of trying, he still had not gotten the cat in the cage. And if he wasn't careful, the cat could cage him with another crushing military defeat in the New World.

Six years before, in 1775, Louis at age twenty-one had climbed onto the French throne, just in time to get a front-row seat to the tumultuous ripping fight between the frustrated lion and her thirteen cubs. For several years he had watched with intense pleasure the agony of the British lion as she wore herself down fighting a treasure-draining transatlantic war.

Louis, like the rest of France, still brooded over the humiliating Treaty of Paris of 1763 that had ended the Seven Years' War and cost the French, among many other things, all of Canada. Unceremoniously kicked out of the New World, France had been publicly humbled.

The American colonies were George III's most valuable economic asset, and his most vulnerable. England had built her entire mercantilist economic system around those absolutely priceless thirteen colonies and had been mercilessly pumping pure gold out of them decade after decade, while many in France had watched and waited for the Americans, no longer fearful of French intrusions from Canada, to rebel against those repressive policies.

The rebellion finally came. And with it came Louis's chance for *révanche.*

From the young king's viewpoint, if America became an independent nation hostile to England, the British economy would be absolutely crushed for years to come. George III would be nearly bankrupt, unable to conduct any war against France in the foreseeable future. *La Belle France* would dominate Europe and the seas. If he worked the right levers, Louis was looking at one of the biggest military bargains in French history. He was also looking at a humiliated England coming to the treaty table under French terms.

But timing had been everything: From the beginning, the biggest danger had been jumping into a war against the British just in time to see the colonies reconciled with the parent country, leaving a furious and unfettered England free to turn and attack France.

In short, the American Revolution was both a golden opportunity and a grave danger for France. And, predictably, it produced a squabbling court fight between the aggressive English-baiting Anglophobic minister of foreign affairs, the Comte de Vergennes, who saw only the opportunity for *révanche,* and Louis's cautious comptroller general of finances, Turgot, who saw only the pitfalls. Queen Marie Antoinette settled the issue. Intruding herself into court politics, she engineered the dismissal of Turgot and his restraining hand. Vergennes was free to go baying after British blood.

Even with Turgot gone, however, Louis XVI still proceeded cautiously—secretly—watching and waiting for signs that the Americans were ready to fight to the death.

Benjamin Franklin, that American master of manipulation, and his cohorts, Silas Deane and Arthur Lee, assured Louis that the Americans would fight to the death, but only if they had the war tools to fight to the death with. In short, they asked Louis XVI for a secret military loan. Louis smelled a bargain, and he lifted the lid on the royal coffers: Out came Roderigue Hortalez et Compagnie, a dummy operation that, beginning in 1777, secretly pumped money and supplies from France to the revolutionists.

From Hortalez had come the equipment for Washington's Christmas night attack on Trenton, which had saved the Revolution and which impressed Louis profoundly; from it also had come the equipment for Saratoga, by which the Americans had captured Burgoyne's entire army—the turning point in the war. The Americans had shown not only that they were ready to fight to the death but that also, properly helped, they could defeat England. Louis felt he was going to get a splendid bargain for his money.

That utterly convincing win at Saratoga told Louis XVI the time had come to openly back the Americans. He could now get in on the winning side, reaping all the advantages that would belong to the first European nation to recognize the new nation.

Louis XVI made his move. In 1778, with both joy and trepidation, the young king openly signed two major treaties with *les américains*. In the first, Louis officially recognized the complete independence of the United States, severing them permanently from England. In the second, Louis welded France and America together in an alliance against England, thereby heading off any potential reconciliation between George III and his former colonies.

With the two treaties, Louis had promised the Americans three weapons the Americans absolutely had to have: an army, a navy, and a bankroll. Then, with the arrival of General Rochambeau and his troops in Rhode Island in July 1780, France's commitment became irrevocable.

Yet Louis had already missed or botched a number of opportunities that could have finished the war. With General Rochambeau sulking in Rhode Island, demanding more troops and a full-sized navy, with the British tearing into the Carolinas, and with the American economy about to collapse, Louis found himself on a very hot griddle indeed. For all his caution, had he bet on the wrong side? Were the Americans about to lose? Was he? Unless he did something soon, he was in danger of having a great opportunity skitter through his fingers. Opportunity would turn into disaster.

But if he kept his head, played his cards in the right sequence—and moved swiftly enough—the British could soon be booted out of the New World. The best revenge is revenge.

Assigned to the recruiting sergeant's barracks of General Arnold's American Legion, Sergeant Major John Champe waited several days before making contact with Baldwin, his co-conspirator. One of Washington's most capable spies, Baldwin lived across the Hudson in Newark, New Jersey. He had already been contacted, his price already established. It was so high it underlined Washington's passionate determination to lay his hands on Arnold: "One hundred guineas, five hundred acres of land and three Negroes."[31]

The kidnapping went far beyond Washington's description of "an indispensable, delicate and hazardous project."[32] Done right under the noses of the British, it was an oddsmaker's nightmare. New York City inside Clinton's paranoid defenses was such a tightly closed fortress, American deserters had a difficult time penetrating the walls to get inside to surrender. Getting out would be equally difficult. Furthermore, Benedict Arnold at thirty-nine was still a very powerful violent man with an explosive temper, as unstoppable as a burst dam—a living legend whose ferocious exploits as an American officer had awed even the British. He would never go quietly.

The location of the house was another problem. A mansion at 3 Broadway, Arnold's residence stood amidst a neighborhood of prosperous homes, and had a garden with a picket fence next to a lane that ran down to the Hudson River. It was directly across the street from Bowling Green, an egg-shaped park wrapped by a wrought-iron fence, inside which gentlemen of the town played bowls. But most troubling of all, the house was right next door to General Clinton's heavily guarded British army headquarters. Twenty-four hours a day Arnold's home stood in full view of armed guards.

The two kidnappers were expected to break into the back of Arnold's home, pull him from his bed, tie him up, and drag him down an alley to the Hudson River. From there they were to boat him across the Hudson into the waiting arms of Lee's dragoons. Arnold was then to be hastened to George Washington's headquarters and, after a suitable public trial, hanged by the neck until dead.

After discussing the assignment, Champe and Baldwin agreed to meet again to plan the details of the kidnapping. They needed to find some way to reduce the extremely long odds they faced.

In parting, Champe gave Baldwin a letter to transmit to Major Lee, reporting the events since his escape—his weekend in prison, his interview with General Clinton, his meeting with Arnold, his enlisting in Arnold's American Legion. Champe intended next to file a detailed plan for the kidnapping that Lee and Washington could discuss.

The sergeant major thereupon spent a few days getting acquainted with Manhattan and particularly the neighborhood around Arnold's house. The site for the abduction was far from ideal. Inexperienced as he was in the art of conspiracy, Sergeant Major Champe could see that this was going to be exceedingly difficult. And there was only one path away from failure: to the gallows.

In New York City, Benedict Arnold, a man with much to prove, struggled with his biggest problem—finding men to flesh out his American Legion. So far few American deserters had turned up, and his sailing date was getting ever closer.

Meantime, he was working night and day to get his Virginia strike force provisioned, packed, and boarded on ships. Sailing the restless gray Atlantic, in grim December, and landing in Virginia in the depths of winter, he had to provision his troops accordingly. Tons of food, military supplies, horse feed, uniforms, blankets, tents, ammunition, cannons, small arms, gunpowder—the list was long—had to be requisitioned, transported to dockside, swung onboard, and stowed belowdecks. All that tonnage would require forty-two ships.

The quartermasters, supply officers, ordnance officers, dockmasters, and many others soon became familiar with that notorious figure. A swarthy, powerful face set pugnaciously on a forward-thrusting neck announced Benedict Arnold's personality to the world. Pale gray eyes that few men ever forgot served as a warning. Standing about five feet nine—middling tall for those days—with an intimidating arrogant bulk to him, Arnold's Heathcliffian personality was ever aggressive, humorless.

If offending people, picking quarrels, and making enemies can be an art form, then Benedict Arnold was its grand master. And if ever a man was his own worst enemy, that, too, was Benedict Arnold. Driven by a hurricane of pride that he was often unable to control, he was guided by an ethical astrolabe that often was not able to control him.

Benedict Arnold was not the man to have for an enemy—a brilliant tactician, a masterful improviser, an inspired leader of men, possibly the best general on either side of the revolution. Born January 14, 1741, in Norwich, Connecticut, great-grandson of a Rhode Island governor, Benedict Arnold, who at age five lost his father, had set out in his teens to become a pharmacist, soon showed a head for business, acquired some ships, and, pursuing maritime trade, became a master mariner, trading extensively with the Caribbean islands and Quebec.

When the shooting started in Concord-Lexington, his business in New Haven, Connecticut, was going sour partly because of the British embargoes, while his marriage was going sour because his morose wife believed a slanderous tale that he had contracted a venereal disease in the islands. She was declining to sleep with him.

When the town council refused to issue weapons to his militia unit, he broke into the town arsenal, took them by force, armed his men, and marched to Boston, where he quickly sold the idea of storming Fort Ticonderoga.

At dawn, on May 10, 1775, accompanied by Ethan Allen's Green Mountain Boys, he climbed over the walls and captured that fort by stealth. Arnold had revealed to the revolutionists a great general. He also put the Continental congressmen in a quandary. Still unclear about their revolutionary objectives, and still expecting a negotiated settlement with the crown, they insisted that Arnold make a meticulous inventory down to the last cannonball, against the day when they might have to return the fort to Britain.

Arnold went on from one legendary performance to another, including the almost unbelievable march on Quebec through the wilds of Maine in the middle of winter, and on December 31, 1775, the foolhardy blizzard-blind assault on that city that came within a whisker of succeeding.

His performance at the Battle of Valcour Island on October 11–13, 1776, was nothing short of extraordinary, almost Baron Munchausen in its improbabilities. To stop General Carleton from marching down from Canada to Fort Ticonderoga, Arnold, who was a masterful seaman, promptly built and scrounged a Lake Champlain navy, forcing Carleton to stop and gather another. Although outnumbered and outgunned, his fifteen-ship fleet blown to pieces and sinking, he accomplished his objective. He had outgeneraled—outadmiraled—Carleton and, in the process, had so battered his forces that Carleton, though technically victorious, decided it was now too late to continue his invasion down through the Hudson Valley before the onset of the northern winter. Had Arnold not stopped him, Carleton would have laid the groundwork for Burgoyne to sweep down to New York City, where he could have extinguished the Revolution still in its swaddling clothes. Arnold thereby had bought the revolutionists time—vitally needed time—to get their revolution up and walking.

Yet instead of receiving wild adulation, he found himself unappreciated. While he was battling the British, other officers were lobbying the Continental Congress, pushing themselves ahead of him. That ever-bickering, party-riven body preferred men from their own states while trying to shove aside other men from other states. As a result, the Congress jumped five lower-seniority generals over Arnold's head, some of them with no battle experience, all of them commissioned after him, all now outranking him. It was a shabby bit of political jobbery, but it showed his lack of support in Congress, a bad omen for Arnold's career.

He demanded that his seniority be restored. Despite Washington's strong backing, a cadre in Congress blocked the correction. Eventually his commission was properly predated, ranking him ahead of the five others once more but not before damage had been done.

Arnold resigned his commission. Then, when the Battle of Saratoga loomed, he quickly withdrew his resignation and hurried north to Albany. He was now at war with both Britain and the politicians in his own Congress.

In Albany, he covered himself with controversial glory. While Burgoyne was heading south down the Hudson Valley to Albany, part of his army under St. Leger was coming from the west through the Mohawk Valley to deliver a crushing blow to the revolutionist's rear.

With 800 men, Arnold hastened to confront St. Leger's troops and found them besieging Fort Stanwix, the last barrier between them and their linkup with Burgoyne. Arnold created a brilliant ruse. Possibly at the suggestion of Lt. Col. John Brooks, Arnold sent to Fort Stanwix a mental defective named Hon Yost Schuyler whom St. Leger's Indians believed to be a soothsayer. Arnold had carefully instructed Hon Yost to tell the Indians that General Benedict Arnold was coming with 2,000 Americans. Hon Yost was to assure the Indians that Arnold was coming only for the British and the Loyalists, that he had no quarrel with the Indians.

With no enemy, no plunder, and no prospect of scalps, the Indians promptly debouched. The troops under St. Leger then fled. Although some later historians suggest that St. Leger's siege against Fort Stanwix was failing and that the Indians were about to leave anyway, the Hon Yost story redounded to Arnold's credit.

Returning to Albany, Arnold persuaded Gates to adopt a truly inspired battle plan that centered on creating an impregnable roadblock. During the ensuing Battle of Saratoga Arnold's leadership on the battlefield on day two and particularly day three breached the British perimeter and helped bring about the surrender of Gentleman Johnny Burgoyne's entire army. It also bestowed on Arnold a severe leg wound that left him with a lifelong limp.

In order to allow Arnold's wound time to heal, Washington sent him to Philadelphia as military governor of that city. It turned out to be one of Washington's worst mistakes. After nine months of brutal occupation, the British army had abandoned a sacked Philadelphia to reoccupy New York. Flocking back into Philadelphia came the Continental Congress and the Pennsylvania Assembly, followed by hoards of exiled revolutionists who were quickly caught up in a maelstrom of political conflicts. Arnold's strength was never in politics or diplomacy, yet here he was confronted with a bubbling stew of patriotism, opportunism, and corruption that would have baffled even the most adroit solon.

Many of the radicals were intent on attacking, disemboweling, and hanging the Loyalists and Quakers who had shared the city with the British. Yet these self-proclaimed patriots were also the selfsame opportunists who quickly moved in to confiscate properties of accused—and falsely accused—Loyalists at knockdown prices in depreciated paper money. Part of the job of the military governor was to protect the Loyalists and Quakers from such double-handed vigilantism.

With warehouses stuffed with goods of disputed ownership, Arnold was also confronted with hundreds of decisions that were bound to offend one side or the other—often both. Arnold soon found himself surrounded by rabid hostility.

This was an age when insider business deals were accepted as the norm—done by businessman, soldier, politician—and in a city filled with an avalanche of such deals, Arnold saw all around him the war profiteers making fortunes and publicly parading their new wealth, saw logrolling politicians making their own deals while ignoring bills for the relief of an army that was barefoot, hungry, unpaid, and about to collapse.

Washington personally was unable to send messages to his French army counterpart for lack of pocket money to pay an express rider. Grain that by law should have gone to the army was sent instead to the Caribbean Islands, where it was sold for hard currency or—even harder to endure—sold for gold to British troops in New York City. Arnold never forgot the terrible winter in Valley Forge where the troops had no winter clothing—where 2,500 men died. Other officers were crossing the ethical line every day.

Arnold was very unhappy with his personal financial state. His pay as a Continental general was $300 a month and he hadn't been paid in years, not even in worthless paper Continentals. Arnold, still the businessman with his own business interests to take care of, war or no war, began making business deals.

In cahoots with James Mease, the clothier general, and his deputy, William West, Arnold made a killing in the clothing market by buying clothing on army credit, selling it to the clothing-hungry public at huge prices, taking their profit right off the top, and returning the borrowed funds. Clothing not sold was put in the army inventory. With his unfirm grip on ethics, Arnold could point out that such practices were going on all around him. Yet this was the very sort of crime he, as military governor, was supposed to uncover and bring to justice.

Arriving in Philadelphia in a highly visible coach-and-four with liveried servants, Arnold began living in a style he felt was expected of the military governor. He set up headquarters in the John Penn house, which had previously been used as General Howe's headquarters. To his home and table to partake of his lavish entertainments came congressmen, city leaders, radicals, revolutionists, Loyalists, Quakers, privateers, businessmen, even the French ambassador. Arnold paid for some of this from his personal funds, some from his business dealings. But his critics ranted that he was living like a grand panjandrum, far beyond his known income, and that far too much of his socializing was done among Loyalists who had recently been cozy with General Howe.[33]

In one of his most visible transgressions, he was accused of going well beyond just protecting the known Loyalists of the town when, at thirty-eight, he pursued the vivacious nineteen-year-old Margaret ("Peggy") Shippen, daughter of the Loyalist Edward Shippen, former chief justice of Pennsylvania.

Arnold was playing into the hands of his enemies. A whispering campaign began—behind-handed gossip in the city's drawing rooms, in the halls of the State House, in neighborhood taverns, and in the patrician City Tavern. Then Timothy Matlack, a politically connected Presbyterian lawyer, attacked Arnold in the newspapers. Pennsylvania Assembly President Joseph Reed next took up the cudgels: Asking blunt questions on the floor of the Assembly, he called for an investigation of Arnold.

Like Gulliver, Benedict Arnold found himself bound by countless Lilliputian threads, and he reacted with impotent rage. Soon he was amazed to find himself fighting for his military life. The politicos called for an official army inquiry. The inquiry led to charges. Arnold, playing the outraged innocent, turned to fight. Showing great oratorical gifts as his own defender, he fought his critics through the civil court trial, then the ensuing military court-martial. His detractors lacked proof, and Arnold was all but vindicated. Into his army record went a trifling charge of improperly issuing a military pass, which included a reprimand from Washington so softly worded it was actually highly complimentary. Arnold had beaten the politicians, and he had beaten them at their own game.

It could have stopped there. But even the minor reprimand infuriated him. He wanted total vindication. He felt that his brother officers had not rallied behind him, that Washington had been slow and halfhearted in his defense. Full of self-justification and injured pride and goaded by young Peggy Shippen, now his wife (his first wife had died in June 1775), and her Loyalist friends, he cast about for revenge. He found it in treason.

Predictably, turning his coat from blue to red proved as tempestuous as everything else he had undertaken. Instead of an impulsive act of personal outrage, his treason became a calculated business deal, requiring more than a year and half of negotiations with the dilatory Clinton. To make the entire package irresistible to Clinton, Arnold managed to get himself appointed commanding officer of the West Point defenses on the Hudson River that for years had completely blocked the British from sailing up the Hudson Valley to cut the Revolution fatally in two. Arnold thereupon began to sabotage those works. The package he was going to deliver to Sir Henry Clinton included the plans to West Point and the kidnapping of Washington and his staff, as well as the gift of himself as a full general in the British army. The sticking point was money. Arnold placed a higher price on his head than Clinton did.

Just as the deal seemed clinched, it all came apart. Clinton's adjutant general, Major John André, was stopped on his way back to New York with the plans for West Point in his boot. Arnold escaped on the British sloop *Vulture* down the Hudson into New York City.

The dickering over money continued after Arnold reported for duty in New York City. Despite Arnold's relentless pressure for more, Clinton gave him what he had bargained for: In current U.S. dollars, about $200,000, a one-time payment, plus about $200,000 more a year for life.[34] As for the general's commission, what he got was not quite the real thing. Brigadier general, yes, but only of provincial troops. His permanent grade was that of a British cavalry colonel.

Worse, in British New York he found that his situation had not improved; in fact, it had not changed. The same characters he had come to loathe in Philadelphia had their exact counterparts in New York, now with British accents, but exhibiting the same bickering, goldbricking, pettiness, peevishness, old-boy networking, infighting, and backbiting. The only difference in New York was a deeper overlay of rampant British snobbery, rigid hierarchy, and ironclad class barriers. Arnold and his wife found themselves in a limbo, now utterly condemned in Philadelphia and not accepted fully in New York.[35]

Years before, one of Arnold's many enemies warned prophetically, "Money is this man's god and to get enough of it he would sacrifice his country." When he got to New York, British officers noted first about Arnold that he was obsessed with money.[36]

One wonders just how blind Benedict Arnold was to the enormity of the act he was committing. Trying to strike back at those who sought to destroy him, he also betrayed his friends and supporters, including the foot soldiers who had proudly followed him into battle. Most of all he had betrayed George Washington, his staunchest proponent and admirer. He had set him up for capture with his entire staff, not once but twice; capture probably would have led to Washington's execution. Benedict Arnold's blinding pride had carried him far beyond revenge into moral wickedness.

He had lost none of his brilliance as a military planner. His plan to raid Philadelphia made great sense. It could have been a crippling blow, even a fatal one, as he believed. Moving very fast, he could descend on that city, capture the Congress or at least a great number of them, and be gone long before Washington—up in the Hudson Valley poised to attack New York—could react. In one stroke, the Revolution would be over. A grateful England would restore Arnold's reputation and his fortune. In London with his young bride, life would be good again.

How dismayed he must have felt when he found himself ordered to Virginia. Virginia! Not Philadelphia. While he was burning tobacco warehouses in a rural countryside, his Philadelphia enemies in their legions would go on flourishing like the green bay tree. He had delivered himself into the temporizing hands of an endlessly talking, indecisive man. Arnold had only one move left.

A short distance away, Arnold's prized new sergeant major, John Champe, studied the lane that led from Arnold's home to the river.

Champe and Baldwin were now meeting periodically to work out the specific details of kidnapping Benedict Arnold. Their plans—including operating costs and fees to be paid to the civilian agents—were then communicated to Major Lee for discussion with General Washington.

Initially, the two kidnappers had been planning to break into the back of Arnold's home, pull him from his bed, tie him up, gag him, and drag him down an alley to the Hudson River and the waiting boat. But how were they to get him out of his bed, sleeping next to his wife, then down the stairs and out of the house without arousing the family, without arousing the headquarters guards next door? Champe, as an active recruiting sergeant frequently conferring with Arnold, had ready entry to Arnold's house and had reconnoitered the whole building—back door, hallways, stairs, and bedrooms.

This hurdle seemed like an unscalable wall until they got a bit of luck. Champe's nightly vigils discovered that Arnold had a fixed habit late at night just before retiring of taking a turn in the garden and visiting the outhouse. This seemed to overcome the major danger of rousing the household, and it offered a perfect time and place for grabbing him—late at night and far away from the house. Arnold's cloacal habits had played right into their hands.

They now had a much simplified plan: They would wait for Arnold to come into the garden, seize him, gag him, and manhandle him down the alley that ran along the picket fence to the river and into the waiting boat. With luck they would not encounter any of the roving night watches. If they did, they planned to pass off the heavily cloaked Arnold as a drunken soldier being carried to the guardhouse.

But there were other, complicating factors. The Hudson River is a tidal estuary with strong currents that could easily carry a small boat upriver or downriver and into the bay. The kidnapping had to wait for a night when the tide would be least troublesome so that the boat could make its way directly across the river to Hoboken on the New Jersey shore. There Light-Horse Harry Lee himself and a party of dragoons would await the arrival of the boat with Arnold onboard.

There were other details to attend to—getting the right boat, getting to the right pier without arousing alarm, and getting the right man to operate it. Then there was the additional problem of British patrol boats. Champe was familiar with their vigilance, for one of them had pulled him from the river during the night of his escape. Ideally, the abduction would take place on a moonless night when they would be less visible on the water.

So tide, moon, patrols, Benedict Arnold's bowels—all were random factors that could affect the outcome. One thing they could pray for but not plan on—a huge dose of incredibly good luck.

The two men made a selection of ideal nights, then Baldwin sent their plans to Major Lee, who would discuss them with General Washington for final approval.

Meantime, Champe and Baldwin rehearsed their movements. In preparation, Champe even walked the length of picket fencing along Arnold's garden and at a key place loosened four palings, wide enough to pull Arnold through into the adjoining alley. Then he loosely replaced them, ready to be knocked down with a kick.

Champe had entered that strange half-world—half terror, half boredom—of spying and intrigue where everything was hurry up and wait, where nothing happened quickly, where clandestine movements took weeks instead of hours, where the danger of exposure could occur at any moment. Baldwin had to make arrangements to line up another man to help handle the boat; in the world of double agents and plots within plots, could that man betray them to the British? Could Baldwin?

Days went by; weeks went by. Champe spent his waking hours recruiting deserters for the American Legion and his nights with Baldwin, planning for every contingency. Everything was fixed except the date. And that was finally set for late at night on December 11.

Light-Horse Harry Lee headed a party of dragoons from camp, leading three spare horses, one for Sergeant Major Champe, one for his associate, and one for the turncoat Arnold. At about midnight the dragoons reached Hoboken and took up a post overlooking the Hudson River.[37] They sat shivering in the cold night and waited. The hours wore on. There was no sign of Champe and his prisoner. At dawn, even the optimistic Lee had to admit that the plan must have gone awry. He reluctantly took one last look over at Manhattan, mounted, and led his party back to camp. Then he went to Washington with his report of "the much lamented disappointment, as mortifying as inexplicable."[38] His biggest concern was not Arnold; what had happened to his sergeant major?

A few days later, Lee received an anonymous letter from Baldwin. Benedict Arnold, fearful that many of his new recruits would desert, had ordered them all—including Champe—immediately onboard a naval transport, where they would remain until sailing time. Champe had been taken onboard just hours before the kidnap attempt.

What could Champe do now? Unless there was a great change in Arnold's battle plan, John Champe was going to return to his home state of Virginia in a manner wholly unexpected—in a British army uniform onboard a British troop transport, brought there to sack and burn his beloved home state. What of the kidnapping plan now?

Still desperate for a dramatic event to boost army morale, Washington continued plotting. His mind's eye, searching the terrain from Savannah all the way to Boston, came to rest once again on New York City, then on British army headquarters there, then on the commanding general of those forces there—Sir Henry Clinton.

Washington made his decision. This time he summoned his aide, Lieutenant Colonel David Humphreys, and unfolded an even more ambitious plan than the one to kidnap Arnold. He would kidnap General Sir Henry Clinton himself. The projected raid was worthy of today's American army special forces—an enactment of the very nightmare of being kidnapped from his bed that haunted Clinton's dreams. With muffled oars, at night, Humphreys and a number of other soldiers—probably as many as 100—were to row downriver to New York. They would tie up not far from the rear of Clinton's house. Entering the garden from the back, they were to divide into groups. One group would hasten down either side of the house to the street, where they were to surprise and seize British sentries there. Another group with crowbars would burst into the house from the rear, bound up the stairs into Clinton's bedchamber, seize him, bind him, and bundle up as many of his papers as they could find. At the same time another group was to batter its way into the home of Hessian general Wilhelm Knyphausen to kidnap him. All these groups would then hasten with their human cargo back down to the river and row across to Hoboken and deliver Clinton and Knyphausen to General Washington.

The date Washington chose for this pair of kidnappings was ironic—just a few weeks away, on Christmas night, the third anniversary of Washington's victory at Trenton. This would serve as a wry Christmas greeting to the king, from one George to another.

On Wednesday, December 20, after well over a week of heavy work by many hands, General Arnold's ships had been loaded; all the horses, the 1,600 troops, and the tons of supplies were stuffed into the holds. The forty-two ships of the flotilla lay at anchor off Sandy Hook. That evening, Arnold himself boarded the commodore's flagship, *Charon*. The next day, with the tide, Arnold would sail for the Chesapeake.

Albeit fettered by his two British guardians, he had been given his first British command. And now he had to perform. To him it would seem that the whole world—his whole world—was watching him intently: every British officer in New York and throughout the growing empire, all his former comrades and present enemies in the American army and, indeed, perhaps most important of all, the king himself. It was up to Arnold to make or break his future.

He was also aware that he was taking his life in his hands. Many an eager sniper's rifle would draw down on him. Were he to be captured by the Americans, he had no doubt that he would be summarily hanged. And he was right: Washington ordered General Lafayette, were he to capture Arnold, to hang him on the battlefield. Arnold had stated that he would not be taken alive.

In addition, Arnold was taking measure of himself, as usual, in terms of money. While he did not forget that his assignment in Virginia was to destroy the war effort there and to destroy the logistics system that was shipping troops and supplies to Greene in the Carolinas, he also saw it as an opportunity, in the custom of the British army, to gather gold for himself. He was not long at sea before he and Captain Thomas Symonds, commodore of the flotilla, fell into some deep conversations about getting wealthy through prize money—from the land where prize money seemed to grow on trees.

The importance Clinton attached to this mission was shown by the officers he gave to Arnold. It had not been an easy choice. From the beginning, Sir Harry had had great difficulty finding any officers who would serve with Arnold. Yet in the end, Arnold set off with two of Clinton's best officers—both with something to prove—as well as some of his best troops.

Lieutenant Colonel John Graves Simcoe, twenty-eight, commander of the Queen's Rangers, was one of the most dashing cavalry officers on either side of the entire Revolution, much admired even among his American enemies. A Devonshire Englishman, he had landed in Boston, at age twenty-three, on the day of the Battle of Bunker Hill, June 17, 1775, and was made captain that year. In 1777, right after the Battle of Brandywine, where he had been badly wounded, he requested and got command of the Queen's Rangers, a light corps of regimental cavalry and foot made up almost exclusively of Americans, which, as lieutenant colonel, he would soon turn into a first-class fighting unit.

Interestingly enough, he made this request to command a light corps well aware that many British officers regarded the light corps as little more than partisans—militarily disreputable, associated with "dishonesty, rapine and falsehood." To them it was a bad career move. However, it offered great opportunity for career-building adventures out on the fringes of military life, as well as an unparalleled school for learning self-reliance and making instant decisions that would earn him, as he noted in his diary, "trusts of importance." In short, this was a position of opportunity, high visibility, and quick promotion—a path made for the ambitious who were willing to take risks.[39]

And he soon acquired the reputation he was after—for boldness, resourcefulness, coolness under pressure, brilliance with a soupçon of raffishness and romance—a sort of eighteenth-century George Custer. Light-Horse Harry Lee, another cavalry devotee and commander of a similar American legion, described Simcoe as "one of the best officers in the British Army, "who had led an enterprise [that] was considered, by both armies, as among the handsomest exploits of the war."[40]

That exploit, much discussed long afterward in officers' messes on both sides, occurred when General Clinton sent Simcoe and his Queen's Rangers on a high-risk night raid across New York Harbor to Perth Amboy in New Jersey. Their mission was to destroy a vast store of small boats Washington was assembling for his projected amphibious assault on New York City—a prospect that was tormenting Clinton's sleep.

In darkness, traveling inland more than twenty miles over terrain bristling with American night patrols, Simcoe and his Rangers moved swiftly to Middlebrook on the Raritan River (the northern edge of modern-day Bound Brook) where he found the boats, a great cache of them, painstakingly assembled. The Queen's Rangers soon set off a bonfire so huge it flung great flames wafting into the night sky. Probably it was the fire, visible for many miles, that aroused the Americans, including Light-Horse Harry Lee and his troopers, who hotly pursued the Queen's Rangers as they raced back toward Perth Amboy and the ferry ride to safety in Manhattan.

Driving his horses hard over more than fifty miles during the night, and needing to rest and water them, the young British commander came upon an American commissary base. He roused the sleeping commissary and ordered feed and water for his horses. Mistaking their uniforms for those of Light-Horse Harry Lee's Legion, the commissary served up the required feed and water while the troopers stood by impatiently. Simcoe then signed the name of the Lee's Legion quartermaster and resumed his race for Perth Amboy.

He had almost reached his destination when he ran into an American militia ambush set up to stop him. Most of his troopers made it to safety but Simcoe, bringing up the rear, had his horse shot out from under him. He and three of his men were wounded and captured. A few months later, on December 31, 1779, he was exchanged and returned to his unit to resume command.[41]

General Clinton, grateful that his night's sleep would not be disturbed by an amphibious Washington—at least for a while—wrote a letter to war secretary Lord Germain in London containing high praise for Simcoe: "The history of the corps under his command is a series of gallant, skilful, and successful enterprises against the enemy, *without a single reverse.* The Queen's Rangers have killed or taken twice their own numbers. Col. Simcoe himself has been thrice wounded."[42]

By joining Arnold's foray to Virginia, Simcoe again raised some eyebrows in British headquarters. He had been one of John André's closest friends. During André's trial as a spy, when the British military realized that Washington was actually going to hang him, Simcoe approached Clinton with a desperate plan. He and his Queen's Rangers, in another daring night raid to match the Perth Amboy exploit, would cross the Hudson and gallop into Tappan, break into the prison, rescue André, and race back to New York. It meant penetrating a much more heavily guarded Continental bastion and, again, crossing the Hudson River twice in one night.

Clinton had had a fatherly relationship with the twenty-seven-year-old André, who had been his adjutant general, his closest military confidant—and, historian Randall suggests, his lover.[43]

Sir Harry yearned to get André back, but he had to weigh the possible rescue of André against the possible loss of one of his best cavalry outfits. For a man who hated risk, Clinton was looking at odds only the most audacious gambler—like Arnold or Simcoe—would dare to face. He declined.

Simcoe may have agreed to serve under Arnold because, in his quest for military advancement, he was eager to get away from barracks life and back into action. But one speculates that Simcoe, a serious, deeply read student of military history and a calculated risk-taker, also wanted to study this legendary renegade—a fellow gambler—in action.[44] Also, it could not have been lost on Simcoe that Virginia was legendary for its war booty and looting, a prime way for eighteenth-century soldiers to augment their slender fortunes. In Simcoe's case he had spent a large sum of his personal fortune outfitting his troops, and Virginia was a way to refill the flattened purse.

The third officer of the troika was Lieutenant Colonel Thomas Dundas. Son of an MP from Scotland's Orkney and Shetland Islands, this thirty-year-old career infantry officer was a skeptical hard-eyed Scot with battle experience in America and the West Indies when, in 1779, he had returned to Scotland to take command, as lieutenant colonel, of the Royal Edinburgh Volunteers, newly created by the city fathers. During the crossing to New York, the new unit, officially designated the 80th Foot, suffered an epidemic of jail fever, a virulent form of typhus that was commonplace aboard eighteenth-century sea voyages and was often lethal to both men and animals. In 1775, troops shipped to Boston from Ireland arrived so fever-wracked that they were not allowed to disembark until the fever subsided and the dying stopped. The French army under Rochambeau lost a number of men to ship fever (probably also typhus) on their crossing to Newport. And on their passages to America, the Hessians had their ranks thinned and culled by seaboard fever. Before the war ended, jail fever and related epidemics had sent a phantom legion of uncounted uniformed ghosts to the bottom of the Atlantic.

Although he lost a number of his men, Dundas distinguished himself by performing the most menial tasks attempting to take care of them. When he arrived in New York, Dundas came down with the fever himself and almost died. For his heroic efforts, he was given a citation from Clinton.

One can conjecture that he accepted duty under Arnold because he, too, was motivated by the desire to get more high-visibility battle experience for his still-green 80th Foot. For career soldiers, wars are all too short, and peacetime at half-pay far too long. One needs to get the experience and promotions on the battlefield.

Simcoe and Dundas, willing as they may have been to serve under Arnold, came onboard with a secret they did not share with him. The uneasy Clinton had given both of them "dormant commissions." This originally had been a military ploy to prevent Hessian officers from commanding British troops. In the spring of 1776, Clinton himself had been given a dormant commission, raising him to full general in the event of General Howe's incapacity. By boosting on the spot Clinton's rank above General Heister's, the German officer would have been blocked from taking command. The dormant commissions of Simcoe and Dundas, raising them to brigadier generals, authorized them to take command in the event that Arnold was killed or incapacitated (and presumably to enable them to remove him from command if he got out of control).[45]

On the evening tide of Thursday, December 21, in a turbulent winter storm that didn't bode well for their passage, Arnold's ships slipped their cables at Sandy Hook and stood out to sea, carrying 1,600 men bent on military mischief, mayhem, misery, plunder, pillaging, sacking, and warfare in Virginia. One of the 1,600 was a very dismayed Sergeant Major John Champe.

On Christmas night, Lieutenant Colonel Humphreys and his raiding party of 100 men gathered on the Jersey side of the Hudson River to row over to New York to kidnap commanding general Sir Henry Clinton and Hessian general Wilhelm Knyphausen.

Waiting for them was a rising windstorm. The river was a choppy mess of jagged, spine-cracking waves.

Undaunted, they managed to get into their boats and set out in the rough water. But the wind was coming out of the northeast, blowing directly against them. Despite their efforts, it was driving them south, down the Hudson toward New York Harbor below Manhattan. After manfully struggling, they saw that they could not reach the opposite shore. Manhattan Island proved to be inaccessible. Reluctantly, spent, they had to turn about and make for New Jersey without their quarry.

Full of Christmas cheer and asleep with his mistress, Mrs. Mary O'Callaghan Baddeley, wife of Captain Thomas Baddeley, barrack master in Charleston, General Clinton was blissfully unaware that Aeolus had sent him an unparalleled Christmas present in the form of the December windstorm raging over his rooftop. The god had saved him from his greatest continuing nightmare.

The failed kidnapping must have become common knowledge in New York. Hessian lieutenant John Von Krafft gave a full account of it in an entry in his diary dated January 2:

> In the night upwards of 100 men of the Rebels at the instigation probably of one of the traitors in New York (who are to be found there and throughout the island) were so rash as to cross over the North River from Jersey in flat boats in order to take Gen. Clinton out of his own quarters

in New York. The accomplishment of the act would have been very extraordinary, if they could have succeeded in spite of the many sentries stationed about. It was enough that they certainly meant to succeed. But Heaven itself had not wished it to be so; for the row galleys which were usually there had gone away and of course it had been immediately made known to the Rebels. But they had the wind and tide so against them, that they could not land and so they had to go back. All this was afterwards reported to Gen. Clinton, (but how, I do not know), and he formed the intention of revenging himself in a way which was before unknown."[46]

Two

Arnold versus Jefferson

Early Sunday morning, December 31, 1780, New Year's Eve day, a lone rider hastened into Richmond, Virginia, and cantered up to the governor's house on Shokoe Hill. He encountered Gov. Thomas Jefferson stepping out on the roadway for his morning stroll.

The messenger had an urgent message from Gen. Thomas Nelson, head of the Virginia militia. Several days earlier, twenty-seven ships had passed the capes of Virginia and entered Chesapeake Bay. Preliminary reports failed to identify them as British or as French.

Jefferson's response was to send an order back to General Nelson, whose home, prophetically, was in Yorktown on the Chesapeake. He placed at Nelson's disposal "the militia, the public arms and the stores" of the state. In short, he gave Nelson "full powers to adopt and execute such measures as exigencies might demand."[1]

The governor then sent word about the anonymous ships to Baron von Steuben, who, as general in command of the Continental Army in Virginia, was actively training new recruits at the Continental army base nearby. He sent a third message to Benjamin Harrison, speaker of the Virginia House.[2]

Having sent those messages, Jefferson decided to await further developments before summoning the Governor's Council to action.

But this was not the first warning Jefferson had received. On December 9 he received an alarmed letter from Washington: "I am at this moment informed from New York another embarkation is taking place . . . destined southward."[3] Washington was referring to the Arnold expedition. His warning might have carried more weight if it had been more specific. But that word "southward" covered a vast area. The destination could be Virginia or Charleston or Savannah or even the West Indies, so the Virginia legislature, with arresting insouciance, had blithely assumed it was Charleston.

But that December 9 letter had not been Washington's first warning. Earlier letters had doubly cautioned the governor that not only must Virginia prepare to defend herself against some heavy military action, but also she must do it alone. The state could not look for help from Washington's tiny Continental Army: "our situation in this quarter precludes every hope of affording you further assistance."[4]

Actually, Virginia's leaders needed no warnings from Washington. They should have roused themselves a year and a half before as a result of the British Collier/Mathew raid of May 8, 1779. Vice Admiral Sir George Collier, one of England's best naval officers, commanding a flotilla of twenty-eight ships, anchored off Willoughby's Point near Norfolk and disgorged 1,800 plunder-hungry troops under Maj. Gen. Edward Mathew. Without having to fire a shot, the raiders helped themselves to a colossal treasure trove that required an entire week just to load onboard their ships.

Sated, they literally wallowed back to New York burdened to the gunwales with booty that included a great fortune of naval and military stores, 3,000 hogsheads of highly valuable tobacco, and an unbelievable cache of 137 merchant ships—destroying those few that they could not bring away with them—plus a large number of American privateersmen. They might have also captured an American twenty-eight-gun fighting ship being built on the ways and two heavily laden French merchant ships had not the Virginians quickly burned them. The Collier/Mathew raid had not cost the British a single life; only two men were wounded. Back in New York, the raiders babbled about the incredible wealth they had left behind.[5]

But that had been hardly more than a raid. The only permanent damage done was to Suffolk. In fact, in a real sense from the British point of view, it might have done more harm than good; it caused the Tidewater Loyalists to rise prematurely, and when Collier pulled out, they were left alone to face the wrath of the Virginia rebels. The Loyalists would be much more hesitant about a second rising.[6]

Yet the estimated cost to Virginia of that single Collier/Mathew raid was a crushing £2,000,000. The British officers and men of that raid had shared in the proceeds from the auctioning of the ships and matériel. Many were made wealthy. Former governor Patrick Henry bore the full brunt of that military disgrace; Virginia had fired hardly a single shot in defense.

Then, on October 20, 1780, little more than eight weeks past, had come a second British attack, this time during Jefferson's administration. Under command of British General Alexander Leslie, a flotilla of sixty ships landed more than 5,000 troops who began to build a base at Portsmouth. This time the enemy seemed intent on staying. And again, although Jefferson had been warned weeks before in September, he and his council were completely unprepared when the attack did come. The legislators had been preoccupied with plans to build their new capital. Jefferson had done nothing.[7]

Then the war clouds cleared away: Leslie had barely begun to build when, in late November, about a month after arrival, he abruptly abandoned his unfinished fortifications, packed up his shovels and guns, and sailed away. Cornwallis, his army laid low by fever and casualties following the major defeat at Kings Mountain, had summoned Leslie's entire command south. The Virginians, unaware of this, were completely puzzled. They heaved a sigh of relief, wondered what Leslie had been up to, rejoiced that he had done little permanent damage, and went back to sleep.

In consequence, the December 31 warning of an approaching fleet should have galvanized Jefferson and the Assembly. They should have called out the militia. They should have moved precious military stores inland and concealed them. They should have fortified their rivers. Instead, the legislators were not even discussing the possibility of another British attack. As Christmas came and went, the absence of saddle horses outside the legislative hall told the story: They had gone home.

In truth, although Jefferson hated to exercise the authority he knew he should and didn't, there was not a great deal that he could do legally. The state constitution, which Jefferson helped create, severely limited the governor's powers. Elected for only one year, Jefferson could neither dissolve the legislature nor veto any of its laws. The governor was little more than the secretary of the Council of State, and it was that body which, whenever they could be lured to Richmond to sit, by majority vote actually ran Virginia.[8]

Virginia's contribution to the Revolution had been enormous and absolutely vital. The state had provided troops that had posted sterling records on many battlefields. No state suffered a greater calamity of casualties than Virginia: Just months before, the state had sent the entire Virginia Line of the Continental Army—some eleven battalions as well as Virginia's entire supply of firearms—down to South Carolina under General Lincoln to help defend Charleston. There they had been surrendered; the bulk of Lincoln's 5,500-man army was composed of Virginians. Another 400 Virginians had been virtually wiped out in the Gates defeat in Camden that followed a few months later. Those eleven battalions of Virginians were now dying with frightful speed on the unspeakably brutal fever-ridden British prison ships of Charleston.[9] As a result, Virginia had few troops in uniform. What remained of her army would be available, Jefferson had written to the imploring Gates, "as soon as they come out of the hospital."[10]

Virginia had also turned her pockets inside out to help finance the Revolution. Her tobacco had served as money on European markets, giving the Continental Congress foreign exchange to buy urgently needed matériel. But now her economy had become a self-inflicted wound. The Virginia legislature had gone on printing worthless paper money until its economy, already gasping from the British blockade, was just about bankrupt. The Virginia Assembly was shortly to peg the price of a horse, worth $150 in hard money, at $150,000 Continental. And even at that exchange rate there would be no sellers.[11]

Virginia was virtually indefensible. Chesapeake Bay is a vast inland sea fed by Virginia's major rivers, including the James, the Chickahominy, the York, the Rappahannock, and the Potomac, all of which are largely navigable. They reach like watery tentacles into the very heart of the state right up to the toes of the Blue Ridge Mountains. In peacetime this ready-made natural transportation system was a priceless economic asset, with annual maintenance costs that were practically zero, costing nothing to make, and nothing to maintain while reaching everywhere. But in wartime, those same rivers turned Virginia into an easy victim of cruising British marauders, burning and looting as they traveled by taxi boat. Easy work: no walking; no opposition worthy of the name; a lush cornucopia of richly furnished plantation houses, tobacco-stuffed warehouses, abundant food and livestock, and a string of military stores and stockpiles; plus plenty of wagons and horses for hauling booty to the nearest river.

To make bad matters worse, the British would soon discover that Virginia's vast and open tableland was also ideal cavalry country. And Virginia, as one of the leading horse-breeding centers in the new country, could provide the British with an abundance of cavalry horses just for the taking.

On New Year's Eve 1780, in the Jockey Hollow army camp in Morristown, New Jersey, the officers' mess was packed with a noisy, boisterous, boozy group of officers of the Pennsylvania Line. Slowly, heavily, Col. Richard Humpton struggled up on his unsteady legs, looked out at the long tables of officers before him, then held up his glass for silence. When the babble stopped, he proposed in his heavy Yorkshire accent a toast to "our friends who are departing: may they always be as happy as they have made their friends!"[12]

"Our friends who are departing" were fellow officers of the Pennsylvania Line who had just become redundant when, effective the next morning—New Year's Day—the Pennsylvania Line was being consolidated and the number of units reduced, requiring fewer officers. The redundants were being given an auld lang syne banquet by their brother officers. Knowing they would be gone in the morning, and encouraged by the abundant bottles that had been passing up and down the tables, the banqueters had been at it for more than six hours. Amidst the loud cheering of their friends, the redundants received Humpton's toast in solemn silence.

When the applause subsided, Colonel Humpton cocked his ear, shook his head to lift the wine fog, and listened again. Formerly a captain in the British army and a man with a lifetime knowledge of camp life, he was hearing unwonted noises coming from the outside when there should have been silence. The troops were supposed to be in their huts. He picked his way carefully through the throng, pushed open a big plank door, and looked out at the dark chilly night. Soldiers were running up and down shouting at each other. Some of them had gotten muskets.

Humpton read the danger signals in an instant. He rushed back into the mess to get help. Shortly thereafter, someone galloped into the night to find Gen. Anthony Wayne.[13]

That same night, on a stormy, endlessly pitching sea, Gen. Benedict Arnold's raiding party groped for a place to land on the coast of the Virginia capes. It had been a harrowing eleven-day voyage under gale-force winds. The flotilla of forty-two ships were scattered, some unaccounted for, half the horses dead, and many heavy guns washed away.[14]

Nonetheless Benedict Arnold's thoughts were elsewhere. During the voyage, he had struck a deal with Captain Thomas Symonds, commodore of the flotilla. The army and the navy would split fifty-fifty any and all prizes, land or sea. With the £2,000,000 of booty brought back by Collier and Mathew in mind, Benedict Arnold fully expected to become a very wealthy man.

On January 2 Gov. Thomas Jefferson urgently summoned the executive council of state. He had terrifying news: A third British fleet had landed the day before in Portsmouth, and thousands of soldiers were now busy rounding up every small boat they could find.

It was all very reminiscent of the Continental Congress dithering in Philadelphia over unessential matters as it faced imminent collapse. At the appointed hour Jefferson looked around the council room with dismay. Despite the desperate situation, too few councilors had come to even form a quorum necessary if a governor wanted approval to call up the militia.

Jefferson, without authority, then, issued a callup of the militia from six counties, hoping he would be obeyed. Having waited far too long, he now ordered all of Virginia's official records as well as military supplies to be carried to Westham further up the James River, safely, he thought, above the river falls. But Westham itself presented additional problems. It was the site of an irreplaceable cannon factory that held, additionally, some fifteen tons of gunpowder.

It seems not to have occurred to him that Arnold's raid was aimed at Richmond, at the Virginia rebel government—at him. The rest of the town did seem to realize it. Thomas Jefferson was left almost alone in Richmond.

In his army training camp in Chesterfield Court House, a few miles from Richmond, Gen. Friedrich von Steuben, head of the Continental forces in Virginia, was raising hell.

And he had been raising hell for some time. He had been demanding troops, uniforms, weapons, and ammunition from Jefferson, from the state legislature, from individuals in power. He wanted the Virginia rivers fortified. He wanted the militia called up and in training camp. He wanted the Virginia legislature to replace the Virginia Line of the Continental Army, which had been lost in Charleston. He wanted army stores moved, hidden. He wanted Virginia to start acting responsibly, arming itself like a state at war, which it was.

This was not the posture of a crank. Steuben was one of the most important men in the Continental army, a professional soldier whose counsels were sought out attentively. Brought to Virginia by Gen. Nathanael Greene, he was soon in a spluttering, table-pounding Teutonic rage at the unflappable Virginia insouciance, at the unkept promises of Thomas Jefferson. The baron put his rage in writing, using such intemperate language that later he considered making an apology to Jefferson.

Everyone in the army knew the nation's great debt to him. On February 23, 1778, in the very depths of winter at Valley Forge, Baron Friedrich Wilhelm Ludolf Gerhard Augustin von Steuben, forty-eight, "late of the armies of Frederick the Great of Prussia," rode into the American army camp of Valley Forge with his retinue, wearing a splendid blue general's uniform, sporting a large medal, and speaking not one word of English. He was the very man Washington desperately needed.

The contribution the baron was about to make to the success of the American Revolution is almost incalculable, for he solved one of the most intractable problems Washington faced.

The eighteenth-century battlefield was a place of complete confusion. After the usual cannonade and musket volleys, the field quickly became wrapped in a dense, blinding fog of gunpowder smoke. The deafening roar of cannon, the shattering sound of the musket, the confusing shouts of soldiers, the screaming of the wounded and the dying would soon disorient any man, cut him off from his unit, deafen him to the commands of his officers, and leave him totally lost, bewildered, and badly frightened. When suddenly a phalanx of redcoats burst through the fog, marching in step right at him, bayonets extended, the American would drop his weapon, turn, and run in full flight. This had happened repeatedly.

On the battlefield, the British were masters of maneuver. Their skill with the bayonet had made them the terror of Europe. They drilled day after day, year after year, on all the maneuvers of the battlefield. The key to all their moves was not the shouted commands of their officers but a series of varied drumbeats. A small thirteen- or fourteen-year-old drummer boy, translating the commands of officers into drum signals, controlled the soldiers on the battlefield. By responding to the drumming, even in the densest smoke British soldiers could wheel like a swinging gate across an entire battlefield, advance, turn, extend bayonets, volley with their muskets, charge, withdraw, and retreat—all as a single unit.

The British redcoat was trained to believe that he could survive, fight, and win only by staying with his unit, moving with his unit, unhesitatingly obeying each command, no matter what his personal instincts called for. The drum signals were the same throughout the entire British army. A soldier could be plucked from a battlefield in America, thrust in an instant into a British military unit on a battlefield in India, and immediately start functioning to the same identical drumbeats and commands.

The American Continental Army, by contrast, was in complete confusion. Different units were trained—if at all—from different drill books using completely different commands. Even worse, because of the shortness of enlistments, often ninety days, the American state militia couldn't be effectively trained at all. With this miscellany of commands and poorness of training, when the Americans marched out on the battlefield the results were too often predictable.

The British weren't better soldiers. They were better-trained soldiers, completely confident they were going to win.

The baron quickly changed all that. In a short time, his great voice could be heard all over the Valley shouting "von two tree four!" then purple-swearing in German, then in French, then getting his interpreters to do his swearing in English. The troops soon developed a great affection for him. Quickly the baron trained a cadre of 100 drill instructors.

Then he rode back and forth tirelessly from drill field to drill field, from six in the morning until six at night, supervising the drill instructors he had just trained as they trained the fourteen battalions of the American army in the essential arts of marching, wheeling, advancing, responding to the signals of the military drum, and wielding the supreme weapon of the battlefield—the bayonet. Most of all, the portly, open-handed, charming German bachelor instilled a new confidence in the troops, making them believe in themselves, convincing them they could whip the British.

By the early days of spring, out of Valley Forge marched Washington's first battle-ready, fully trained professional army, soon to demonstrate, at Barren Hill, then at Monmouth Court House, that it was the match of the British redcoat.

The *Dictionary of American Biography* is unhesitating in its accolades. The baron's efforts, it says, were "perhaps the most remarkable achievement in rapid military training in the history of the world."

At Washington's request, the Congress appointed the baron inspector general of the army. From that day forward to Yorktown—where he was to display another gift, a profound knowledge of the art of siege warfare—the baron's contribution to victory was tangible and acknowledged.

Much of his résumé that he carried to Valley Forge came from the imagination of Benjamin Franklin in Paris. Steuben actually was a baron, but he was not a lieutenant general of the Prussian army recently retired, as Franklin claimed, but a half-pay captain fourteen years away from his last military service during the French and Indian War. Of Steuben's embellished military resume, the historian Bruce Lancaster observed: "In this benevolent deception Franklin probably performed his greatest service to the American army."[15]

It was this miracle of Valley Forge that the baron was trying to repeat in Virginia. And it was this that the Virginians were resisting. They accused him of arrogance and idleness and contempt for Virginians and so ignored him. Baron von Steuben was not the kind of man you ignored.

In Portsmouth, Benedict Arnold had proposed, with the 1,200 men available and despite the setbacks suffered at sea, to go on the attack immediately, before Virginia could mount any defenses. He ordered search parties to hunt down without delay and commandeer enough small craft to carry his troops in a lightning move up the James River. He proposed to start for Richmond the very next morning. Simcoe and Dundas were astonished. This was the kind of drive and energy—the kind of warfare—neither had ever seen before, the kind that had made Arnold a living legend.

Prior to landing, Arnold once more reviewed his orders. And these, unlike Clinton's usual vagueness or contradictoriness, were fairly explicit and brief:

Set up a hit-and-run raiding base in Portsmouth on the Elizabeth River within ready rescue by the British navy.

Destroy rebel military storehouses, particularly in Richmond and Petersburg.

Interdict the flow of troop reinforcements and supplies south to Greene in the Carolinas.

Raise and train an army of Virginia Loyalists.

Ruin the Virginia economy, which was helping to finance the rebel cause.

And if Arnold found "a favorable opportunity of striking at any of the enemy's magazines" before building the Portsmouth base, he was "at liberty to attempt it provided it may be done without much risk." Without much risk. Daringly safe warfare. Granny warfare, Rochambeau called it.

And always in the background, looking over his shoulder, were the built-in brakes on Arnold's juggernaut: Simcoe and Dundas, "officers of great experience and much in my confidence [who] previous to your undertaking any operation of consequence," Arnold had to consult.

In many ways Clinton's plan was a good one. With raids rather than a full-scale invasion of Virginia, Clinton proposed to relieve that pressure on Cornwallis and slowly strangle Greene's army. It did not, however, take into consideration Washington's response.

At five o'clock in the morning of Thursday, January 4, in pouring rain, a pounding on the door of the governor's home roused a servant who woke Jefferson with very grim news. The British had not stopped at Williamsburg, as Jefferson had hoped. They were already at Westover, well above Williamsburg and only twenty-five miles away from Richmond down the James River. Even as he heard the news, some 800 British troops had disembarked there and were pounding out the muddy miles for Richmond. They could arrive as early as noon.[16]

Jefferson also learned that at their head was none other than the infamous Benedict Arnold. Jefferson understood at last: It was to Richmond that now came misery, mischief, and scorched earth, and, unless he moved quickly, the capture of the author of the Declaration of Independence.

The legislature had already fled to Charlottesville, seventy miles to the west. For the time being, at least, government in Virginia was ended. Jefferson sent a message to General von Steuben putting him in charge of Virginia's militia, then put himself in action on horseback the day long, directing the removal of gunpowder and military supplies stored upriver at Westham. But fifteen tons of gunpowder is not easy to move, to ship to distant points of safety, to conceal. The timing of Arnold's raid could not have been more exquisite. Worse still, Arnold had moved faster than expected. He was on the fringes of Richmond by eleven o'clock that morning.

Colonel John Simcoe was becoming more and more enthusiastic about Arnold. He described the way Arnold led the 800-man contingent up the James River to Westover in glowing terms: sailing "with incomparable activity and despatch, the whole detachment showing an energy and alacrity that could not be surpassed."[17]

In great panic, hordes of people were fleeing, crowding the muddy roadways in the miserable downpour, dragging as many of their valuables as they could carry.[18]

By one P.M. Governor Jefferson, sitting on his horse across the James River in the section known as Manchester, was watching Benedict Arnold march into Richmond. Through a spyglass, he saw the hastily assembled Virginia militia form up on the streets of the town, 250 of them, many with no weapons in their hands. Militia officials had simply not been given enough time to assemble or arm a larger body. The governor watched with dismay as the redcoats moved to disperse them. It was as easy as flapping hands at chickens: They broke ranks, turned, and ran for their lives. Jefferson watched Benedict Arnold move into the center of the town in his British general's uniform, surrounded by his red-coated troops. And he watched Arnold send search parties out. The traitor, he now believed, was looking for him.

British troops went to the governor's house, learned that Jefferson was long gone, ransacked the place, descended to his wine cellar, drank his wine collection, smashing what they could not consume, looted and burned his papers, torched his library, and carried away ten of his slaves, who were sold for hard cash.[19]

In the meantime, Arnold made an offer to the businessmen and property owners of Richmond: He would spare the capitol from the flames if they could get Governor Jefferson to agree to allow British vessels to come up the James unopposed. These would then take away all the tobacco, leaving the warehouses unscathed.

Arnold's offer was carried by messenger across the river to Jefferson in Manchester, who must have thought it very strange. Arnold, having watched the militia run away, knew perfectly well that neither the governor nor Steuben nor anyone else had the means to oppose those boats coming upriver. Was Arnold's offer actually a ruse to try to flush out and capture Jefferson?

The governor refused to even acknowledge receipt of the message from a "parricide" and so bore the grim responsibility for Arnold's next move: Ten captured ships and thirty-four open boats were brought up-river, and soon after, great hogsheads of tobacco went rolling onboard along with a broad inventory of things including "West Indies goods, wines, sailcloth." What Arnold didn't take belonged to Loyalists: They were given passes to escape downriver with shiploads of wine. With the looting ended and the ships loaded, the "parricide" gave Jefferson his answer: A growing pall of smoke rose over the town. Having stripped Richmond to the walls, Arnold was now burning much of it to the ground.[20]

Arnold reported to Clinton that "warehouses, shops and magazines were put to the torch, along with a printing press and types . . . also purified by the flames." Most of the spared buildings belonged to Loyalists.[21] In addition, Arnold located and raised five brass four-pounders that had been deliberately sunk in the river. These were carried away.[22]

Light-Horse Harry Lee later wrote that Arnold burned so much of the town that "even his greedy appetite was cloyed, and his revengeful heart sated."[23]

In the meantime Jefferson had gone back upriver seven miles to Westham to check on the disbursal of the gunpowder. He was just ahead of the British, and when he got there he was stunned. Virginia's public records—wagonloads of them—had been mistakenly dumped on the floor of the cannon foundry—right in the path of the oncoming British army and ideally situated for the pillager's torch. It was far too late to save them. Of the fifteen tons of gunpowder, he had moved nine, reluctantly leaving six tons in full view. Jefferson galloped away to safety, just ahead of Colonel Simcoe with 400 soldiers.[24]

At Westham Colonel Simcoe found a heavy day's work destroying the place. To disable the cannon Simcoe ordered that the trunnions be struck off, thereby preventing them from ever being mounted and swiveled and aimed. He also destroyed "a quantity of small arms and a great variety of military stores." The strangulation of Greene down South had begun.[25]

While that heavy labor was being done, the colonel turned other troops to an equally precious rebel store—the gunpowder magazine. The lack of gunpowder had dogged Washington from the beginning. The British would never have carried Bunker Hill if the farmers had not run out of ammunition. When Washington mounted the cannon on Dorchester Heights to drive the British out of Boston, General Gage never knew how little powder and how few cannonballs Washington had—certainly not enough to have driven Gage from the city. Of the countless thousands of American muskets that surrounded Boston after Bunker Hill, many had no ammunition. Shortage of gunpowder had been a factor in the defeats at Brandywine, at Germantown, and multitudinous other times even up to the Battle at Yorktown, where Washington's chief artillery officer, General Henry Knox, would note: "As to powder, it was so scarce that there was hardly enough for use of the forts along the Hudson, let alone for Virginia."[26]

Destroying the gunpowder presented its own problems to Simcoe. "Upon consultation with a military officer," he wrote, "it was thought better to destroy the magazine than to blow it up. This fatiguing business was effected by carrying some five tons of powder down the cliffs and pouring it into the water. The warehouses and mills were then set on fire . . . the foundery, which was a very complete one, was totally destroyed."[27]

Rolling the barrels of powder down to the canal took some time. Simcoe notes that by day's end, his troops were so bushed from their efforts that most of them crawled into their tents to sleep without cooking their evening meal. Some other troops, presumably also skipping supper, eased their aching muscles by breaking into private houses "and there obtained rum."

Another casualty when the foundry was torched was Virginia's irreplaceable collection of public records that had been so hastily and mistakenly dumped on the foundry floor. All were burned.

Simcoe now turned his attention to the nearby town of Chesterfield, a military clothing depot, its warehouses filled with army supplies. That night, Simcoe torched them along with the town's mills.

Having destroyed cannon that shouldn't have been there, tons of precious gunpowder that shouldn't have been there, and priceless public historical records that shouldn't have been there, the exhausted troops must have slept through the night oblivious and indifferent to the numerous great bonfires that blazed in the night sky around them, destroying great quantities of military stores that shouldn't have been there. Benedict Arnold must have tipped his hat in the direction of the absconded Virginia government. It couldn't have been more accommodating.[28]

Arnold later informed Clinton that Simcoe and his troops "burnt and destroyed one of the finest foundries for cannon in America." He gave the count as "twenty six cannon . . . along with 310 barrels of gunpowder, plus several warehouses of oats."

When Simcoe's work-weary troops returned to Richmond, Arnold promptly marched his men back down to the boats in Westover under a ceaseless rain in roads so deep in red clay mud that to cover the twenty-five miles took almost two days, during which the rain never stopped. Along the way he encountered the last vestige of rebel opposition in all of Virginia. General von Steuben, whose recruiting and training base was in Chesterfield Court House, had set up an ambush along the river. But even the baron couldn't turn raw troops into fighters overnight. Against his ambush of the greenest of troops, Arnold sent a force that chased them off in a scrambling route.

All of Virginia, now helpless, lay open to Arnold's reaching hands.

Sometime around noon on January 3, Major Benjamin Fishbourne cantered into army headquarters in New Windsor, New York, and handed to General Washington a stunning letter written by the head of the Pennsylvania Line, Brig. Gen. Anthony Wayne.

> The most general and unhappy mutiny took place in the Pennsylvania line about 9 o'clock last night. It yet subsists; a great proportion of the troops, with some artillery, are marching toward Philadelphia. Every exertion has been made by the officers to divide them in their determination to revolt; it has succeeded in a temporary manner with near one half; how long it will last, God knows.[29]

The Pennsylvania Line was one of the Continental Army's backbone units, fully trained, battle-scarred, tough, most of them with more than three years on the line. When trouble came, Wayne's Pennsylvania Line was one of the first units Washington would call out. And trouble, Arnold, was coming soon.

More frightening was the possibility of a ripple effect of mutinies. Ever since Arnold had turned coat, Washington and his staff had been fearing that mass defections to the British might follow. Every officer was particularly on the alert for the slightest signs of revolt. Was this the way it was going to end, with entire military units swinging over to the British army?

On New Year's night, Wayne had come galloping into the Jockey Hollow camp, ridden right up to the mutineers, and ordered them to put away their weapons and return to their huts. They refused. Wayne felt his life was threatened and pulled open his coat.

"If you want to kill me, shoot me now!" he said. "Here's my breast. Shoot!"

The mutineers said that they had no quarrel with him or the other officers of the Line. "They have been our friends."

"Don't go over to the enemy!" Wayne said desperately.

"We'll hang any man who tries to do that," Sergeant Bowser assured him.[30]

It was clear: The Pennsylvania Line was not going to New York for new red coats. It was going to Philadelphia for back pay and food. Wayne, whose sympathies lay with his long-suffering, unpaid, unclothed, unfed troops and not with the indifferent legislators, agreed to represent them and promised them no harm would come to them as a result of the mutiny.

The specifics from Jockey Hollow were grim. One officer had been shot dead, another shot in the thigh, a third gutshot. Apparently a result of firing off weapons in the dark, none of these shootings were intentional. The ten infantry regiments and the artillery regiment gave the Line a total strength of about 2,500. Not all had mutinied. Perhaps half. Yet, with strictest discipline, those who had mutinied packed up their tents, equipment, and arms and in correct military formation, under command of their sergeants, at ten o'clock at night, set out for Philadelphia on winter roads to confront the Pennsylvania Supreme Executive Council with their grievances. They weren't planning on an idle chat. With them they were bringing cannons.

This was not the way Wayne had planned to spend his thirty-sixth birthday.

Up from Philadelphia hastily came Pennsylvania Assembly president Joseph Reed and his Supreme Executive Council, getting as close as Trenton. The mutineers stopped at Princeton, a few miles to the north. There the Board of Sergeants, chosen to represent the mutineers, set up headquarters in the partially burned Nassau Hall of what was later to become Princeton University.

The issues they put on the table had been festering for some time and should have been addressed long before by Reed and his Supreme Executive Council. Many of the oldest and most battle-seasoned troops had signed up for three years or the duration of the war. By insisting that the wording in their enlistments clearly implied "whichever comes first," they claimed that their time was up at the end of their third year.

Reed accepted this "or" interpretation, but only for those who had signed up before January 1777 for three years or the duration; they were free to retire or to ship over under better service conditions. However, this escape clause clearly did not apply to those later enlistees who had signed up simply for the duration. Yet many of these received full discharges before their actual papers were located, by falsely swearing as to the terms of their enlistments. As a result, more than half the Pennsylvania Line, legally or otherwise, promptly left. It was an awesome loss. The mutineers had fared so well that Washington, fearing they would trigger copycat mutinies in other units, scattered the remaining Pennsylvania units throughout eastern Pennsylvania.

The consequences were numbing. As an organized corps, the entire Pennsylvania Line had disappeared. In very short order, this loss was to have severe consequences for Washington and the Revolution.

A few nights later, in Philadelphia, President Reed and the Supreme Executive Committee of Pennsylvania threw a banquet for General Wayne.

It was to be a night of food, wine, and speeches. Wayne's handling of this affair, his close negotiations with the mutineers, and his liaison with both the Board of Sergeants and President Reed were consequences of the absolute trust his men had in him. As a result of his negotiations, no reprisals were taken, and the negotiations brought a conclusion to the mutiny.

But what was the celebration for—the disappearance of the Pennsylvania Line from the Continental Army? Wayne had long feared the possibility of a mutiny and had repeatedly warned the mulish, pinchpenny Pennsylvania legislature to correct the festering causes. Now, just when the Revolution was sliding into a most dangerous condition, just when Washington would need that Pennsylvania Line the most, high praise was being heaped on Wayne's head by the very men who had caused the mutiny, had lost that army.

Wayne had no illusions about the pack of shabby politicians who were thanking him for saving their necks. Just days before the mutiny, on December 28, 1781, Chaplain and Reverend David Jones had written to General Wayne: "It would take a large volume to give you a sketch of our public matters in the State of Penn'a, in short, nothing is done by our civil officers that answer any good purpose for the Army—Our taxes are insupportable, and all seems likely to be consumed in support of civil government. . . . What is lamentable is that our civil officers receive their pay, but no period is fixed to pay the Army. Today, the [Pennsylvania] Assembly rise, and I believe they have done little more than quarrel about the election."[31]

So the politicians paid themselves, skipped the army's pay, and instead of dealing with the mutiny that was so clearly about to explode in their faces, engaged in politics as usual, then went home. They could have given lessons to the Virginia government.

And Gen. Anthony Wayne found himself in command of a phantom army and empty barracks.

On January 20, Gen. Benedict Arnold reentered Portsmouth and found that his 400 troops missing at sea had finally landed unscathed. Also waiting was some deeply satisfying news from New York: The Pennsylvania Line had mutinied.[32]

"This event will be attended with happy consequences," Arnold assured Clinton. "We anxiously wait in expectation of hearing that the malcontents have joined His Majesty's army in New York."[33]

But soon they would receive greatly offsetting bad news from Cowpens that Banastre Tarleton had lost the entire left wing of Cornwallis's army to Dan Morgan on January 17.

With his troops reunited, Arnold now followed Clinton's cautious orders to set up winter quarters, construct an army base, train an army of

Virginia Loyalists, and plan his next campaign against American supply lines after the spring thaws. Arnold planned to move up and down the countryside at will, gnawing on the very innards and bones of the rebel resistance until it collapsed and he had grown rich.

The first raid had been highly successful. Echoing the devastation in the Carolinas, he had left soaring clouds of black smoke behind him as he burned a trail of flaming plantation houses, stables, tobacco barns, docks, and ships. The roads were crowded with refugees in wagons and on foot, carrying whatever valuables they could lift, and walking backward to see their homes and wealth eaten by flames.

The raids had been also highly profitable. He had taken a large number of ships, commandeered hundreds of hogsheads of tobacco, plundered homes of valuable possessions, and gathered up staggering quantities of provisions, military and naval stores in abundance, cordage, canvas cloth for sails, barrels of rope—all shipped to New York for the courts to libel and condemn and turn into very spendable prize money.

As a New Year's greeting to his wife, Arnold sent her a veritable Noah's Ark—"a sloop loaded with sheep, calves, geese, turkeys, ducks, guinea-hens, dunghill fowl, pigs, butter, eggs, hams, and smoked tongues."[34] This was just the kind of food that would find an eager market in hungry New York City.

Tranquility was not a characteristic of Arnold's life, however, and he was sailing once again directly into a major new quarrel.

In February 1781, with much grumbling and predictable hostility, the Congress took up the recommendations of the Hartford Convention, which demanded that Congress seize the power to tax as a power implied by the Articles of Confederation.

The French ambassador, Lucerne, who watched the moves of Congress with great care—and often with great intrusiveness—readily identified the kink in the hose that was blocking the flow of greater Continental powers. He wrote: "Samuel Adams, whose obstinate and resolute character was so useful to the revolution in its origin, but who shows himself very ill suited to the conduct of affairs in an organized government, has placed himself at the head of the advocates of the old system of committees of Congress, instead of relying on ministers, or secretaries. . . ."

He was referring in particular to Adams's strong resistance to transferring powers from congressional committees to an executive cabinet with secretaries or ministers for each executive function. Such a cabinet was urgently needed—if for nothing else than to remove a groaning burden of administrative work that was swamping the clogged committees. But once a cabinet was created, Adams well knew, control over efforts to get taxing powers would slip away from Congress. And with a singular lack of common sense, he fought to kill it.

After discussing the Hartford Convention proposal, the Congress appointed a three-man committee, James Madison of Virginia, James Duane of New York, and James Varnum of Rhode Island, to search the question of implied powers. All three were lawyers.

The committee was back in six days—now early March. Article XIII, they said, was the open sesame. The power to tax was clearly implied in Article XIII, which stated: "Every state shall abide by the determinations of the United States in Congress assembled, on all questions which by this confederation are submitted to them." Madison, Duane, and Varnum contended that Congress possessed "a general and implied power . . . to carry into effect all the Articles of the said Confederation against any of the States which shall refuse or neglect to abide by such their determinations." But then they acknowledged that "no determinate or particular provision" showed how that power was to be implemented.

Their solution: Propose an additional Article authorizing such power. That meant convening the states for a constitutional amendment to give the Congress the power, when states failed to send in their dues, "to employ the force of the United States by sea as by land to compel such state or States to fulfill their federal engagements."[35]

The report was tabled, to be brought up for consideration at some future date.

In Portsmouth, the February days must have seemed especially bleak to Brig. Gen. Benedict Arnold after he—with his infernal propensity to fight rather than negotiate, to turn friend into enemy—managed to get into another quarrel, once again working against his own best interests. But perhaps this time he was truly the victim.

Arnold's haul in Virginia was enormous, but some of the most lucrative plums, taken on the James River, were clearly maritime prizes. Nonetheless, Arnold had either personally captured—or made possible the taking of—most of them and felt justified in claiming his share. Despite the terms Symonds and Arnold had agreed to, Symonds's officers—possibly with Symonds's blessing—began to chafe against giving half of such a great amount of maritime prize money to Arnold and sought to cut him out by claiming that the maritime prizes belonged solely to the navy. This would be a shabby way for Symonds to abrogate his deal with Arnold, but the commodore's take would obviously be much larger if he could euchre Arnold out of his share of the pie. Deal or no deal, the sailors were ganging up on him.

Arnold must have suspected that Symonds was behind the challenge. So when he appealed the issue to General Clinton in New York, he contrived to offend the commodore so greatly that Symonds refused to carry Arnold's troops up the Chesapeake to attack Lafayette's troop transports. Symonds gave as his excuse the shoal water of the bay.

Arnold thereupon fanned the flames of the quarrel further by scornfully suggesting that Symonds was a coward who used the excuse of shoal water "whenever he thinks there is danger."[36]

Arnold must have been deeply unhappy when the whole brouhaha was sent back to New York. There it would become entangled in army-navy politics and naval prize courts where Arnold had no friends and Symonds had many. It may be that trying to negotiate would have done little, but quarreling may have cost him everything. For all his dashing exploits, Arnold faced a substantial financial mugging. Once again he would pay the price of having no friends.

He must have felt cold comfort to realize that his dashing exploits had won over one of his British officers, Colonel Simcoe, who enthusiastically reported that "the garrison is in great spirits, full of confidence in the daring courage of General Arnold."[37]

But the third man, the Scot, Colonel Dundas, was another story and would soon speak out.

Three

Cornwallis versus Greene

In Winnsboro, South Carolina, the previous November, sick from fever, Major General Charles, Lord Cornwallis, had been carried by army wagon into his winter camp. Behind him followed his weary, sick army.

The General had lain in the wagon for days, bouncing, rocking, swaying through muck and mud, over roads pocked with holes and ditches, so sick he passed control over his fever-wracked army to his second in command, the twenty-six-year-old Lord Francis Rawdon.

Lord Cornwallis was tormented by more than his fever. Militarily he was in a tight corner: His autumn campaign, expected to have begun the wrap-up of the entire Revolution, had ended in a disaster.

Clinton in New York was scolding. Lord Germain in London was frowning. The king in Kew was drumming his fingers. Fever or no, Cornwallis knew he had to formulate a plan to mend himself, rebuild his army, and recover control of the Carolinas war. His reputation was at hazard. His usual unflappable self-confidence had been shaken.

At forty-two, Cornwallis, unlike Clinton in almost every way, was ideally suited to his Carolina command. An eager fighter, aggressive, unhesitating, a gifted general who reveled in warfare, he had earned the great affection and loyalty of his troops, who, enduring every sort of hardship, would fight like hell for him. And the earl looked like an aristocrat. His painting by Sir Joshua Reynolds portrays a patrician with that imperious expression that seemed to be fitted onto every highborn face at birth. And he was in every sense an aristocrat. Bearing the title of the first marquis and second Earl Cornwallis, he was descended from a Suffolk family whose antecedents could be traced back to the fourteenth century.

A warm and affectionate man, the earl was utterly devoted to his country, to his estate, and to his family. Marrying below his station to Jemima Tullekins Jones, the daughter of Col. James Jones, a commoner, he had doted on her and his two children, Charles and Mary. Only the strongest call to duty could have induced him to leave his family and his Suffolk estate.

Born on New Year's Eve 1738, he attended Eton, where on the playing fields a future bishop of Durham gave him "a permanent cast in one eye."[1] He began his military career at seventeen when he was commissioned an ensign in the Grenadier Guards. He went on to become one of the few officers of the period to study the arts of war formally when he enrolled in the military academy in Turin. Later he saw military action in Europe. In 1760, having reached his twenty-first birthday, he entered the House of Commons, and upon the death of his father in 1762 he entered the House of Lords as the second Earl Cornwallis.

As a parliamentarian, he sided with the American colonists through a number of crises, voting against such measures as the Stamp Act of 1765. But when the violence began in Massachusetts, duty required him to help put down the rebellion. He offered his services to his king. On January 1, 1776, a grateful King George III commissioned him a lieutenant general of the army of North America, and the next month sent him to Boston.

In 1779 Jemima died. Her death "effectually destroyed all my hopes of happiness in this world." Cornwallis, grieving for her and sick of the war on principle and sick of second command under two officers he did not respect (Howe and Clinton), sick of the bungling and incompetence, sailed for home and almost did not return to the American war.[2]

His relationship with Clinton was antagonistic. Homesick for his children, he chafed against Clinton's creeping conduct of an unending war, and stated openly that the battle should be brought not to the Carolinas but to Virginia. Yet he eagerly took the Carolinas command to get away from Clinton, to get away from New York, and to get back onto the battlefield, perhaps to bring an end to the conflict.

Now, fever-ridden, what he needed was a quiet winter season—a few fever-free, trouble-free months—to rejuvenate his army and train new Loyalist recruits. Then in the spring sunshine, under fluttering banners, he would march out of camp restored, resupplied, and enlarged to hunt down the last remnants of the American army, to wrest convincing victory over the rebels, and to turn the tempo of the war back in his favor. In control once again, he would do what he had wanted to do from the beginning. In order to give the coup de grâce to the American cause, he would move up into Virginia, to the Chesapeake to set up a base there at Norfolk or Portsmouth—or perhaps a place called Yorktown. Time would tell.

From the beginning, the Carolinas campaign had been governed by London, by a plan conceived over sherry and tea in the British cabinet offices of Whitehall by Lord George Germain. And it was based on a simple concept: Break the spirit of the rebels, force them back down on their knees into complete submission.

Germain sought total victory through a fast-moving two-part plan of conquest. First was the recruitment of American Loyalists. He had been assured that young Loyalist tigers could be found in abundance among the wealthy plantations of the Carolinas, so he sited his new war plan there. These young Americans in British uniforms would then be turned on the rebels to drive them out root and branch from the Carolinas. Once the Carolinas had been pacified, the same tactics would be applied in a roll-up through Virginia and the mid-Atlantic—burning, hanging, scattering, destroying until the last spark of resistance was smothered and the thirteen colonies would be led in chains back to the king.

The role of the regular British army would be twofold: Train the new Loyalist recruits on British army bases, then set up a series of fortified control centers, staff them with the new Loyalist army, and turn them loose on the rebel countryside with musket, bayonet, and torch, leaving the rebels with no roofs over their heads, with no place to hide, nowhere to form up and organize. In short, submission or extermination. The ideal Loyalist unit would be mounted—dragoons who could fight from the saddle with their sabers, and mounted infantry who could rush to a battle site, dismount, and function like classic infantry with musket and bayonet. The British army at this point would be free to leave.

Initially the Germain plan had been extraordinarily successful. Sir Henry Clinton himself led the conquest of Charleston, which netted the enormous bonus of an American army trapped inside the city.

At that point, General Clinton had turned over the job to Lord Cornwallis—an enormous, challenging assignment. Sir Henry had ordered the earl to pacify a huge area, some 15,000 square miles, much of it primitive backcountry, hilly and mountainous, and another large area full of pestilential swamps that regularly filled cemeteries with fever victims. To control all this the earl established a perimeter of forward bases, swinging in an arc 350 miles wide, from Ninety Six, the anchor base for all the other forward bases, eastward to Camden—with its satellite outposts at Cheraw, Hanging Rock, and Rocky Mount—then further east to Georgetown on the coast. In between were a number of smaller outposts.

Staffed with a combination of British army regulars and British-trained Loyalist regulars, these strong points—log forts most of them—functioned like regional police stations.

To italicize the importance of the Loyalists, Cornwallis had put in command of his key base at Ninety Six Gen. John Harris Cruger, a New York Loyalist with a distinguished war record in whom both Cornwallis and Clinton had the greatest confidence.

In addition, the earl had brought from New York several British army units that were made up of almost exclusively of Americans—Loyalists in red coats. They included the Volunteers of Ireland, the New York

Volunteers, the Prince of Wales American Regiment, and, particularly, Tarleton's British Legion, one of the finest fighting units in the British army anywhere in the world. From the Carolinas were drawn the South Carolina Royalists and the North Carolina Volunteers. These units of Americans, hating the rebels, were eager to welcome all the Carolinian Loyalist recruits they could lure into camp.

By June 1780, less than two months after landing in Charleston, Lord Cornwallis had the system of log forts up and working. The initial response of Loyalist volunteers was encouraging.

Then on August 16 at Camden, South Carolina, the earl achieved the absolute capstone of his Southern campaign with a crushing victory over a second Continental army, under General Horatio Gates. This was barely three months after the fall of Charleston and made Camden the greatest American disaster of the war; the beginning of the end, many predicted. In London Cornwallis's reputation had soared, equaling that of Clinton's. Lord George Germain was hailed as a modern-day Hannibal, a military genius. London waited for the arrival of thirteen scalps.

Indeed, those two victories alone should have brought the Americans to the negotiating table. In fact, many a prudent soldier would have thrown in his hand at that point and surrendered. Two American armies in three months—not just defeated but completely erased, including all the necessary war-making equipment—two complete rebel armies now caged and dying inside British fever hulks in Charleston harbor. With no third army in the offing, the Americans' revolution was on the ropes. Or so it had seemed.

Cornwallis kept right on pressing the rebels, searching out the last spark of resistance. His British Legion under the brilliant Banastre Tarleton, in galloping attacks, struck at the remnants of organized patriot resistance. In rapid order, the ferocious Tarleton smashed the rebels at Monck's Corner—which cut off General Lincoln's escape route from Charleston—then struck again at Lenud's Ferry and yet again at Waxhaws. Broken and scattered, the tatters of the rebel army were on the run everywhere.

At the same time, Loyalist units had ranged out of the outpost forts to terrorize the homes and farms of local rebels. Raiding, looting, bayoneting, hanging, the Loyalist terror campaign from the first cowed the populace over large areas. Many rebels, sensing the collapse of the Revolution, returned home.

On the surface South Carolina had been pacified and fortified. Officially, on June 30 Cornwallis reported to Clinton "an end to all resistance in South Carolina."[3]

Then affairs began to falter. To begin with, the earl had uncovered serious administrative problems inside his army—internal problems that had appeared almost as soon as he left Charleston and that had bedeviled him ever since.

One of them was cavalry. To operate the long communication and supply lines between Charleston and the outposts, he needed an abundance of cavalry, but Clinton had taken most of the cavalry back to New York with him along with most of the wagons and dray horses as well as shiploads of other essential equipment.

As a result, long delays in resupplying ensued; worse, opportunistic bands of rebel guerrillas—mounted, swiftly moving—began attacking and cutting those lines. To beef up the wagon train escorts, Cornwallis had to take troops away from his front lines, to defend the wagons and also to rebuild the repeatedly destroyed bridges. And to snuff out the increasing guerrilla menace, Cornwallis saw that he needed still more cavalry, more horses, more wagons. Also, he needed many more volunteer Carolina Loyalists than he was getting—many thousands more.

He began to see that the military tarpaulin Clinton had handed him was cut too small to cover the entire territory.

Clinton had even shortchanged Cornwallis on medical supplies and medical personnel. From the day he began campaigning, Cornwallis faced a severe shortage of both. His urgent requests to Clinton were ignored.[4]

Money problems also hampered operations. Clinton hadn't left Cornwallis with enough ready cash. So instead of purchasing military supplies, Cornwallis had to commandeer them, which immediately alienated the very people—Loyalists—he was there to win over.

And then the British army's notorious corruption became a factor.

On paper, the lowly foot soldier was paid 8 pence a day, but as that money filtered down through the system, from London through many hands to the commanding officer, paymaster, even sergeant, each level took his cut. Usually the payee never saw a penny of his pay. On top of that, the system was further corrupted by carrying dead and even fictitious soldiers on the payrolls.

The officers of the quartermaster general's corps operated their own scams. They often went into business for themselves, buying up—probably expropriating—civilian wagons which they then leased to themselves, and thus to the British army at skylofty prices that they pocketed. On more than one occasion, they actually held back wagons, hobbling Cornwallis's already hard-pressed supply lines while further alienating the Loyalists.

Also making enemies everywhere was the army's custom of looting and stealing as they marched. British officers turned looting into a roaring business. "They earmarked certain supplies for the use of the army. Other valuable items—silver, slaves, rice and indigo—they sold through their army commissaries and divided the profits according to rank, as naval crews divided spoils taken on the high seas." Much of this booty had been taken from the Loyalists they had come to save.[5]

Perversely, even the weather joined the rebel side. Rain seemed endless that spring through autumn. Roads became rivers of mud, slowing movement between outposts; rivers became lakes requiring long detours, creating delays of days and even weeks; men became struggling somnambulists, ending their sodden days in an ordeal of fireless meals and leaking tents. On one occasion in just thirty hours the Pee Dee River rose twenty-five feet.[6] The only consolation was knowing that the rain fell just as hard on the rebels.

On top of that, swamp fevers struck and devastated Cornwallis's army. At times as many as one-quarter of his troops had been laid up.

Furthermore, Clinton had foisted a major piece of mischief on Cornwallis: He left him with a disastrous proclamation to enforce.

Initially Clinton had offered a full pardon and British protection to all rebellious Americans who would renew their allegiance to the king—including all the South Carolina militia captured in Charleston. (The Continental regulars captured there were imprisoned on British prison hulks in the harbor.) But two days later, Clinton went one step further. He now demanded that the forgiven must actively support the British army. Otherwise they would be recategorized as rebels. The effect had been chilling.

Having been convinced the Revolution was over, a number of disaffected rebels—including some important leaders like Sumter—had chosen to accept the original proclamation and return to British citizenship. But now they would be required to take up arms against their old comrades, or at least inform on them. Betray or defy. They chose to defy and promptly swung back into the rebel camp.

Lord Rawdon saw firsthand what great damage Clinton's second proclamation had caused. He wrote Cornwallis that previously, most of the people in Waxhaws, while "ill disposed" toward the British, had not taken up arms. But "nine out of ten of them are now embodied on the part of the rebels. . . . The greater part of the Waxhaw people have joined the rebels. The rest live under the enemy's protections."[7]

Cornwallis had known nothing of this proclamation until Clinton told him casually after the fact. Literally calling up a "second rebellion," Sir Henry then returned to New York.

Cornwallis wrote a "thanks-a-lot" letter to Admiral Arbuthnot, who had countersigned the proclamation: "I hope you will not be offended when I assure you that the Proclamation of the Commissioners of the 1st, and that of the General of the 3rd, did not at all contribute to the success of my operations."

As soon as Clinton left, Cornwallis rescinded the second proclamation. But rebel propagandists made much of it, while many of those who knew of the proclamation probably never knew of its cancellation or, if they did, distrusted it.

As for the policy to raise an army of Loyalist Americans, British army regulars were putting serious dents in that. British snobbery was combining with contempt for things American. A particularly flagrant example had just occurred on the march into the Winnsboro winter quarters.

While Cornwallis lay in his wagon, his army struggled to move through mud and clay slippery as ice. At the Sugar Creek crossing, the horses, now exhausted, could not draw the wagons and artillery across the slippery bottom and up the steep bank. Loyalist militia in an extraordinary act of selflessness unhitched the spent animals from the traces and shouldered the harnesses themselves. To the British officers, if you acted like a horse you were treated like a horse, and consequently they cursed and abused the struggling men and even beat them. The Americans, waiting for darkness, slipped away before dawn, taking their horses with them.

Forever gone, Commissary Stedman reported, noting they were "chusing to run the risque of meeting the resentment of their enemies rather than submit to the derision and abuse of those to whom they looked up as friends."[8] Having scampered, they quickly spread stories of their treatment by the British, stories that did nothing for the British recruiting program.

At the same time rebel guerrillas were conducting a special campaign of attacking and scattering Loyalist militia units. And they spread word that they would burn the homes of any Loyalists who volunteered for the British army.

As though to drive home the point, a mounted rebel patrol came upon a party of Loyalist drovers herding cattle to the British army camp. With flailing sabers they killed twenty-three of the drovers.[9] The warning was not wasted: Loyalist recruitment fell on even harder times.

Then the policy of crushing the rebels began to shred. That is, Lt. Col. Banastre Tarleton and his mounted British Legion turned from being a major weapon against the rebels into a serious problem themselves.

Initially Colonel Tarleton had seemed just the man under Cornwallis to commence the program of harassing and scattering the rebels. The son of a wealthy former lord mayor of Liverpool and a so-so student at Oxford, at nineteen Banastre Tarleton appeared to be starting off his life on the wrong hoof. He squandered his inheritance—a fortune—on London gambling and high living and seemed destined for the pinched career of a wastrel. But when his mother bought him a commission as coronet, Tarleton discovered his métier as a born cavalryman and galloped into the pages of American history. So adept was he at his new military trade that Tarleton was promoted to lieutenant colonel before his twenty-fourth birthday.

A powerfully built peppery redhead of middle height, Tarleton was assigned command of the superb British Legion in New York, the instrument that was to lead him to fame and fortune. Composed of young men from American Loyalist families in New York, New Jersey, and Pennsylvania, the Legion quickly became a fast-moving, hard-hitting company of cavalrymen and mounted infantrymen. A martinet and a perfectionist who drilled his men endlessly, Tarleton personally sharpened their performance to a whetted edge. When he was finished, he had made the British Legion "the most powerful combat team in the British Army."[10]

Furthermore, the young colonel would soon have a personal overriding motive for attacking the rebels: On the previous October 2, his closest friend, Major John André, was hanged by Washington as a spy.

In their green jackets, to mark them as Loyalist Americans, and their dragoon helmets with jaunty plumes and black armbands to mourn André, the British Legion swept through the South like avenging angels—devils, said the Americans—terrifying vast hordes of Southerners who fled for their lives at the sound of the Legionnaires' hoofbeats.

Tarleton was known as a ferocious leader, sparing neither men nor mounts as he covered impressive distances in short order, arriving on the scene at a full gallop, then, without pause and often greatly outnumbered, charging onto the battlefield and into explosive action against the enemy. The Green Dragoons rarely lost. On one occasion he drove his men more than 100 miles in fifty-four hours. On another occasion he arrived at a battle scene with animals so spent, the artillery horses could not drag the cannon up on the battle line. Undaunted, he charged onto the battlefield and won. At the end of another such day, twenty horses dropped dead where they stood. Such tactics made the British Legion the terror of the backcountry, especially when their explosive violence overwhelmed the Americans at the battles of Monck's Corner, Lenud's Ferry, and Waxhaws. Word spread that they were invincible.

But another side to Tarleton and his Green Dragoons soon showed itself. When he sailed for the Carolinas with his men, the innkeepers and public houses of Long Island were glad to see them go. Tarleton left behind a reputation as a deadbeat and a cheapskate who had stiffed landlords all over New York and Philadelphia.

Tavern owner Epenetus Smith spit whenever he mentioned Tarleton's name, for the cavalryman and his British Legionnaires had run up an unpaid tab of £250 for room and board, then left. Worse, they had staggered away with forty gallons of rum, forty-two sheep, five beef cattle, sixteen turkeys, three geese, a hog, forty bushels of corn, two petticoats, and a silk handkerchief. Repeating this process time and again, they could claim that this was the custom of most British army units in America, including royal governor and general William Tryon, but the bilked innkeepers had a different view.

Showing an even bleaker side in the Carolinas, Tarleton's men soon developed a taste for rape and rapine, mayhem and murder, leaving behind them a trail of blood and tears. Soon the Carolinians' fear of Tarleton and his British Legion turned into revulsion, then anger, then fury.

The stories of the British Legion scandalized the entire region. Searching for loot, Banastre Tarleton ordered the corpse of a recently dead elderly Loyalist, Richard Richardson, to be dug up. The colonel must have had trouble controlling his smirk when he stated that he merely wanted to look upon the face of such a brave man. But that's all he got; the silverware he was seeking was not there. Tarleton believed that the grieving widow, Mary Richardson, had warned Francis Marion, the notorious Swamp Fox, of the Legion's approach and that she knew where Marion's base was. After dining well in her home, Tarleton, according to Francis Marion, had Mrs. Richardson flogged. Then Tarleton had all the farm animals driven into the Richardson barn, which was set on fire, and for a grand finale, amidst the screams of the dying animals, he left Mrs. Richardson to watch her mansion that he had just dined in burn to the ground.[11]

The wealthy Loyalist Lady Jane Colleton and several other women guests at her plantation, Fairlawn Barony, were amazed to find themselves beset by Green Dragoons bent on rape. Defending her guests, Lady Colleton had her hand slashed by an angry cavalry saber. British colonel Patrick Ferguson wanted the dragoons lined up and shot; Tarleton indifferently watched his men led away to be mercilessly whipped by Cornwallis. But when the Carolinians, especially women, heard about it, the damage was irreparable. Thereafter his Green Dragoons were considered unsafe around any women, rebel or Loyalist.

At the Battle of Monck's Corners, Chevalier Pierre-François Vernier, who commanded the remnants of Pulaski's Continental Horse, surrendered and downed his arms. Numerous sabers thereupon slashed him, mangling his body, and as he lay dying Green Dragoons stood over him to mock his last gasps, shocking other British officers who were present.

Tarleton's most notorious offense took place at the Battle of Rugeley's Mill in Waxhaws, north of Camden, right after the fall of Charleston. He had caught up with a small band of Continental infantry under Col. Abraham Buford hastening away toward Virginia. Buford, after putting up a brief but ineffectual defense, surrendered and called for quarter—clemency. Killing a soldier calling for quarter was considered murder.

Tarleton's dragoons instead fell upon the disarmed men and, as Tarleton watched, began a systematic slaughter that went on for fifteen minutes. One hundred and thirteen disarmed men were killed, many on their knees; of the 150 others who were wounded, many subsequently died, Americans paying back Americans. The dragoons were accused not only of sabering and bayoneting wounded men lying on the ground but of pulling away bodies to stab the wounded underneath. Tarleton and the British army denied the charges ever after, but too many witnesses told the story in graphic detail to silence the scandal.

Banastre became "Bloody Ban" and "Banastre the butcher" and soon was the most hated man in the British army. "Tarleton's quarter" was now an American battle cry. Many were the Carolinians on the sidelines who now became active enemies of the British flag. And uncounted were the many surrendered British and Loyalist soldiers who were bayoneted in reprisal.

The British army never understood the decisive role of newspapers in the Revolution. These maintained an unblinking watch on British behavior and followed every action with as much information—and bias—as they could get. They identified British officers by name and rank and record. Tarleton's butchery of Buford's men was reported in detail in papers throughout the colonies. Typical was *The Pennsylvania Gazette*. It never afterward would refer to Tarleton as simply Tarleton but always with an attached epithet: "Tarleton, who massacred Col. Buford's party after they begged quarter."[12] The British had given the Americans another martyr and a major monster both.

One of Tarleton's officers, Capt. Charles Campbell, with a contingent of Green Dragoons, was sent to arrest—and no doubt hang—Thomas Sumter, a former colonel in the Continental Army. Sumter's wife, Mary, who had been handicapped all her life, was sitting on her porch with her housekeeper when Campbell and his British legion approached. He demanded that Mrs. Sumter tell him where her husband was; Sumter, who had taken the parole and had been inactive, had been warned by his eleven-year-old son and escaped only minutes before. Mrs. Sumter refused to answer Campbell's question. The soldiers then looted the home and the smokehouse and barns. When Mary Sumter still refused to talk, Campbell ordered his troops to carry her off the porch in her chair and left her, like Widow Richardson, with a front-row seat to the burning of her home.[13]

Thomas Sumter's response was predictable. In nonstop fury, he created a guerrilla group and, within six weeks, made his first major strike against the British, then went on to compile an astonishing record of destruction and mayhem that tore gaping holes in British defenses. He was ever after known as the Carolina Gamecock. Campbell's torch had ignited a fanatic.

Hate drove another Tarleton officer, Capt. Christian Huck, "My Lord Hook," a lawyer from a prominent Philadelphia Quaker family who seethed with loathing for rebels, particularly Presbyterians.

Leading a band of Green Dragoons, Huck went into raptures of looting, butchering, plundering, burning, and sacking entire valleys. He cut swathes of destruction forty miles long, from one end of a valley to the other, while summarily hanging even the clearly innocent in front of their families. When a young boy reading his Bible in a church was shot dead by a Huck legionnaire, the murder provided passionate material for rebel newspapers.

Tarleton ordered Huck to search out Sumter and as many of his partisan lieutenants as he could capture and kill. On July 11, Huck and 115 men, headed by thirty-five of Tarleton's dragoons, went to the home of rebel captain John McClure. Frustrated at not finding him home, they camped for the night a half mile down the road at James Williamson's plantation.

Huck had not found the rebels, but they found him. At sunrise, Captain McClure along with a number of other rebel leaders—including Bratton, Hill, Neel, and Lacey—plus some 250 men, mostly from Sumter's camp, closed in on Williamson's plantation. Asleep, with no guards posted, Huck and his men were "caught totally by surprise." They tried to defend themselves; the dragoons managed three bayonet attacks but were beaten back. They broke and ran. Trying to rally his troops from horseback, Huck was shot twice in the head by sharpshooter Thomas Carroll. Few of Huck's party survived; according to Tarleton's account, 91 men out of 115 were either killed or captured.

The rebel losses were minuscule: one man killed; one wounded.

Sumter's men had scored an astonishing victory. Huck's Defeat, as the battle came to be called, was more than the defeat of Huck. Proving that even Cornwallis's deadliest unit, the British Legion, could be beaten, Huck's Defeat in particular caused a great resurgence in rebel confidence. Thereafter, from all over the backcountry, single men or groups or families searched out and joined Sumter in his camp at Tuckasegee Ford in North Carolina or found Marion on his Snow Island camp in the South Carolina swamps. Or they volunteered to Davie or Pickens or any of an increasing number of guerrilla leaders. Every day that summer of 1780, while Cornwallis believed his program was working, the ranks in the guerilla camps were swelling. The week following Huck's Defeat, Sumter's band alone had increased by 600 men.[14]

The damage to the British cause was becoming irreparable. Public opinion—even Loyalist—began to turn against them. Germain's policy had succeeded only in raising hordes of active enemies where there had been few before.

One of Tarleton's majors, James Wemyss, needing little prompting to emulate his commanding officer, spread devastation with pitiless gusto. Wearing his upper-class British snobbery like a banner, Wemyss hated the colonials with a passion, considered them little better than livestock, and treated them like vermin. He kept a meticulous list of all the houses he burned, all the men he hanged.

When Huck was killed, Cornwallis sent Major Wemyss to find and kill the now very active fury-driven Sumter. Cornwallis's orders to the Major would bring joy to heart of any brigand: He was ordered to confiscate the arms of anyone "untrustworthy." He was to "punish the Concealment of Arms and Ammunition with a total Demolition of the Plantation," and hang any person who had broken parole summarily on the spot without trial.[15]

Searching for Sumter, Wemyss and his contingent of 150 British Legion dragoons rode seventy miles from Kingstree to Cheraw, sacking as they went—burning fifty homes, a Presbyterian church ("sedition shops," he called them), gristmills, blacksmith shops, and loom houses. Wemyss invited the local Loyalist militia, who had been unable to subdue the area alone, to now plunder it at will. Burdened with more loot than they could carry, the dragoons left behind a valley canopied with smoke from burning houses and barns and crops, the air filled with the screams of dying animals and the cries of homeless women and children. The area of desolation was in most places fifteen miles wide.[16]

While Adam Cusac's wife and children were standing beside Wemyss's horse, reaching imploring hands up to him, Wemyss watched Cusac readied for hanging. When the noose slipped over Cusac's head, his anguished family collapsed on the ground in front of Wemyss's horse. Wemyss, in a great rage, attempted to trample them under his horse's hooves, thwarted only when a young officer pulled the horse back by the bridle. Cusac died kicking in air in full view of his family. Then Wymess burned his house.[17]

Dr. James Wilson's pleas on behalf of Cusac's innocence were answered when Wemyss burned the Wilson house, too. Wemyss got his response from Dr. Wilson, in turn, when the doctor rode off to join the guerrilla band of the Swamp Fox, Francis Marion. Like Tarleton, Wemyss—now placed second on the list of the most hated men in the British army— was creating more rebels than he was killing.

Finally, in the middle of the night of November 9, at the Battle of Fishdam Ford, Wemyss caught up with the Carolina Gamecock. Moving in darkness, he and his Legionnaires closed in on Sumter's camp. But the surprisers were surprised: The waiting rebels shot Wemyss from his saddle, severely wounded him in arm and leg, captured him, and wounded many of his men, capturing others. Wemyss, the joyful burner of home and barn, was now prisoner of the man against whom Wemyss had sent two assassins, the man whose home Wemyss's fellow Legionnaire, Campbell, had burnt to the ground.

Sumter's restraint after capturing Wemyss is impressive, even puzzling. When the wounded Wemyss was searched, Sumter found in his pocket the list of the houses he had burned and the men he had hanged. Sumter by firelight read the damning list, then saved Wemyss from instant death by his rebel troops when he put the paper in the fire.

Making matters worse, the original policy of looting only rebels was abandoned when the British army discovered that the real wealth was in the homes of the rich Loyalists, especially the rice kings. Thereafter to the redcoats loot was loot, whether Loyalist or rebel.

Eliza Wilkinson, a very young widow who lived on Yonge's Island, thirty miles south of Charleston, wrote a letter to a friend to describe the sacking of her home when a band of "inhuman Britons" entered. One of them took a trunkful of her clothes, and then looked down at her shoes.

> "I want them buckles," said he, and immediately knelt at my feet to take them out, which, while he was busy about, a brother villain, whose enormous mouth extended from ear to ear, bawled out, "Shares there! I say, shares!" So they divided my buckles between them.
>
> Other wretches . . . took my sister's ear-rings from her ears: hers and Miss Sammuell's buckles. They demanded her ring from her finger. She pleaded for it, told them it was her wedding ring, and begged they'd let her keep it. But they still demanded it, and, presenting a pistol at her, swore if she did not deliver it immediately, they'd fire. She gave it to them, and, after bundling up all their booty, they mounted their horses. But such despicable figures! Each wretch's bosom stuffed so full they appeared to be all afflicted with some dropsical disorder. . . . They took care to tell us, when they were going away, that they had favored us a great deal—that we might thank our stars it was no worse.[18]

Often the looting was of the humblest items. The British seemed to specialize in looting the homes of women whose husbands were "away" and therefore presumed to be rebels. A Loyalist raiding party from Thicketty Fort looted the home of Samuel McJunkin, taking clothing, blankets, and quilts. McJunkin's young daughter, Jane, in cold fury tried to snatch back her quilt from a soldier. He was winning the tugging contest when he slipped on a pile of fresh manure. As he went down, she put her foot on his chest, yanked the quilt free, and took it back into her house, amidst raucous laughter.[19] This and other acts of looting by Loyalist raiders in Thicketty Fort soon brought an American attack and conquest of that fort. The biggest enemy facing the British army in the Carolinas was turning out to be the British army.

One of the most devastating effects of the British policy of slash, burn, and hang was the smoldering backcountry civil war that it fanned into an inferno of brutality by men like Benjamin Cleveland. Long before the British came, the Carolinas had been a crazy quilt of different groups. The major division was between two economic classes: the rice and indigo kings who owned the great plantations along the tidewater on the edges of the endless swamps—which placed them among the wealthiest families in the new world—and the impoverished backcountry people whom the rice kings treated with such contempt that they even froze them out of the legislative and judicial system. The backcountry people regarded the rice kings as class enemies, invincibly Loyalist and predatory.

But there were much more significant divisions. The backcountry people had many quarrels among themselves: Huguenots who had left France rather than become Catholics; Scotch-Presbyterian Irish who bore a hatred for the English that reached back to Ireland; Scotch Catholic Highlanders who had emigrated after the Battle of Culloden Moor of 1745—that blood-soaked defeat of the Scots' royal pretender, Bonnie Prince Charlie—and now were largely loyal to the crown; Presbyterians and Baptists who hated paying a mandated tax that supported the official religion, the Anglican Church of England; the same Presbyterians and Baptists who disliked and distrusted—hated is not too strong a word—each other as well as all Catholics; Germans, often isolated by the barrier of language, who were afraid to be disloyal to the English king who had given them their land and could reclaim it; and the native Indians who had been at intermittent war with the settlers for generations.

Mixed into this stew of group hostilities were numerous local feuds and bickering brought on by land disputes, ill-defined borders, personal grudges, and family quarrels as ineradicable as the Hatfield and McCoy feud, all in a vast land where there were few arbitrating courts, and little police order. To compound the complex, as an overlay on all these layers of explosive unrest was the ultimate division—that between blood-in-the-eye rebels and Loyalists who would kill each other on sight—often dividing families into bitter factions.

The depredations of the British army—from Tarleton down to the lowliest British foot soldier—provided the spark that set off this smoldering tinderbox of murderous violence. And soon both sides, Loyalist and rebel, were committing appalling atrocities. Bands of men stalked each other, butchering the sleeping in their blankets, taking no prisoners. Amid shouts of "Tarleton's Quarter," men, surrendered and unarmed, were routinely bayoneted to death, which led to endless bloody reprisals and counterreprisals. With their homes gone and crops burned in their fields, women, children, and the elderly slept in the woods, starving in winter. Inhuman brigandage occurred everywhere. Women wandered the burned-out countryside seeking lost sons, husbands, fathers.

Every day these backcountry fighters were giving Banastre Tarleton and his sackers lessons in brutality and pitilessness far beyond their imaginings. From the frontier of North Carolina, Benjamin Cleveland, a 300-pound rebel eventually to weigh 450, a sadistic Indian fighter and a justice notorious for his cruelty and summary executions, had as great a fondness for the noose as any Loyalist. Partaking of the great victory at Kings Mountain, he pressed for the drumhead execution of thirty-six of Ferguson's captured Loyalists. To his dismay, the other rebel leaders, after hanging nine, had enough and released the rest.

On another occasion, bringing two Loyalists from a jailhouse, Cleveland stood one of them on a log, placed a noose around his neck, then ordered the log to be kicked from beneath his feet. While the struggling man was slowly strangling, Cleveland then gave the other Loyalist two choices: Swing or cut off your ears. With the hanging man probably still kicking and gasping right next to him, the second man called for a knife and stropped it on a brick. He cut off one ear, then the other. With both ears on the ground, he fled, streaming blood. Buchanan reports he was "never heard of afterwards."[20]

A Loyalist counterpart to rebel Benjamin Cleveland was the equally homicidal Thomas Brown. One day, armed only with a pistol and sword, he was fighting for his life against a group of 100 rebels when a "miserable miscreant" knocked him senseless with a rifle butt. They looted his home, then hot-tarred Brown's legs before holding his feet over a fire. In the meantime, not to neglect the rest of his body, they cut off his hair, then scalped him. Afflicted with a pounding headache for the rest of his life, Brown survived minus two toes; miraculously, he was eventually able to walk again. And walk he did into the annals of Carolina bloodshed, for he became a holy terror nicknamed Burntfoot Brown who spent years wreaking such stunning revenge on rebels, anywhere, everywhere, that General Cornwallis banished him to the frontier in Georgia, where, unforgiving to the end, he hanged thirteen rebel prisoners and had Indians torture others.[21]

The Loyalists around the fort at Ninety Six had such a hatred for rebels that a paroled rebel officer reported that "he had seen eleven patriots hung at Ninety Six a few days before, for being Rebels."[22] Professor Edgar quotes a report that in the district around Ninety Six alone lived some "twelve hundred" widows.[23]

Of the three Harrison brothers who helped organize the Loyalist regiment known as the South Carolina Rangers, Robert was killed in battle, while both John and Samuel were shot dead in their beds.[24]

Governor Rutledge of South Carolina described the civil war in his state as "such severities as are unpractised, and will scarcely be credited by civilized nations."[25] Nathanael Greene wrote in December 1780: "The Whigs and Tories pursue one another with the most relentless fury, killing and destroying each other whenever they meet. . . . If a stop cannot be put to these massacres, the country will be depopulated in a few months, as neither Whig nor Tory can live."[26] This brutality more resembled a homicidal brawl than organized warfare. Fought not for territory and advantageous treaties, not even for loot or reparations, the skirmishes had one murderous intent: extermination.

The violent policy against the rebels had been conceived in London by Lord Germain, who had never been to America and could not conceive of the existence of mortals like the backcountry Carolinians. Nor had Lord Cornwallis, raised in the aristocratic drawing rooms and peerage schools of England, with the stern code of the officer and gentleman, ever seen anything like this before. Having sparked the mad butchery, he could not stop it. Years after the earl left—long after he was back in England writing his memoirs—the firestorm of killing still had not burnt out. Cornwallis had touched off the first American civil war.

Then in October, Cornwallis saw a longed-for opportunity to regain his momentum, by making a devastating assault on the rebels in a pivotal winner-take-all battle, and he meant to make the most of it. To Col. Patrick Ferguson, commander of Cornwallis's left wing, which was to do the fighting, the battle seemed like a sure win for the redcoats.

Ferguson felt he was just the man to do the job. A brilliant Scot and "perhaps the best marksman living," he had invented a weapon that could have ended the Revolution years before. Drawing on a design by the Frenchman LaChumette, Ferguson had devised one of the first workable breech-loading rifles and stunned all of Britain with a demonstration of it. Military shoulder arms of the time—rifle and musket—were loaded by laborious process of dumping gunpowder down the muzzle, then ramrodding the ball after it. Ferguson's rifle used an ingenious— and much faster—breech opening just above the trigger to take powder and shot together, then snap shut.

At England's Woolwich Arsenal on April 27, 1776, in a driving rainstorm when no muzzle-loader could be fired, under high winds that would have blown musket balls around like hailstones, just weeks before the signing of the Declaration of Independence, Ferguson put on a shooting performance that made him an instant legend.

He started firing at a distance of 200 yards, hitting his target at the impressive rate of four shots a minute. Now walking quickly forward, he kept firing four shots a minute. Three shots a minute by musket was considered exceptional. Halting, Ferguson now increased his firing speed to an astonishing six shots a minute. During the entire demonstration only three of his shots failed to hit the target. Patrick Ferguson had announced a revolution in warfare.[27]

The lowly British infantryman now had at his disposal an awesome increase in firepower. The effect was the equivalent of multiplying the

British army by four, perhaps even six. The mind-bending battlefield cal-culus was obvious to the dullest Colonel Blimp. To confront a thousand British infantrymen armed with Ferguson rifles, the enemy would have to field at least four times as many men. Four times as much food, four times as many wagon trains, four times as many horses, tents, powder barrels, uniforms, shoes, helmets—worst of all, at four times the expense. The Ferguson rifle, if it did nothing else, at such bargain rates could soon bankrupt an enemy nation.

Ferguson was quickly put in command of a 200-man unit of riflemen that was shipped to the Revolution in America to make its debut during the Battle of Brandywine in September 1777 outside Philadelphia. Prior to the battle, Ferguson had a sniper's opportunity to shoot two American officers but declined to fire because they had their backs to him. One was George Washington and the other was the Marquis de Lafayette. Shortly after, before he could bring his two companies on the field, he was so severely wounded in the right arm, that he was out of commission for months, after which he had to teach himself to shoot left-handed. General Howe, who apparently was displeased to have this strange unit thrust on him without consultation, disbanded the leaderless men, scattering them among his other units, where many disappeared from history.

Shipped to the Carolinas, Ferguson, now in command of Cornwallis's left wing, boldly sent out a warning to the over-the-mountain men—the "banditti" as Cornwallis termed them—that if they did not cease their resistance he would "hang their leaders and lay their country waste with fire and sword."[28]

Some 1,000 rebels, many coming from as far away as Tennessee, reacted immediately. Led by such notorious rebels as Isaac Shelby, John Sevier, and the 300-pound "Ears" Cleveland, who had come for as much Loyalist blood as he could spill, the rebels rode nonstop for thirty-four hours in driving rain to confront Ferguson.

On October 7, the two forces came together at Kings Mountain, North Carolina. Several ironies appeared. First of all, Ferguson's entire cadre of redcoats was composed of American Loyalists. Ferguson was the only British combatant in the battle. Redcoats or not, this was to be a civil war battle between Americans.

A second irony—the contest pitted muskets against rifles. But the men armed with the rifles were the American rebels, with muzzle-loading rifles accurate up to 200 yards and more; the British, with Brown Bess muzzle-loading muskets, hardly accurate beyond 100 feet. Fewer than 100 American redcoats were armed with Ferguson's rifle.

Ferguson's troops, ideally, had the high ground. But the slopes were covered with trees that the rifle marksmen could use for cover as they picked off the redcoats. The victory was a lopsided slaughter.

In half an hour, the Loyalist unit, Cornwallis's entire left wing, was wiped out—156 dead, 163 wounded, and 698 captured.

The Battle of Kings Mountain vindicated Ferguson's concept. It demonstrated unequivocally the superiority of the rifle over the musket. But Ferguson didn't live long enough to see it. The rebels stripped his body and abused the corpse, including, some said, a not-uncommon practice of pissing on it. Then, in reprisal for the hanging of rebels, the rebels conducted a tree stump trial, condemned thirty-six to death, and hanged nine. Most of the remaining prisoners were so brutally treated that Cornwallis never saw them again. The rebels were teaching Cornwallis lessons in barbarity. They were to show him many more backwoods refinements on ambushing, murder, arson, torture, and betrayal.[29]

The devastating firepower of breech-loading rifles waited more than eighty years to appear on the battlefield—and again, ironically, it was during the second American Civil War of 1861–1865 when, at the beginning, most military rifles were still muzzle loaders.

Ordnance historians are left to wonder what the outcome would have been if all 1,000 redcoats had been armed with Ferguson rifles.

The American newspapers proclaimed the news of Kings Mountain on their front pages. *The Pennsylvania Gazette*'s headline announced: FERGUSON, THE GREAT PARTISAN, HAS MISCARRIED. AN ACCOUNT OF KINGS MT.[30]

Cornwallis knew time was running out. The guerrilla opposition had grown like a windswept grass fire and soon would not be containable.

Furthermore, Washington was certain to send more trouble to Cornwallis in his Southern theater. If the two of them—Continental troops and rebel guerrillas—could coordinate their operations, Cornwallis might find more opposition than he could handle. He heard a rumor that Washington was sending down Gen. Nathanael Greene to gather up the remnants of the American army and reorganize things. He knew Greene, had fought him—but no matter how effective Greene was at reorganizing, Cornwallis had not left him with much to reorganize. That chicken had been plucked.

Torrential winter rains fell in the Carolina mountains—a misery. Often mixed with snow, the rain brought on heavy frosts at night. Not exactly the sunny, dry, wintry days that the earl could have wished for in his winter camp at Winnsboro. Nonetheless, the earl was busy reforming his army, laying his plans for the spring campaign. His intelligence men were out scouting the rebels.

While there was still time, he knew exactly what he needed: a major victory, one that would finally take the heart out of the revolutionists—a crushing victory, somewhere, anywhere, somehow, anyhow. Just—soon.

So his plan was to mend for the winter in Winnsboro, and in the spring he would scatter his enemies, including the starveling Continental ragtags. Then he would march into Virginia to end the American Revolution.

In New York City, the foppish Englishman James Rivington, coffeehouse impresario, bookseller, and, most significantly, publisher and editor of the highly influential *Rivington's Royal Gazette,* ran an item in his newspaper that many considered a masterpiece in the art of journalistic warfare. The repercussions were to last for months, causing waves of derisive British laughter in the coffeehouses and homes on both sides of the Atlantic while filling Americans with burning shame. Dated September 17, 1780, the item at first appeared to be just another classified ad.

REWARD

Strayed, deserted, or stolen, from the subscriber, on the 16th of August last, near Camden, in the State of South Carolina, a whole ARMY, consisting of horse, foot and dragoons, to the amount of near TEN THOUSAND (as has been said) with all their baggage, artillery, wagons and camp equipage. The subscriber has very strong suspicions, from information received from his aid de camp, that a certain CHARLES, EARL CORNWALLIS, was principally concerned in carrying off the said ARMY with their baggage, etc. Any person or persons, civil or military, who will give information, whether to the subscriber, or to Charles Thompson, Esq., Secretary to the Continental Congress, where the said ARMY is, so that they may be recovered and rallied again, shall be entitled to demand from the Treasurer of the United States the sum of

THREE MILLION OF PAPER DOLLARS

as soon as they can be spared from the public funds, and

ANOTHER MILLION

for apprehending the person principally concerned in taking the said ARMY off. Proper passes will be granted by the President of the Congress to such persons as incline to go in search of the said ARMY. And as a further encouragement, no deduction will be made from the above reward on account of any of the Militia (who composed the said ARMY) not being found or heard of, as no dependence can be placed on their services, and nothing but the most speedy flight can ever save their Commander.

HORATIO GATES, M.G.

And late Commander in Chief of the Southern Army, August 30, 1780[31]

In early December, inside American army headquarters in Charlotte, North Carolina, some 370 miles southwest of Yorktown, Virginia, the defiant and humiliated Gen. Horatio Gates, surrounded by the fragments

Horatio Gates by Charles Wilson Peale,
from life, 1782.

of the "said army" he had lost, awaited impatiently for his replacement
to arrive.

With the unbearable snickering of the British and the open scorn of
the Americans—many of them his fellow officers and soldiers there in
camp with him—Gates wanted urgently to get to Congress in Philadelphia to begin repairing what many considered irreparable—his military
reputation. In particular, he wanted a military court of inquiry to expunge
the tarnish of cowardice from his record.

He faced the most difficult challenge of his career for, as a notorious
snob with an obnoxious personality, he had few friends to speak for him
and many enemies, including the highly vocal Alexander Hamilton.
Worse still, everyone had read Rivington's mocking want ad; many could
quote it; many did so behind his back. After a distinguished military
career, at fifty-two he found himself writhing in a cauldron of shame.
How would he ever live it down?

The son of the housekeeper to the Duke of Leeds, Gates received a
great initial boost in life when Horace Walpole, a parliamentarian of
considerable influence, helped launch his career as a commissioned officer in the British army, where birth, connections, and money were the
trinity of advancement.

In the French and Indian War he served under Braddock during the
latter's defeat at Fort Duquesne, and later in the West Indies. Aware that

his common birth would forever block further advancement, in 1765 Major Gates retired resentfully at half pay and, with the help of George Washington, purchased a home, Traveler's Rest, in the Shenandoah Valley.

When the Revolution started, he hastened to join the Continental Army, bringing with him his extensive military background and some considerable skills in army organization, troop training, and administration— along with a passion for political intrigue and backstairs politicking.

Driven by his excessive ambition, his complex machinations got completely wrapped around the axles of the American war efforts, and in the end not only failed to help but almost brought the Revolution to a halt.

He managed to oust unsuspecting General Sullivan in the Canadian campaign. Next he turned his eyes on New York's Gen. Philip Schuyler, who as commander of the Hudson Continental forces was waiting, with a skillfully baited trap, to confront Burgoyne's army at Saratoga. Lobbying the Congress, Gates managed to uproot Schuyler. When Burgoyne surrendered his entire army, Gates, who had sat in his tent far from the battlefield, claimed all the credit, but there is evidence that his contribution was less than minor and that the victory really belonged to Schuyler, for his planning and preparation, and to Benedict Arnold and Dan Morgan.

Decorating himself with what many believed to be others' military ribbons, he now lobbied in the Congress to lever Washington out as commander in chief. Sam Adams, no admirer of Washington, got Gates appointed president of the Congressional Board of War, which was supposed to be for civilians only. From there, Gates's efforts to undermine Washington in an affair called the Conway Cabal blew up in his face.

This "Cabal" may have included Gates, General Thomas Conway, Sam Adams, and Richard Henry Lee of Virginia, all contemptuous of Washington's leadership. Whatever it was, it stumbled and collapsed of its own weight before it could gather any momentum. Some historians feel it was little more than behind-handed mutterings and some carping letters that got into the wrong hands, hardly qualifying as a cabal, but Washington and a number of his loyal generals believed that the Conway Cabal existed and blamed Gates, perhaps unjustly.

In 1780, despite Washington's opposition, Gates became the third of Congress's three disastrous appointments: at Camden, he incompetently— arrogantly, heedlessly—lost an entire army to Cornwallis and promptly fled the battlefield and kept running for 120 miles.

Now, haunted by Rivington's mockery, Gates sat in his tent, burning with shame and anger, waiting to be relieved ignominiously of his command by the arrival of his successor, Gen. Nathanael Greene. The army he was leaving to Greene was little more than the feathers of a plucked chicken.

He wasn't going to have to wait much longer to be relieved.

On December 2 Gen. Nathanael Greene rode into Continental Army headquarters in Charlotte, North Carolina, with his entourage. Almost immediately he discovered that the situation he faced was worse than he had feared. To survive while he rebuilt, he promptly began to think about making the most dangerous move a general can make.

Greene was a thirty-nine-year-old Quaker from Rhode Island who had been ejected by his Quaker Meeting for joining the Rhode Island militia in 1775. He was now a veteran of five years of fighting the British and was considered by many to be Washington's ablest general. Taller than average and physically powerful from a lifetime of tough hard work at the forge of his family's ironworks, he was afflicted with an asthmatic wheeze, a faint limp from an old foundry injury, and, like General Cornwallis, a damaged eye, also from his foundry. Behind an open welcoming expression he looked at the world with shrewd eyes.

Barred by his father from any education Quakers considered sinful and earthy—almost anything beyond the three R's—he more than made up for it by teaching himself, especially after he discovered the London Bookshop in Boston. It was owned by Henry Knox, Washington's brilliant artillery general who was also largely self-taught. Knox introduced Greene to a whole new world of books—history, science, philosophy, law, and mathematics—even basic bookkeeping.

Propping *Euclid's Elements* on his forge, he mastered geometry while he hammered hot iron bars. Books were expensive; he couldn't buy all he wanted, so he worked out a barter arrangement with Knox. Making readily saleable toy anchors on his forge, he had found a way to pay for a steady supply of books. His library grew to noteworthy size—over 200 volumes.[32]

At the time his father died, making him head of the ironworks, he had become convinced that war with England was inevitable. He turned to the study of warfare and intensified those studies after the Boston Tea Party. Like General Knox, and General Heath and Washington himself, Greene patiently absorbed the art of warfare from his books—from Plutarch and Caesar, Sharp and Turenne, among others.

By 1774, no one else in Rhode Island could match his knowledge of warfare. But when he offered his services as an officer, the Independent Company of Kentish Guards rejected him because of his stiff knee. He signed up as a private, was disowned by his Quaker Meeting, and by the time war began on Lexington Green, he had led his Guards to Boston as its brigadier general, leading all three Rhode Island regiments, complete with tents, wagons, supplies, and even artillery.

Marching off to war, he ordered his ironworks to be converted into a cannon factory. He continued his studies between battles, often halting a march to make a cup of tea and read a book.

Riding south during the Revolution's grimmest days to take command of the remnants of the Southern army shattered by Cornwallis, this uneducated metalsmith discussed with his aides the merits of the Latin poets in the original Latin.

As soon as he could assess the situation, Greene wrote to Washington:

> Nothing can be more wretched and distressing than the condition of the troops, starving with cold and hunger, without tents or equipage. Those of the Virginia line are literally naked, and a great part totally unfit for any kind of duty, and must remain so until clothing can be had from the Northward. I have written to Governor Jefferson not to send forward any more until they are well clothed and properly equipped.[33]

His army—only he would dare call it that—consisted of some good troops, ready-steady Marylanders and Delawarians, plus riflemen from North Carolina and Georgia. At his officers' meeting, Greene could look around and see some of the Continental Army's finest officers: Maryland's John Eager Howard; Virginia's cavalry lieutenant colonel William Washington, with gunnery Lt. Col. Edward Carrington, who, under Greene, had shattered the British attack at Monmouth. Soon to arrive— and prove to be indispensable—was another desperately needed cavalry unit, Lee's Legion under another Virginian, Light-Horse Harry Lee. Expected any day was the creaking and groaningly arthritic, gigantic Gen. Daniel Morgan, the Old Wagoner, always as dangerous as a cornered wildcat, whose tree-climbing Kentucky riflemen had helped bring about that unforgettable victory at Saratoga. The rest were either militia serving out their short-term enlistments or green troops.

Counting everyone on the rolls, Nathanael Greene saw that he had fewer than 2,300 men. And the daily muster rolls told him an even grimmer story: He had only 800 men fit for duty—800 against Cornwallis's 4,000.

With those few men, Greene had to find a way to prevent Cornwallis from rebuilding his army and augmenting it with local Loyalist enlistees. Greene needed bait strong enough to lure Cornwallis out of his comfortable winter quarters and onto the roadways. To do this, he was toying with the most dangerous military idea he had ever considered. One misstep could snuff out the American cause. Greene looked at the officers around him as he presented his idea and watched their stunned faces.

Everyone in that meeting knew—every military textbook warned with heavy underscoring—that one of the worst moves a general can make in face of a numerically superior, better trained, better equipped, fitter army is to split his forces. Most military experts would call it suicidal. And Greene, arguably Washington's best general, knew this chapter and verse.

Yet he was proposing exactly that: to split his forces between himself and General Morgan in the desperate hope that Cornwallis would take the bait and in response split his.

Splitting his forces, he explained, "makes the most of my inferior force, for it compels my adversary to divide his, and holds him in doubt as to his own line of conduct. He cannot leave Morgan behind him to come at me, or his posts of Ninety-Six and Augusta would be exposed. And he cannot chase Morgan far, or prosecute his views upon Virginia, while I am here with the whole country open before me. I am as near Charleston as he is, and as near Hillsborough as I was at Charlotte; so that I am in no danger of being cut off from my reinforcements."[34] But would Cornwallis take the bait?

Greene's proposal was both frightful and frightfully simple. He would send Gen. Dan Morgan with William Washington's cavalry and 700 troops to circle north of Cornwallis's camp at Winnsboro, there to harass the enemy and to discourage Loyalist enlistments. This would enable Greene to march to Cheraw Hill, South Carolina, 75 miles east of the British at Winnsboro and 100 miles away from Morgan, a dangerously wide gap. There Greene planned to regroup and rebuild the rest of his army—and to await more troops and more supplies that he hoped would be trickling down from Virginia.

Cornwallis would be faced with a dilemma: He could attack Morgan and find Greene ripping open his interior lines, or attack Greene and find Morgan ripping open his other defenses. Or he could split his forces and go after both halves of Greene's army simultaneously.

Greene did something else, unorthodox but brilliant. He conferred with Francis Marion, the Swamp Fox, and Thomas Sumter, the Carolina Gamecock, the two leading guerrilla campaigners, and offered to coordinate his operations with theirs—the Continental Army in combination with the Carolina guerillas to make common cause against the British.

Marion and Sumter came to camp and listened to Greene's proposition, skeptical. They had tried to work with Gates, warned him, in fact, but Gates had airily dismissed their warnings, laughed behind their backs at their threadbare uniforms and homemade weapons, refused their help, then vapidly marched into destruction. Greene had to convince them he was a different animal entirely. They listened, nodded, and this time agreed. Common cause, coordinated. As that meeting broke up, faint embers of hope began to glow. Greene had increased his striking power considerably. Still inferior to be sure, still weak and ailing, but now a more formidable adversary nonetheless. Most important, morale was beginning to rise.

Greene got another inestimable bonus from his liaison with the guerrillas, especially Francis Marion: British army equipment, including clothing and ammunition that the Swamp Fox Marion was looting from British wagon trains. Cornwallis would soon find himself fighting Continentals who were not only becoming increasingly effective as fighters but were also armed with the finest equipment the British army could provide.

Greene was ready. Now it all depended on Cornwallis's decision to split his army—to bring it out of winter camp. Would he?

On December 4, 1780, at Rugeley's Mills, South Carolina, two days after Greene announced his plan to split his forces, William Washington's cavalry struck a decisive blow against Cornwallis. A distant cousin of George Washington and a fellow Virginian, Washington had been studying for the ministry when the Revolution broke out. Like his cousin, he was a large man; according to Light-Horse Harry Lee, "he possessed a stout frame, being six feet in height, broad, strong and corpulent." He was a veteran of numerous battles including the Battle of Long Island, where he had been severely wounded, as well as the Christmas night raid on Trenton, where he was struck in the hand by a musket ball. "He preferred," said Lee, "the heat of action to the collection and sifting of intelligence."[35]

At Rugeley's Mills Washington had trapped inside a fortified log barn Col. Henry Rugeley and a large body of Loyalists intent on joining Cornwallis's army. Unable to penetrate the fort with his cavalry, Washington brought up a cannon and ordered Rugeley and his men to come out or else. Amazed that Washington had a cannon with him, they quickly surrendered, only to be deeply chagrined to discover that the cannon was a pine log.[36]

Washington's victory denied a substantial new supply of Loyalist Carolina volunteers that Cornwallis was waiting for at Winnsboro. At the same time, mounted guerrillas led by Francis Marion and Thomas Sumter, fast striking from their bases, began harassing the British flanks. And soon Light-Horse Harry Lee's cavalry would arrive to attack another Loyalist unit and scatter it.

Greene and Morgan had brought the fight to Cornwallis, challenging him to attack. Now they waited to see if Cornwallis would take the bait and split his forces.

In his headquarters in Winnsboro, South Carolina, General Cornwallis was baffled.

He had watched the new American general, Greene, make the incredible gaffe of splitting his forces, sending his second in command, General Morgan, with part of the ragged American band footling somewhere north and west. In the deepening winter of December 1780 this was a particularly dangerous move. Cornwallis had faced Greene before, a number of times, on Long Island, at Trenton, Brandywine, Germantown, and most memorably, at Monmouth. Greene knew better than to casually split his forces; Greene also knew that Cornwallis knew he knew, so the earl could not dismiss Greene's unorthodox and dangerous move.

The problem was complex. The earl could not go after either half of that army and ignore the other. Nor could he ignore them all together. Greene's move had played off several of Cornwallis's weaknesses. It meant taking his army out of winter quarters, where, following the disaster of Kings Mountain and the appalling number of deaths from the reaping fevers of Carolina's swamps, he needed urgently to rebuild and restore it. He also needed to remain inside an established winter training camp in order to draw to him as many volunteer Loyalist recruits as he could get, then use the winter months to train them. Only with those volunteers, securely buttoned inside British redcoats, could he make his victorious march northward. Those Loyalist recruits would come only if they could be sure that the British army had come to stay, sure that the British wouldn't suddenly leave, abandoning them to the vengeance of the Carolina rebels. If they came to camp, he could end the war. If not, not.

So Cornwallis was facing an opponent who was willing to take an enormous risk for an enormous potential payoff. In that light, Greene's move made sense. By splitting his army and beating up and down the country roads in winter, harassing potential Loyalist enlistees and working in unison with guerrilla units like Marion's and Sumter's, Greene was introducing a new kind of shoot-and-scoot, catch-me-if-you-can, ever-moving warfare, while the Marions and the Sumters, in support, could come galloping out of their camps to sink their fangs into Cornwallis's redcoated flanks, attacking wagon trains and outposts, killing sleeping soldiers in their tents in the middle of the night, and then vanishing again, carrying off British arms and equipment and numbers of Cornwallis's irreplaceable troops.

This kind of fluid warfare did not offer many set-piece battlefield actions, European style, of which Cornwallis was a master. By breaking up camp and scampering after the bits and pieces of Greene's divided army, Cornwallis would be fighting Greene's war on Greene's terms. But then Cornwallis had no choice. If he chose to ignore Greene, Greene would nibble up the edges, chop away hunks of Cornwallis's military capability, drive off those Loyalist volunteers, and overturn the British outposts, taking piecemeal what he could not take head on on the battlefield.

Cornwallis saw that he would be forced to fight an unorthodox defensive war that his troops were not trained for, not equipped for, not adept at. He would be fighting not to advance his strategy but to keep what he had already taken.

The British general was caught between what he wanted to do and what Clinton's directives ordered him to do. Clinton's orders were to subdue South Carolina first, then North Carolina. But Cornwallis soon decided that in order to tame South Carolina he needed to subdue North Carolina. And in order to pacify North Carolina, he needed to subdue Virginia, the source of fresh rebel troops and rebel supplies feeding into the two Carolinas. Cornwallis reasoned that "if we do not attack that province [Virginia], we must give up both South Carolina and Georgia, and retire within the walls of Charleston."[37]

Yet if he made the right moves, he could pounce on those two wiggling pieces of Greene's army, squash them, and then march up into Virginia.

The unknown quantities were those guerrilla leaders Thomas Sumter and Francis Marion. Unlike Gates, who, to his everlasting regret, had laughed at the guerrillas, Greene had sought them out and signed them up for coordinated operations. And that was a formidable combination.

In his mountain base at Tuckaseegee Ford, the Carolina Gamecock, Thomas Sumter, forty-eight, senior brigadier general of the South Carolina militia, announced that he was ready to work with Greene, at least as far as his unpredictable and very tender ego would let him.

A South Carolina store owner born in Virginia of Welsh parents, a justice of the peace, state congressman, and military man, barely educated but well read, Thomas Sumter had retired from rebelling after Clinton had taken Charleston—at least until Tarleton's Captain Campbell and his Green Dragoons burned his house down. Sumter promptly moved into the rebel stronghold west of the Catawba and raised a partisan band. That single house burning had created a guerrilla maelstrom that was giving Cornwallis nightmares.

Ferocious and fearless and absolutely unpredictable, Thomas Sumter fought with wild abandon, scanted strategy, and slapdash tactics and often planned not at all, living day to day, waiting to see what the fortunes of war would turn up. Although this practice several times ended in disaster, it also produced brilliant successes.

Cornwallis had made a major effort to destroy this holy terror. First, the earl sent the sadistic Huck after him; the Gamecock's men had ambushed and killed him. Then the earl sent Wemyss; Sumter shot him out of his saddle and took him prisoner. When Cornwallis sent the terrifying Tarleton, at first the Green Dragoon brushed aside Sumter's planless tactics and bloodied his nose, particularly at Fishing Creek, but Sumter soon replied by smashing Tarleton's forces, handing him his first defeat, a crushing one, showing the world that the British were not invincible. Sumter was badly wounded in that affray and out of commission for months—much to the relief of Greene and Marion, who, without the obstreperous Gamecock's wild punches, promptly embarked on a well-planned and coordinated campaign against the British.

Sumter's guerrilla contribution was essential, yet he was a man who wanted to fight his own war in his own way; several key times he refused to support Greene's efforts, preferring to pursue his own—occasionally disastrous—bent. He was also quite capable of going into a great sulk, as when Light-Horse Harry Lee took Granby while the Gamecock was off somewhere else. He drew a crowd when he announced "Sumter's Law," a campaign aimed not at the British but at Carolina Loyalists. By this he raised a horde of partisans for a ten-month enlistment. The lure of Sumter's Law seemed to have no other military purpose than the loot to be taken from Loyalists. His campaign touched off a bloody civil war within a civil war that earned him a reputation for brutality that dogged him into the cemetery and even after.

His career ended in a great bonfire of emotion when, to placate his band's demand for still more plunder, he attacked Georgetown on July 25, 1781. The British replied by destroying that city. The outcry against Sumter was so great that Governor Rutledge outlawed plundering especially "Sumter's Law," and effectively shut him down. He would retire in ill health, war-weary, his own men deeply discontented with him and his name reviled by many.

In his swamp base of Snow Island, Francis Marion waited.

As junior brigadier general of the South Carolina Militia, he was subordinate to Sumter. Yet in many ways, to Cornwallis, the Swamp Fox was more dangerous than the Carolina Gamecock. Marion was a thinker, a hatcher of disasters. Of all the guerrilla leaders in the Carolinas, Francis Marion looked—and acted—least like one. "Small enough at birth to be put in a quart mug" he was, at fifty, slight and frail.[38]

His methods were utterly opposite to the flamboyant high-hills Thomas Sumter, who was guided by a ready-fire-aim mentality.[39] Marion wasn't interested in fighting showpiece battles. He cared only for doing maximum damage to Cornwallis's military network while taking the least possible casualties.

When Cornwallis sent Wemyss after him, Marion ghosted into the swamps. When Cornwallis next sent his enforcer, Tarleton found himself racing after the fresh tracks of invisible horsemen. Marion led Tarleton on and on ever deeper into malarial marshes for twenty-six miles until Tarleton gave up chasing "that damned swamp fox," saying "the devil himself could not catch him!" Tarleton soothed his frustrations on the way back to camp with an orgy of house-burnings.[40]

Descended from French Huguenots, Marion, barely educated and a lifelong bachelor, loved his plantation and extended family, loved the swamps, loved hunting and fishing, and hated the arrogant, intrusive British. A passionate South Carolinian patriot, he spent much of his life serving his state in various military and governmental capacities going back to the Cherokee Expedition of the French and Indian War. After helping to lever the royal governor out of South Carolina, he was one of the few military leaders who escaped Charleston when Lincoln surrendered, breaking an ankle in the process. He then took up the role of a guerrilla leader.

He wore shabby clothes indifferently, as did most of his followers, who were identified only by a white paper cockade in their hats. Their weapons were either homemade or army issue smouched from the British.

Eating little and usually drinking only water, he was solemn, short on conversation, speaking only when he had something pertinent to say, and then, hard-headed and practical, calculating, he always made sense. Light-Horse Harry Lee, who had great affection and respect for Marion, noted the only flaw he found in the man: "His visage was not pleasing, and his manners not captivating."[41]

If Sumter was a battering ram, Marion was a rapier, making a sudden surprising thrust and then gone. He avoided violence, did not burn homes, did not terrorize. He allowed no looting, no pillaging, and no acts of vengeance on Carolinian Loyalists. When he needed to take anything, he issued receipts, albeit with no specific redemption dates.

Marion was truly as Tarleton described him, a swamp fox. His base on Snow Island in the Great White Marsh lay so deep in that watery wilderness that for a long time the British weren't able to find it.

Unlike Sumter, he proceeded with extreme caution, gathering detailed intelligence and scouting his targets, planning his strategy with care, even canceling an attack at the last minute if he felt something wrong.

His strategy generally had three purposes: to capture essential British army matériel to continue the fight, to discourage Carolina Loyalists from joining the British army, and to shut down British supply trains. He felt that if he could prevent the British army from getting enough fodder, firewood, and food, if he could so terrify British army regulars that they were afraid to go to sleep in the woods at night, if he could make Loyalists stay neutral, then he could eventually isolate the British, diminish the size of their army, starve them, decimate them by attrition. And he would keep that up until he forced them to leave South Carolina. In time there was not a single redcoat or Loyalist militia in Marion's territory.

That the British were reluctantly supplying him with the arms to attack them must have struck him as amusing. So important were those captured supplies that he was able to send quantities of them to Greene's threadbare Continental soldiers.

Marion preferred to move at night silently through the swamps, communicating by whistles, springing on his enemies at dawn, striking fast and hard, scattering their wagons and seizing whatever equipment he had come for before fading back into the swamps. And sometimes he would wait for the enemy to regroup only to strike again an hour later.

The style of his first attack became his trademark. Singling out a mounted column of Loyalist redcoats that was terrorizing the neighborhood, he struck at breakfast time, took all their horses, gunpowder, and military equipment, and set the survivors—there were few—wandering back to base on foot through hostile countryside. Before he left he and his men ate their Loyalist breakfast.

He feinted his next attack against another Loyalist band that was obviously ready for him. Seeming to flee, Marion lured them into a prepared ambush, then crushed them.

One of his most successful attacks was on a British army unit leading 150 Marylanders from Gates's shattered army to a certain slow death on prison hulks. Marion's furious attack rescued all of them to fight Cornwallis another day.

Unlike Cornwallis, both Sumter and Marion were successful at gathering new recruits. Marion alone commanded at one time or another some 2,500 men. In fact, their best recruiting officer was Cornwallis himself. The sadistic two-pronged British army policy called forth a murderous opposition that was quickly coalescing. Many of these new guerrilla recruits, former Loyalists among them, had watched a lifetime of backbreaking work—house and barn and crops—ascend in great plumes of black smoke while their hard-won, most precious possessions were carried off under the tunics of British soldiers who no longer bothered to distinguish between rebel and Loyalist.

Conversely, another significant consequence of guerrilla victories was the loss of confidence in the British ability to protect Loyalist volunteers and their families. Loyalist enlistments dropped even more.

Those smoldering Carolinians, as they hurried to join guerrilla bands, often had nothing more with them than the clothes they wore and, sometimes, a horse. Lacking sabers and swords, they hammered homemade blades out of whipsaws; lacking muskets and ammunition, they raided British wagon trains; lacking uniforms or clothing of any sort, they snatched the red coats off the bodies of the soldiers they had killed or wounded, then dyed them nondescript earth colors. Lacking cavalry tack, bridles and bits, and saddles, they made what they could on anvils.

They outfitted themselves with ingenuity and captured British army equipment—or went without, sometimes saddleless, even shoeless.

But whatever they brought or lacked, they all carried one thing with them in abundance. Anger.

The guerrillas were particularly effective against Loyalist militia. The confrontations were short, bloody, and decisive. American against American crashed at each other in fury. And gradually, throughout the Western Carolinas, the rebels began to win.

At Williamson's plantation, Sumter defeated and killed Captain Huck and his British Legion. At Cedar Springs rebels defeated Loyalists, as they also did at Gowen's Old Fort; at Earle's Ford rebels defeated both dragoons and Loyalists; at Prince's Fort, the rebels' victory caused the Loyalists to abandon their fort; at Flat Rock, rebels ambushed a Loyalist wagon train. At Thicketty Fort, without firing a shot, rebels talked Major Moore, a Loyalist, into surrendering a key fort in the British outpost system that was probably impregnable.

There was a standoff at Rocky Mount when a fortuitous rainstorm saved the British fort there from fire set by the Americans, as well as other setbacks. But at the Battle of Hanging Rock, the Americans, without taking the fort, slaughtered three companies of North Carolina Loyalists. Then, five days later, in the Second Battle at Hanging Rock, although again unable to take the fort, the rebels almost annihilated the Loyalist Prince of Wales Regiment, then posted an even more stunning victory by breaking up a bayonet attack by the supposedly invincible British Legion. At the Second Battle of Cedar Springs the rebels won again. At Wateree Ferry Sumter posted yet another win, although at Fishing Creek Tarleton scattered the rebels and nearly captured Sumter. The rebels replied at the Battle of Musgrove's Mills when they ambushed 500 Loyalist militia. At Fishdam Ford, Sumter captured Wemyss, and at the Battle of Blackstocks, Sumter nearly destroyed Tarleton, for, while losing three killed and four wounded, Sumter killed ninety-two and wounded seventy-six of Tarleton's men, a shocking 62 percent of his force.[42] Most significant, Blackstocks destroyed the myth of Tarleton's personal invincibility. Worse still for the British, Loyalist enlistments fell still further. Cornwallis was not getting the Loyalist manpower he needed in order to implement Lord Germain's brutal policy.

The British response to the growing opposition was more brutality. In fact, it descended into depravity. The historian Scheer notes that the British used slaves as "instruments of germ warfare. British General Alexander Leslie wrote to his superior, Cornwallis, 'About 700 Negroes are come down the River in the Small Pox. I shall distribute them about the Rebell Plantations.' "[43]

The defeat at Kings Mountain demonstrated clearly that the British dream of Loyalists defeating rebels was just that—a dream. A scant two months after he had informed Clinton that South Carolina had been pacified, Cornwallis must have astonished Clinton with his report that "the whole country" between the Pee Dee and the Santee was "in an absolute state of rebellion, every friend of government has been carried off, and his plantation destroyed." In short, he was saying to Clinton, the Germain/Clinton policy was a wash; in the Carolinas, the British lion had laid an ostrich-sized egg.[44]

The guerrillas knew they could bedevil Cornwallis, steal his supplies, terrify his troops, blunt his actions, but they didn't have the muscle or the heavy equipment to fight him on the battlefield. For that, they looked north—for another army to take on Cornwallis, an army to replace the army lost by the self-induced disaster of the foolish Gates. In the meantime they fed on hope. As long as they could believe that ultimately an army large enough, trained enough, was going to someday march down from Virginia to defeat Cornwallis, they could continue to fight like cornered rats.

Cornwallis finally concluded that he could now have only one goal: make the rebels despair. To kill the Revolution, kill the hope.

He regarded the wintry roads of the Carolinas and pondered. If he made the wrong choice, he could ruin his career and bring defeat on his army. To split or not to split? Which?

Did Cornwallis ever wonder during his sleepless nights whether Clinton had deliberately stuck him in the Carolinas to get rid of him and then deliberately underarmed him so that he could gather no glory there—only failure?

On December 25, 1780, Gen. Daniel Morgan, Greene's second in command, sent Lord Cornwallis a Christmas present.

After slogging his band of dragoons and light infantry through fifty-eight miles of mud under a cold winter rain, Morgan celebrated that festive day by setting up camp on the Pacolet River. Situated near Ninety Six, the linchpin of Cornwallis's system of pacification forts, Morgan had put a deep hook into Cornwallis's flank. As General Greene had planned, Morgan was now in a perfect position to raise hell.

It was Cornwallis's turn—to split or not.

In his camp in Winnsboro, Cornwallis considered Morgan's move. The earl was situated between Morgan to his southwest on the Pacolet and Greene to his northeast at Cheraw Hill. He had twice the number of troops as their combined forces. He could split his forces and, while holding Greene at bay, send Tarleton in a quick strike to crush Morgan. Then Greene's tiny remnant, now isolated, would be in a hopeless position, ready for the slaughter. Destroying Greene, Cornwallis could make his move into Virginia.

To split or not to split? Cornwallis decided to make the most of Greene's classic blunder. He split his forces also—not in two but in three pieces.

One piece he sent northeast to Camden to pin Greene down and to prevent him from hurrying to Morgan's aid. The second piece—his newly reconstituted left wing under Colonel Tarleton—was sent down to Ninety Six to either force Morgan into battle and defeat him or, failing that, at least to drive him north across the Broad River. Cornwallis in the meantime would lead the third piece, his main army, out of winter camp at Winnsboro right into Morgan's line of retreat. Morgan would be either crushed in battle against Tarleton or flee into a trap set by the waiting Cornwallis and his main British army.

Cornwallis believed Morgan's position was hopeless. The earl had 4,000 effectives in camp and another 4,000 manning the scattered forts. Of that number his new left wing under Tarleton had 1,100 dragoons and light infantry—some of Cornwallis's best light troops—while Morgan had some 1,000 troops in very poor condition leading animals weakened from a lack of forage.

Tarleton also had two grasshoppers, portable pieces of artillery designed for light infantry, mounted on three legs rather than wheels and carried by pack animals. The troops called them grasshoppers because they hopped when fired. On the battlefield, they could make a difference. Cornwallis had captured them from Gates at Camden. Gates had captured them from Burgoyne at Saratoga in September 1777.

Cornwallis was additionally heartened by the news of Benedict Arnold's march of devastation in Virginia, which had cut Greene's supply lines. Simultaneously, Greene was having his spine severed in Virginia and his head cut off in North Carolina.

Dealing out nonstop days of rain and nights of frost, weather became one of the principal players in the ensuing maneuvers. Tarleton had to wait three days to cross the flooded Enoree but then managed to cross not only the Enoree but also the Tyger and was off in hot pursuit, hurrying to cross the Pacolet to trap Morgan. Rain slowed Cornwallis even more: He spent from January 8 to January 14 traversing a mere forty miles. At that rate he might not get far enough north and west to trap Morgan.

With a speed that caught Morgan by surprise, on January 14, 1781, Tarleton crossed the Pacolet and the next morning rushed into Morgan's camp. It was empty. Morgan had just fled.

Tarleton and his troops paused long enough to eat Morgan's breakfast, then resumed the chase all through that day. By the morning of

January 16, he had closed the gap and with a few hours' sleep rushed the last few miles after Morgan. Exactly as planned, he had his quarry pinned against the Broad River. The place was known as Hannah's Cowpens. The British prepared for a slaughter.

What Tarleton probably didn't know was the desperate physical condition of Morgan. Over the years, the Old Wagoner suffered such agony from his rheumatism that he had often had to take time off from military service. The unending cold and rain had so aggravated his sciatica that on the road from the Pacolet, he had to ride at a walk because he could not bear the trotting of his horse.[45]

Brigadier General Daniel Morgan, forty-five, son of an ironmaster and a first cousin to Daniel Boone, could not have been more different from the patrician-born Banastre Tarleton. A huge bear of a man, over 200 pounds, more than six feet tall, and ready with his fists, in peacetime Morgan was a prosperous Virginia farmer who had worked his way up through the ranks to a position of command by sheer ability. He got his well-known nickname of the Old Wagoner because more than a quarter-century before he had driven a supply wagon for Braddock's army in the French and Indian War.

It had been a rough war for Morgan. His quick temper got him in deep trouble when a British lieutenant slapped him with the flat of his sword. Morgan knocked him down. His punishment was supposed to be more than lethal—500 strokes of the lash, normally enough to kill a man several times over. Morgan later claimed that the drummer boy had miscounted and that George III owed him one lash. He was known to inspire men to fight the hated British by showing them the mass of scar tissue on his back. In 1758, as an ensign, he was carrying dispatches when an Indian bullet smashed all the teeth in his lower left jaw.

In 1775, in response to the Battle of Lexington/Concord, he led ninety-six mounted riflemen from the Shenandoah Valley to Boston—600 miles—in twenty-one days. His legend grew significantly when he joined Arnold on his remarkable march through Maine to Quebec and, taking command when Arnold was wounded there, nearly carried the day. He was raised to colonel during the Philadelphia campaign. From there he was sent by Washington to Saratoga, where his riflemen were a deciding factor in that victory. When Burgoyne's Indian scouts saw Morgan's riflemen, they vanished, depriving the British general of vital scouting information. Armed with their sniping rifles, the Virginia sharpshooters, climbing trees, had a decimating effect even before the battle began by reducing Burgoyne's supply of officers, sergeants, and artillery horses. Morgan was further admired by his fellow officers for his brilliance in handling light infantry and is considered one of the best battlefield tacticians of the American Revolution.

Daniel Morgan by Charles Wilson Peale,
from life, 1794.

At six forty-five A.M. on January 16, 1781, Banastre Tarleton sent Captain Ogilvie with fifty dragoons ahead of his main body to feel out the American position. In the weak predawn light, Ogilvie, looking out over the Cowpens meadow, got a surprise. At the end of the meadow stood the Americans silently lined up for battle, waiting for Banastre Tarleton. Morgan was ready to fight.

He had chosen his terrain well. A gentle slope led in three tiers to high ground. At the top waited Morgan. Tarleton rushed to get into battle formation.

Out in front of Morgan's battle lines stood 120 skirmishers. Tarleton sent Ogilvie and his dragoons to disperse them. Ogilvie made an unpleasant discovery: These skirmishers were not the usual musketeers; they were all skilled rifle sharpshooters from Georgia and the Carolinas. Ogilvie's original fifty dragoons came galloping back with 15 empty saddles, a cautionary warning to all but Tarleton.

Tarleton set up Burgoyne's grasshoppers on his flanks. Shortly their jumping fire drove off the skirmishing riflemen, but as they went the sharpshooters were picking off officers, sergeants, and horses—Saratoga revisited.

In typical Tarleton style, he expected the fight to be over in minutes. Shortly after seven o'clock, with some of his troops still arriving on the scene, Tarleton ordered the band to strike up a tune. Holding their bayonets at the ready, his deadly infantry proceeded with their grim march toward Morgan. They had a long walk ahead of them—400 yards.

Tarleton seems not to have noticed—or didn't care—that Morgan had a very unconventional setup on his battle line. In his first line of defense were the last troops any other general would have used. Militia, notorious for running at the sight of bayonets or cavalry, stood waiting. Like the skirmishers, these South Carolinians were not armed with muskets but with rifles, deadly marksmen all, under the command of militia general Andrew Pickens. At 100 yards from the advancing British, far beyond the range of muskets, and aiming again at officers and sergeants, they commenced firing. Their pickoffs were devastating the British line long before it could get within range with its muskets and bayonets. Then the militia turned away toward the rear and, to Tarleton, seemed to flee from the field. Tarleton's 17th British Legion—the Green Dragoons—galloped after the fleeing militia and ran right into a withering barrage of more rifles, these in the hands of Morgan's own Virginians, manning the American second line. The dragoons staggered. Abruptly William Washington's cavalry raced out from cover and galloped right into them, inflicting heavy casualties. Tarleton's dragoons fled the field.

Tarleton reformed his infantry and pressed the attack, all yelling "Hurrah!" as they finally reached the main line they had come to wipe out. But now they ran into Maj. John Eager Howard's battle-seasoned Maryland and Delaware Continentals and veteran Virginia militia who waited with their bayonets. Kneeling for greater accuracy, they were firing one volley after another. The British line, losing men rapidly, was in serious trouble.

Tarleton ordered his kilted Highlanders, accompanied by their bagpipes, to hit the American right. Howard ordered his right company to shift over to confront them. The move confused both sides at first, and the rest of the American line began to withdraw. The Highlanders charged.

Then Morgan entered the battlefield galloping to the front and brandishing his sword: "Form, form, my brave fellows!" he shouted. "Give them one more fire and the day is ours."[46]

Howard ordered his infantry to form a new line, turn, and attack. Firing from the hip, they closed with the Highlanders, bayonet against bayonet.

Washington's cavalry came galloping back on the battlefield to turn Tarleton's right and penetrate the rear. Composed mainly of American recruits, the British 7th Regiment threw down their arms and asked for quarter—which, through the intervention of American officers, they got. Washington's cavalry cut off the rest of the British right from retreating and made them ground their arms.

But Tarleton's Highlanders and his left refused to stop fighting. Unexpectedly, Pickens's sharpshooting militia, who had seemed to flee from the field, reappeared, now all the way over on the British left, and ran directly at the Highlanders. The Scots were completely surrounded, nine of their sixteen officers down; they were fighting for their lives when their leader, Major McArthur, handed his sword to Pickens. The Scots were through fighting that day.

Tarleton, unhorsed, seized another and galloped back to his own formidable British Legion—200 fresh cavalrymen. He ordered them to charge into the tiring American center. Instead, they fled.

In contrast, the British artillerymen, firing the grasshoppers, refused to surrender and were wiped out almost to a man.

Fortescue, the noted British historian, observed that Tarleton's vaunted cavalrymen, "ill disciplined . . . spoiled . . . were not the men to face so desperate a venture." Washington, smarting from two encounters with Tarleton, raced after him. Tarleton and two of his officers turned. Washington, slashing at one of them, broke his saber near the handguard. As the officer raised his saber at Washington, a fourteen-year-old bugler shot him. Tarleton struck; Washington parried with his bladeless saber hilt. Tarleton fired his pistol, missed Washington but hit his horse, dropping it. Bloody Ban galloped off, just barely eluding capture and battlefield vivisection. Tarleton had probably fired the last shot of the Battle of Cowpens.

In fifty minutes, it was over—an extraordinarily lopsided victory. One hundred and ten British soldiers lay dead; 229 were wounded; 712 more were captured. Thirty-nine of the dead were officers, twenty-seven of the wounded. In fifty minutes Tarleton had lost 86 percent of his force—just about all of Cornwallis's vitally needed light troops.[47]

The Americans lost 12 dead and 60 wounded.[48]

Morgan scooped up his desperately needed winnings: 100 healthy cavalry horses, 800 muskets, 35 wagons, a traveling forge, musical instruments to outfit a complete military band, all kinds of supplies, and the regimental colors of the British 7th. Also, he had recaptured the two Burgoyne grasshoppers that Cornwallis had taken from Gates, and Gates from Burgoyne. More adventures were in store for them.

As Boatner says: "Tarleton took one hell of beating at Cowpens, and there is nobody the Americans would have rather seen it happen to."[49]

Some writers place more blame on Tarleton's incompetence than praise on Morgan's brilliance, stressing the Old Wagoner's incredible luck, but this is none too accurate. As he showed that day, Morgan was a far better field tactician than Tarleton. He took what he had—which in retrospect turned out to be a great deal—and made the most of it. No American cavalryman could have turned in a better performance than

William Washington, getting more than enough revenge for two previous black eyes from Tarleton. And Morgan couldn't have had a better battlefield infantry leader than John Eager Howard. Howard's infantry, from Maryland and Delaware and Virginia, settled the argument once and for all: The best American infantry had become every bit a match for the best British infantry. As George Washington had often dreamed, the Americans beat the British at their own game, on the battlefield, bayonet against bayonet.

Tarleton had fought rebels; Morgan had fought Tarleton. He had planned his strategy around Tarleton's predictable behavior on the battlefield.

Further, knowing the propensity of militia to run away—especially riflemen whose weapons could not mount bayonets—Morgan put them where they had never been before—on the first line. Because they were such deadly long-range shooters, he asked them to squeeze off two rounds, then leave the battlefield. It helped to steady them by having other soldiers behind them ready to shoot any militiaman who tried to run off without firing his two rounds. Those two rounds were so reaping they set up the whole battle; they deprived Tarleton of his essential battlefield leadership—officers and sergeants. By placing his battle line in three tiers, each punishing the British line as it advanced those long 400 yards, Morgan increased the advantage of his long-range rifles and caused the British to be nearly exhausted when they at last made contact with the Americans, and there he had Howard's ready-steady infantry waiting for them.

Morgan had good luck, true. But he had set the table for such luck and he had also inspired his men to reach unexpected heights of fighting. He must have been as astonished as anyone when Pickens led his militia riflemen back onto the battlefield to turn the tide against the Highlanders.

Most commentators barely notice the importance that day of the rifle, Morgan's favorite weapon. Of the 900 American troops, a highly disproportionate number of them were skilled riflemen, probably no accident. Morgan had introduced a revolutionary innovation: more firepower. And the lopsided casualties show it. A very high percentage of Tarleton's casualties fell long before their short-range muskets and arm-thrust bayonets came in contact with the enemy. The riflemen would have called it a turkey shoot.

Morgan outthought, outplanned, outfought, and outfirepowered Banastre Tarleton, who had the final humiliation of seeing the flight of his vaunted British Legion, who still might have turned the tables.

For the American troops who were at Cowpens that day, from this point forward, on every army base, every tavern, every home and farm, they had gotten supreme bragging rights: They were the boys who had slam-stopped Bloody Ban and kicked his rump. Here's to Cowpens, soldier. Long live that name.

The consequences were almost incalculable. Tarleton had done what Ferguson had done: For the second time, Cornwallis had lost his entire left wing. Throughout the colonies Loyalist morale plunged; rebel morale reached new heights. Volunteers flocked to the guerrilla camps of Marion and Sumter and the others. With renewed hope, the Congress and the state legislatures opened their hollow coffers, groping for more troops and supplies to send South. The teeter-tottering Revolution had been saved again. Gloriously. Morgan is given credit for one of the battlefield masterpieces of the American Revolution, having achieved a double envelopment of his opponent and crushing him.

Concerning his British prisoners, Morgan wrote to Greene: "Although they waged the most cruel warfare, not a man was killed, wounded or even insulted after he surrendered."[50] No Tarleton's quarter. But Morgan could not have controlled his men if they had known what orders Tarleton had issued to his troops against the Americans that day: No quarter.[51]

General Cornwallis could have gotten his talons on Dan Morgan, despite his great victory, if he, Cornwallis, had been where he had planned to be—on the other side of the Broad River just behind Morgan. But because of the rain and floods and poor communication he was still at Turkey Creek more than thirty miles away. Morgan didn't wait for him to come visiting. He scampered.

Less than two hours after one of the greatest victories of the Revolution, Morgan was leading his troops across the Broad River, right past the spot where Cornwallis might have been, should have been. And with every step he was moving further away from the earl.

When General Cornwallis saw Banastre Tarleton returning from the slaughter at Cowpens with barely a handful of survivors from what had been the entire British left wing, he was nearly unhorsed. He groaned that Cowpens "almost broke my heart."[52]

The day before, the earl could tot up some 3,300 troops on his muster roll, including Leslie's reinforcements that had marched up from Charleston, and Tarleton's left wing. With Tarleton's defeat, the British army had shrunk to 2,550, about the same size as Greene's army. But, after discounting Greene's very discountable militia, Cornwallis's seasoned professionals, British and German, still had Greene outnumbered two to one.[53]

His great pride demanded that he reply with something spectacular and do it quickly. Otherwise his standing in London would crash and his career would be in ruins. Astonished as he was by the defeat, his response was equally astonishing—even to his army.

His first reaction was to get those irreplaceable troops back—the 700 captured and the 200 wounded—and next to catch Greene and Moran and grind them up. Only one way offered itself, and that he did instantly.

In an act that shocked even his most devoted troops, he started a great bonfire. On it he burned all of his tents, burned most of his wagons, burned much of his supplies, and retained only essential material for a fast march, turning his heavily armed army into 2,550 light troops capable of sprinting after the quicksilver Americans. Even his troops's rum rations were sacrificed. His army solemnly watched a golden river gush out of the axed barrels onto the half-frozen ground. Two hundred and fifty men deserted.

Nathanael Greene's great joy when he heard the news was tempered with a realization that Cornwallis's outraged pride would drive him to do something stunning in reply.

In his communications with Greene, Dan Morgan, who never ran away from a fight in his life, urged Greene to lead the troops up into the mountains for the winter to regroup, recoup, and fight another day. Retreat beats defeat.

But Greene sensed that Cornwallis would race north to get between him and any fresh troops coming down from Virginia, then turn and pulverize Greene. However, Greene had anticipated him. Back in December when he first decided to split his army, Greene had also planned an escape hatch. He had given orders for detailed retreat routes into Virginia to be plotted and carefully mapped and boats for fording the rivers to be assembled, just in case. He was also fortunate in the quartermaster general he had on his staff—brilliant, resourceful, unflagging Edward Carrington—who was given the unenviable assignment of creating that escape route. Now had come the time to find out how escapable that escape route really was.

"Just in case" had arrived like a fire bell. Fleeing north was a more dangerous course than retreating west into the mountains, but Greene chose to follow his original escape strategy, to try to get ahead of Cornwallis's greyhound and lure him ever further away from his resupplies in his coastal bases, string him out, make him hungry, short of rations and equipment, exposed to the winter. If he could beat Cornwallis in a race north, Greene could link up with fresh troops from Virginia and be in a position to turn around to face Cornwallis and pick him apart piecemeal. These were long odds that careful soldiers like Clinton would never have accepted. But Clinton had never been in such a desperate situation. Greene was gambling with the sudden death of the American cause. He turned north and ran like hell.

Having lost two days stripping down his travel weight, Cornwallis, now outnumbering Greene more than three to two, went raging after his enemy. He lost more days trying to find Morgan and his captured troops. The trail was cold, and Cornwallis headed in the wrong direction. More days went by before he got himself turned around. Morgan had gone north to meet Greene.

Also, Cornwallis discovered he was too late to recover his captured troops. Morgan had quickly dispatched them to prison camp in Virginia while Morgan himself scuttled across the Catawba.

Unencumbered by nonexistent baggage, Greene set out on a challenging 125-mile march to the Dan River in Virginia, knowing he must beat Cornwallis there. The race was on.

The chase lasted for three agonizing weeks, a great trial to the troops of both armies. In the dead of winter, in biting cold and under freezing rain and snow and on half-frozen mud roads, with "pitifully inadequate clothing—many of them barefooted," often hungry, Greene's 1,400 Continentals had four swollen rivers to cross, with Cornwallis's furious, and often barefoot, 2,300 regulars snatching at them over every mile.

Struggling across millrace rivers, horses drowning, the men were pushed beyond endurance, nipped by Cornwallis's cold fury, fever taking its nightly toll, men dying with chattering teeth, quickly buried in shallow graves under a few shovelsful of earth and quickly forgotten as the armies slogged on, gaunt starving men picking the countryside clean of the last mouthful of anything edible and even not quite edible, stuffing uncooked corn in their mouths as they marched, then paying for it with wracking dysentery.

Yet they could look and see their general sleeping on the ground with them while a few miles behind them crouched the British, suffering as much, and determined to keep coming—to catch up with them and pin them against the banks of the Dan.

One night in a cold rain, Greene shared a bed of old straw in a hovel with the governor of South Carolina, John Rutledge. When repeated kicking woke them, they discovered that a hog had pushed between them to get out of the cold.[54]

The pursuing British army, for the first time as hungry as the Americans, seized anything edible—turnips, corn, beef from slaughtered farm animals. They, too, slept in the open under the rain. Cornwallis, eschewing his tent, slept on the ground with them, along with his officers.

The British also spread terror before them. The roads were crowded with fleeing people, horses, and wagons. British soldiers looted and pillaged and, mile after mile, torched the houses in their path. They were setting a new high for their Carolina depredations. General O'Hara, Cornwallis's second in command, was so shocked by the looting of the female camp followers that he warned them he would stop their snatching hands with savage beatings. But they must have realized he didn't have the time to stop and beat anyone. Cornwallis, seeing the ascending palls of smoke all around him as he marched, repeatedly commanded the looting and burning to stop. It didn't.[55]

Crossing fords, then felling trees to slow Cornwallis, seizing boats, using them, hiding or burning them, Greene's strategy was just barely keeping him ahead of Cornwallis. When Morgan's troops reached the Yadkin, Quartermaster General Carrington, with superhuman efforts, had boats waiting for them just ahead of their pursuers, who found no boats for miles around.

At one point, Greene moved his troops forty-seven miles in forty-eight hours, stretching Cornwallis ever northward toward Virginia. Lee's cavalry, riding at the rear for a chance to pounce on Cornwallis's advance guard, slowing them, got only six hours' rest out of forty-eight. But one misstep, one missed fording, and the lion would close for the kill.

For nearly two days, Greene relentlessly pounded out the last few miles toward the waiting boats at the last river to cross—the Dan—at a place called Irwin's Crossing. His rear guard decoyed Cornwallis to march toward Dix's Crossing, twenty miles west. Carrington had made sure there wasn't a single boat there. Cornwallis was further misled by fake campfires—a trick that Washington had pulled on him at Trenton.

With forty miles to go to the Dan, the race became a cross-country endurance contest between the two armies. The British sprinted those forty miles in barely twenty-four hours; the Americans did them in sixteen.

Greene found his boats waiting, got his main unit across, then watched Lee's cavalrymen board the boats, leading their swimming horses beside them. In the last boat to cross rode Light-Horse Harry Lee with his fellow Virginian, the gifted quartermaster, general, Edward Carrington.

In a two-man race covering 200 miles, Cornwallis had come in second. Despite the superb performance of his intensely loyal troops, he had been outrun and outgeneraled, and found himself on the flooded banks of the Dan in the dead of winter, exhausted, empty-handed, hungry, out of supplies, and Greene still maddeningly beyond his reach. All he could do was stand on the banks of the river and shake futile fists.

The failure was significant. If Cornwallis had caught Greene—Greene wasn't in condition to pull off another Cowpens—the earl could have swept up into Virginia, recovered his Cowpens prisoners, rescued Burgoyne's army languishing for years in its prison camp, joined up with Benedict Arnold there, and conquered all four states—Virginia, the two Carolinas, and Georgia.

Instead, Cornwallis could not now march up to meet Benedict Arnold without leaving a Greene fox in his Southern chicken coop.

Lewis Morris of the Continental Army wrote to his father, General Lewis Morris, about the retreat: It "was performed without any loss—not even a broken waggon."[56]

Alexander Hamilton saluted Greene: "To have effected a retreat in the face of so ardent a pursuit, through so great an extent of country, through a country offering every obstacle, affording scarcely any resource, with troops destitute of everything, who a great part of the way left the vestiges of their march in their own blood—to have done all this, I say, without loss of any kind, may, without exaggeration, be denominated a masterpiece of military skill and exertion."[57]

The historian Fisher summed it up in four words: "Cornwallis had been outgeneraled."[58]

In extreme adversity, Nathanael Greene had learned how to turn even retreat into victory. At Guilford Courthouse he would try to teach Cornwallis how to turn defeat into victory.

It was February 14, Valentine's Day, without a cupid in sight.

Standing on the banks of the Dan, Gen. Charles Cornwallis had some harsh truths to face. Triple defeat had made his bleak winter even bleaker. He was more than 250 miles from his winter camp in Winnsboro; the loss of the light troops from two left wings—at Kings Mountain under Ferguson and at Cowpens under Tarleton—had done significant damage to his army; and burning his equipment and sprinting after the hare-quick Americans proved to be a major error. His pride was deeply wounded; his sterling reputation was now bespattered with red Carolina mud and his own soldiers' blood; and he was miles from the sea and new supplies. Around his campfires and the officers' mess there was no joy.

Moving to camp in Hillsboro, he could wait for resupply and, possibly, new Loyalist recruits. In unending rain, he turned his exhausted troops southward and marched away.

In his base across the Dan in Virginia, Greene found his situation, although still desperate, improving. First, he had preserved his army, fended off Cornwallis's coup de grâce, and bought more time. He also received some good news: While he rested his 1,400 troops, guerrilla leader Pickens welcomed 700 new militia recruits into Greene's camp. Also, some 600 Virginia riflemen were on the march to him. And in the Chesapeake tidewater, General von Steuben was raising up and training another cadre of Continental troops. Soon he might have enough troops and equipment to take Cornwallis on head-to-head.

The day after Cornwallis marched away, Greene sent his first troops back across the Dan—Lee's Legion—followed by two companies of Maryland Continentals plus Pickens's now-enlarged guerrilla force. Their orders were to harass Cornwallis, chew on his flanks, scatter his foraging parties, prevent Loyalist recruits from joining him, and make his life miserable—weaken him.

Two days after that, Col. Ortho Stevens, replacing the arthritic Morgan, led his light infantry across the Dan. Shortly after that, the arrival of the 600 Virginia riflemen gave Greene enough new troops to do what he wanted more than anything else in the world—take Cornwallis on in a set battle, winner take all.

Greene recrossed the Dan with the remains of his rested army and went looking for British redcoats. His strategy, as he explained it to General Washington, was brutally simple: Prevent Cornwallis from drawing any more strength from Loyalist recruits, then, while keeping the earl on the defensive, batter his way back down into South Carolina and break up the system of British forts still in place, especially Ninety Six. In effect, he wanted to drive the British out of the South.

At first, Cornwallis's desperate call for Loyalist recruits had succeeded. But in his first action against the Loyalists since recrossing the Dan, at the Haw River Light-Horse Harry Lee and his cavalry, letting their green uniforms be mistaken for Tarleton's, mingled with several hundred mounted Loyalist militia at rest and, at a signal to draw their sabers, brutally inflicted many casualties. Two hundred was a lot of cavalry—enough to make the difference in any battle. But these Loyalists would never get the chance to show it. The Haw River action put them in full flight. It also changed the plans of many other Loyalists who had been thinking of joining Cornwallis.

British sergeant Roger Lamb reported the event with moral outrage:

> They mistook the American cavalry for Tarleton's dragoons, and were surrounded before they perceived their error. In this situation they immediately begged for quarter; but the relentless American refused it, and in the very act of supplicating mercy, two or three hundred were inhumanly butchered.—When did such a deed as this stain the British arms?[59]

By mid-March, Greene's strength had so grown that he was ready for the showdown fight.

Cornwallis, although lacking new troops, had been ready and eager for weeks. On March 15, 1781, Nathanael Greene headed for Guilford Courthouse, North Carolina.

A misery of rain fell all night before the battle, dismaying American and British. The men slept out in the rain; the few tents available were used to store ammunition and weapons to keep them dry. During the night fifty American soldiers died. By dawn the rain stopped and the day of the battle remained clear and dry but cold, the battleground soggy.

Although Greene had raised 4,400 troops, 85 percent of them had never seen action. The core of his army was his 1,670 veteran Continentals. His preliminary tactics had paid off—Cornwallis had been unable to recruit any Loyalists. So his total count of redcoats was only 1,900, and while seriously outnumbered, his troops were all seasoned. Believing that he was facing 10,000 Americans, the earl still did not hesitate to go on the attack.

Greene, after careful reconnoitering, chose the battleground.

Using Morgan's Cowpens battle plan as a model, Greene built his battle around the rifle and a long foreground for Cornwallis to cross. He set up three lines of defense and put his greenest troops on the first line—1,000 North Carolina militia. Posting them behind a zigzag fence so that their gun barrels could rest on the rails for better sighting, he, echoing Morgan again, asked them to get off two—some later said three— shots before withdrawing.

Then he placed seasoned troops behind them, "to shoot down the first man that runs."[60] And to them he added 400 more militia riflemen from Virginia—200 on each end of the first line. At 500 yards 1,400 riflemen would commence firing at 1,900 advancing British troops.

Green, assuming the defensive posture, waited for Cornwallis to attack.

By noon, after a twelve-mile march without breakfast, the British formed up 500 yards away and, after exchanging artillery fire, at one-thirty started the march uphill toward Greene's first line. At 150 yards, 1,400 rebel rifles and two three-pound grasshoppers volleyed. The British line took the shock, leaving holes in their line, then, pacing around their comrades as they fell, regrouped, and marched into musket range of fifty yards, fired a musket volley, took another tremendous volley from the Americans, then, with their frightening shouts of "Hurrah!," charged with their bayonets.

Many of the North Carolina militia, armed with rifles without bayonets, broke and ran. A number fled long before the British reached them, flinging away their weapons as they ran. But in general they got off two rounds each and caused heavy casualties in the British line, then, duty done, left. The rest of Greene's first line withdrew to the second line and turned to fire again.

When the British wedged through the center of the first line, Greene's flanks still held, and Cornwallis had to send in all his infantry. Now Greene's flanks began to give outward, widening the gap. More British troops pressed through the gap and, facing another 300 yards of unrelenting rifle fire, charged into Greene's second line, manned by 1,200 Virginia militia in the woods where the British use of bayonets was difficult. Although the second line fought well, the British pressed through, paid heavily in casualties, and now started across another 550 yards, with casualties soaring, toward Greene's third line. Here they hit Greene's best troops—Howard and his tough Continental infantry from Maryland and Delaware. The combatants became intermixed in a hand-to-hand brawl. The British regulars had met their match, veterans from Cowpens who would not quit, would not retreat.

Greene ordered Washington's mounted troops to attack. Cornwallis was about to be stopped, driven back. For the first time, Cornwallis was looking at defeat. To stop Washington's attack and to extricate his troops from the Americans, Cornwallis ordered his artillery to fire grapeshot into the mass of men and horses, American and British alike. Brutal as it was, killing his own troops as well as the enemy, the artillery broke up Washington's charge, forcing the brawling troops to separate. The British were able to regroup and to press the Americans back.

Greene still had troops in reserve and had at this point a golden opportunity. If he ordered a counterattack to break through the British line, Cornwallis had no more infantry to stop them. The way would be clear all the way back to Cornwallis's boot tips. The temptation to make a final charge to victory was tempting, but Greene was committed to not risk the annihilation of his army. The chance that it might fail, that darkness would fall and stop him, that he might suffer tremendous casualties from British artillery, that the British would prevail and crush his entire army, ending organized American military opposition in the South, possibly bringing on the end of the Revolution—all stayed Greene's command to attack. He ordered his troops to disengage and make an orderly withdrawal. As he left the battlefield darkness was near, and once again an all-night rain began to fall. It was another night of biting wet cold.

In the dying light, Nathanael Greene could see he had done ferocious damage to the British. He had left the ground strewn with redcoats, dead, dying, and wounded, and had preserved his own army. He knew that his troops had fought furiously and well against some of the toughest and bravest redcoats he had ever faced. He recognized the brilliance of Cornwallis's battle-saving artillery attack. But he had to admit that he had lost. Cornwallis had been willing to pay more for victory.

But in the most important sense, Cornwallis, not Greene, had failed. His overriding objective—at Cowpens, then during the race for the Dan River, and now here in Guilford Courthouse—was to destroy the last spark of hope in American hearts by destroying Greene's army. Instead he destroyed his own. His casualties were stunning: Out of 1,900 men and officers, 532 were killed, wounded, or missing. Left on the battlefield were some of his most valuable officers. The casualty rate of the Guards alone was 50 percent. Almost 30 percent of Cornwallis's army lay on the ground all around him, dead or wounded. He had suffered so many casualties that he didn't have enough men left—some 1,360—to follow up on his victory and force Greene to surrender. He ruined his army only to create a huge British cemetery.

In fact, as Cornwallis was standing in the midst of the bloody battlefield, the victor was in danger of being attacked by the loser.

Greene's own losses were much lower: 79 killed and 184 wounded, about a 6 percent casualty rate. His biggest loss—1,046 missing—included 885 militia who had run home. Greene was still in the field and, with 3,500 still standing, in condition to fight again.[61]

Greene's tactics had been to preserve his army and inflict maximum casualties on Cornwallis. And he succeeded. One is struck by how well his use of riflemen succeeded. Again, the riflemen.

Greene waited all night in another steady downpour for Cornwallis, waited with the cries of dying men on the muddy battlefield filling the night, then waited two more days. But Cornwallis would come no more.

Greene remained within ten miles of Cornwallis until a few days later, when the earl packed up and led his ruined army down the road to Wilmington, North Carolina, abandoning the only gain he had from the battle, the blood-soaked battlefield at Guilford Courthouse that he had bought at such a great price.

The only trophy Cornwallis carried from the battlefield was the pair of grasshoppers he had taken from Greene, taken from Tarleton, taken from Gates, taken from Burgoyne.

As Cornwallis trailed off, lugging Greene's two cannons after him, the scene gave off eerie echoes of the Battle of Bunker Hill and Greene's comment at the time: "I'd like to sell them another hill at the same price." As his two grasshoppers traipsed away under British colors, one could wonder if Greene considered offering Cornwallis two more grasshoppers at the same price.

Guilford Courthouse had been one of the greatest and most puzzling battles of the Revolution.

Cornwallis had won the battle and lost his army; Greene lost the battle and won the campaign. The American Southern army had lived through an amazing three months—from December 3 when Greene arrived in

Nathanael Greene by Charles Wilson Peale,
from life, 1783.

Charlotte, North Carolina, to March 15 at Guilford Courthouse. Greene
had rebuilt the ruins of the American army, capitalized on the British
disaster at Kings Mountain, and watched his rejuvenated army win at
Cowpens, survive a murderous foot race to the Dan, then destroy Cornwallis's victorious army at Guilford Courthouse. Even he was impressed.
After teaching Cornwallis at the Dan how to turn retreat into victory, he
now taught him at Guilford how to turn defeat into victory.

Bemused, Greene wrote: "The battle was long, obstinate, and bloody.
We were obliged to give up the ground and lost our artillery, but the
enemy have been so soundly beaten that they dare not move towards us
since the action, notwithstanding we lay within ten miles of him for two
days. Except the ground and the artillery, they have gained no advantage. On the contrary, they are little short of being ruined." His final
phrase: "it is out of the enemies power to do us any great injury."[62]

The British must have wondered where their victory was. The stunned,
exhausted Gen. Charles O'Hara, Cornwallis's second in command,
lamented when he should have been celebrating. "I wish," he said, "it
had produced one substantial benefit to Great Britain."

"On the contrary," he went on, "we feel at the moment the sad and
fatal effects of our loss on that Day, nearly one half of our best Officers
and Soldiers were either killed or wounded, and what remains are so

completely worn out by the excessive Fatigues of the campaign, in a march of above a thousand miles, most of them barefoot, naked and for days together living upon Carrion which they had often not time to dress, and three or four ounces of ground Indian corn has totally destroyed this Army—entre nous, the Spirit of our little army has evaporated a good deal. No zeal or courage is equal to the constant exertions we are making. Tho you will not find it in the Gazette, every part of our Army was beat repeatedly, on the 15th March, and were obliged to fall back twice."[63]

General O'Hara himself was so severely wounded, he had to be carried off the battlefield on a litter. The most desperate blow of all for him: His son had died on the battlefield.

Even Banastre Tarleton lost something on the battlefield. Lieutenant Colonel Tucker of the Virginia militia wrote his wife, "Tarleton had two fingers cut off his right hand."[64]

Only in a letter to his friend Gen. William Phillips did Cornwallis himself confide the truth: "We had not a regiment or corps that did not at some time give way. . . . I never saw such fighting since God made me. The Americans fought like demons."[65]

Few military commentators of the day pay heed to role of the rifle: In three successive battles American rifles had been a decisive factor. The British line for more than 1,000 yards had provided ample targets for massed American rifles, and the abundance of redcoats writhing on the ground—especially officers—testified to their deadly effectiveness.

Kentucky riflemen had figured out Ferguson, Morgan had figured out Tarleton, and Greene had figured out Cornwallis. Cornwallis had not figured out how to reach his key goal: strangling American hope.

Back in London, the waspish parliamentarian Horace Walpole observed, "Lord Cornwallis has conquered his troops out of shoes and provisions and himself out of troops."[66]

Another parliamentarian, Charles James Fox, a chronic bone in the throat of George III, made an equally acid comment, soon repeated all over London, that echoed Pyrrhus after defeating a Roman army at Asculum in 280 B.C.: "Another such victory would destroy the British army."[67]

Marching away from Guilford Courthouse, Brig. Gen. Charles Earl Cornwallis found himself at an impasse. He was in hostile country in winter with no supplies, many of his men barefoot, and a quarter of his army either wounded or sick. He was in no condition to attack or follow Greene; he was in fact in a poor position to defend himself against an attack from Greene. Instead he had to go to the nearest base quickly to feed, clothe, resupply, heal, and rest his troops.

It had been a devil of campaign. He had started the previous summer from Charleston with 4,000 troops; 2,500 now lay in shallow graves scattered throughout the Carolinas or had deserted: He had less than 1,500 left.

Germain's program of controlling the Carolinas through a system of forts had failed. The program of using Loyalists to harrass and destroy the rebels had blown up in his face. While the Loyalists were murdering rebels, rebels, with even more ferocity, were murdering Loyalists. He had ignited a subhuman civil war that if left unchecked would leave no people to conquer.

And worst of all, Nathanael Greene, with his paltry band of starvelings, was brilliantly surviving, thwarting him and growing stronger. In his contest against Cornwallis, he might not be winning, but he was certainly not losing. The Americans were no longer the pushovers they had been. How do you defeat a man who is willing to freeze all night in a sty with a pig to defeat you?

General Cornwallis, trying to subdue the countryside outside Charleston, had discovered what General Gage, trying to subdue the countryside outside Boston, had discovered the day the Revolution began: British authority extended as far as the tip of the Brown Bess bayonet and not an inch further. In six years, nothing had changed. In six years, except for their enclaves in New York and Charleston, the British had not conquered an inch of America.

Second only to his need for food for his troops, Cornwallis's most pressing need was for more troops—Loyalist troops. Captain Graham summed up the results of that effort in two sentences:

> His Lordship after the battle of Guildford issued a proclamation calling upon Loyalists to come forward; and he states in his despatch that many of them rode into Camp and took him by the hand, expressing joy at the defeat of Gen. Green, but went no further. In short either from timidity or change of sentiment, not one appeared in arms for his Majesty's Government.[68]

Cabinet secretary Lord George Germain's plan—seconded by Sir Henry Clinton—to subdue the Carolinas with a crusading Loyalist army, then roll up the Revolution northward hadn't worked, wasn't going to work, couldn't work. Very publicly, very loudly, right in front of their king and Parliament, Lord George Germain and General Sir Henry Clinton had dropped a clanger.

For the nonce Cornwallis faced his most pressing need: to get his troops out of the winter weather. For food and shelter, he turned and headed for the British army base in Wilmington, North Carolina. There he would decide the question of his next move.

Charles Washington Coleman Jr., editor of St. George Tucker's diary, notes that, as Cornwallis marched away from Guilford Courthouse, he was still losing men: "In a strange and hostile country many of these poor fellows sank on the roadside, died, were hastily buried by the rude hands of soldiers, left to mould away in unmarked graves and were forgotten."[69]

As they marched, his ruined army, starving and angry, vengeful and dedicated to looting, spread over the land, flowing toward Wilmington, searching every house, barn, and pigpen.

Writing to a cousin in Ireland, planter William Dickson described the terrifying passage of Cornwallis's army:

> The whole country was struck with terror; almost every man quit his habitation and fled, leaving his family and property to the mercy of merciless enemies. Horses, cattle, and sheep, and every kind of stock were driven off from every plantation, corn and forage taken for the supply of the army and no compensation given, houses plundered and robbed, chests, trunks, etc., broke; women and children's clothes, etc., as well as men's wearing apparel and every kind of household furniture taken away. The outrages were committed mostly by a train of loyal refugees, as they termed themselves, whose business it was to follow the camps and under the protection of the army enrich themselves on the plunder they took from the distressed inhabitants who were not able to defend it.
>
> We were also distressed by another swarm of beings (not better than harpies). These were women who followed the army in the character of officers' and soldiers' wives. They were generally considered by the inhabitants to be more insolent than the soldiers. They were generally mounted on the best horses and side saddles, dressed in the finest and best clothes that could be taken from the inhabitants as the army marched through the country.[70]

At Guilford Courthouse on May 18, three days after the battle, Greene faced the question of pursuing Cornwallis. The temptation was great. Cornwallis's army had been critically wounded and quite vulnerable. But Greene didn't have the food or the supplies, the weapons or the ammunition he needed to pursue Cornwallis. If Greene's army moved across the same winter-barren ground behind Cornwallis, trying to forage food from land already picked over by Cornwallis, Greene's army would starve. And if Cornwallis got all the way to Wilmington, Greene was in no condition to lay siege to that city. Also, militia enlistments were up, and the Virginia militia were planning to go home. There were no replacements for them in the offing. And most pressing, he had to find food for his troops, find a haven from the terrible winter weather.

Moving back into South Carolina offered one significant possibility. "The enemy will be obliged to follow us or give up their posts in that State," he noted.[71] He didn't assume it would be easy. There were still 4,000 redcoats dug into the Carolina forts. But with the support of Sumter and Marion and Pickens and the other guerrilla leaders, he felt they might be strong enough to overrun those forts one at a time, to drive the British out of them, out of the Carolinas and back into Charleston, ending their Southern campaign permanently. Or so he hoped.

As Cornwallis marched north, Greene moved south—each to campaign in the other's backyard.

Greene and his troops now marched toward a place called Hobkirk's Hill and a date with destiny.

A grimmer date with destiny faced the Carolina Loyalists. These, the Loyalists Cornwallis called out, then abandoned, were the greatest victims of Lord George Germain's savage policy. Even before the earl marched away, Carolina rebels were attacking Loyalist plantations everywhere, murdering the owners, murdering the overseers, burning the houses and barns to the ground, slaughtering their horses and farm animals, burning crops and driving hordes of people in full flight for their lives into Charleston—which didn't have enough food to feed them.[72]

Four

Lafayette versus Arnold

At Washington's headquarters at Peekskill, in deep winter, the news of the stunning victory in the Battle of Cowpens on January 17 brought a surge of hope. Everywhere throughout the states, morale soared, crowds gathered around festive bonfires, drums and fifes celebrated, the taverns were full of toasts, the hearth fires seemed to burn a little more brightly, and the state legislatures and the Congress were stirring, seeming at last to be more willing to participate once again. Everywhere the summertime soldier and the sunshine patriot came out of hiding to lead the celebrants in song.

But Cowpens did not remove the grave danger Benedict Arnold posed in Virginia, where he was cutting Greene's supply lines and doing fearful damage to the irreplaceable Virginia economy while reducing a great part of the Tidewater to ashes.

Washington needed to make a move, and that move had to be against Arnold. Unfortunately, he did not have many options. His armory was nearly bereft of weapons and troops. Entombed in the winter of the Hudson River Valley, his army was facing starvation. And the general himself was still thinking seriously of dismissing his troops to allow them to go in search of food.[1]

In that desperate plight, Washington now came up with a desperate plan, based more on optimism than practicality. To catch Arnold and to destroy the British raiding force in Virginia, he proposed to make a military sandwich with Arnold the meat in the middle.

One slice would be an American army force moving down from New York through Chesapeake Bay to Portsmouth. The other slice would be a French army force sailing from Newport, Rhode Island, under command of Admiral Destouches, which would reach Portsmouth by sea. In addition to transporting the French troops to Virginia, Destouches was also to seal up the watery escape route by burning Arnold's naval transports. If the various parts could move fast enough, Arnold would be trapped between the American force and the French force . . . if the various parts could move fast enough.

But who was to lead the American expeditionary force?

Washington had to cast his weary eyes over his list of generals. One wonders how many of them dreaded the prospect of facing Arnold. The ideal man to send against Benedict Arnold would have been, of course, Benedict Arnold.

In the end, Washington decided on a general from France, one largely unproven in battle and only twenty-four years old. His name: Marie Joseph Paul Yves Roch Gilbert du Motier, Marquis de Lafayette. Washington had the profoundest respect for him, and they had developed a genuine father–son relationship.

The official reason for choosing Lafayette was that he spoke French, enabling him to communicate with the French troops sailing down from Newport. Also, speed being a major factor, he was experienced in handling swift-moving light corps.[2]

And he was not without other credentials. He had been wounded at Brandywine, had been seasoned in a number of minor actions, and had first come to notice, at age 21, leading a reconnaissance force of 300 men in a skirmish against a force of Hessians who had him outnumbered. With a cool head and deft tactics, he came away with his first victory. Washington commended him for his "bravery and military ardor."

Also, a dazzling talker and an inspiring speaker, he had the gift of diplomacy. Sailing home to France on a mission to win French help for the Americans, he was an important factor in convincing the French king to send gold and troops and navy to the American rebels.

Nearly ten months since his return from France in April 1780, he was ready, willing, and able—eager for action.

More was needed than "bravery and military ardor" against Benedict Arnold, but of all his generals, Washington made Lafayette his first and only choice to go to Virginia.

Washington wanted more than just to defeat Arnold. He wanted to capture him and execute him. In his orders to Lafayette, he directed him summarily, without delay, to hang Arnold right on the battlefield.

Next Washington had to come up with some troops. In casting his eyes over his available military units, Washington could grieve for the loss of the Pennsylvania Line. Those thousands of battle-seasoned troops— civilians now, back home and getting ready for the spring planting— should have been in camp getting ready to march. They would have been a deadly weapon against Arnold. In each kit bag would have been a noose.

Still, General Wayne was busy reforming the Pennsylvania Line. So Washington ordered Wayne to attach his new Pennsylvanians to Lafayette and march into Virginia as soon as possible.

Wishing he had much more to give, Washington handed Lafayette command of 1,200 men—light infantry regiments from the Massachusetts, Connecticut, New Hampshire, Rhode Island, and New Jersey Lines—and ordered him to start his march south from Peekskill, New York. The date was February 19, 1781.

On the road, Lafayette revealed another one of his unmentioned gifts: the essential military art of scrounging. Lafayette quickly discovered that his troops, as they set out on the muddy roads in the steady rain and chilly weather of February, were without, Lafayette noted, "a sou, a horse, a wagon, a wisp of hay." As usual. So he set about outfitting his army as they marched.[3]

In Philadelphia he schmoozed Quartermaster General Pickering out of 1,500 pairs of shoes, plus medicines and tools—hardly all that he needed, but enough to keep him going. Then he scrounged a complete artillery unit—troops, cannon, ammunition, and horses. For other things he would be like Mr. Micawber, and wait to see what turned up as he went on his way.

The year 1781 seems to have been a year of rain. Relentless, flooding, it became a major—often deciding—factor in all the campaigns from Virginia to the Carolinas. It bedeviled Cornwallis's pursuit of Greene and gave the Americans fits at all the swollen river crossings, and in Lafayette's efforts to make a hasty march to Portsmouth. Rain got into food, into tents, into shoes, and gave soggy-soled soldiers pruned toes.

Washington's orders to Lafayette were to march to Head of Elk in Maryland and wait there until he heard from the French troops that they had arrived in Portsmouth by sea and were sending ships up the Chesapeake to carry his men back down to Portsmouth.

Leaving his troops at Head of Elk, Lafayette hastened south to wait in the headquarters of General von Steuben to greet the French soldiers. Lafayette had not yet told his own troops where they were going. And he had good reason.

Calling on his noted powers of persuasion to raise a new force, Gen. Anthony Wayne, standing in the ashes of mutiny, had to sell President Reed and the Pennsylvania legislature on quickly raising a new fighting force. His was an exhausting task requiring endless buttonholing, wheedling, and cajoling.

Onerous as the job was, Anthony Wayne was just the man for it. A former member of the Pennsylvania legislature and a very skillful negotiator, he was also one of the fieriest heroes of the Revolution, who as such was shaming the politicians into doing their patriotic duty.

Hailing from Chester County just outside Philadelphia, the thirty-six-year-old Wayne was born into a well-to-do tanner's family, himself in his early years apprenticed to that trade. He started a life in politics with a two-year term in the Pennsylvania legislature before being appointed colonel of the 4th Pennsylvania Battalion. In 1776 he fought with distinction at the Battle of Trois-Rivières in Canada and commanded Fort Ticonderoga, where he handled his first mutiny. By 1777, he had been promoted to brigadier general and head of the Pennsylvania Line. His only serious military setback occurred during the surprise night raid in Paoli, Pennsylvania, by Gen. Charles Grey. The casualties, most inflicted by the British bayonet, were high—over 200 dead—although Wayne, heavily outnumbered, managed to save his guns and to stop the slaughter with an orderly fighting withdrawal and was later acquitted of negligence by a court-martial he requested.

He and his Pennsylvanians participated in the Battle of Brandywine and later played a major role in the Battle of Germantown. At the Battle of Monmouth, under his battlefield command, his troops held the center of the American defensive line, their victory over Clinton's army blocked only by the onset of nightfall.

Anthony Wayne's greatest moment was the Battle of Stony Point on the Hudson River. After killing all the dogs in the neighborhood to silence them, Wayne's force of some 1,300 men, at eleven-thirty on an exceptionally dark night, waded silently through four feet of marsh water, then hacked through the fort's abatis—downed trees with sharpened branches—climbed walls, and, once on top, still without firing a shot, hacked and bayoneted their way through the defenders in a fifteen-minute bloody melee that netted them 472 prisoners. By daylight they counted twenty British dead, seventy-four wounded, and fifty-eight missing. Wayne's losses were fifteen killed and eighty-three wounded. Considered one of the most impressive victories of the Revolution, Wayne's brilliantly planned and executed night attack with bayonets avenged Grey's night attack with bayonets at Paoli.

A charismatic warrior and a sartorial cock of the walk often called Dandy Tony, he loved to dress in the resplendent togs fitted to him by Curry, Philadelphia's leading custom tailor. Quite handsome, disliking solitude, an extrovert, he was quite comfortable in Philadelphia's sumptuous taverns like the City Tavern, in the rougher inns on Race Street, and in the gilded drawing rooms of Society Hill where, in an age that admired gifted conversationalists, he was celebrated for his inspired chat, his gift of repartee, and his never-failing knack of turning a phrase.

Fascinating to women and loving their company, he once said he avoided all danger of contracting venereal disease by consorting only with women of his own upper class. A war hero, a ferocious fighter, and in every way a man's man, he could drink and drink and never lose his composure. Many were the tavern adventures he had with other such colorful figures as Light-Horse Harry Lee, who on one celebrated occasion was prevented from braining a crusty Pennsylvania legislator only by Wayne's timely intervention. Conviviality was such a central part of his character that it raised more than one eyebrow in Washington's headquarters. He was also noted for his rash impulsiveness and his hot temper.

Pressed by the need to hasten to Lafayette's aid, he cast about for a quick supply of tested veterans, and he turned his attention to the soldiers who had resigned, wondering what he could offer that would induce them to reenlist. Pennsylvania's enlistment bonus of £9 was woefully inadequate to attract new enlistees. By crossing the border to New Jersey, they could pick up £15. He urged the assemblymen to at least match New Jersey. President Reed and his council did nothing. The £9 enlistment bonus enticed no new recruits.

Like Lafayette, Mad Anthony also had to scrounge for his supplies. Soon he had enough guns and equipment; the old bugaboo was clothing. Needing enough uniforms for his new force of 1,500, he slip-sheeted invoices to mislead the quartermaster general's supply clerks and ended up with 2,000—shirts, socks, and jackets. While patrolling the halls of the state legislature and schmoozing lawmakers in the taverns around Independence Hall, he parlayed false news of a major military victory to spike a new patriotism. Wayne quickly swept a number of enthused recruits into his net and snatched up newly voted funds before the lawmakers could call them back.

The legislators next tried to pay the new troops in debased Continental paper. Wayne objected fiercely. This was a contributing cause to the original mutiny. No recruit in his right mind would take worthless paper for pay. He held out for hard cash; he got it, but more days were wasted.

Each imploring note from Lafayette begging him to hurry drove Wayne all the harder. Finally, after a lather of meetings and wheedlings and broken promises, Wayne felt he had to go with what he had. Ending his prolonged grapplings with the miserly Pennsylvania legislature, he hurried back to his camp in York, Pennsylvania, intent on marching out of camp and covering 100 miles the fastest way possible. But he hit another brick wall.

On March 8, Admiral Charles-Rene-Domanique Gochet Destouches set out to implement Washington's original two-pronged plan to deliver French troops to Virginia and to trap Arnold by burning his fleet. He led a French fleet out of Newport carrying 1,200 French troops. But this time the British were more alert. Hampered by a thirty-six-hour handicap, the British clapped on all sail and hastened flank speed after the wake of Admiral Destouches. The British were under the command of Adm. Marriot Arbuthnot, seventy, who was well into his dotage and probably suffering from Alzheimer's disease, and who was probably, as his many enemies claimed, on his best day the worst admiral in the navy, a relic of the incompetent and scandalously corrupt Lord Sandwich, head of the British Navy.

On March 16, Arbuthnot's task force caught up with and actually passed Destouches off the Virginia capes. The confrontation was, on paper, a dead even match: Destouches's eight French ships of the line faced off against Arbuthnot's eight British ships of the line—for although the British could unload more metal per broadside than the French, they were also handicapped by the incompetence of Arbuthnot.

The two fleets turned out to sea, squared off, and for an hour proceeded to batter each other, doing an equivalent amount of damage and ending up with a draw. But Arbuthnot had failed to block the French ships from entering the Chesapeake. Destouches needed only to seize his advantage to sail into the bay to drop off the French troops. Inexplicably, Admiral Destouches turned out to sea and returned to Newport for repairs, carrying the troops with him.

Arbuthnot, equally battered, did what Destouches should have done— he sailed into the Chesapeake. There he joined Arnold and effectively blocked the French from entering the bay. Worse, Arbuthnot had kept the bay open for a now thoroughly alarmed Clinton to send reinforcements to Arnold.

Destouches went down in history as the admiral who was outmaneuvered by the worst admiral in the British navy. The senile Admiral Arbuthnot had eaten Washington's military sandwich. And Washington had missed the opportunity to provide major relief to Virginia by destroying Clinton's raiding force and, more to the point, the opportunity to capture and hang Benedict Arnold.

Lafayette hastened back up the Chesapeake to get his troops. His expectation was to return to camp on the Hudson, but he found new instructions from Washington. Clinton, Washington's spies informed him, was sending another 2,000 men to bolster Arnold's defenses. Lafayette was now ordered to turn south and place himself under the command of Greene in the Carolinas. But shortly later he learned that Greene was in control of his situation. Lafayette could best serve Greene by remaining in Virginia and protecting the vital lines of communication from Virginia into the Carolinas. That meant that Lafayette, with 1,200 men, was going to have to confront Benedict Arnold, now with nearly 3,800 men, including the 2,000 reinforcements brought by General Phillips.

When he got back to Head of Elk, he found, in addition to the messages from Washington, something else waiting for him: a mutiny.

Marie Joseph Paul Yves Roch Gilbert Motier,
Marquis de Lafayette, by Charles Wilson
Peale, after Charles Wilson Peale, 1779–1780.

With British ships now once again in control of Chesapeake Bay, there would be no French ships to carry the troops down to Portsmouth. Instead they would have to cross the Susquehanna River and march all the way to Portsmouth, 250 miles. His troops were resisting. Not having expected to go so far or so long from home—more than two months already—they were not ready to go further. But they were ready to mutiny—and not for just the usual good reasons: no food, no shoes, no pay, lied to endlessly by their state legislatures and by Congress, who would literally leave them on the battlefield with no ammunition.

Their complaint now was new: They believed the Southern climate was deadly—and it was. Every summer, fever sent numbers of funeral processions—men, women, children—to the cemeteries in Virginia's Tidewater and in the Carolinas, where it had wiped out part of Cornwallis's army. They wanted no part of that.

Going south also meant they would be outnumbered, still ill treated by Congress, half starved, but now living among hostile Virginians who regarded soldiers from other states as looters, food stealers, and, worse, foreigners, even though they were coming to defend—and die for—Virginia soil. In short, they knew that they would be treated little better than the British enemy.[4]

It was a strange confrontation: these homesick war-weary plowboys facing a highborn foreign patrician. They cared not a fig that he was one of the wealthiest and most sophisticated noblemen in all of France, nor that he had danced at Versailles in front of Queen Marie Antoinette. Here on the flooded banks of the roaring Susquehanna, in an unending rain, he had to make the most persuasive speech of his life, or find himself in command of rows of empty tents.

He told them that if he could come across the ocean to fight for their freedom, they could certainly fight for it, too. Where was their patriotism? He told them they were heroes marching to glory. He told them that being outnumbered meant they were heroic Davids confronting Goliaths.

He assured them he was going to go even if he went alone. In fact, those who were afraid, timid, without the fighting spirit, would not be *allowed* to go with him. If they were willing to miss the glory, all they had to do was "apply to headquarters for a pass to join their corps in the North . . . to obtain it immediately." This was a long roll of the dice. The entire unit could opt to apply for a pass home.

Even for a legendary talker, the marquis here outdid himself. He watched the change on their faces. He had wafted a whiff of romanticism under their noses, called them heroes, puffed up their chests. The mutinous mood changed to enthusiasm. Those who had already gotten permission to return home now wanted to be readmitted. He refused them and ordered them home. A sick sergeant, weeping, begged to be carried in a cart along with them. Eight deserters suddenly reappeared and begged forgiveness. He hanged one, dishonorably discharged another, and sent the remaining six home. They would not be allowed to participate in the glory that lay ahead.

So it was settled. They were not being dragged, flogged, driven southward. The lurking fever was forgotten, the hostility of the native Virginians overlooked. Lafayette had convinced them they wanted to be heroes more than they wanted to go home. Among his other military gifts, he had proved himself to be a master psychologist.

To get all the soldiers and their baggage across the roaring, rain-swollen Susquehanna River in a constant downpour took three arduous days. Nine men didn't make it, the river's toll. And the heaviest equipment had to wait for later, less turbulent days.

But now on the other side and moving down the road to Portsmouth, he could look behind him and see over 1,000 men and a company of artillery eagerly following him. The young marquis had his first major victory, without having fired one shot at the enemy.

From all sides, various actions were converging on the Chesapeake while the tempo of events was accelerating. Yet few of the principal actors had ever heard of a crossroads named Yorktown.

One question remained: where was Anthony Wayne and that desperately needed Pennsylvania Line?[5]

Lafayette cast about for a faster way to get to the battlefield 250 miles away. First he left behind his artillery, tents, and sick; these could arrive later. Then, with profuse apologies to the native Virginians, he "borrowed for a few days" horse-drawn wagons wherever he could find them, and soon had half his troops riding, half walking, and periodically changing place. It was a novelty in eighteenth-century warfare, but on the first day alone, his troops covered twenty-eight miles.

He received more discouraging news. General Clinton, alarmed at the failed effort of the French navy to land troops to attack Arnold, had sent yet 2,000 more troops from New York. Disturbing, too, was the information that the troops were under the command of Gen. William Phillips, who now superseded Benedict Arnold in command. Lafayette's father had been killed in the Battle of Minden on August 1, 1759, by a cannonball that had been fired, it was widely believed, by Phillips's artillery.

The British in Portsmouth now numbered 3,800, well dug in and not likely to be defeated by Lafayette's paltry 1,200.

Next, Lafayette learned that General Phillips was on the march, marauding and burning his way from Petersburg north to Richmond. Arnold had destroyed only a portion of the military stores in Richmond and elsewhere, stores that were vitally important to Lafayette's troops and to Greene's. To protect them, Lafayette had to redouble his efforts—had to get to Richmond first and save it. He sent General von Steuben a message, urging him to use his 1,000 Virginia militia to delay Phillips as long as possible. Then he pressed his troops into new performances of speed.[6]

Arriving at Manchester, Virginia, on April 30, Gen. William Phillips with Benedict Arnold as second in command looked across the James River at Richmond and was astonished. Looking back at them, blocking their crossing, was Gen. Gilbert Lafayette and his army.

Lafayette wrote to Washington that Phillips "had fallen into a violent passion and swore vengeance against me and the corps."[7]

Before Phillips could begin his first efforts to cross the river, General von Steuben arrived with Virginia militia. Thwarted by the Americans and the river, Phillips contented himself with burning 1,200 hogsheads of tobacco and some of the buildings in Manchester, then headed downriver. Lafayette's forced march had paid off. For the nonce, by a hair's breadth, he had saved Richmond. And for the nonce, fair weather returned.

Then Lafayette received more bad news. Clinton had sent yet another 2,000 troops. Phillips was now commanding a formidable army of over 5,500. The disparity between the two armies was almost laughable.

With the sun came that notorious Tidewater summer. Complaints about the rain gave way to complaints about the heat, the wet, suffocating humidity, and the ticks.[8] But at least now their baggage and tents had caught up with them—along with the shirts made for them by the ladies of Baltimore.

Lafayette took time to celebrate Phillips's withdrawal with a victory march just outside Richmond in a flag-flying, piping, and drumming grand review. If he couldn't yet outfight Phillips, Lafayette decided that by traveling light he could outmaneuver him. He had his men cut off the bottoms of their coats to move faster, then hurried them across the James River toward the retreating redcoats. It was a dangerous move. If Phillips turned back, he could pin Lafayette against the banks of the James and wipe him out.

Phillips and Arnold were far less interested in Lafayette than they were in pillaging, and soon they were struggling under the weight of it all. Much of it the officers would sell for their own profit, while every enlisted man's tunic bulged to bursting. Behind them they left skies filled with black smoke, homes in embers, families scattered, lives destroyed, misery and grief. No other previous British raid equaled it for sheer brutality and greed or the enormous property damage it did. And probably few served a military purpose less. The redcoat terror of 1780–1781 in Virginia would be recalled for generations.

Lafayette, helpless to stop them and intent on protecting Williamsburg, was growing more desperate than ever for Anthony Wayne's Pennsylvania Line—wherever it was. To distract Phillips from his marauding, how long could the marquis play the game of dog 'em and dodge 'em without making a fatal slip?

On May 2, 1781, the Congress took up a major battle. It was addressing the report of the three-man committee of Madison, Duane, and Varnum that had been tabled. That study had been prompted by the demand from the Hartford Convention that Congress seize the power to tax as an implied power. The three-man committee had reported back that the implied powers were found in Article XIII of the Articles of Confederation and had recommended that an amendment to the Articles be submitted to the states for ratification.

The debate was going to proceed without Sam Adams. In April he had hurried back to Boston to try to shore up his crumbling political power there, but not before the Congress had sent the three-man proposal to the embalmers—to a special Grand Committee consisting of one member from each of the thirteen states. No one had any illusions as to what was going to happen. Even without Sam Adams there would be enough frightened congressmen to strangle the bill in its cradle. It simply would never emerge again.

Now, on May 2, the Congress began shadow-boxing. Proponents wanted the Congress to immediately use the taxing powers implied in Article XIII without even consulting the states.

Thomas Burk of North Carolina tried to picture a Congressional army arriving on the doorsteps of the state legislatures without any warning, with cannons primed. He was completely awed by the idea. He opined that the reaction of the states "who are so jealous of their Liberty" would be explosive—"dreadful alarm" was his term. And he was undoubtedly right. "Homicidal" might have been a better word.

Marching along the James with Lafayette nipping at his heels, General William Phillips abruptly stopped. Then turned around. Then sailed back up the James, throwing panic into Lafayette's forces.

But Phillips was not interested in Lafayette. He had received orders to bring his army to Petersburg, twenty-three miles below Richmond—orders that had come from Gen. Charles Cornwallis. The earl announced to Phillips that he had abandoned the Carolinas, in fact, having already marched 223 miles, was in Virginia and would arrive with his army in a few days. The rendezvous he had chosen was Petersburg.

Lafayette now would face an army of 7,200 led by the most dangerous British general in America. The situation had gone from grimly laughable to absurd.

It must have seemed to Lafayette that everyone was coming to Virginia, except more American troops. He was wrong. Everyone was coming to Virginia, including, very soon now, the Americans and the French.

On May 19, when he hastened from Philadelphia into his camp at York, Gen. Anthony Wayne stared about him with rising anger. Weary from trying to beard the state legislature and the Congress for more money, more arms, more men, he now found the camp he returned to "badly officered" and unkempt. Instead of a bustle of activity preparatory to moving out, he saw slackness, indolence, discipline out of control.

In his absence idle men and officers had begun to chafe. Utterly bored and restless, the officers had passed around the sole worn copy of Tobias Smollett's *Peregrine Pickle*. In the officers' mess, the number of near quarrels was a major warning sign. Tempers were short.

"When I arrived at York," the furious Wayne wrote, "there was scarcely a horse or a carriage fit to transport any part of our baggage or supplies."[9] Worse, the Pennsylvania Assembly, despite the recent mutiny, despite their solemn promises, reneged once more and paid the soldiers with Pennsylvania paper so worthless the local storekeepers wouldn't accept it. It was clearly provocation for mutiny again.[10]

Wayne noted that on the day before they were to leave for Virginia, "a few leading mutineers on the right of each regiment called out to pay them in real and not ideal money: they were no longer to be trifled with. Upon this they were ordered to their tents, which being peremptorily refused, the principals were immediately either knocked down or confined by the officers, who were previously prepared for this event."[11]

Among the enlisted men, a full-scale riot had boiled to the explosion point. A light horseman had assaulted a militiaman. He was thrown in the brig. His sidekick rode into camp to try to free him, and a militia sentry shot him out of his saddle, killing him. The light horsemen in a body were planning to retaliate by killing all the militiamen. Three civilians were facing charges of treason. One of Wayne's best sergeants, John Maloney, nicknamed Macaroni Jack because of his dapper dress, the same Maloney who had been one of the leaders of the Jockey Hollow mutiny, was put in the guardhouse for a minor infraction. Very popular, clever, witty, he was known for caring for the affairs of the common foot soldier. His arrest had cast a sullenness over the troops.[12]

Maloney's wife, a washerwoman attached to the army whose quick needle and thread and nursing hands had been helpful to many enlisted men, was crying for his release. But at his trial, Maloney was sentenced to whipping. That had caused more unrest. The enlisted men felt the punishment excessive. When he was tied to the whipping post, Macaroni Jack called, "Help me brothers." The officers, remembering Maloney's leadership of the Jockey Hollow mutiny, construed Maloney's words as an invitation to mutiny; after he was whipped, Maloney was sent to headquarters for a court-martial along with two deserters accused of sedition.[13]

Also sent to headquarters was another sergeant, John Lillie, charged with being drunk and out of his tent at night and for having sworn at an officer. With him came Jack Smith, charged with rolling a cannonball too close to officers with the intent of killing them. He, too, had sworn at an officer.

This was too much bad morale to load in the baggage wagons on the road to battle. Out of time and out of patience, Wayne wanted quick, sharp justice, then march out. He turned ruthless.

For Lafayette, more surprises popped up. His spies now informed him that General Phillips was ill with fever in Petersburg. Then he learned that General Phillips was desperately ill. A day later, on May 15, he learned that Phillips had died, leaving Benedict Arnold in temporary command, waiting for Cornwallis.

In the York, Pennsylvania, army camp, under Wayne's stern eye, the court-martial was quick and brutal: all accused were sentenced to death. Execution was set for the next morning. Now the entire camp was in an uproar over the sentences, which were considered far too excessive, while the speed of the executions allowed for no appeal.[14]

After a sullen breakfast the entire corps was called out. At their head, a unit of twenty marksmen was formed up. With musicians in the lead playing the "Dead March," the Pennsylvania Line was marched to the jail. The condemned men were brought out. And in a voice loud enough for all to hear, their death sentences were read to them. A number of women attached to the Line were now milling around the soldiers, some shrieking for mercy. The entourage marched out of town to a rye field in full bloom.

The three men were forced to kneel, and had their upper arms tied about their waists. Blindfolds were tied around their eyes. Sergeant John Maloney's wife could stand it no longer and tried to run up to her husband but was knocked down by an officer. Guards blocked other women from intruding.

Ten sharpshooters were marched up to within ten feet of Sergeant Maloney. When the officer in charge dropped his hand holding a fluttering handkerchief, the ten muskets fired. The handkerchief around Maloney's eyes burst into flames and his head was blown apart, bits and pieces of it sprayed across the rye blossoms.

Ten more marksmen stepped forward and on command blasted off the head of Jack Smith. Lillie's head was the last. The troops were then required to march past the three bodies and, on command, to look down at them. The marching units then turned and came back from the opposite direction so that all troops from either side of the ranks got a close-up view. Wayne himself later wrote that the marksmen fired with tears flowing down their cheeks.

From the ranks now came shouts of defiance. In response, the troops were ordered into their tents. Those who refused were knocked down, arrested, and subjected to immediate court-martial. Four were tried and executed on the spot by firing squads made up of their friends. All told, seven men were executed that day.

Following the executions, four of Wayne's officers resigned. Before he forwarded their resignations to Washington, he blistered them for leaving, contending that they were acting not out of moral outrage but out of cowardice. Evidently he was trying not to persuade them to stay but to deter other officers from resigning. There were no other resignations. Wayne believed he had scotched another mutiny.

On Saturday, May 26, 1781, after a full breakfast, the Pennsylvania Line marched out of camp in a drenching downpour, hellbent for Virginia and Lafayette. Each soldier carried his weapons but no ammunition. Under lock and key in the munitions carts were their cartridges and powder. Leading them was the general they wanted to kill.[15]

Five

Lafayette versus Cornwallis

On May 20, Lord Cornwallis led his spent troops into camp at Petersburg and joined Benedict Arnold. He then sent to his commanding officer one of the most shocking communications Clinton, in six years of warfare, had ever received. Despite Clinton's strictest orders and without having sent him a single message for three months, the earl, by suddenly popping up in Virginia, had done exactly what Clinton did not want him to do, but exactly what he himself did want to do—leaving the Carolinas under command of Lord Rawdon with hardly enough troops to maintain the fort system against the growing strength of Greene and the guerrillas.

Cornwallis's letter to Sir Henry explained his position: "I shall now proceed to dislodge Lafayette from Richmond and with my light troops to destroy any magazines or stores in the neighborhood. . . . Thence I propose to move to the Neck at Williamsburg, which is represented as healthy and where some subsistence may be procured, and keep myself unengaged from operations which might interfere with your plan for the campaign, until I have the satisfaction of hearing from you."[1]

The letter must have confounded Clinton. Cornwallis seemed to be asking Clinton what to do next.

When the earl told Arnold that he was going to set up camp somewhere below Williamsburg, Arnold cautioned him. That spit of land at Yorktown, he knew from direct experience, was indefensible. A better location would be on the James River as far up as Richmond, which was more defensible and also well beyond the reach of the deep-draft French fleet.

Shortly later, Arnold was recalled to New York.[2]

Outside Richmond and still waiting for Wayne, General Lafayette realized he could not have been caught in a deadlier trap even if it had been planned.

He was an easy target for either force—Cornwallis by land and Arnold faster and more mobile in riverboats. The marquis was now vastly outnumbered, faced by an army nearly six times his size and armed with highly mobile, fast-moving cavalry under Banastre Tarleton and Simcoe. Although nimble, Lafayette was only lightly armed, with few cannon, no cavalry, and no boats. He couldn't stand and fight, and he couldn't retreat fast enough to outrun the cavalry, which could outflank him at any river's crossing. Furthermore, he couldn't move across the Virginia countryside for any distance without encountering rivers—each crossing a place of entrapment for a fleeing army.

The few mounted militia Lafayette had were at the end of their short-term enlistments and, several days later, ignoring all pleas, went home. Could matters get worse? His mission now was to survive, fight for time, keep Cornwallis away from those military stores. Despite the firestorms of warehouses, barns, homes, piers, and ships Arnold and Phillips had set off, there were still stores of military matériel earmarked for Greene.

No one needed to tell the marquis that between Cornwallis's formidable army and New York stood nothing but him and his 1,200 light infantry men.

Getting nothing from the Virginia legislature, indeed not even sure where it was, finding that General von Steuben had but a few hundred men still under training, having learned that Jefferson was no help at all, and not knowing where Wayne was, he must have felt like a mouse in a cage with six cats.

He redoubled his begging to the Virginia officials, to the new Governor Nelson, who was also the active general of the militia. He extended his scope of begging up to Governor Lee in Maryland. He zipped off quick begging notes to the Congress, to Washington, to fellow officers, to private citizens.

He sent messengers in search of Daniel Morgan, whose stunning victory over Tarleton at Cowpens loomed larger and more significant every day. Morgan had left right after that battle in agony from arthritis and gone home. Lafayette heard that he had somewhat recovered and was working his way back down to Greene's command in South Carolina. The marquis wrote him an urgent note urging him to come instead to his aid, bringing with him as many of his famous Virginia riflemen as he could.

At the same time, he started to hurry his troops back up toward Richmond—to put them closer to the eventual linkup with Wayne. But where was Mad Anthony? Lafayette penned an urgent note to him, then another, yet another, and still others, all begging Wayne to hurry.

Now, aware that even Wayne's arrival would not give him an army large enough to confront Cornwallis on the battlefield, Lafayette noted (one can hear the chuckle from the gallows): "On [Wayne's] arrival we shall be in a position to be beaten more decently, but at present we can only run away."[3]

He enticed, danced, moved out of range, enticed again, trying to draw Cornwallis ever northward toward Wayne and away from the military stores.

Rain had been falling for four days on Wayne's army. Slogging along the deeply mired roads, the men were muttering to each other and glowering at their officers. Even the officers had no smiles for Wayne.

The general himself was grim. He had fought like a wildcat to raise 1,500 men. He was marching with barely 800, none of whom he dared to arm. This was not the way he wanted to hurry to the relief of Lafayette. This was not the proper condition for the American army sent to turn the tables in Virginia.

In a fury, he drove his men to exhaustion.

On May 20, at the end of his 223-mile march from Wilmington, North Carolina, to Petersburg, Virginia, where he took command, Cornwallis had made his own nose count of the forces under his command. His count was quite similar to Lafayette's: his total strength had risen to over 7,000. Against him Lafayette, twenty-three miles away at Richmond, commanded 1,200 Continentals and 1,800 inexperienced militia. Von Steuben, southeast of Charlottesville, had 500 barely trained Continental recruits.

Cornwallis decided the time had come to go after Lafayette. The race to the Dan was about to have a sequel.

In late May, in his camp outside Richmond, Lafayette learned that Cornwallis was on the road and marching right toward him. With no military stores left in the area, the marquis had already decided that Richmond wasn't worth defending "for the sake of a few houses, most of which are empty." In truth, Arnold had not left much in Richmond that was worth a single arsonist's match.[4]

The marquis had no illusions about his desperate plight. He wrote to General Knox: "Lord Cornwallis's abilities are to me more frightening than his superiority of forces. . . . To speak plain English, I am devilish afraid of him."[5]

As he moved, Lafayette adopted Greene's tactics to slow and stall Cornwallis. As he marched, he left behind him felled trees that blocked roadways; at each river crossing, after getting to the other side, he destroyed all the bridges, capturing everything that floated, then occupied a strong position on the opposite bank. Cornwallis would find all means of crossing gone, and while his troops sat and waited for his engineers to rebuild the bridges, Lafayette slowed them even further by harassing the bridge builders. It was an exceedingly dangerous strategy. At any time, at any river, Cornwallis might send Tarleton or Simcoe in a wide sweep upriver or downriver to another crossing for a dash behind Lafayette, surrounding him and destroying him.

Yet there was nothing between Cornwallis and the end of the Revolution but Lafayette's scant force. One misstep and Cornwallis seemingly with the merest flick of his lion's tail could end the six-year-old contest. Never was the old Russian proverb truer: The cat and the mouse are not playing the same game.

The entire congregation of thirteen infant states could do little but hold their breaths and pray for a miracle. The state legislatures could repent each bullet, each soldier, each pair of shoes they so irresponsibly failed to send to the army, each battalion they should have sent.

By a series of quick marches, Cornwallis pursued, snatching at Lafayette and coming up with fistfuls of coattails and air, his reach exceeding his grasp. He was unable to catch up with, let alone encircle, the marquis.

Over and over Lafayette played the one card he had. Cornwallis was encumbered by his eighteenth-century army, miles of wagon trains carrying food, weapons, and military stores, followed by a second army of camp followers—women, cooks, laundresses, wives, prostitutes, and children, all bent on looting as they passed over the land.

With pirouettes and adagios, sleights of hand, Lafayette keep luring the earl across one river and stream after another, ever northward, until Cornwallis reached the North Anna River. There he finally stopped. He saw he wasn't going to catch Lafayette, wasn't going to be able to prevent him from linking up with the long-overdue Wayne, wasn't going to bother with attacking the half-ruined weapons plant at Hunter's Works or even the town of Fredericksburg.

Cornwallis was able to seize one compensation for his failure to catch Lafayette. As Lafayette crossed the Rapidan, he was leaving open better pickings to the south and west, especially Charlottesville, whither Jefferson and the Virginia legislature had fled—"less dilatory in their motions than they had formerly been in the resolutions"—and where there was reported to be a large cache of military supplies. Consequently the earl sent his two mounted rapiers—Tarleton and Simcoe—on deadly strikes.[6]

He ordered Banastre Tarleton to race fifty miles to Charlottesville and there to capture Thomas Jefferson and the entire Virginia legislature. He was also expected to find there and destroy a huge cache of arms while Simcoe went after von Steuben.

To prevent a warning from getting ahead of him, Tarleton had to exceed even his famous ground-covering pace. And he had just the mounts to do the job. The Greene Dragoons were in horse heaven. By raiding the nearby horse farms, the British legionnaires in their smart green uniforms were soon riding hard for Charlottesville on the finest horses they had ever mounted.

He allowed one pause, for breakfast at a tavern. And there he was seen by Capt. John Jouett, who was well mounted on a fresh horse. Jouett, a native of the area, chose a shorter road to town. Still he didn't count on the incredible speed Tarleton could get from horses, especially since Tarleton was willing to run them to death.

In his famous home, Monticello, Thomas Jefferson was hosting the speaker of the state legislature and a number of assemblymen at a legislative breakfast meeting when the warning reached them. The speaker promptly ordered the legislature to reassemble in Staunton, Virginia, adjourned the meeting, and dashed away. Jefferson continued to coolly finish his breakfast while issuing orders to his staff. A carriage for his wife and children was brought to the front and dispatched to the home of Colonel Carter on the adjacent mountain. Jefferson ordered a messenger to race to the farrier where his riding horse was being shod and bring back the animal to the bottom of the Monticello hill, ready for his arrival.

A militia lieutenant, Hudson, now hurried into the house to report that the Green Dragoons were coming up Monticello's winding road. Minutes before the dragoons rushed in, Jefferson left his home by a footpath and, while his home was being searched, reached the bottom of the hill to ride off on his waiting horse. Captain McLeod of Tarleton's Legion conducted a thorough search of the mansion, then, strangely, departed without burning Monticello to the ground.[7]

In the meantime, at Point of Fork, Lt. Col. John Simcoe, bluffing von Steuben with an excessive number of campfires, nearly nabbed the German general and his raw militia. Von Steuben, believing from the many campfires that there were many more Queen's Rangers than there really were, withdrew his green troops, who were terrified of cavalry, and hastened away. In the process he abandoned a large store of military supplies. Simcoe thereupon crossed the river, destroyed much of the matériel, and pitched a number of cannon into the river. Duty done, he returned to base.

Yet the missions of Tarleton and Simcoe were not the thumping successes Cornwallis had expected. All Tarleton had to show for his spectacularly executed raid were four lesser lawmakers and a piece of Jefferson's coattail. And no arms. Following the expected British practice, as he rode back to base he left a trail of burning buildings and crops across Virginia, destroying in the process one of Jefferson's plantations and its crops, valued at over $400,000.

And although von Steuben was strongly criticized for abandoning his supplies, he was able to recover many of the key pieces, such as the cannon Simcoe had dumped into the river. Like Tarleton's, Simcoe's raid was not nearly as successful as Cornwallis later would claim.

*   *   *

Wayne's march had turned into a misery compounded by misery squared. The rain continued to fall; roads were flooded; mud covered their feet; the least rivulet became a torrent. There was no way to get dry. Even with increasingly early reveilles and hasty breakfasts, the troops were unable to slog more than fifteen miles a day. They struggled waist-deep through Pipe Creek only to be confronted with even more challenging Monocacy Creek. It was too deep for humans; when his troops tried to cross in horse-drawn wagons, the wagons rolled over, pouring men and equipment downstream. They lost a whole day there to clean their weapons, dry out and repack their equipment, and reload the wagons.

Wayne, in single-minded fury, pushed all the harder. And harder. But finally, reluctantly, he had to pause to let the men yet again clean up, dry out their weapons, and take stock. Maddened by the water, Wayne counted up the miles; in five days, he'd gone barely fifty miles. Seventy to go.

The men fell exhausted into the tents at night sopping wet and woke just as sopping wet when they stepped back out to find the rain waiting for them. Overladened wagons were sinking up to their hubs in mud mires. Hands, arms, and backs strained to pull them out only to see the wheels sink again in the next quagmire. Slow, tortuous, backbreaking labor consumed each day, striving for miles, totting up yards.

Furiously, Wayne drove on. Past Frederick, Maryland, he urged his troops. One day he paused at noon to let his men eat their first meal of the day—cold. Hardly had they had an hour's rest when he ordered them up and on the road again, pressing for the Potomac River. There he made a serious error.

He switched his marching plan from a crossing at Georgetown, where he knew boats and fresh supplies awaited him, to try a crossing twenty miles upstream at Nolan's Ferry, which he prayed would be shallower. It wasn't, and he found only four boats, all in poor condition. The rain was now falling in biblical quantities, harder than ever. The supposed three-hour crossing stretched into many more; midnight saw the last of his exhausted his troops cross over. Worst of all, he lost a sergeant and three soldiers as well as six field pieces and all his ammunition to the unquenchable raging flood. More time was lost fishing out the field pieces, dragging them up on the ground, and then laboriously disassembling them, drying out the parts, and oiling them. The day lost at Monocacy was matched by another day lost at the Potomac. He tried to get his army on the march again at four in the afternoon.

The rain was an inescapable torment, with God's anger seemingly in every drop. Thunderstorms lashed them. After another short soggy restless night, the troops woke at dawn to see the rain unabated. Wayne was now

Anthony Wayne by James Sharples Senior,
from life, 1796.

running out of food and had to wait for carts that dragged the food from Georgetown. Another thirty-six-hour write-off.

Then, unbelievably, the rain stopped. As the troops marched through Leesburg, struggling through the river of mud that had been the main roadway, at least they were beginning to dry out. But not for long. South of Leesburg, the torrents began again. Day after day. And at every turn, a horseman would ride up to Wayne, salute, and hand him a message. The messages were from the same man with the same urgent refrain: his commanding officer, General Lafayette, urging him to press harder, leap forward faster, arrive sooner. At any moment Cornwallis could pounce and leave a pile of blue Continental feathers on the roadway to mark the place of the kill. And always Wayne would press harder. Days could count. Hours.

Wayne could recite by heart Thomas Paine's comment, "These are the times that try men's souls," for abruptly the weather turned colder. His troops, rainwater leaking out of every fold and wrinkle of their clothing, were now shivering from the chill that was bringing foot-deep snows west of them in the Blue Ridge mountains. When would it end?[8]

Wayne was still struggling. Mudbound, he made twelve miles one day and on the next a mere nine. Violent thunderstorms descended on his camp that night and blew down tents and got everything so soaked and entangled that yet another day was lost drying out and repacking.

The sun came out—out to stay. But the effects of the storm lingered: Wayne's forces stood at the bank of the north branch of the Rappahannock, blocked by the flooded river. Another detour, more lost time.

In Albemarle Old Courthouse lay supplies the loss of which would have been difficult for the Americans to replace. And Cornwallis, at last catching Lafayette out of position, was many miles closer to Albemarle than Lafayette was. He ordered Colonel Tarleton to race to Albemarle Old Courthouse, destroy the vitally important stores there, then cross the James, scatter von Steuben's newly trained Continentals, and return to Cornwallis.

Tarleton arrived there with his usual astonishing dispatch, only this time he was in turn astonished. The seemingly impossible had happened: Lafayette, who had disappeared the day before, had turned up at Albemarle ahead of him. And in numbers. With an ambush set in place. Flummoxed, Tarleton had to withdraw hastily.

Lafayette had shown Cornwallis another advantage he enjoyed over him. The day before, men from his Virginia militia, having a native's knowledge of every creek and tree, pointed out to Lafayette a long-unused road—a shortcut. Working through the night, ax men cleared the road of old overgrown brush and trees. Then, during the remaining night hours, Lafayette's troops, invisible to Cornwallis's scouts, were able to quick march to Albemarle ahead of Tarleton. Afterward the road came to be known as the "The Marquis's Road."[9]

The next day, June 10, twelve miles south of Raccoon Ford on the Rapidan, 120 miles and fifteen long days of marching from York, Anthony Wayne's scouts came riding in. They had met advance units of Lafayette's army.

The rain paid one final visit. At the very last minute, on the banks of the swollen Rappahannock, a fresh deluge made this ultimate river between them impassable.

Both Lafayette's and Wayne's performances had been exceptional. The marquis won the race against Cornwallis, as Greene had done, and once more Cornwallis, thwarted, stood on the banks of a second Dan— the North Anna. Because of Wayne's Herculean efforts, Cornwallis would now have to pay a price in terms of casualties higher than he was willing to pay in order to crush Lafayette. Wayne had raised the ante.

Simply put, some 800 mutinous men, disarmed because they were furious enough to want to kill their commanding officer, in a historic display of true grit, may have staved off the death of the American cause.

Lafayette also won in a larger sense. Like Greene, he had survived. He had bought time. The vital military stores were still largely intact. And the delay had paid off in another way: First, he had now acquired three regiments of Pennsylvanians—more than 800 men. Adding them to his 1,200 New Englanders, three brigades of Virginia militia, von Steuben's 400 Virginia Continentals whom the gifted German teacher had personally trained in his Virginia camp, plus nine Continental field guns, Lafayette's numbers and strength were growing. Most significantly, he was also raising a cavalry: young, superbly mounted Virginians who were born on horses were increasing the size of a corps of sixty dragoons and an equal number of mounted volunteers, giving him vitally needed eyes and ears and great tactical speed.

Then he learned that Gen. Daniel Morgan, heeding his pleas, was moving rapidly toward him with Virginia militia general William Campbell, thirty-six, a giant of a man, bigger even than the huge Morgan, married to Patrick Henry's sister. Accompanying them were 600 Virginia militia riflemen, all mounted—a number that was to soon grow to 780. These were not raw militia but tough mountain men, many of them veterans with Campbell of the destruction of Ferguson at Kings Mountain and of the Battle of Guilford Courthouse, where their rifles had inflicted such high casualties.

Lafayette's army was getting respectable—nearly 5,000 men and growing. Although he was still not able to meet Cornwallis head to head, his army would soon have to become a major factor in Cornwallis's thinking.

Then the earl presented the marquis with another crisis.

From the banks of the North Anna River, Gen. Charles Cornwallis ordered his troops to withdraw. With an empty net, he turned south.

Cornwallis had assured Clinton, naturally, that his campaign against Virginia's war stores was a great success: "5000 stands of arms, about 600 barrels of powder, and 2000 hogsheads of tobacco, as well as a great number of guns, some clothing, harness, salt and other supplies."[10]

In truth, during three weeks of pursuing Lafayette, the earl's busy torches had sent great quantities of property up in flames, burning wide areas of tidal Virginia to the waterline. But very little of it was of any military value. The marquis had done more than lure him on a chase after a headless chicken; he had kept him away from the property that mattered. He had plucked the initiative from Cornwallis.[11]

Cornwallis had failed once again, and from the military point of view had made things worse by moving into Virginia. Greene's army, gathering strength, was preparing a major campaign against the British fort system, unchallenged. Worse, Cornwallis's efforts had failed to interdict the flow of vital supplies, including troops, to Greene. And now a second army was growing up around him.

As Cornwallis marched, Lafayette followed, having few wagons and fewer supplies to carry in them anyway, scraping the bottoms of his powder barrels, nervously watching his foot-dragging Virginia militia, who talked of nothing but going home for the harvest.

Although Cornwallis, with his superior cavalry and ample wagons stuffed with his bulging powder barrels and confiscated food for his troops, seemed utterly indifferent to Lafayette's moves, the young marquis, ever the propagandist, made it seem that Cornwallis was retreating and that he was pursuing. This played very well with the terrorized Virginians, who applauded his every step. Morale rose. Virginia militia enlistments increased. Congress began to sniff the first whiffs of possible victory, and Lafayette would soon find supplies flowing from Philadelphia. In the state capitals of Delaware, Maryland, and Virginia, other noses sniffed the first scent of hope, and Lafayette could now look for an influx of more troops.

But the marquis was still playing a dangerous game; Cornwallis was as cunning a stalker as the British army had to offer, with far more battle experience than the twenty-four-year-old Frenchman. Lafayette was in serious danger of falling into one of the earl's lightning traps. Yet with the first stirrings of hope in so many parts of the country, Virginia was beginning to look increasingly like the place for the showdown battle of the American Revolution.

In New York, the headquarters of Gen. Sir Henry Clinton were in total confusion. Now fully convinced that Washington and Rochambeau were at last going to attack his ramparts, Sir Harry was urgently preparing the city's defenses.

Moving toward Williamsburg to put his troops in summer quarters, where he believed they would be safe from the notorious Tidewater fevers, Cornwallis received orders from Clinton to return 2,000 troops to New York posthaste, then put his remaining Virginia army in a military piggy bank safely based on the bay, where the British navy could evacuate them in a hurry whenever Washington started his New York siege.

To convince Cornwallis of his plight, Clinton enclosed several intercepted American dispatches with the comment, "You will observe I am threatened with a siege in this post."[12]

Clinton was putting Cornwallis in mothballs. The acerbic earl replied by suggesting he would be better off returning to Charleston. But following General Clinton's orders, on June 21 Cornwallis evacuated Richmond and went looking for a safe base on the bay.

Not sure where Cornwallis was going or why, Lafayette followed, sniffing for a trap. He now recognized three enemies: Cornwallis, smallpox, and the looming harvesttime. Even Morgan's riflemen were talking about harvesttime. The marquis was in danger of seeing his army evaporate.

*　*　*

In Philadelphia, at the prompting of the French minister to the United States, Chevalier Anne-César de La Luzerne, the Continental Congress had been debating since February over a very unpalatable subject: On what terms, and under what conditions, would America discuss peace with Britain?

The members of Congress recognized that this was a question that needed to be addressed seriously because European court chat was whispering that the mediator of a peace conference was likely to be none other than the empress of Russia—a formidable presence who would demand the most serious negotiations. But, empress or not, they did not like what was staring them in the face.

Britain, it was hinted, might consider an in situ peace accord, retaining those former colonies over which she had control at the time of the peace conference. Did this mean the United States could lose Georgia? And both Carolinas, including the prize city of Charleston? And Virginia? And what about New York? All of it, or just the city?

The Congress had already dealt with these matters, the year before, in February 1780. A congressional committee at that time brought out a bill containing a list of minimum peace demands: These included first and foremost, of course, complete and absolute independence from England, with total withdrawal of all British forces from U.S. territory, recognition of certain disputed state boundaries, stipulated fishing rights, and free navigation of the Mississippi River. On February 14, Congress accepted all the provisions of the committee report except the fishing rights and then appointed John Adams to handle negotiations with England, which included drawing up a commercial treaty. In the same spirit, John Jay was appointed minister to Spain to negotiate a peace treaty there. In both cases, the efforts had proved to be premature.

Now, a year later, in the spring of 1781, to the members of Congress, squinting at the total collapse of the new nation and the possibility that all thirteen of the former colonies could be reclaimed by England, the idea of giving up four or five of them might sound a little less catastrophic—unless you came from one of those question-mark states. At least there would still be a United States of America. The discussion that started in mid-February 1781 was to continue until June 15.

For General Washington, such a division of the former colonies would mean that as a consequence of six years of sacrifice and blood, he would not only lose Mount Vernon but also become a permanent exile from his beloved Virginia, which would become once more a British colony.

On June 15, the Congress made its decision: John Adams was no longer alone. He was now to be part of a peace-negotiating committee that included Benjamin Franklin, John Jay, Henry Laurens, and Thomas Jefferson. Instructions required the negotiators to stand fast for freedom and national sovereignty—give up not an inch of the thirteen states—and to negotiate all other matters. All agreements were to be made with the "knowledge and concurrence" of France.

During the sweltering Tidewater weather of June, Lafayette continued shadowing Cornwallis, ever puzzled by the earl's moves as he traipsed steadily southward. As both an American patriot and a French patriot seeking révanche and as a young general eager to match himself against one of Britain's best, Lafayette watched for the chance to draw first blood.

He got his chance in a place called Spenser's Ordinary, a tavern six miles northwest of Williamsburg and only a few more miles southeast of a hamlet called Yorktown. To forage for the army and also to gather some military stores along the Chickahominy River, Cornwallis dispatched Colonel Simcoe and his Queen's Rangers along with a contingent of Hessians to a crossroads known as Spencer's Ordinary.

To bushwhack Simcoe, Lafayette sent Col. Richard Butler with a Pennsylvania regiment, now trusted with ammunition, plus 120 mounted troops and some Virginia riflemen. An all-night march brought them in contact with the surprised Simcoe. This promised to be a ferocious contest, since the Queen's Rangers were primarily American Loyalists and, equally significant, primarily Loyalist Virginians who wanted to free their state from the hated rebels.

The two forces attacked each other furiously. Hand-to-hand fighting moved back and forth, with Simcoe's troops holding a slight edge. Virginia riflemen came up in support of the Americans; then Wayne sent in more of his Pennsylvanians. Simcoe, thinking that Lafayette's main body might be nearby—it wasn't—broke off the fight and moved out, leaving his wounded behind. Butler, believing Cornwallis's main body was nearby—it was, and coming up fast—also withdrew soon after. Both sides had about thirty casualties. Both sides claimed victory. More probable: It was a standoff.

Spencer's Ordinary told Cornwallis that Lafayette was feeling strong enough if not to brawl, at least to trade punches. And the logical place to brawl would be where Cornwallis would be most vulnerable, at a river crossing.

Lafayette, while eager, remained ever-ready to dance out of a possible Cornwallis trap. He licked his chops while increasing his vigilance. That proved to be a wise move. The earl knew how to set traps.

On July 6, 1781, in sweltering weather that was affecting both men and animals, Cornwallis came to the James River, just a few miles north of the original settlement of Jamestown, with 7,000 troops and multitudes of horses and wagons. Crossing it was a major undertaking.

During the morning, Simcoe's Rangers were the first to be ferried across the James. By midday, Lafayette, watching, thought that most of Cornwallis's troops had been carried over. Soon would be the perfect time to attack the remnant.

As an opening move, he sent Anthony Wayne and 500 of his Pennsylvanians to Green Spring Plantation not far from the crossing, there to make contact with the British and gather intelligence. As Wayne tried to reach Cornwallis's point of embarkation he began skirmishing with British outriders, many of them belonging to Tarleton's Legion.

About one in the afternoon, while holding the rest of his army at the ready, Lafayette himself joined Wayne. Since Cornwallis's camp lay behind some woods, no one had really gotten a good look at it. Lafayette hesitated; he grew suspicious. Instead of committing his entire force, he sent in another 500 troops but held the rest of his army in reserve. Then, to get a better view of the earl's camp, he went riding over to a promontory.

By five P.M., fighting his way through stubborn opposition, Wayne had almost reached Cornwallis's main camp, still sure he was in contact with just the rear guard, still sure that Cornwallis's main force was on the other side of the James.

But now Lafayette, gaining the promontory, was shocked when he saw the truth. Almost the entire British army was still on this side of the James and poised to strike Wayne. He went galloping back to Wayne to warn him. Too late. The earl, sure that the greater part of the American army was in his grasp, had sprung his trap.

Wayne himself now realized he had been duped. A huge force of British stepped out from the cover of woods into full view and on the attack. He was trapped. But to make a stand would have led to encirclement and slaughter. To retreat could quickly become a bloody rout. Instead, keeping his head, he did the unthinkable. About to be flanked on both sides, Wayne ordered his 900 Pennsylvanians to attack the main body of Cornwallis's army head on. He paid for it by taking heavy casualties from grapeshot and musketry, but the Pennsylvanians' counterattack, by getting within seventy yards of the British line, astonished Cornwallis, who was briefly stopped. Wayne held him off for fifteen minutes until his line began to waver. With his artillery horses down, he was going to lose his field pieces; with every one of his field officers unhorsed, he was about to lose his battlefield communications system.

Wayne seized the moment when the British were massing for an overwhelming attack to begin an orderly retreat. Lafayette had already gone rushing back to Green Spring Plantation to cover Wayne's retreat. On the way, the marquis had two horses shot out from under him. As Wayne wiggled out of Cornwallis's snare, darkness fell. The fighting stopped. Cornwallis came up once again with an empty net.

Only darkness saved the Americans. Cornwallis believed that if he had had another half-hour of daylight, he would have bagged a French marquis and a third American army—or at least a huge piece of all the American troops in Virginia. But Cornwallis had also been deceived. By keeping his main force back from the battlefield, the marquis had kept it safely out of the trap.

Wayne's casualties could have been much greater. But they were bad enough: twenty-eight killed, ninety-nine wounded, twelve missing—nearly 140 all told. Cornwallis took only seventy-five casualties. Yet Wayne was fortunate to have managed to survive at all; his 900 Pennsylvanians had been jumped by more than 6,000 British.

Cornwallis gets credit for a brilliant strategy, Wayne, for his defensive attack, Lafayette, for his caution and prudent defensive posture, although if he had done his reconnoitering earlier in the day, he might have eluded the trap entirely. Because of Wayne's audacity and his own battle-field leadership, Lafayette preserved his forces. Because of it probably less than a third of his troops, at most, had been at risk. Cornwallis had thrown his haymaker too late; yet had he sprung his trap sooner he would not have had as many of Wayne's troops in his grasp.

After Cornwallis had crossed the James, Lafayette withdrew to a camp at Malvern Hill, a healthy site halfway between Williamsburg and Richmond. He had more reason than ever to be devilish afraid of Charles Earl Cornwallis.

General Nathanael Greene, on hearing of this engagement at Green Spring, probably gave the best advice to General Wayne mixed in with his praise: "It gives me great pleasure to hear of the success of my friend, but be a little careful and tread softly, for depend upon it, you have a modern Hannibal to deal with in the person of Cornwallis." So said the voice of experience.[13]

"All of Virginia north of the James, deserving no credit for defending its state against the redcoated arsonists, now gave its applause for the withdrawal of Cornwallis to Lafayette, who, while deserving credit for his courageous efforts to distract Cornwallis from his depredations, deserved no credit at all for that withdrawal."[14]

Before the applause had died away, Lafayette watched much of his army melt away. With their short terms up, with harvesttime nigh, most of the Virginia militia went home, leaving only some 1,500 in camp. Lafayette allowed many of the Virginia gentlemen volunteers to go home also. Then, like a great melodrama, the tables turned once more.[15]

The congressional Grand Committee submitted its report to the Congress on the vexing taxation issue. To no one's surprise, not mentioned in the report was the constitutional amendment giving Congress the power to tax. Obviously Sam Adams had killed it very dead indeed. But the fight was not over yet. A coterie of members managed to get through the committee and out on the floor a recommendation that yet another committee—the third—be formed to outline a series of changes needed to improve and strengthen the Articles of Confederation. Every one of the congressmen knew that creating committees and sending inflammatory proposals to them were harmless activities. The danger lay in what came back out.

The third committee was duly authorized, and three new committee members—James Varnum of Rhode Island, Oliver Ellsworth of Connecticut, and Edmund Randolph of Virginia—were sent in to prepare "an exposition of the Confederation."

General Cornwallis had crossed the James River to Portsmouth for the specific purpose of loading 3,000 of his troops on board transports and sending them to New York—obeying Clinton's orders, however reluctantly.

But while the earl was loading them, Sir Henry changed his mind.

He now told Cornwallis to keep the troops in Portsmouth. Then, while the earl was unloading the troops, General Clinton changed his mind once again. He reverted to Benedict Arnold's original plan; his new order to Cornwallis told him to reload those 3,000 troops to be ready for transport not to New York but to Philadelphia as a diversionary action. This, he felt, would impel Washington to break off his attack on New York City.

But before Lord Cornwallis could comply with that order, Clinton changed his mind yet again. He now ordered Cornwallis to hold those 3,000 troops in reserve in Virginia.

In the meantime, he wanted General Cornwallis to obey his original order to build a defensible naval base on the Chesapeake so that the earl and all his troops could be quickly sailed back to New York. Where to build it? Sir Henry was not sure where. He suggested Old Port Comfort, but then, unwilling to make a firm decision, told Cornwallis to make the choice.

Clinton seemed to be changing plans at the end of each meeting, depending on which of his advisors he had last conferred with; none of them were in agreement, and consequently they were pulling him in different directions.

On August 1, following the orders of Clinton and Admiral Graves, General Cornwallis and his engineers and naval consultants examined Old Point Comfort in the Hampton Roads area as a potential naval base. They took soundings and samples of the bottom, then looked skeptically at the width of the anchorage. In the end they decided that a naval base here would not be defensible since the channel was so wide enemy ships could easily sail beyond the range of shore battery on either side. Cornwallis wrote to Clinton that Portsmouth "cannot be made strong without an army to defend it." In addition, "it is remarkably unhealthy."[16]

Cornwallis went looking for another site and eventually selected one that he felt better met their specifications. It lay some ten miles up the York River, which, itself only twenty miles long, was the shortest river in Virginia—actually more estuary than river, strongly tidal, feeding into the Chesapeake with a channel that ran as much as ninety feet deep. The map gave its name as York, but it was better known as Yorktown—the very town Benedict Arnold had told him to avoid.[17]

More village than town, Yorktown, a century-old tobacco port in which fortunes had been made, was hardly prepared for the landing of 7,000 troops, and its few residents must not have been pleased to see their forests disappear into the woodwork of the Yorktown fort. Consisting of little more than fifty houses, some of them fine mansions, a courthouse, and several churches strung along a forty-foot marl cliff, Yorktown, built on a slope, was two streets wide; the upper, with the view from the cliff, featured the town's mansions; the lower, with access to the river and the docks, was a working thoroughfare. Lying a dozen miles from Williamsburg, the former capital of Virginia, Yorktown had been an important economic center and had in fact defied the British tea tax in 1774 when it conducted its own tea party by pitching tea bales from the ship *Virginia* into the York River.

Two almost impassable marshes protected the flanks of the town from a land attack, while across the York River less than a mile away lay the town of Gloucester with its own point of land wedging well into the river. In case of emergency, Gloucester could provide Cornwallis with a ready escape route.

Completely at odds with Clinton's policy—as far as he understood it—resenting Clinton's orders to take a defensive position against the French boy general and his tiny army of militia, yet with engineers' plans obediently in hand for building his fortifications, Brig. Gen. Charles Earl Cornwallis stepped ashore, unloaded his troops, and prepared to make his stand, for better or for worse, in somnolent Yorktown, Virginia.

The high summer of August had come and the heat, even in an area notorious for its smothering summer humidity, was exceptionally punishing that year. Hessian Johann Doehla described the temperature belowdecks on the transports as "scarcely to be endured." The troops eagerly scrambled ashore for air.[18]

In a stubborn summer that simply refused to leave, the heat was to be an unwelcome guest right into October. And despite that heat, the troops were soon manhandling tree trunks and shaping logs, digging trenches, struggling to build a wooden fort. Cornwallis's officers watched carefully; they well knew that these brutal conditions made men desert.

Now the British army seemed to be a paradigm of General Clinton's mind—split into two major pieces, New York and Yorktown, fortified and both on the defensive. If the British navy lost control of the sea, they could both be isolated and vulnerable.

Yet at such a critical time, when there should have been a single policy and a unified command, Clinton and Cornwallis were holding opposite ends of a rope, pulling against each other in a tug of war—all to the Americans' advantage.

Both seemed to have forgotten that America was known to the British military as the "grave of reputations."

Six

Cornwallis versus Washington

In mid-August 1781, Gen. George Washington was dismayed to see that the Revolution had settled into yet another stalemate.

Sir Harry Clinton in New York was loitering behind his wooden walls, waiting for the rebel cause to collapse. Cornwallis was wrapping himself in another wooden cocoon. The army in Charleston was completely protected from attack. In South Carolina, Clinton's arc of wooden forts was also in a defensive posture. Clinton had his "granny" warfare.

Inadvertently making Clinton's position more secure, his two allied enemies were not getting along. As early as May 22, at their historic meeting in Wethersfield, Connecticut, the relationship between Washington and Rochambeau had declined into a tangled mess. They had come together to plan a military strategy and parted, nettled, in disagreement. Washington wanted to attack Clinton in New York. Rochambeau wanted to attack Cornwallis in Virginia.

To Washington, an attack on New York had great merit. Clinton had shown time and again that the slightest feint toward that city would make him panic. Like a snake poked with a stick, he would contract instantly, calling troops back from Virginia, probably from the Carolinas, even from Georgia. He would wrap his navy around Manhattan Island like a floating wooden fort. And that would take tremendous pressure off both Greene and Lafayette and leave both Cornwallis and Charleston vulnerable.

The irascible French general thought attacking New York was wrong-headed. He said it required a navy they didn't have. Washington said that attacking Cornwallis in Virginia also required a navy they didn't have.

The Wethersfield conference had not been an easy one for either general. Personal relations between the two had become strained. From the beginning, Rochambeau had not been as impressed with Washington as were many members of his staff. During that very tense meeting, general and aide-de-camp Chastellux described Rochambeau's treatment

141

of Washington as showing "all the ungraciousness and all the unpleasant-
ness possible."[1]

Understandably, the two generals labored under almost unbearable
pressure. They both knew they did not have much time left to conquer
British power in America, for even General Rochambeau could see that
the Americans were nearly finished.

"These people here are at the end of their resources," he wrote to
Admiral de Grasse. "Washington has not half the troops he counted on;
I believe, though he is hiding it, that he has not 6000 men. M. de La
Fayette has not 1000 regulars, with the militia to defend Virginia. . . .
This is the state of affairs and the great crisis at which America finds
itself. . . . Only seapower can save the revolution."[2]

No one saw this more clearly than Washington: "Whatever efforts are
made by the land armies, the navy must have the casting vote in the present contest."[3] He wrote to John Laurens in Paris, "We are at the end of
our tether. . . . now or never our deliverance must come."[4]

Rochambeau's position was little better. He had neither the troops
nor the navy he had been promised. His hard-pressed king might pull
him and his troops out of the American theater overnight and send
them scuttling to other battlefields in other countries. In the meantime,
he was under great constraint to produce a victory—and soon—or face
the wrath of the crown.

Both men knew they had to get along with each other or not get
along at all. Publicly all was harmony and light.

Only one agreement came from the meeting. Since they could do
nothing without a navy, Rochambeau announced he would contact
Admiral de Grasse in the Azores, asking him for naval aid. To Washington such a letter was little more than a wish list. Or did Rochambeau
know something he wasn't telling Washington?

In the meantime, as a first step, to see how much they could achieve
simply by threatening New York without a navy, the two generals had
agreed that General Rochambeau should march his army from Newport,
Rhode Island, to the Hudson Valley right above New York City. Just by
camping there, right next to Washington's army, near Dobbs Ferry twelve
miles north of the city, the allies would seem to be poised for an attack.
Then, depending on what happened, the two armies would be in an
ideal position to either attack New York or march on Cornwallis. Once
the two armies were bedded down beside each other, the two generals
would reconnoiter Manhattan together to see what else they could do to
spoil Sir Harry's sleep.

Back in his camp, General Rochambeau did as he promised. He
wrote to Admiral de Grasse in the Azores, and as he later admitted to
Washington, he urged de Grasse to make his first destination the Chesa-

peake, with New York as a second possibility. If de Grasse agreed, then any dream of storming New York would be abandoned.

Actually, Washington already knew that the allies could not take New York. At Wethersfield, he had promised Rochambeau more than 10,000 American troops for the siege. But when the nose counting was done, the states had let him down again; he had barely half of that in camp.

On August 2, in his diary, Washington told himself the truth: "I could scarce see a ground upon which to continue my preparations against New York . . . and therefore I turned my views more seriously than I had before done to an operation to the southward."[5] While giving up the plan to attack New York, he was at some pains not to let the skittish Clinton know—or Rochambeau.

Then in a letter on August 14, 1781, came the breakthrough. The six-year-old war was to explode into sixty climatic days of violence, chance, enormous risk, and final resolution.

The letter from de Grasse must have made Washington's hands tremble. The admiral announced that he was leading a fleet of twenty-nine ships of the line and six frigates from the French West Indies up to the Chesapeake, a stunningly large fleet—an armada to Washington. And even more elating news: de Grasse was bringing with him three French regiments—2,500 men. He would arrive at the Chesapeake in little more than two weeks, on September 3. This could give the allies the means to win the Revolution.

The admiral warned, however, that he could not stay on the Chesapeake after October 15.

But this gift from the French king might turn out to be the torment of Tantalus. While offering a staggering opportunity, de Grasse seemed at the same time to be taking it back. With his fleet came some impossible problems:

His deadline of October 15 gave the two generals just two months to move their armies 450 miles, build a great siege works, lay siege against Cornwallis, and compel him to surrender—all in just sixty days.

Since de Grasse wasn't coming to New York, where he could have transported them to the Chesapeake, they would have to get there largely by land—a formidable piece of military logistics.

Most immediately, the two allied armies would have to march down through Jersey past Clinton's army, much of it based on Staten Island just a few miles away across a very narrow isthmus. Clinton could send his army charging into allied armies that would be strung out for miles.

Clinton didn't have to win a major battle; he didn't even have to fight one. All he had to do was mount a series of nipping attacks, slow the allies down, force them to stop and assume a defensive posture, and chew up a few of those precious sixty days, thereby wrecking their October 15 timetable and ending their chance to capture Cornwallis and his army.

Furthermore, while they were en route, Clinton at any time could send his navy to move Cornwallis to Charleston, to New York, to Philadelphia—anywhere away from Yorktown.

Then there was the problem of General Rochambeau's vitally important siege guns. These were still in Newport, Rhode Island, so heavy they had to be transported by ship. True, Admiral Barras had the naval transports right there in Newport—the same ones that had brought the siege guns from France. But the British fleet was prowling outside Newport, and unless Barras could find some way of evading them, they would eagerly pounce on his small, lightly armed transport fleet and send the siege guns to the bottom of the Atlantic, sinking allied hopes with them.

As for Admiral de Grasse himself, to prevent Cornwallis's escape by water, he would have to fight his way up the American coast past or through the British Navy into the Chesapeake. Was the French navy up to that job? In the past it had been mauled time and again by the British navy.

Next was Cornwallis's potential escape by land. This was Lafayette's problem. To keep Cornwallis pinned down until the allies got there, Lafayette had to block the Yorktown peninsula and then with his greatly outnumbered army possibly take on and defeat Cornwallis on the battlefield. To completely blacken that scenario, Clinton might send significant reinforcements to Cornwallis by sea, giving Cornwallis an even more overwhelming advantage; he would be able to crush Lafayette under his British boot soles, then escape onto the mainland, where he could exercise a number of options.

To make the juggling act even more dismaying, all of these moves were to be made from widely separated locales against a very narrow timetable—de Grasse sailing north from the Caribbean, in danger of being slowed or stopped by the British navy or even a hurricane; Barras sailing south from Newport, in danger of being sunk by the British navy; the allied army marching down to Head of Elk; army agents down there desperately racing around to find enough boats to carry the allied army south to Yorktown; Lafayette, still greatly outnumbered, scrambling to find enough cavalry and troops to block the Yorktown peninsula; other agents scrambling to find clothing and shoes and ammunition and weapons and an infinity of other requirements for Washington's naked army; Robert Morris, Congress's superintendent of finances, urgently trying to find the specie to pay for moving the army; Congress, with a supply of uniforms, not having the specie to pay the wagonage to deliver them to Washington; Heath with barely 2,000 men to guard the vital West Point passage on the Hudson against a Clinton incursion; and multitudinous other pieces that would have to be coordinated by an exquisite piece of timing. The failure or lateness of any of these moves could end the campaign in a galley-west collapse.

Washington turned to his most immediate problem—a staggering money shortage. He knew his mutinous army—starving and ill-kempt, unpaid and shoeless—would never willingly travel down into the Virginia Tidewater. It was notorious for fevers that annually scooped armies of residents into the grave. He feared he could lose from a third to half of his troops to fever, desertion, and mutiny. He simply had to find some hard money—no more worthless paper Continentals—to cover their back pay. Even a month's pay in hard cash might do it. Worst of all, he also needed a large sum of hard cash to transport his army to Virginia—and he didn't have it. Unless Robert Morris used some fiscal black magic, his whole army would never get as far as Philadelphia.

In the last days of August, George Washington, in his headquarters on the Hudson, performed his first miracle. Only five days after receiving de Grasse's letter, he had his army up and ready to march. Could he and General Rochambeau pull off the next and slip by Clinton?

In Philadelphia, just as Washington and Rochambeau were hastening to Yorktown, Congress received the third congressional committee's report on "implied powers" and its recommendations. To the horrified Congress, it was a bomb with the fuse burning.

The committee was proposing no less than twenty-one new provisions aimed at strengthening the Articles. Furthermore, the committee listed seven powers of the states that ought to be transferred to or shared by the Congress. Predictably, one of them was the power to tax and to collect taxes: the specific wording empowered Congress "to distrain upon the property of a State delinquent in its assigned proportion of Men and Money."

The Congress hastily agreed that a full floor debate over such an important—volatile—committee report should be scheduled "tomorrow," which, of course, was not supposed to ever come.

On August 19, at King's Ferry on the Hudson, some eight miles below Peekskill, the allied army began to assemble. Rain was falling heavily.[6] Washington had left behind only 2,000 men under General William Heath—barely enough to watch Clinton, certainly not enough to fight him.

The French stared with shock at the American troops of Washington's army—in rags, in miscellaneous uniforms, many in bare feet, barely equipped.

At two o'clock the next morning the crossing of the Hudson began. One of the first to go over was Washington. When Rochambeau's French troops with all their heavy equipment crossed the Hudson—it took days—and fell in behind, the entire allied army headed south. It was now August 25. But with every stride, Washington lived with the agony of the long-odds gambler. It was Yorktown or nothing.

Washington, for the benefit of Clinton's multitudinous spies, had assembled along his line of march numerous landing craft as well as bridge pontoons, which any spy could plainly see were to be used to carry allied troops across to Staten Island. His object was to get as far south as possible before Clinton divined his true destination. If the allied army got far enough, Clinton would realize his error too late to attack from Staten Island and too late to send reinforcements to Cornwallis by his watery express. Was Clinton being fooled, or was he waiting for the right moment to strike?

General Rochambeau contributed to the deception: At Chatham, a few miles west of Newark, he ordered masons to begin building the first of a number of bread ovens that, the local residents were deliberately told, could supply his army for a lengthy stay.[7]

Washington wanted to deceive his own troops as much as he wanted to deceive Clinton. He dreaded their reaction when they realized they weren't attacking New York but marching into Virginia. Proceeding south, he divided the allied army into three parallel columns, miles long. He had his left flank actually move for a time toward Staten Island.

Clinton still seemed persuaded that the allies were coming right at him. Evidently he was so convinced of this that he was planning a British diversionary attack on Newport where the siege guns were, hoping this would compel the allies to break off their campaign against him.

On August 29, Washington, riding ahead of the marching columns into Princeton, New Jersey, felt the allies had brought off a miracle. Over the lunch table with Rochambeau, Washington heard officers of both armies express their amazement that Clinton had stayed behind his bulwarks. They all agreed that Sir Henry had let pass an unparalleled opportunity.

A French officer wrote of Clinton's inaction: "An enemy, a little bold and able, would have seized the moment of our crossing . . . for an attack. His indifference and lethargy at this moment is an enigma that cannot be solved by me."[8]

Had Clinton lost his stomach for fighting?

The next day, on August 30, in Trenton, Washington received an alarming message from a spy watching ship traffic at Sandy Hook. He had counted eighteen ships of the line entering New York Harbor from the south and flying British colors. The spy surmised they were under the command of Admiral Rodney. If these ships were added to Graves's in New York, the British now had twenty-nine fighting ships in American waters, about the same number as de Grasse. Would they get to the Chesapeake first and block de Grasse from entering? Twenty-nine ships between de Grasse and Barras. Had Barras sailed? Where was de Grasse?

The next report stated that the commanding officer was not Rodney but his very capable—many said brilliant—second in command, Adm. Samuel Hood. Rodney was ill and had ordered himself home to recuperate.

The significance of the change was reflected in the seniority roster. Rodney outranked Graves and would have commanded in any fight with the French navy. But even with forty years in the service, Hood was outranked by Graves—which meant that the very pedestrian Graves would lead the British against de Grasse, with the better admiral taking orders.

Washington next learned that the ailing Rodney had ordered Hood from Caribbean waters to New York to supplement Graves's fleet. He was under orders to hunt for de Grasse as he sailed north. Hood had hurried with all sails clapped on, his canvas climbers scanning the seas for French battle pennants. Moving at flank speed, he had rushed into the Chesapeake and, not finding de Grasse, hurried on north to New York, hoping to catch him on the way there. He didn't. But if Hood hadn't found de Grasse on the way up from the Caribbean, then where was he? And where was Barras? Would Graves catch Barras in the net intended for de Grasse? More worry.

As it turned out, had Hood waited for de Grasse inside the Chesapeake, he might have altered the outcome of the entire war.

The next day, August 31, Washington and Rochambeau, in transit with their armies, received a hopeful message. On August 21 Admiral de Barras had written that "if the weather favored," he would sail on August 25 from Newport for the Chesapeake with eight ships of the line, four frigates, and eighteen transports carrying the siege guns and 1,500 barrels of salt meat for Washington's army.[9]

But the next day, September 1, in Philadelphia, both allied generals also learned a grim piece of information that de Barras did not have. On the day de Barras was to have sailed—August 25—Graves had set sail with Hood from New York, bound for the Chesapeake to find de Grasse. Probably their fleet size was twenty-one ships and four frigates.

Two somber facts were clear to both generals. De Barras might be discovered by Graves's fleet—which would be the end of the siege guns and the salt meat, both vital for the success of the siege. And the pivotal battle of the entire American Revolution might be looming not on a battlefield but on the open sea, with not one American involved—Graves versus de Grasse.

On that same day in Trenton, September 1, on the banks of the Delaware, the American soldiers realized they were going not to Staten Island but to Virginia. And they muttered that they would go no further than Philadelphia unless they were paid—they hadn't been for almost one year.[10]

Washington and his staff, who were already in Philadelphia, read the rippling disaffection with grave concern. The possibility of mutiny was real. Matters only became worse when the troops found there were not enough boats to carry them from Trenton to Wilmington, Delaware. Although there were enough boats to carry most of the baggage, the troops would have to walk all the way to Head of Elk at the top of Chesapeake Bay. And that would take them through Philadelphia—just what Washington didn't want: delays and dangerous temptations waited for them there.

On Sunday, September 2, Philadelphia's smartly turned out City Troop, a militia cavalry unit, led the ragged Continental Army into the city along streets crowded with cheering, shouting throngs. Marching feet raised clouds of smothering dust over streets sweltering in the heat. The residents were celebrating as madly as though the war had already been won.

While the troops marched amidst drums, fifing, and fluttering banners along Vine Street, General Washington was in the City Tavern on Second Street, barely submitting to the enthusiastic toasts of rum punch. And while the crowd applauded the war-famous Americans in the parade, Knox, Hand, Pickering, Benjamin Lincoln, and Scammell, who was leading the troops, Washington was hurrying through the streets to the home of banker Robert Morris, Congress's Superintendent of Finances, to talk money, money, money.

And well he might. The gaunt American troops, parading their poverty two miles long, were looking with fury at the well-dressed, well-fed civilians and their wives in the latest fashions applauding so loudly, seemingly unaware that most of the troops were hungry, unkempt, barefoot—wearing dirty rags.

Washington marched them through the city and out the other end without stopping so that he could camp them that night well south of all that temptation.

Morris, nearly worn out with his money quests, assured Washington that he was beating the wallets of anyone he came near. In a city stuffed to overflowing with war profiteers and newly minted millionaires, he couldn't flog even spare shillings from their pockets.

Morris warned: "Should the operations against Cornwallis fail for want of supplies the states must thank their own negligence. If they will not exert themselves upon the present occasion, they never will." But he vowed he would try again.[11]

That night, Washington's penniless staff slept on mattresses in the hallways of Morris's home.

The enormous Henry Knox, Washington's gifted artillery general, also was shopping hard in the halls of Congress—for ammunition. He needed 300,000 cartridges, 20,000 flints, musket balls, and much more— and he was not getting anything. Washington, agreeing with Knox's frustrated rage, said: "Certainly, certainly, the people have lost their ardor in attempting to secure their liberty and happiness."[12] How could the Congress, he wondered, send their army into what promised to be the ultimate battle of the entire Revolution without the ammunition to fire its weapons?

Instead of the required 100 wagonloads of ammunition, Knox's ordnance men were parading twelve.[13] But Sgt. Joseph Plumb Martin reported that he sailed down the Delaware River "in a schooner, which had her hold nearly full of gun powder." Later, "a smart thundershower" made him anxious about a lightning strike "which might . . . compel me to leave the vessel sooner than I wished."[14]

And on Monday, September 3, when the French army paraded into the city, with their spectacularly colorful uniforms, superb military music, and precision marching, raising cries of delight, Washington was still talking, still buttonholing, still urging congressmen, Pennsylvania Assembly delegates, businessmen, anyone to heed his pleas for weapons, ammunition, shoes, uniforms, horses, wagons, forage, food, and a nonstop list of other supplies. And especially, above all, back pay. Not paper. Specie.

Then, almost providentially, improbably, out of the blue, the money appeared. In Philadelphia, Washington turned to see the approach of his aide-de-camp, Lt. Col. John Laurens, who had just arrived in Philadelphia from the French court. He brought with him the greatest good news. Louis XVI was sending the Americans two and a half million French livres. How he got it was as astonishing as the money itself.

Colonel Laurens was the son of Henry Laurens, one of the most prominent merchants in Charleston, a former president of the Continental Congress who had succeeded John Hancock, and now active in revolutionary affairs, especially diplomatic ones.

Known as one of the bravest men in the army, the twenty-seven-year-old Laurens was a literal whirlwind. He had been educated in England and Switzerland. Elected to the South Carolina assembly, he resigned to go to war and got into as many battles as he could find, north and south. He had fought at the Battle of Brandywine, was wounded at the Battle of Germantown, wounded again at Monmouth, led light infantry in Savannah, fought against Clinton in Charleston, and was captured and paroled. During his cavalry forays in Georgia, he fought so ferociously and with such reckless abandon that some officers resigned rather than ride with him.

In between these duties, he found time to periodically serve without pay as Washington's aide-de-camp, secretary, and translator.

After his parole, because of his winning charm, his polished manners, and his fluent French, Congress sent him to France to help Franklin coax money from the French court. Even though he understood the rigid rules of protocol, he had shrugged off the advice of Benjamin Franklin and had almost gotten himself declared persona non grata by brashly going around the frigid and extremely cautious French foreign minister, Charles Vergennes, and his bureaucracy to make his plea directly to Louis unexpectedly during an open court fête. Franklin was sure the young man was going to be dismissed from court when Louis astonished everyone. He gave Laurens two and half million livres in silver for the American cause.

Here he was just returned to Philadelphia from the French court. The silver was following behind, destined to be delivered in Boston. That solved Washington's immediate financial problems, except for one thing: He needed hard cash in hand to pay his troops now. Not months or even weeks from now. His troops had been lied to so many times by the politicians in Congress and the various states that another promise would simply infuriate them.

Robert Morris, who had learned to sniff money in the breeze, now swung into action. He turned his eyes on Rochambeau. The French general was being feted in the home of the French ambassador to the United States, Chevalier Anne-César de la Luzerne. Going there, Morris seized the moment to ask for a swing loan, to be paid back when the French silver arrived from Boston. But that was weeks, even months, away. Rochambeau was expecting a substantial sum of money of his own when de Grasse arrived. Until then he felt he barely had enough money to pay his troops. He turned Morris down. And there things stood. The French money—like the French half-army and the French half-navy—was like half a bridge over troubled waters. Washington looked elsewhere.

Morris didn't give up. He got on his horse and followed the French army south, talking.

The eyes of the entire nation were on the Chesapeake, praying for success, daring to hope for freedom and peace in one package. Benjamin Rush, the prominent Philadelphia physician, stood watching the ragged Continentals march by in a great cloud of dust, then went home to pen a note to Gen. Horatio Gates, who was still trying to get his reputation back following his defeat in Camden: "Before this reaches you, the fate of Great Britain and the repose of Europe will probably be determined in Chesapeake Bay. Heaven prosper our allies."[15]

Leaving Philadelphia, Washington and his staff rode ahead of the army, sending messengers with urgent letters to governors, officials, businessmen, plantation owners, ship owners, and financiers down in the Chesapeake to stress the urgent need for—in addition to specie—fodder, feed, food, military supplies, and boats, boats, boats. When he got there, Washington planned to badger and buttonhole those same people personally. He felt he was just hours away from an explosive mutiny. In fact, he was just hours away from another piece of heart-lifting news.

General Rochambeau had opted to travel down to Chester by boat to better see the battle sites and the Delaware river defenses, Fort Mifflin and Fort Mercer included. Later in the afternoon, as his boat approached the port city of Chester, Pennsylvania, about twenty miles south of Philadelphia, he beheld a very tall American officer onshore, waving his hat, twirling a white handkerchief over his head, and capering while bellowing something indecipherable. Improbably, he looked just like General Washington. As they approached shore, Rochambeau's party wondered who he was.

When they got closer, Rochambeau remembered: "I caught sight of General Washington waving his hat at me with demonstrative gestures of the greatest joy. When I rode up to him he explained that he had just received a dispatch . . . informing him that de Grasse had arrived."[16]

Completely out of character, Washington reached out to Rochambeau and the two men heartily embraced each other. Washington had been well south of Chester when he had received the news and had ridden all the way back to Chester to inform Rochambeau.

Miracle number three had materialized; barrier number three had fallen: de Grasse had indeed arrived three days before, on September 2, while Washington and Rochambeau were marching through Philadelphia. He had sailed through lesser-used channels between the Caribbean Islands to avoid contact with the British and so had taken longer than Hood had and was some days behind when Hood first arrived in the Chesapeake thinking de Grasse was still somewhere ahead of him.

De Grasse had disembarked Marquis de Saint-Simon Montblern, field marshal of France, and his 2,500 troops at Jamestown, where the French officer placed himself under the command of twenty-four-year-old Lafayette.

With de Grasse's fleet in the Chesapeake, Cornwallis's escape by sea was blocked, at least for the time being. And with the added 2,500 French troops, Lafayette should be able to seal off the peninsula, considerably increasing his odds of cutting off Cornwallis's escape by land. The earl was pinned inside his stockade.

But now, would de Grasse stay long enough to make the siege possible? It was already September 5 and de Grasse was scheduled to leave on or before October 15, hardly enough time to get from Philadelphia to Yorktown, conduct a siege, and press Cornwallis to surrender. Much of it depended on having enough boats for the sail down the Chesapeake. Would enough be waiting for the allied troops at Head of Elk?

Also, where was Barras with those siege guns and that salt meat?

But one of the most important immediate results of de Grasse's arrival was that Robert Morris, aware that de Grasse had brought a large infusion of money for Rochambeau, now went back to him to badger him once more for a loan that General "Vasington" needed to pay his troops. Rochambeau listened, then nodded. *Oui.* Yes. You can have the loan. Morris rode with the French army treasurer to get the silver. Miracle number four had come to pass; barrier number four had fallen.

Philip Audibert, the deputy paymaster general of the Continental Army, appeared at Head of Elk, the troops were mustered, and the barrels of coin were broken open to spill onto the ground. The troops saw 114,000 French silver half-crowns winking at them in the sunlight. Every man filed past to receive his pay, not in paper, but in real, bitable specie. It was just one month's pay, but the troops were overjoyed.

The significance was not lost on Maj. William Popham, aide-de-camp to Continental general James Clinton. In a letter to Clinton's older brother, George, first governor of New York State, the major noted, "This day will be famous in the annals of History for being the first in which the Troops of the United States received one month's pay in specie." He also noted the magic effect the money had on the army's sick. "There is scarcely a sick man to be found," he wrote.[17]

Looking at the silver that had crossed his palm, Sgt. Joseph Plumb Martin observed: "This was the first that could be called money, which we had received as wages since the year '76 or that we ever did receive till the close of the war, or indeed, ever after, as wages."[18]

Foreign duty done, the mercurial Colonel Laurens had donned his uniform and slipped into the line of march ready to do battle. He had more military and diplomatic adventures ahead of him.

And George Washington was getting a run of luck that was hard to believe. Would it last?

In New York City, General Clinton's spies had kept him informed of the allied army's progress almost step by step. But only on September 2, when the Americans actually set foot in Philadelphia, did Clinton admit to himself that he'd been jobbed. Washington had bluffed him, and now Sir Henry didn't have enough time to hasten another contingent of troops to Cornwallis. Other bad news for Clinton arrived on September 2. De Grasse had landed. Cornwallis's army was snared in Yorktown. Clinton had to take quick action to save the earl.

Benedict Arnold's American Legion had returned with him from Virginia reduced by desertions and casualties to barely ninety men. One of the deserters was busy making his way south into North Carolina to find Light-Horse Harry Lee to get his old job back—Sgt. Maj. John Champe. If he were stopped before he got to camp to clear his name, he could be hanged as a deserter by either American or British military authorities.

In just fifteen days, the allied armies had moved 200 miles from the Hudson to Head of Elk at the beginning of Chesapeake Bay, averaging thirteen miles a day.

The first units of Rochambeau's army reached Head of Elk on September 8. And there Washington's luck seemed to wobble. After years of raiding in the Chesapeake, the British navy had destroyed a great number of bay boats. Quartermaster Pickering had not been able to find nearly enough of them to transport the two armies to Yorktown.

The two generals held a conference. Onto the available open boats they stuffed the essential siege equipment, 1,200 French troops, and 800 Americans and dispatched them, literally loaded to the gunwales, down the Chesapeake bound for Williamsburg. While scouts searched the bay for more water transport, the remaining troops, more than half of the total army, were set off on a march to Baltimore. The lack of boats had slowed the army's progress. Days were being lost. With every step, Washington was in an agony of apprehension. Would he find more boats in Baltimore? Would they get to Yorktown too late? And where was de Barras?

On September 7 in Williamsburg, General Lafayette faced a different problem. Even with de Grasse blocking the bay, Cornwallis still had enough strength to attack Lafayette, break through, and rampage into Virginia.

To prevent that, Lafayette brought his entire force—his troops, Wayne's troops, and those new French troops of de Saint Simon—outside Williamsburg and set up a strong defensive line across the entire peninsula. He was aware that at any time he could have his hands full of redcoats; then he would find out how good a general he was against Cornwallis. The obvious question was: Did Cornwallis realize he was trapped?

The earl, aware that 2,500 French troops had landed and aware that de Grasse was blocking the bay, sent scouts to explore Lafayette's position.

He then held a conference with generals O'Hara and Tarleton, among others. Tarleton urged him to smash his way through Lafayette's lines into freedom. But Cornwallis, undoubtedly mindful of his fearful losses at Guilford Courthouse, decided that Lafayette had set the price too high, especially if Clinton was going to rescue the Yorktown army at any moment now anyway. Tarleton didn't believe that Clinton knew the entire situation in Yorktown—didn't believe that Clinton could break through and rescue them.

On September 8, at Eutaw Springs, South Carolina, Gen. Nathanael Greene mounted an attack at the major British camp on the Santee River there.

Marching through bypaths and swamp trails, Greene was able to steal up to and surprise Lt. Col. Alexander Stuart. Greene's force was formidable, with Light-Horse Harry Lee's dragoons, William Washington's dragoons, John Eager Howard and Ortho Williams and their Marylanders, and Kirkwood's Delawarians. In addition, he was backed by major partisan support from Francis Marion and Andrew Pickens.

Stuart's men were largely Loyalists, and the fight quickly took on the tone of another all-American brawl. The two sides were more or less evenly matched—something less than 2,000 men each—with Greene having the edge in horses.

When Greene's line struck Stuart's, Stuart's right was embedded in a dense blackjack thicket, unreachable by cavalry attack. Throughout the entire fight, it held, driving off repeated attacks from American dragoons. Washington's horse was shot out from under him; he himself received a severe bayonet wound and was captured. Half his unit was wiped out.

But Stuart's whole left and center, fighting furiously, was slowly pushed back into the tents of their campsite. The brawling was so violent that Lee notes, "A number of soldiers fell transfixed by each other's bayonets."[19]

Then the improbable happened. Greene's troops, among the enemy's tents, broke into barrels of rum, and stopped fighting to start swilling and looting. Greene, when he finally realized what was happening so close to victory, ground his teeth in frustration.

Orders between Greene and Lee became confused. An attack was made on the wrong side of the line. Even so, the British defense was caving in. Then Greene took the full brunt of a counterattack from Marjoribanks that drove the swilling Americans from the tents and into the woods. This gave Stuart time to turn the rout around, regroup, and carry the field. The courageous Marjoribanks was killed.

Once again Greene still had enough men in reserve to have counterattacked and possibly snatched the victory, but as at Guilford Courthouse, he felt the casualties would be too high and called his men off. And once again, the victorious British were so decimated that Stuart had to withdraw and march his destroyed army back to the safety of Charleston. Wounded, dead, and dying lay everywhere, on the battlefield, in the woods, in the blackjack thickets, among the tents and campground. Greene's casualties stood at 500—fully 25 percent of his fighting force. Washington was wounded; John Eager Howard was wounded; so were Pickens and four of the six commanding officers; Richard Campbell was dead. The British suffered the greatest rate of casualties in any battle of the war: They lost 693 of their 1,800 men—nearly 40 percent killed, wounded, or missing. Other accounts insist they lost 866 men—nearly 50 percent. Eutaw Springs was probably the bloodiest battle of the entire war.

Greene said it was by far the most obstinate fight he had ever witnessed.[20]

Despite Stuart's victory, the Battle of Eutaw Springs was the beginning of the end for British power in the Carolinas. Cornwallis's work was rapidly going down the drain. Lord George Germain's war-winning plan lay in ruins. The way was now left open for Greene now to chew up the other British strongpoints one at a time until, in the end, he got every one.

Back in New York, the indefatigable British diarist, Major Mackenzie, saluted Greene's performance: "22nd Oct. Greene is however entitled to great praise for his wonderful exertions, the more he is beaten, the farther he advances in the end."[21]

On September 7, leaving the allied army in the hands of General Lincoln and his staff, Washington, Rochambeau, Chastellux, and entourage pressed on to Baltimore. But few riders could keep up with Washington's mile-eating gait when he was pushing, and the French officers soon let him go, to follow at a more comfortable pace.

With his aide, David Humphreys—who had led the abortive attempt to kidnap General Clinton—and Billy Lee, his black body servant, Washington bid adieu to Rochambeau and the others and pounded out the miles to Baltimore. He needed to do some hasty begging there for stores, with boats now high on the list. To his dismay, but not to his surprise, he found Moore's Light Dragoon militia drawn up to greet him. Impatient to be away, he was snared by ceremony.

That night, windows were illuminated all over the city in his honor. During the evening, as in Philadelphia, he was impelled to listen to laudatory speeches and pressed to make one of his own. It was barely five paragraphs long and probably written by David Humphreys.[22]

He could not have slept well that night: His next stop was Mount Vernon. Little had he realized, when he had ridden away in 1775, as spring was spreading over Virginia, that he would not see his beloved home even once in the next six years.

Early Sunday morning, September 9, the three riders mounted their horses and cantered south out of Baltimore. Before the sun went down that evening they had pushed their horses the sixty miles to Mount Vernon and hurried eagerly down the long tree-lined approach to his home. Six years and four months, it was, and the time had brought many changes.

Washington was greeted by Martha, staff, and servants and also by four children, born since his departure, all of them offspring of Martha Washington's son, Jackie Custis.

On Monday, September 10, Rochambeau and his staff arrived. Still no news of Barras.

In the manner of the Virginia plantation owner, until his death, Washington often entertained an endless stream of guests. "We have not dined alone in twenty years," Martha Washington once said. In a single year, in 1798, the Washingtons accommodated 667 overnight guests. And this night in 1781 was no exception. He accommodated Rochambeau's entire staff, among others, for two days. Tradition says that during dinner that evening in the formal dining room, Washington and Rochambeau planned the siege of Yorktown.

Neither of the allied generals left so much as a note about what they did and said during the two days. Jonathan Trumbull, Washington's aide from Connecticut, reported to his diary: "A numerous family now present. All accommodated. An elegant seat and situation, great appearance of opulence and real exhibitions of hospitality and princely entertainment."[23]

Mount Vernon was a huge plantation, consisting of four farms that encompassed 8,000 acres, worked by a large group of slaves. And Washington was proud to show the French some part of it. But there was no rest for Washington, not even at home. He contacted the Virginia militia to repair the road the troops would have to follow all the way to Williamsburg if boats were not found.

As he left Mount Vernon, he must have felt some pain. Despite his best efforts, despite the noblest principles, he could lose all this. He could be looking at it for the last time. A lifetime of struggle and effort gone in a puff of cannon smoke, scooped away by the great croupier.

On the road from Head of Elk, slowly, slowly, three or four miles an hour when the roads were good, the rest of the allied army followed Washington's hoofprints. On September 13 the great caterpillar—soldiers, wagons, artillery, camp followers, women, children, a walking city—reached Baltimore, the halfway point. From their beginning at Kings Crossing on the Hudson on August 19, they had marched over 200 miles and there were still nearly 200 more to go, with time slipping by. The only way to move the army faster was to put them on ships and sail them to Williamsburg. Quartermaster Pickering was beating every river and creek, every dock and boatyard, for water vessels of any type. He wasn't finding much.

On September 12, on the road from Mount Vernon, Washington encountered a rider carrying dispatches from Williamsburg for the Congress in Philadelphia. The news stunned him. Admiral de Grasse had been alerted to the approach of a British fleet. To keep the nail in Cornwallis's coattail, de Grasse had left four ships off Yorktown. Then, against strong winds, his fleet had beaten its way out to sea and disappeared over the horizon. No one had heard a word since.

Now it was evident to both Washington and Rochambeau that the most decisive battle of the American Revolution might just be a sea battle, now raging offshore from the Chesapeake. Whose ships would now come back over the horizon? The implications were numbing. Would the national flag on the next man-o'-war to arrive proclaim the winner of the American Revolution? Would Graves turn de Grasse's fleet into sunken ships and floating ruins out at sea while he swept in and rescued Cornwallis and his army?

They waited in agony for news of the victor of that sea battle. If Admiral de Grasse won, he would still have Cornwallis trapped. If Graves won, his control of the sea would be decisive—he could carry Clinton's army down from New York, and the Franco-American army would be caught without sea power, without supplies or supply lines, forced to fight a defensive campaign for survival.

Washington immediately sent messages to the boats bearing his troops on the Chesapeake to put ashore and wait until they were sure Graves's ships were not coming after them.

The entourage traveled on to Fredericksburg, where accommodations at an inn awaited them. Any hope of waiting news faded as soon as they arrived. The next morning, September 14, the group was back on the road again, riding for Williamsburg, aching for news. Sometime after four in the afternoon, they entered the city.

As the entourage passed through the camp of the Virginia militia, General Lafayette came riding up with Thomas Nelson, governor of Virginia and head of the Virginia militia, and with General de Saint-Simon. Lafayette was probably the one man in Washington's army who could eagerly embrace him, especially in public.

Washington was invited to review de Saint-Simon's troops in camp, hastily lining up to salute him. He then moved into the American camp, which turned out with full honors for their general, including a twenty-one-gun salute. That evening he was invited to dine with General de Saint-Simon and his French staff, where he was fêted with fine wine, food, and military band music. He went to bed finally, but hardly to sleep. The two French admirals were still missing.

De Grasse had been gone for nine days, since the afternoon of September 5. He had upped anchor and, in a running tide, with the bulk of his fleet, simply disappeared over the horizon. No one had heard from him since.

What happened was the most important sea battle of the Revolution.

Earlier that morning of September 5, Adm. Thomas Graves had approached the entrance of Chesapeake Bay and was astonished by what he saw. Expecting to find no foreign ships—or nothing more than de Barras and his tiny fleet of transports—he found instead a great fleet of France's finest war ships. At eleven A.M., Graves ordered his fleet to form a line of battle and sailed at the entrance to the bay.

Admiral de Grasse had also been caught by surprise. Two thousand of his seamen were onshore collecting wood and filling water casks when a French patrol frigate on duty at the bay's entrance signaled the approach of a large fleet flying British colors. Compelled to wait until noon for the tide to turn in his favor, de Grasse abandoned most of his beached sailors and ordered his ships to stand out to sea against strong headwinds. By early afternoon his ships were rounding Cape Henry one after the other like beads on a string, twenty-four French warships in a long irregular line, scrambling against the wind to shape up for battle.

Graves had never faced de Grasse before, but he knew his reputation. Nearing sixty, three years older than Graves and ailing, Rear Admiral François Joseph Paul Comte de Grasse had a long and distinguished career with the French navy. Everything about him was extreme; he was the scion of one of the oldest aristocratic families in France; in his youth he had been considered one of the handsomest men in Europe; with the imposing girth of a Bacchus, the gigantic admiral was reported to be the tallest man in the French navy; and his flagship, *Ville de Paris,* the pride of the French navy, the biggest warship in the world. Volatile, given to violent mood swings and violent tempers, he was in every way a formidable fighter. As he came shouldering his way out of the Chesapeake he was ready to do just that: Fight.

This naval duel involved far more men than any of the Revolutionary War land battles. Against Graves's nineteen ships of the line with 1,400 guns and 13,000 seamen, de Grasse presented twenty-four ships of the line—a five-ship advantage—carrying 1,700 guns and 19,000 seamen.[24]

With the wind in his favor, had Graves attacked de Grasse's ships as they struggled against severe headwinds, he might have driven the whole French fleet one at a time up on the shores of Cape Henry. That's exactly what Hood would have done—and what he expected Graves to do. Instead, following the Royal Navy's antiquated "Line" sea battle formation, Graves headed east to parallel de Grasse.

Early in the battle, Graves had a piece of bad luck when his signals were misread by his other ships. Because of that, only eight French and eight British ships were able to get within cannon range of each other. In the running gunfight that ensued from four-fifteen to six-thirty on the 5th, these ships hammered each other, firing one thundering salvo after another, emitting great clouds of gunsmoke that were quickly snatched to shreds by the heavy wind.

By dusk, ninety British sailors were dead, 246 wounded, sixteen guns dismounted. De Grasse's casualties were 220 killed and wounded, while the heavier French guns and superior gunnery had pounded Graves's ships, damaging several severely, especially H.M.S. *Terrible*, which had been leaking badly even when she had limped up from the Caribbean, all her pumps going. De Grasse had the intense pleasure of watching his *Ville de Paris* batter Graves's own flagship, *London*, so heavily she would have to replace all her masts.

As darkness fell, the ships broke off and, guided by deck lights on both fleets, watched each other through the night, sailing in parallel columns just beyond cannon range. Trying to patch up the damage, sailmakers, ships' carpenters, and riggers on both sides were busy with hammers, saws, and axes until dawn of the second day.

As daylight broadened, each side struggled to get the weather gauge and thereby be upwind of the opponent. Admiral Hood was furious with Graves's handling of the battle, and during the next few days the two English admirals fenced with each other, by signals and by conferences, over what action to take next.

Late on the second day, at four o'clock, the flaccid north wind shifted around to the southwest and hardened, giving de Grasse the weather gauge, but it was too late. As he approached the British fleet, darkness descended.

After waiting another night, the two fleets tried to face each other for a third day, September 7. Scattering and drifting southward throughout the day, at nightfall they were near the Outer Banks of North Carolina, off Cape Hatteras. Squalls and storms separated the two.

The morning of the fourth day, September 8, began with a severe storm. The mortally wounded H.M.S. *Terrible*, its hull already dangerously damaged, sprung new leaks that became irreparable. Also, as Graves had feared, *Intrepid*'s main mast collapsed.

The British held the north. De Grasse, believing that Barras would be coming from that direction, struggled for the rest of the day to get the upper hand to place himself between Graves and Barras if he should appear. By six P.M., he had succeeded.

During the fifth day, September 9, although the wind was in Graves's favor, the two fleets began to drift apart, and Graves missed his chance to attack. De Grasse decided to beat back up the coast to protect the entrance to the bay, and with all sails set was soon over the horizon as darkness fell. Hood capered in anger on his quarterdeck when he realized that Graves was not following the French fleet.

The next morning, September 10, Graves called a meeting on his ship, *London*, to decide what to do next. Hood was stunned to discover that Graves didn't know where de Grasse was. He urged Graves to set full sail for the bay, although he feared they would be too late.

Graves was preoccupied with trying to save the sinking *Terrible*. He spent the day struggling with her pumps. To lighten her, cannon were shoved overboard. But in the end, Graves had to order her stripped of her stores, ready to be abandoned.

By noon that day, de Grasse arrived once more off the two Virginia capes—Charles and Henry—that framed the entrance to Chesapeake Bay, the point where he had begun. The next day, he was back at his anchorage in Lynhaven Bay.

On September 11, Graves abandoned *Terrible* with her seacocks open. As she drifted away sinking, she exploded and burned to the waterline, still drifting in a running sea as darkness settled. She was the only ship lost in the battle.

On September 12, Graves sent H.M.S. *Medea* to search for de Grasse. The next day, H.M.S. *Medea* returned and signaled to him that she had found de Grasse—back in his anchorage inside the bay.

Graves called another conference. The smoldering Hood, utterly dismayed by now, said he "would be very glad to send an opinion but he really knows not what to say in the truly lamentable state we have brought ourselves."

There was really not much to be done. The bay was blocked by a superior naval force, Cornwallis was beyond reach, and at least ten ships of the British fleet had taken a major beating. In the meeting on *London* that followed, the council of war reluctantly decided to sail back to New York.

The French navy had won what is often billed as one of the most important sea battles in modern history.[25]

In camp in Williamsburg, finally, during the night, a messenger awakened Washington to deliver a letter from de Grasse. The French admiral announced that he was back in his anchorage, the victor of the sea battle. Before Washington could take in all that, de Grasse had additional sensational news: Admiral de Barras was at anchorage with him, bearing all the siege guns and the 1,500 barrels of salt meat without having lost so much as a belaying pin. The combined French fleet now had thirty-two ships of the line versus Graves's eighteen—very close to two to one.

To talk the volatile Frenchman into staying long enough to see the siege through, a face-to-face meeting was needed. Washington prepared himself to do the toughest negotiating he had ever done in his life.

On Thursday, September 13, in New York, still waiting for a report from Graves on the outcome of the sea battle against de Grasse, Clinton called a council of war. Seated at the table was the elderly Lt. Gen. James Robertson, royal governor of the colony of New York, a corrupt old reprobate who was stealing a fortune through the army's martial law, looting city property and courts and openly spending much of it in the pursuit of notorious strumpets. Thomas Jones, a justice of the Royal Supreme Court of New York and an outraged chronicler of the British in that city, left a verbal portrait of Robertson "waddling about town with a couple of young tits about twelve years of age under each arm."[26] A born intriguer, Robertson's low opinion of Clinton—and Clinton's of him—was well known in both New York and London. He held that Clinton didn't have the brains of a corporal.

Governor Robertson urged immediate action. He wanted to send a convoy of troops under the aegis of H.M.S. *Robust,* to barge their way into the Chesapeake and relieve Cornwallis.

The idea seemed sheer madness to Clinton, who didn't mind saying so. Stuff a flotilla of transports with troops under the protection of a single man-o'-war? Send that one warship against a fleet of more than thirty? Besides, even if by incredibly good fortune those troops got through, they would have no provisions for themselves, so they would be dependent on the earl's fast-dwindling supplies. They could all starve together.

Among the others attending was Maj. Gen. Alexander Leslie, forty-one, who had recently returned from Charleston. He also urged action. Like most of Clinton's generals, he chafed under Sir Henry's endless vacillating.

Then Sir Henry himself proposed immediate action—a favorite plan of his, proposed originally by Gen. Benedict Arnold, to attack Philadelphia. Clinton now saw this as a way of forcing Washington to break off his march to Yorktown and, in effect, save Cornwallis by indirection. The rest of the table had heard this idea before—many times. By now Clinton had come to believe the Philadelphia raid was his own idea. Anyone at the table could have pointed out to Clinton that the Benedict Arnold raid on New London the week before had not deterred Washington.

Robertson, of course, disagreed with Clinton's plan and withdrew his own. He suggested instead that they all wait for the arrival of Admiral Digby, who was sailing for New York from England with more ships.

It was the only unanimously accepted idea of the day. The council broke up.

Major Mackenzie made note of this in his diary: "13th Sept. We certainly are now at the most critical period of the war. Should the French gain such an advantage over our fleet as to enable them to continue their Operations unmolested against Lord Cornwallis, our hopes in that quarter rest entirely on the firmness of him and his troops; on the Contrary should our fleet beat theirs, we have a fair prospect of ending the Rebellion, and at the same time, of giving a severe blow to the Military power of France, by the destruction or Capture of their troops on this continent."[27]

The next day, September 14, Governor Robertson came back at Clinton again. In writing. He admitted that rushing lightly guarded troopships to the Chesapeake might be highly risky business, but doing nothing was riskier. And a spot of luck might make all the difference. Besides that, the loss of Cornwallis's army could not be allowed to happen. Robertson finished: "We give up the game if we do not try to risk it. . . . No person has seen this. I have no copy. Destroy it if you blame the sentiments."[28]

Without a better idea to chew on at the moment, the desperate Clinton began to rethink it. He then called another council of war for that afternoon. The subject: Robertson's plan. Clinton comforted himself with the thought that Cornwallis was secure enough behind his fortress to last to the end of October, still time enough to thrash out some plan of action.

At the conference table once more, Robertson pushed his plan even harder. Clinton observed that this written plan was different from the plan Robertson had submitted in writing earlier. When challenged, the old general produced yet another written version. Clinton noted, "Not an officer concurred with him, but rather laughed at his extravagant zeal." Baffled by inconsistencies, some of those on the committee— Major Mackenzie included—believed that the old reprobate was becoming senile.[29]

Sir Henry next summoned several officers who had recently been with Cornwallis. Their opinion was unanimous. The earl could stand up against a siege by an army of 20,000—for three weeks, anyway. No one else in the council put forth a plan—at least, one that they could all accept. Comforting themselves with the idea of abundant time, the council voted on the same plan of action they had voted for the first time-await Digby's flotilla. That oncoming squadron looked increasingly like the savior they needed. Shrugging, Robertson agreed.[30]

Like a literary editor with abundant time at his disposal, Sir Henry sat down with Robertson's three versions, wrote an extensive—and time-wasting—critique of them and filed it for future protection.

Three days later, on Monday, September 17, 3,000 people, waiting at a dock in New York for news of the sea battle, greeted a boat from Graves's homecoming fleet. They went away lamenting.

Graves's message to Clinton stated that he could see no way to break through that vastly superior fleet of both de Grasse and Barras to reach Cornwallis and so was returning to New York. "The enemy," he wrote, "have so great a naval force in the Chesapeake that they are absolute masters of its navigation."

Still, Clinton thought, there was time and there were possibilities. He called another council of war.

The council met. It talked. And talked. The council members managed to agree that reinforcements must be sent to Cornwallis as quickly as possible, certainly by the end of October. The only means of delivering those reinforcements—Graves's fleet—was at that moment laboring its way back to New York in very bad condition, needing extensive repairs. The committee failed to indicate how else those reinforcements were to be delivered to Cornwallis. Clinton, the soldier, believed that Graves, the sailor, would find a way in, fighting his way up the York River or the James, perhaps. Believing that, he put 4,000 troops aboard sweltering naval transports ready to sail when Graves returned.[31]

Washington, Rochambeau, Lafayette, Knox, and Alexander Hamilton (whose mother was French Huguenot and who had grown up speaking fluent French) sailed some thirty miles down the bay to visit de Grasse's flagship, *Ville de Paris,* 110 guns, down in Hampton Roads. At the very minimum, they had to convince de Grasse to delay his departure fifteen days beyond his original date of October 15. And even that would be tight. Sieges take much time.

They sailed between the anchorages of some thirty French warships and steered their way to the flagship. Washington must have felt an abiding gratification to the bottoms of his bootsoles: Here were the magnificent ships he had needed all along, the ships that had given the British navy in America its comeuppance.

They climbed aboard the flagship to an unexpected welcome. The bearish French admiral greeted Washington with a mighty bear hug, bussed him on both cheeks, and cried, "My dear little general!" to the great diversion of his aides; even the equally bearish Henry Knox shook his sides with laughter.[32]

Washington was surprised by the courteous and cooperative manner of de Grasse, who soon reassured Washington. He not only wasn't planning to leave by October 15; he would stay until the end of the month, if need be. Would that be enough time to conquer Cornwallis?

On September 19, Graves's fleet struggled into New York.

Clinton was fully expecting Graves to turn around and escort the transports with the 4,000 troops back down to the Chesapeake. But Graves announced that ten of his ships needed major repairs. He had to put them in the shipyards. That left him fewer than eight ships to take on de Grasse's thirty-two. Four to one. Out of the question. Graves wouldn't even guess when those ten ships would be ready for sea duty again. Clearly his officers thought Cornwallis was doomed. So Clinton unloaded his suffering, heat-whipped troops. He comforted the bemused Graves with a platitude: "We must stand or fall together."

Lieutenant McKenzie wrote: "I fear the fate of the Army in Virginia will be determined before our fleet can get out of the harbour again."[33]

Clinton once more took comfort where there was none. Although Graves had lost one ship, *Terrible*, seventy-four guns, *Robust*, and *Prudent*—storm-damaged some weeks before—were now ready for service again; in addition, *Torbay* and *Prince William* were sailing up from Jamaica. Digby, according to reports, was bringing three more ships of the line. If the ten damaged ships could be repaired quickly, Graves—even without the five ships on the way—would have twenty-five warships, giving de Grasse only a seven-ship advantage. If. If. If.

Clinton began planning a naval attack on the Chesapeake. Hundreds of Loyalist families began packing for exile.

On September 23 the news received in New York insisted on being bad. All bad. Cornwallis reported that his people had counted not thirty-two but thirty-six ships in de Grasse's armada. Worse, he warned now, his fort of logs would not stand up to a steady battering for long. "If you cannot relieve me very soon, you must be prepared to hear the worst." How "soon" was soon? Three weeks? A month? Surely not just a week.[34]

All the stormy petrels were coming home to roost at the same time. The French had taken all the gambles and were getting a great run of supporting luck. When Rodney had failed to send enough ships from the islands, de Grasse had gambled on bringing his entire fleet up from the islands and, catching the smaller British fleet shorthanded, had trapped Cornwallis inside the capes. Barras had dared to sail from Newport for the Chesapeake with those siege guns and, with luck again and exquisite timing, by sailing far out to sea, then swinging around off North Carolina, then up the coast to the Chesapeake, had slipped into port right past Graves, who was being pummeled by de Grasse.

And now Cornwallis was saying that he was not well fortified and was expecting the worst in short order, and that there were no means for Clinton to get past de Grasse's huge fleet of thirty-six to help him.

Major Mackenzie, seeing no other options, was hoping that Sir Harry Clinton would make a major move against Philadelphia.[35]

In Williamsburg, a disturbing rumor began to circulate among the troops and finally came to Washington's attention.

The rumor claimed that Adm. Robert Digby had arrived in New York from England with five more British warships to reinforce Graves and Hood. Indeed, Rivington's Loyalist *Gazette* reported that Digby's squadron consisted of eight ships. Graves's badly battered fleet had been patched up, according to the rumor, and with Digby's additional ships had loaded General Clinton's relief force and was now sailing flank speed for the Chesapeake.

Washington had learned to dismiss most rumors. But apparently Admiral de Grasse believed this one entirely. By messenger he announced that he wasn't going to let the now-enlarged English navy seize the initiative; before they came down from New York and into the Chesapeake after him, he would sail out of the bay to meet them on the high seas or even sail to New York.

Furthermore, de Grasse added, "If I am compelled by the weather, or by the result of the battle, not to return, please send the regiments back to Martinique on the vessels which remain in the river."[36]

Not return? If he did not return, the whole game would be up. Washington and Rochambeau held a panic meeting, then sent messages to de Grasse, urging him to put the siege against Cornwallis ahead of the British navy in New York. Lafayette personally carried Washington's message to de Grasse. The allied generals now waited in agony for de Grasse's answer.

On September 25, Lafayette returned. Admiral de Grasse had read their messages and now sent his answer. It seems that even de Grasse's own officers had voted against his planned move. The admiral decided he would stay.

But the battle was far from over. De Grasse's mercurial behavior was proving too unreliable; he could easily change his plans again and sail back to the Caribbean on a moment's notice. And even with his ships plugging up the Chesapeake, Cornwallis could still escape across the York River, through his compound in Gloucester.

The tone of the siege was now raised from urgent to feverish. From this point on the allied army would work around the clock.

Washington had to summon all the patience he could muster while he, Rochambeau, and their armies reorganized themselves for siege warfare. Staffs were busy from dawn to late night handling the maddeningly slow, detail-ridden process of formulating the requisite order of battle, assembling and inventorying all the siege equipment, and bringing the rest of the army from Annapolis to camp in Williamsburg. Ultimately the reorganizing consumed eleven days—September 17 right up to the 27th— to ready the army for the final leg of its long journey, just twelve miles from Williamsburg to the wooden walls of Yorktown.

On September 23, Clinton's council of war met once more, then on the 24 sat in another meeting with the navy. Clinton, Robertson, Graves, and Hood (who clearly was blaming Graves for blowing the most important sea battle of the war) together drafted a letter to Cornwallis. And in it they made a frail promise—which was to greatly reassure the Earl—"to relieve you and afterwards cooperate with you."

Then they set a date for sailing, tentative, to be sure, but not beyond reason: October 5.

But how were they going to bring off this miracle? Clinton had the troops, yes. He was planning to embark 6,000 of them. But the now-augmented council of war was back to belling the cat again. Who was going to get the 6,000 past the French fleet?

Clinton had to take a realistic look at that promise of rescue made to Cornwallis. If his 6,000 troops were blown out of the water by de Grasse while Cornwallis's 7,000 were crushed in a siege, that wasn't just a catastrophe; it was a war-ending cataclysm. In the cold light of realism, this was the mad scheme of that senile old debauched Robertson. It just didn't make sense.

Yet now Admiral Hood was pushing it also. At least, pushing for action. Clinton needed assurances that the admirals were reasonably confident they could deliver all their ships in fighting condition in time to get the relief force to Cornwallis. And on that point Admiral Graves seemed ominously silent. Yet there was no other plan; there could be no other plan. To relieve Cornwallis, the joint army-navy council of war simply had to find some way to go around or through or over de Grasse's thirty-six ships.

Robertson's challenge haunted them: "If we do not try we cannot succeed."

Seven

Siege at Yorktown

On September 28, the allied forces set off on a march through the streets of Williamsburg bound for Yorktown twelve miles away for what they dared hope would be the final great battle of the Revolution. It was a warm day.

The whole country talked of nothing else. The troops were aware that everyone they passed, everyone they had left behind, was watching them, waiting for the only word anyone wanted to hear: Victory.

"We are all alive and so sanguine in our hopes," Col. St. George Tucker wrote to his wife, "that nothing can be conceived more different than the countenances of the same men at this time and on the first of June."[1]

"I am all on fire," wrote Gen. George Weedon of the Virginia militia at Yorktown in a letter to General Greene. "By the Great God of War, I think we may all hang up our swords by the last of the year in perfect peace and security!"[2]

But behind the exuberance lurked the nibbling dread that Cornwallis, the wily fox, would pluck a last trick from his hat, that in the end he would turn the tables and reassert British control over them, over Virginia, over America.

Fifes and drums sounding, banners streaming, three divisions of Continentals under Generals Lafayette, Lincoln, and von Steuben led the way. General Wayne and his brigade of Pennsylvanians, now feeling vindicated by the Battle of Green Springs Plantation, marched with heads up under General von Steuben's command.

Among the marchers were more than 3,000 Virginia militiamen eager to be in on the kill. Included with them was a corps of riflemen who called themselves the "Sons of the Mountains," tough fighters able to subsist on a handful of cornmeal. Leading them was Gen. Thomas Nelson, a signer of the Declaration of Independence and now both general of the militia and governor of Virginia, replacing the ineffectual Thomas Jefferson. A native of Yorktown, Governor Nelson, a man of great girth and jolly disposition, would soon see cannonballs strike his home, which now sheltered British officers. He was probably the only man in Washington's army who could say that by marching to Yorktown he was going home.

Next came the Second Canadian Brigade, originally composed of Canadians but, especially since the army reorganization on January 1, 1781, now containing other "foreign" troops. Of the original 800 Canadians in 1775, attrition and casualties had left but 200.

The First Rhode Island Regiment was a "segregated" unit, containing black troops with white officers. It had been in the army's duty roster since 1775 and had served with distinction throughout the Revolution. It was about to add considerable luster to its name.

Next trooped the artillery brigade of Gen. Henry Knox, another officer of notable girth whose greatest exploit may have been the dragging of cannon from Fort Ticonderoga through the snows and frozen rivers of New England to drive the British under Gen. Thomas Gage out of Boston and whose cannonading at the Battle of Trenton was celebrated.

Two hundred cavalrymen cantered by next, followed by the key men in any siege, specially trained sappers and miners, including the newly minted sergeant, Joseph Plumb Martin. Then came the splendidly caparisoned French troops. Full regimental bands shook the ground as four major generals—the Baron de Viomesnil, his brother the Count de Viomesnil, the Chevalier de Chastellux, and the Marquis de St. Simon with Brigadier M. de Choisy—led seven regiments of smartly stepping, superbly tailored soldiers, composed of the four regiments that had marched from Newport and the three regiments that had come with de Grasse.

Brigadier George Weedon's militia brigade of 1,500 men had crossed the York downstream to dig in around the British garrison at Gloucester, which some believed was going to be Cornwallis's escape hatch. Along with them, to Gloucester, Washington sent Duke Armand Louis de Lauzun's legion of 600 cavalry. The duke was about to write his own notable record at Yorktown.

That gave the allies 17,600 troops in all—about 9,000 American troops and 8,000 Frenchmen.

At Yorktown, well dug in, ready for a long siege and waiting to greet them, were 8,300 British and Germans, including 800 sailors, mainly gunners.[3] These were the best British troops in America, and they weren't going to make it easy for the allies. They represented approximately one-third of all British forces in the country.

Sergeant Joseph Plumb Martin had personal reason to remember that celebratory parade to Yorktown. During a pause in the march, while visiting some Pennsylvania troops, he had his wallet stolen with $5 in it.[4]

On September 24 Adm. Robert Digby, forty-nine, finally arrived at Sandy Hook, New York, long after rumors said he had. And instead of a fleet with some muscle, he brought with him a royal distraction: the third son of King George III, sixteen-year-old Prince William. The overjoyed city, needing a lift, turned out to fête the young prince in force. For the nonce everyone seemed to forget about their trapped army in the Chesapeake.

Now, with Admiral Digby in port, Clinton called another council of war. He had conceived of the idea that the earl would make his escape across the York River through Gloucester and was proposing to send a force to attack Philadelphia and thereby be ready to greet the fleeing Cornwallis there.

It was a splendid vision, but his entire council of war shook their heads. The earl's last report clearly stated that he was trapped. "Expect the worst," he had written.

A feint at Philadelphia would never convince Washington and Rochambeau to drop the quarry they had in their grip to gad after a will-'o-the-wisp 300 miles away. Furthermore, the army in New York would be ready to embark on October 3. So why change plans now? No. They rejected his shopworn plan and he accepted their decision. Somehow the navy had to get through de Grasse to Cornwallis.

The navy was talking about catching de Grasse's fleet badly moored with one of the bay's notorious tides running against him, preventing him from turning his ships for broadsides when the British fleet came running through the capes right at him. They would race past him into an anchorage on the York, where de Grasse would find his deep-draft ships hardly able to maneuver. Timing would be everything. And it was time for luck to start running with the British tide.

But the navy—Hood and Graves and now Digby—were still asking the most frightening question of all: Once in the bay, how were they to get out? The implications of that question were far more alarming than appeared on the surface. If Clinton lost Cornwallis's army, then lost his own, that could very well be the end of the British in America. But if he lost the British navy, too, that could mean the loss of the British possessions from Canada down into the incredibly valuable Spice Islands in the Caribbean. England itself could be ruined. Court-martials for that offense could lead to execution.

No British sailor forgot the death of Admiral Byng, who a quarter-century before was executed for a far less serious crime. He was defeated in a naval battle off Minorca. A court-martial acquitted him of cowardice but convicted him of negligence and ordered him brought to his quarterdeck and there, in front of his entire ship's company, shot by firing squad.

In the New York conference room, Admiral Byng's shade wagged his finger as he displayed his bullet holes. And that caused an interesting byplay among the three admirals. Digby, newly arrived from England, outranked Graves and should have therefore taken command. But he deferred, leaving Graves in command. Admiral Hood was clearly unhappy about this. He felt that Graves's incompetence had cost one of the most important battles of the war. He would have much preferred to have Digby take command. Whisperers suggested that Digby didn't want to be blamed for what was about to happen. If there was to be another Admiral Byng, he was refusing to make himself available for the role.

On the 27th, Major Mackenzie recorded: "Altho' the Navy are now hard at work in refitting the ships, and are preparing every thing for Sea with great diligence, yet I greatly fear that something decisive will take place against Lord Cornwallis before we can possibly be ready to go from hence."[5]

The next day, September 28, Clinton called another meeting of the joint council of war in order to conduct a survey among the councilors. The gravest doubts surfaced. The navy could promise only that they could land the army. The army said if that was all they could promise, it was too little. The landed army would be destroyed. The army didn't like the navy's plan and the navy felt the army had no plan. What was that army going to do once it got there? Were they going to trust to luck? Nobody was happy.

Worse still, the repairs in the shipyards were taking longer than expected, and the council, realizing the fleet wasn't ready, was in effect deciding that it might have to postpone the sailing date until they had a more solid plan. They were drawing back again. In the meantime, they decided that Cornwallis should be told to take his own action without immediate help from New York. October was at hand. The sands were running out of the glass. And they still hadn't figured out a way to save the earl. The meeting ended.

The slippage continued. Admiral Graves announced that because of shipyard problems, the sailing had to be postponed yet again. He called for another meeting to reopen the whole plan once more while moving the sailing date from October 5 to October 8, then from the 8th to the 12th, then to the 17th.[6]

Major Mackenzie, watching the slow pace of work in the shipyards, shrewdly suspected foot-dragging. Hood seemed as eager as ever and hounded the shipyards to get his ships ready to sail soon as possible. But individual ship captains were slacking off. Evidently they didn't believe Cornwallis could be rescued. Digby seemed desperately unhappy to be in any way involved. The rescue mission was being called a forlorn hope mission. One of Digby's ship captains, Lord Robert Manners, newly arrived from England with him, warned publicly that a major naval defeat could give all of the West Indies to France. William Smith warned Clinton that the navy was very likely to keep delaying a sailing date until all hope ran out. Cornwallis's reports were growing grimmer by the day.

On October 1, forty-three days after starting out on their long march, Washington and Rochambeau had accomplished what few had believed they could: They were standing before the fortifications of Yorktown, about to confront General Charles Earl Cornwallis in a showdown they hoped would end the American Revolution.

Accompanied by a band of French siege engineers and a military escort, the two generals walked dangerously close to Yorktown—within 300 yards—as they studied Cornwallis's fortifications and the ground in front of where they would dig their siege works. Such reconnaissance was always dangerous; Lieutenant Denny of the Pennsylvania Brigade wrote that high-ranking officers were always pickoff targets for snipers.[7]

The reconnaissance party could see that Cornwallis had been busy, had even pressed into service the labor of many slaves. And he had built with careful thought to make the allies pay heavily to get inside the town. His works were bristling with cannon. He had even stripped the ship's cannon from both *Charon* and *Guadeloupe,* anchored out on the river, and pressed their gun crews into land service to man their batteries on the fortifications.

All told, waiting for the allies were fourteen British batteries brandishing sixty-five pieces of artillery, the largest eighteen-pounders, and all placed for maximum lethality.[8]

Outside Cornwallis's main works, his engineers had devised more trouble for allied troops. Seven redoubts—free-standing artillery emplacements—each completely fortified and separate, stood like the first line of pawns in a chess game, blocking the main avenue of enemy attack. More redoubts were at either flank of the Yorktown fortifications. From each protruded the snout of a cannon. Near them were redans, two-sided log walls shaped like arrowheads with open backs, to offer protective firing ports for ground troops defending the redoubts.

Here the engineers saw that each redoubt would have to be taken separately by storm, one by one, prior to assaulting Yorktown's main works. The price in casualties would be barely acceptable, the price in time probably unpayable: de Grasse could be long gone before all redoubts were taken. The French engineers were going to have to find a way to reduce Cornwallis's prices.

A half-mile across the York River from Yorktown lay Gloucester, which Cornwallis had also fortified to give him a quick escape route and to prevent the allies from mounting cannon there. The engineers could look with regret at Gloucester's British fortifications: With Yorktown completely exposed along its riverfront, allied cannon mounted in Gloucester could have pulverized Cornwallis's troops.

Cornwallis had put the defense of Gloucester in the hands of Lieutenant Colonel Dundas, who had come to Virginia with Benedict Arnold. His second was the seemingly ubiquitous Lt. Col. Banastre Tarleton. Their base contained 700 troops plus numerous dragoon horses.

At anchor in the river were a number of ships. In addition to two ships of the line, *Charon* and *Guadalupe,* their cannon now on the fortifications of Yorktown, there also lay at anchor three shallow-draft troop transports as well as numerous small craft capable of carrying Cornwallis's troops across to Gloucester in short order.

The engineers recommended that the allied siege works consist of two trenches paralleling Cornwallis's fortifications. The first parallel would be the most distant from Yorktown, some 600 to 800 yards, in fact. For maximum safety, the initial digging would have to be at night when the British could not see them.

Once begun, the first trench, four feet deep, could be extended left and right in daylight, running 2,000 yards in length, more than a mile. After it was completed and artillery placed, the first parallel would allow for a zigzag trench to extend closer to Yorktown. With the artillery of the first parallel covering the diggers, the second parallel would begin much closer to Yorktown—only 350 yards, in fact. It would be four feet deep, seven feet wide, and 750 yards long—some 500 feet under a half-mile. After the completion of the second parallel, the major bombardment from there could begin in earnest—from seventy French guns and forty-five American.

The troops were set to work immediately felling trees for logs and for making breastwork baskets called fascines and gabions. The two parallels were going to take the exhausting labor of thousands of troops.

In the meantime, things were not going at all well on the Gloucester side of the encirclement. This was a key part of the siege; it was quite possible that the siege in Yorktown would flush the bird through the back door of Gloucester. The allied troops here could suddenly be faced with Cornwallis's entire army moving at great speed to wedge through their lines and break into Virginia.

The ranking American officer there, in charge of 1,500 Virginia militia, was Gen. George Weedon, a peacetime innkeeper from Fredericksburg. Under his command was placed the dragoon regiment, Lauzun's Legion, led by the Duc de Lauzun.

Armand Louis de Gontaut, Comte de Biron, Duc de Lauzun, created a stir wherever he went in America. Exceedingly handsome, wealthy, superbly tailored in gorgeous uniforms, a dashing cavalryman to his boot tips and scion of one of the important courtly families of France, the duke was said to be a lover of Queen Marie Antoinette. With his scintillating personality and delightful wit, he was a raconteur of note in every officers' mess. To add to the luster of romance, he bore the same name as his celebrated late uncle, whose adventures were standard fare in every tavern and dining room of France.

When, with his entire regiment of 600 horse and foot, he reported for duty under General "Wiedon," the Duc de Lauzun received a shock, although his sense of mirth did not desert him. He noted that General Weedon had "blockaded Gloucester in a drole way; he was more than fifteen miles from the enemy's posts, frightened to death, and did not dare to send a patrol half a mile from his army. He was the best man alive and all that he desired was to take no responsibility."[9]

The fifty-one-year-old Weedon would have been outraged by Lauzun's description of him. He had fought well through the New York and New Jersey campaigns, and distinguished himself at Brandywine when he and his Virginians paused to let the collapsing line retreat through their files, then formed up to stop the British attack. He fought with frustrated distinction at Germantown, where he believed the Americans were minutes from victory when through fog and miscues the American attack fizzled. Although he had been described as one of the "jealous, ambitious men," he had stayed the course and most recently had helped fight the British raiders in Virginia. True, having only 1,500 very unreliable Virginia militia under his command outside Gloucester, he felt he was in a very untenable position. He well knew what green militia would do at the first sight of the combined cavalry of Tarleton and Simcoe exploding out of Gloucester and bearing down on them at high speed.[10] Washington himself, aware of this, had personally ordered Weedon to set up a perimeter at a safe distance from the British huzzahs.

The duke decided this was not the setup that could stop the Cornwallis cannonball if it came that way. He needed reinforcements. So he reported to General Rochambeau that General Weedon and his American militia would be useless, and requested reliable French troops to replace them. General Rochambeau sent him more than he bargained for—he "sent me artillery and eight hundred men drawn from the marines"—but he sent those troops "under the orders of [Brigadier General] M. de Choisy, who by seniority commanded General Wiedon and myself."

So Lauzun and Weedon had a new boss, a man not destined to endear himself to either.

"M. de Choisy," observed the duke, "is an excellent and worthy man, absurdly violent in temper, constantly in a rage, quarrelling with everybody, and without common sense. He began by ridding himself of General

Wiedon and the entire militia, telling them they were all cowards, and in five minutes they were almost as much afraid of him as of the English, which is certainly a great deal to say."[11]

Yet with the formidable combination of Dundas, Tarleton, and Simcoe in Gloucester, the duke was certainly right in calling for more help. He was destined to meet Tarleton head on.

On September 29 Cornwallis read with great satisfaction a message from General Clinton, dated September 24.

"A meeting of the General and Flag officers held this day" had decided to send 5,000 troops to rescue Cornwallis's garrison. These troops were to be carried by a British task force of twenty-three warships that was going to set sail "in a few days." Clinton's message told Cornwallis to be on the alert; the British fleet would enter the Chesapeake and announce itself by firing its guns.[12]

From the tenor of this message, Cornwallis estimated that the fleet should arrive in a week—certainly no later than October 5. For Cornwallis, holding out for another week would be relatively easy because the enemy had not even begun to dig his siege trenches, had not yet dragged onto the battlefield a single siege cannon. Rescue by sea meant that Cornwallis would soon if not fly the coop, certainly sail the coop compliments of the British navy. Seven days of waiting—until October 5.

Cornwallis, eager to reduce his potential casualties, replied to Clinton, "I shall retire this night within the works." The implications of that statement were significant, as the allies were about to learn.

The next day, Sunday, September 30, Lt. Col. St. George Tucker of the Virginia militia was astonished by the view before him. Cornwallis had abandoned three redoubts and a smaller redan.

"This morning," he wrote in his journal, "it being discovered that the enemy had abandoned all their advanced redoubts on the south and east ends of the town, a party of French troops, between seven and eight o'clock, took possession of two redoubts on Penny's Hill or Pigeon Quarter, an eminence which it is said commands the whole town."[13]

The allies were baffled. Washington was deeply suspicious. There was no reason to have abandoned them and many reasons to have retained them, even defended them with blood. What did it mean? What did Cornwallis have up his sleeve? Were these three redoubts Trojan horses? He had given up, without firing a shot, redoubts that would have cost the allies many casualties and precious time. Since the redoubts faced all ways, they could now be armed with allied artillery and turned against Cornwallis's walls.

The British commander had made the allies' work much easier. The siege now would now be finished in fewer days, a priceless gift of time to Washington and Rochambeau, ever with their spyglasses on those mercurial French ships at anchor.

But Cornwallis had not been completely generous. He still retained three other redoubts, all larger, all much more formidable, all more strategically placed—all needing to be dealt with before the main assault began. Two in particular worried Washington: redoubts nine and ten. His fears would turn out to be justified.

Yet for the time being, Cornwallis seemed to have reduced his prices.

One of General Clinton's difficulties in coordinating his moves with General Cornwallis was the simple problem of communicating with him. Getting a sailing vessel past the French fleet lying at anchor in Lynhaven Bay was increasingly dangerous. Sending riders overland was also very risky; they were liable to capture, and any rider caught with British messages would be treated as a spy and hanged.

So, in desperation, General Clinton turned to Maj. Charles Cochrane. With a message from Sir Harry in hand, the major set out from New York Harbor on rough seas in a whaleboat with a crew and twelve oars. He proposed to row to Yorktown.

On Wednesday, October 3, Brigadier General Choisy, aware that Cornwallis might try to escape through Gloucester, decided to move his defensive perimeter closer to the British encampment and dig in there against a major British attack.

Down a single lane four miles from the British cantonment he led his forces—French marines, American militia, and the Duc de Lauzun's cavalry Legion. The duke saw a very pretty woman in a farmhouse doorway and asked her about British operations in the area.

"Oh," she replied, "Colonel Tarleton left this place only a few minutes ago; he said he was very eager to shake hands with the French duke."

Lauzun laughed. "I assure you, madam, I have come on purpose to gratify him."

At around ten o'clock in the morning, the French forces encountered the British. Almost the entire British garrison had been out making a "Grand Forage," pillaging every farm and field of great stores of forage, feed, and food. The formidable Lieutenant Colonel Dundas was himself at the head of the operation, supervising the long train of heavily burdened army wagons and backpacking "bat horses" trundling back to the British base. Covering their return were units of Simcoe's Queen's Rangers and Tarleton's British Legion.

When he saw the French advancing toward him, Tarleton quickly moved into a woods on Choisy's left, formed up, and came out charging. Without waiting, Lauzun immediately charged at Tarleton.

The two units crashed together in a large field in a violent skirmish, each side fighting furiously. Lauzun and Tarleton were moving ever closer to each other. Tarleton raised his pistol. Then the horse of one of his troopers was impaled by a French cavalry spear and went down, taking Tarleton and his horse with it. The main force of British cavalry now bore down and drove into the French, who took the shock, firmed up, and were pushing the British legionnaires back.

A unit of British infantry came running forward to break up the French cavalry attack. In the melée Tarleton had jumped up, seized another horse, and signaled for retreat behind the infantry so that he could re-form. The British infantry had saved Tarleton from defeat by Lauzun.

Tarleton now saw a battalion of despised American militia that had come running up. He immediately bore down on them and got a surprise. This was no ordinary militia. Almost all the men were seasoned fighters, most of them former Continental Army regulars, and they were led by Lt. Col. John Mercer. They didn't run; standing their ground, they shattered Tarleton's attack with their steady fire, giving Lauzun time to reform. He was on the verge of another attack on Tarleton when Tarleton withdrew from the field.

The duke was able to claim the victory. The historian Thomas Balch said of the duke: "He beat back, with French impetuosity, the cavalry of Tarleton, three times as numerous as his own, and forced it to retire precipitately in Gloucester."[14]

In the general orders the next day, Washington saluted both Lauzun and Mercer and pinned the laurel of praise on them for their victory.

Tarleton had gotten his wish. He had had his hand shaken by Lauzun.[15]

In his memoirs, the duke does not say whether he revised his opinion of the Virginia militia.

As the October days wore on in New York, the sailing day of the rescue flotilla became a mote floating over the calendar while Clinton waited to see where it would land. Governor Robertson and Admiral Hood squirmed with frustration. The governor fired one verbal salvo after another at Graves, trying to goad him into precipitate action. The town itself, clearly seeing the gravest disaster in the offing for England and for American Loyalists both, was urging action; the wealthiest Loyalists were putting up large sums of money to help fit out the ships; people were rounding up men to serve as crews. Chief Justice Smith said, "The populace raves at the navy."[16]

Graves gave every appearance of wanting to avoid another fight with de Grasse. And Clinton now gave every appearance of wanting to push him into it. When the repair yards announced they didn't have enough lumber to finish the repairs, Clinton provided all the lumber they needed from the lumberyards he kept for barracks building. When the navy announced a shortage of gunpowder, Clinton provided it from army supplies. Graves, now openly truculent toward Roberts and Hood, refused to attend a Clinton meeting, saying he was attending one of his own. When he arrived at another, he tried to raise again the question of rescuing Cornwallis. Did anyone think it was possible? Hood was furious. The question had been already explored thoroughly and the plans drawn. There was no other choice but to sail to the Chesapeake, attack de Grasse, and rescue Cornwallis. Hood felt that the ship repairs had been deliberately slow and that it might already be too late. He pressed Graves to name a sailing date.

Robertson said that Graves behaved like a man who "considers himself as ruined already." Clinton drafted his will, gave one copy to his mistress, Mrs. Baddeley, and sent another with financial instructions to England.

On the night of October 5, the siege engineers walked out and began to lay out the trenches.

"We began," Sgt. Joseph Plumb Martin noted, "by following the engineers and laying laths of pine wood end-to-end upon the line marked out by the officers for the trenches." The stark white pine laths looming in the dark like dotted lines would guide the troops who were to dig the trenches. But the work was cut short. "It coming on to rain hard, we were ordered back to our tents and nothing more was done that night."[17]

At dusk on October 6, the British, looking over their works, saw 4,300 men, French and American, marching in parade formation. General Lincoln's six American regiments spread out to the right, Baron Viomesnil's troops to the left. To do the digging, some 1,500 men were equipped with shovels and gabions (cylindrical wicker baskets for transporting earth and filling and lugging sandbags); to protect them from sudden British sallies out of Yorktown, another 3,000 were placed ahead of them.

So while nearly 1,000 troops were occupied in the woods chopping down trees, hewing thousands of stakes, making siege equipment like saucissons (sausage-shaped sandbags), fascines (tied bundles of twigs and underbrush for filling in enemy ditches), and gabions, and while others were struggling to drag and slide the cannon to the siege site, fully one-third of the available troops were put to digging the trenches—in shifts, at first in the dark, preferably on nights with no moon or nights covered with thick clouds, but later often around the clock.

The labor was enormous. Colonel Lamb of the American artillery wrote that the troops "fell to digging, in reliefs, with a will, and in the greatest silence." While they were digging, the allied troops often heard the British regimental bands serenading from behind their walls. One of the most popular tunes they played was "Yankee Doodle Dandy."

Sergeant Martin recorded that he and his companions "completed laying out the works. . . . The ground was sandy and soft and the men employed that night eat no 'idle bread' (and I question if they eat any other), so that by daylight they had covered themselves from danger from the enemy's shot."[18]

With these trenches as a cover, the digging now went on at an urgent, exhausting pace. Various units rotated the digging: on the 8th Lafayette's division wearily yielded to von Steuben; on the 9th Lincoln's division spelled von Steuben's; Chastellux's troops were succeeded by those of the Marquis St. Simon, who yielded to the diggers of Viscount Viomesnil, who were then spelled by the troops of his brother, Baron Viomesnil. The trenches grew by the hour despite the galling cannon fire from the British fortifications, which kept booming away all through the construction of the first parallel.

Yet even when the allies had placed a number of their guns, they didn't fire a single shot in reply for fear that the British would pick off the new batteries piecemeal as each was completed. The allies waited until all guns were in place.

At dawn on the 7th, the British commenced a heavy artillery barrage on the new line, but it had little effect. Sergeant Martin observed them firing their mortars:

> They had a large bulldog and every time they fired he would follow their shots across our trenches. Our officers wished to catch him and oblige him to carry a message from them into the town to his masters, but he looked too formidable for any of us to encounter.[19]

This whole operation of the siege had necessarily to be under the direction of French army engineers. Only one American officer had engaged in a siege before: the general from Germany, Baron von Steuben, who was seen all over the battlefield giving vital advice and instructions to Washington and the troops.

At all times, lookouts kept a weather eye out on the bay, watching for Clinton's ships, sailing between the capes, all cannon belching smoke and shot, rushing thousands of redcoats to Cornwallis's rescue. The engineers soon laid out emplacements for batteries specifically designed to drive off British men-o'-war.

Washington pressed everyone to maintain a frantic pace, and by the afternoon of the 9th the troops finished digging the first parallel. Wooden platforms for the batteries were ready when the struggling work crews manhandled all the guns into position. Forty-one cannon were in place, with the rest scheduled to be placed in the next two days. Artillerymen decided that forty-one were more than enough to start with. The artillerymen lit their slow matches. Cornwallis was about to learn how well his engineers had built the British works.

At three o'clock on Tuesday, October 9, in fine autumn weather, the French flag slowly rose up its pole and stirred in the breeze. Then the American flag matched it. Everyone was in place for the official ceremony that traditionally opens a siege, commencing with martial music.

The diggers were now converted back to soldiers who, on an alternating basis around the clock, were to man the trenches they had just completed, ready for any organized attacks on their siege guns. They watched the two flags rising.

As a gesture toward their contributions, Washington offered the French the honor of firing the first gun, and at three o'clock, with General Saint-Simon officiating, the superbly trained French gunners carefully, proudly aimed one of their wall-crushing twenty-four-pounders and stood ready. At the signal from an artillery officer, the first allied shot of the campaign thundered from the barrel. It scored a direct hit, smashing into the British fortifications, bringing a great cheer from the troops. The opening French battery of four twelve-pounders and six mortars and howitzers then went into action.

It was the Americans' turn. Massachusetts doctor James Thacher, twenty-seven, medical officer with Colonel Scammel's elite corps, left a telling description of the event in his lively and readable diary. General Washington and his chief artillery officer, Gen. Henry Knox, were doing a final inspection of all the American batteries when it came time to fire the first ceremonial shot. Knox was evidently scheduled to do the honors. As they stood before the ceremonial cannon, all primed, loaded, and ready, Washington's excitement was evident. Knox took the touch-hole match from the gunner and handed it to his commander in chief. The delighted Washington reached the match to the touch hole and sent the first American shot into the British fortifications. It was just five o'clock in the evening.[20]

Colonel Philip van Cortlandt of the Second New York Regiment later recalled: "I could hear the ball strike from house to house, and I was afterwards informed that it went through the one where many of the officers were at dinner, and over the tables, discomposing the dishes, and either killed or wounded the one at the head of the table."[21]

Graham of the 76th Highlanders recorded when the artillery barrage began: "On the evening of October 9, they fire an eighteen-pound ball into the town as a beginning which entering a wooden house where the officers of the 76th Regiment were at dinner, badly wounding the old Highland lieutenant, also slightly the Quartermaster and adjutant, and killed the Commissary General, Perkins, who was at table."[22]

Sergeant Martin wrote, "All were upon the tiptoe of expectation and impatience to see the signal given to open the whole line of batteries, which was to be the hoisting of the American flag in the ten-gun battery. About noon the much-wished-for signal went up. I confess I felt a secret pride swell my heart when I saw the 'star-spangled banner' waving majestically in the very faces of our implacable adversaries. It appeared like an omen of success to our enterprise, and so it proved in reality. A simultaneous discharge of all the guns in the line followed, the French troops accompanying it with 'Huzza for the Americans!' "[23]

The sustained bombardment of forty-one allied siege guns had begun. It would continue around the clock.

That night the allies finished and mounted more batteries, and by the early morning hours of October 10, the French started firing ten more cannon—both eigthteens and twenty-fours. Then the Americans set off four more eighteens.

During the night of the 10th, the French began lobbing red-hot cannonballs at the British ships at anchor. One of them scored a direct hit on the flagship *Charon,* forty-four guns, which had carried Benedict Arnold to Virginia and whose cannon were now doing duty on the walls of the city. The ship burst into flame and set several other ships on fire. Dr. Thacher recorded what happened:

> The ships were enwrapped in a torrent of fire, which spread with vivid brightness among the combustible rigging, and running with amazing rapidity to the tops of the several masts, while all around was thunder and lightning from our numerous cannon and mortars . . . one of the most sublime and magnificent spectacles which can be imagined.[24]

Charon and one other ship broke their moorings. Running aground across the York at Gloucester, they both turned into infernos, lighting the night sky for hours and finally burning to their waterlines.

Late that night of October 10, amidst the incessant bombardment, a twelve-oared whaleboat in rough seas moved past Cape Charles stealthily into Chesapeake Bay, then, wrapped in darkness, oars muffled, slipped furtively past the French flotilla at anchor in Hampton Roads and up to the York River to land Maj. Charles Cochrane, with an urgent letter for Cornwallis from Clinton. The whaleboat had made the voyage from New York in seven days.

In a sense, the letter made no sense. Its intent was unclear.

Clinton wrote: "I am doing everything in my power to relieve you by a direct move, and I have reason to hope, from the assurances given me this day by Admiral Graves, that we may pass the bar by the 12th of October, if the winds permit and no unforeseen accident happens: this however, this is subject to disappointment, wherefore if I hear from you, your wishes will of course direct me and I shall persist in the idea of a direct move, even to the middle of November, should it be your Lordship's opinion that you can hold out so long; but, if, when I hear from you, you tell me that you cannot, and I am without hopes of arriving in time . . . I will immediately make an attempt by Philadelphia."[25]

"An attempt by Philadelphia"—what did that mean? How would attacking Philadelphia relieve Yorktown?

Two sentences stand out in Cornwallis's reply: "Nothing but a direct move to York River which includes a Successful Naval Action can save us. . . . We cannot hope to make a very long resistance."[26]

By the next day, October 11, fifty-two pieces of allied artillery were firing, "making," Adjutant General Hand reported, "aweful music." They had stopped most of the British return fire.[27]

It was time to begin the second parallel, 500 yards closer to the British lines. One of the most critical and dangerous moments in building a siege line came with the opening of the second parallel, when the besieged were most likely to sortie from their fortifications. Without adequate armed protection, unarmed digging men in a trench could be bayoneted like pigs in a pen.

Amidst a thundering, flashing, ground-shaking bombardment, the French engineers began laying the lines of the second parallel. Captain Duncan observed, "The entire night was an immense roar of bursting shell." Following close behind the engineers came the sappers and miners laying the white pine laths. And these, in turn, were followed by a great army of work details, French and American, who hastily dug along the flickering white lines. They dug, in silence, without pause, urgently, all through the night, stopped only by the dawn light.

Steuben's guards stood at maximum alert all throughout the blackest hours, muskets at the ready, bayonets fixed. No one was allowed to sleep or sit down. In a no-man's land, they were exposed to both British and Allied fire booming over their heads. The gunners in the first parallel sometimes cut their fuses too short, and a number of their own shells burst prematurely over the heads of the diggers. But morning came without the loss of single man killed or wounded. Washington's adjutant general, Edward Hand, wrote a friend, "As soon as our batteries on the second parallel are completed, I think they will begin to squeak."[28]

* * *

During the night, General Cornwallis and Major Cochrane stood upon the fortifications to observe the bombardment. The major stepped forward to fire one of the British cannons, then peered into the night to see where the shot went. An allied cannonball, narrowly missing the earl, decapitated the major.[29]

By dawn the British looked over their fortification to see the new allied parallel "within short musket range of the town," Comte William Deux-Ponts asserted. The allies were snaking ever closer.

The camp followers became involved, trying to feed the troops digging the parallels. Sarah Osborne Benjamin, a servant girl from Albany, had married a soldier named Benjamin in 1780 and traveled with him in Washington's train. In her pension application fifty years later, she described the battle and stated: "I cooked and carried in beef, and bread, and coffee (in a gallon pot) to the soldiers in the entrenchment." She must have been very young at the time because she lived long enough to have her photograph taken in 1850.[30]

The digging parties had encountered a problem: those two manned British redoubts—numbers nine and ten. The closer the parallel got, the more deadly they became. The allies saw that before they could go any further with the second parallel, those two redoubts had to be taken by storm.

The two attacks had to be coordinated to take the two redoubts simultaneously so the redoubts could not lend supporting fire to each other. The action had to be sudden, at night, with bayonets only. Muskets would be unloaded, so as not to draw counterfire aimed at the musket flashes. In particular, the two attacks had to be done in three phases: clearing the abates that surrounded the redoubts, filling in and crossing the trenches at the base of the redoubts, then climbing up the walls and inside. Each of the three posed special problems.

These abates were complete trees, felled then dragged out on the battlefield and anchored by their trunks there. All the branches of the entire crown were sharpened in a helter-skelter of needlelike spear tips pointing in all directions, waiting to impale any attackers. This was a point of high casualties, especially among sappers and miners, who went ahead of the attacking infantry to chop through those abatis. While they were chopping, the defenders up inside the redoubts would be pumping barrages of musket fire down at them and down at the waiting masses of infantry bunched up behind them. Just before the assault, a heavy artillery barrage would try to blast passageways through those deadly trees.

Then came the trenches. The sappers and miners would run ahead of the troops carrying fascines—tied bundles of branches and twigs—that were thrown into the trenches so that the troops could scramble across them.

Last came the scaling operation. This required dragging heavy ladders across the battlefield, through the abatis, over the filled trenches, and up against the walls of the redoubts, where the defenders would try to push them away while greeting the attackers with down-stabbing bayonets and musket fire.

Preparation, surprise, speed—all were essential. The plan was to have 400 men of the French regiments Gatenois and Royal Deux-Ponts storm number nine on the allies' left while 400 Americans stormed number ten on the right. The attack was set for eight o'clock on the night of October 14, 1781, starting with a signal of six cannon shots.

The Americans became embroiled in a dispute—who would lead the charge?

The unit involved was to be drawn from Lafayette's division. And Lafayette gave the honor of leading it to his aide, brevet Lieutenant Colonel Gimat, in his mid-thirties, a volunteer from France who had come to America with Lafayette and joined the American army in 1777. With a commendable record, he had most recently distinguished himself at the Battle of Green Springs.

But the field officer that night was Lt. Col. Alexander Hamilton. He claimed the right, as field officer, to lead the charge.

Lafayette replied that the battalion was the oldest in the Continental Army, that it was one of the three with the longest service in the Virginia theater, that Lieutenant Colonel Gimat was the leader of that battalion, and that he, Lafayette, had already made the appointment. Besides, Colonel Hamilton was not only not an officer in the assault group, he was not even an officer of infantry but of artillery.

Hamilton noted that he was commander of Moses Hazen's brigade in Lafayette's division and so qualified as a leader. He wrote a letter of protest to General Washington.

Alexander Hamilton had a very impressive battle record. While still a college student in New York he had formed a volunteer artillery company and was commissioned captain of the unit. He fought at the Battle of Long Island, manned his cannon at Harlem Heights, fought at White Plains, and fought Christmas night at Trenton and later at Princeton, manifesting extraordinary courage in all of them. Because of his significant writing skills, his fluent French, and his high intelligence, he was made aide-de-camp to General Washington in 1777 with the rank of lieutenant colonel. He was barely twenty years old. He held that position with noteworthy distinction for four and half years, becoming in time a trusted consultant to Washington as well as a very deft emissary on delicate military matters. He had recently returned to service as an artillery officer.

The deciding factor was the date of Hamilton's commission of March 14, 1776. It predated Gimat's of December 1, 1776, and Washington ruled that therefore he had seniority. He gave the command to Hamilton.[31]

At six-thirty, to distract the British, the French, with heavy artillery cover, started diversionary attacks on both the fusilier redoubt on the far right flank of the British fortifications and on a redoubt across the river at Gloucester.

Lieutenant Colonel Comte Guillaume de Deux-Ponts embraced his brother, the colonel of the Royal Deux-Ponts, said good-bye, and readied himself for the artillery signal.[32]

At eight o'clock, just after dusk, at the signal of six cannon shots in succession, the main attack began. In grim silence, stealthily, preceded by fifty chasseurs carrying fascines and eight others carrying ladders, the French platoons, chosen as the first wave to scale the walls and so named the Forlorn Hope, moved out.

As they approached the abatis, a voice in the redoubt cried out in German: *"Wer da?"* "Who goes there?" The French did not answer. Redoubt number nine opened fire. The French began chopping their way through the abatis, taking more fire. The chopping went on for five minutes while the British fired volley after volley down on them. Casualties mounted. At last the axes cut through the abatis. Into the openings the Forlorn Hope streamed, crossed the trench on their fascines, and put up their ladders. As they climbed, the defenders fired down on them, lunged with their bayonets, pushed the ladders away. More men began climbing the walls. They struggled onto the platform, pulling others after them. The Chevalier de Lameth reached the top only to be wounded in both knees and fell. Other men nearing the top were pushed off. Fallen men struggled to stand up only to be trampled by others who climbed on them, reaching for the top.

In the darkness and the dense smoke, confusion quickly set in. Deux-Ponts' French regiment was made up of German-speaking troops from the Saar Basin. Their blue uniforms were similar to those of the German-speaking Hessians inside the redoubt. German commands were being shouted by both sides, mixed with shouted English and French commands on either side. With the only light coming from intermittent musket fire, identities were confused. During the melee of hand-to-hand combat, many men were bayoneted by their own companions.

The Hessians reformed up and charged. The French counterattacked, shouting, *"Vive le Roi!"* The Hessians were driven back and down behind some barrels. As Deux-Ponts was shaping up a bayonet charge at them, they dropped their weapons and surrendered.

At that moment, all the British guns on their fortifications fired at once with a tremendous show of flashes and light. "I never saw a sight more beautiful or more majestic," Deux-Points recalled. "I did not stop to look at it. I had to give attention to the wounded and directions to be observed towards the prisoners."

In less than thirty minutes, the battle was over. The French had overrun redoubt nine and were now bracing for the inevitable British counterattack. To their great surprise, it never came.[33]

Two hundred yards away and about twenty feet from the banks of the York River waited redoubt ten, square, a little smaller than redoubt nine, and manned by seventy enemy troops. Colonel Alexander Hamilton and his 400 "Forlorn Hope" American light infantrymen, all veterans and half of them also veterans of the Virginia campaign, lay on the ground in the dark, listening and watching for the flash and boom of the signal cannon.

In the van was the segregated First Rhode Island Regiment, 197 African American light infantrymen under white officers who first saw combat at the Battle of Rhode Island on August 29, 1778, when they successfully beat back three separate assaults by veteran Hessian troops. They were part of probably as many as 8,000 African Americans who served in the American army during the Revolution. But since muster rolls didn't designate race, an exact count may never be established. Baron von Closen of the French army praised the First Rhode Island Regiment in Yorktown for being "the most neatly dressed, the best under arms, and the most precise in its maneuvers."[34]

Scammel's Light Infantry Regiment was under command of the ubiquitous Lt. Col. John Laurens, who only months before had stood in the French court and chatted up King Louis XVI for two and a half million French livres in silver. His unit's assignment was to swing to the rear of the redoubt and stop any enemy retreat.

The sky was so clear that Sgt. Joseph Plumb Martin lay with a clear view of Jupiter and Venus. In the excitement he would mistake them for the flash of the signal cannon and nearly jumped up to charge.

At the artillery signal the Americans moved out. The password they were given was "Rochambeau," which they immediately converted to "Rush on, boys." Many of the Forlorn Hope were armed with bayonets attached to long poles.

Sergeant Martin and his fellow sappers and miners found that the earlier artillery barrage had done very little damage to the abatis and set to work chopping their way through. As they hacked, a British sentry called out a challenge. When he received no answer, he fired his musket.

This was a signal for British pickets all along their fortifications to start firing.

The Americans impatiently struggled past the chopping sappers and scrambled in and out of bomb craters large enough to "bury an ox in," Martin wrote. When he saw the men falling into the craters, he thought they were being wounded or killed "at a great rate," only to see them leap up the other side and continue the attack, shouting, "Rush on, boys," and, with their spears and bayonets, struggle to get up the walls and inside.[35]

Men stood on other men's shoulders, fighting off down-thrusting bayonets. Colonel Alexander Hamilton climbed up on the back of a trooper and pulled himself up and onto the redoubt. He stepped right into the midst of a furious bayonet fight. More Americans scrambled inside. Even the sappers and miners who had been ordered not to join in on the attack ignored their orders and swarmed up the walls. British soldiers began to leap off the redoubt. At the rear Lt. Col. Laurens and his men captured Major Campbell, the wounded commander of the redoubt, and several of his men.

In ten minutes the Americans had secured redoubt ten.

A highly excited Lafayette came hurrying up, took stock, and quickly sent a teasing message to his French counterpart, Viomesnil: "I am in my redoubt. Where are you?"

"Tell the marquis," Viomesnil replied, "that I am not in mine but will be in five minutes." He was.

Washington stood with generals Lincoln and Knox watching the entire affair. When both redoubts were secured he said: "The work is done and well done."

Lieutenant Colonel Gimat, who had originally had been chosen to lead the American attack, had led his own American troops into the melee behind Hamilton's van, but when they reached the abatis he was wounded in the foot.

The French lost fifteen killed and seventy-seven wounded. The Americans suffered nine killed and twenty-five wounded. In redoubt nine alone, the French had killed eighteen British and captured fifty. From both redoubts the allies had captured six British officers and sixty-seven men and killed more than seventy.[36]

Deux-Ponts in his journal saluted his comrades: "I owe them the happiest day of my life, and certainly the recollection of it will never be effaced from my mind."[37]

Even before the two redoubts were completely secured, allied work parties had come groping back into the trenches of the second parallel. A teeming rain had begun and, for the rest of the night, fell on the troops as they doggedly shoveled mud. The French sector took heavy casualties. One blast wounded a hundred, killing twenty-five.

At dawn, the British looked over their fortifications and saw that their two redoubts, nine and ten, were now key elements in the new allied parallel. From both, howitzers were aimed right at them. For the British, looking downstream for Clinton's rescue armada, it was a rain-filled blue Monday, October 15.

The allies were asking the same question as Cornwallis: Where was Clinton?

With the second parallel now in full view, General Cornwallis wrote a letter to General Clinton that, two and a quarter centuries later, needs no elucidation. It was now ten days after the expected rescue by Clinton, and Cornwallis seemed to be jabbing his finger into Clinton's chest with every word:

> Last evening the enemy carried two advance redoubts on the left by storm, and during the night have included them in their second parallel which they are at present busy in perfecting. My situation now becomes very critical; we dare not show a gun to their old batteries, and I expect that their new ones will open to-morrow morning. Experience has shown that our fresh earthen works do not resist their powerful artillery, so that we shall soon be exposed to an assault in ruining works, in a bad position, and with weakened numbers. The safety of the place is, therefore, so precarious that I cannot recommend that the fleet and army should run any great risk in endeavoring to save us.[38]

In Gloucester Point, Simcoe's and Tarleton's farriers were putting down their starving horses. Dr. Thacher observed earlier that 600 or 700 carcasses were seen floating down the York River and into the bay.[39]

That night, Monday, October 15, inside his crumbling stockade, General Cornwallis, despite his despairing letter to Clinton, still had a few moves left: He still could make a major bust-out across the York, and once loose he was still one of the most dangerous fighters in the British army. He waited for darkness.

After midnight, 350 picked troops of the British light infantry and guards under Major Robert Abercrombie made a sortie from Yorktown and, undetected, entered the French trenches. They swarmed down between two unfinished redoubts in a largely unfinished part of the second parallel to reach two French gun emplacements.

Colonel Richard Butler, commander of the Second Pennsylvania Battalion of Wayne's Pennsylvania Line, told his journal what happened:

> In the process of spiking the guns, they killed four or five French soldiers and drove off the rest. Then they got into the zigzag trench that led from the second parallel back to the first where they paused. They then located a battery commanded by Captain Savage of the Americans and

attacked with bayonets. They also used their bayonets to spike three of Savage's guns. This was accomplished by thrusting the bayonets into the touch holes and breaking off the tips.

Count de Noailles heard them shout "huzza!" and hurried forward with a band of grenadiers to engage the British. Eight British were killed, twelve wounded, and the rest driven off. All told, the British had spiked seven cannon.

The damage was negligible. The spiked cannon were all repaired within a few hours while the allies' pounding bombardment continued relentlessly.

Cornwallis's artillerymen, answering the allied bombardment, seemed to be running out of shells—or undamaged cannon. Or both.

The sense that the end was near rippled through the allied troops. Excited off-duty soldiers stood on the battlefield by the hour to watch cannonballs slamming into Cornwallis's log fortifications, filling the air with splinters, dirt, and smoke, knocking British guns from their platforms and tumbling them over. Much of the town had been battered into rubble that filled the streets. The allied spectators seemed to forget they were exposing themselves to danger. To protect them, Washington had to order all spectators off the battlefield.

British Captain Graham of the Seventy-sixth Highland Regiment observed that the allied cannonade was so incessant that his comrades scarcely could fire a gun of their own, their "fascines, stockade platforms, and earth, with guns and guncarriages, being all pounded together in a mass."[40]

General Cornwallis now had his back to the wall. To avoid being crushed inside Yorktown he would have to surrender—or try to escape across the river through Gloucester.

If he could catch the allies by surprise, he could move his troops across the York to smash through the allied barriers. Then, abandoning all his impeding equipment—as he had done in the race to the Dan—he could storm up the peninsula and be well nigh uncatchable. Many of his troops were veterans of the Dan campaign and had already demonstrated the astonishing speed they could achieve while enduring the greatest hardship.

For the allies, the prospects were frightening. Once loose, Cornwallis could head north for Wilmington, Delaware, or head south for Wilmington, North Carolina, and wait in either place for the Royal Navy to pick him up. Or Clinton could race out of New York to join him and together they could turn and attack the allies.

The gravest danger of all: The very act of escaping could cause soaring American hope to crash, cause America to despair. The moribund

American economy would collapse entirely, and Clinton would be dictating terms for peace in New York.

With autumn barely a few weeks old, the timing could not have been better for a foraging army. The crops had been harvested and stowed in barns; fresh horses for Tarleton and Simcoe and for most of the infantry were there for the taking in abundance; more than two months remained before hard winter set in—two months to forage and survive and terrify. Equally important, the earl had burned into his memory General Greene's playbook on how to outrace a pursuing army.

If there was a time for Cornwallis to make the allies' worst fears come true, that time was now.

On the night of October 16, at eleven o'clock, Cornwallis made his move. Captain Graham recorded in his journal that "His Lordship's intention was to attack Lauzun's legion at Gloucester, and get possession of their horses, and then move rapidly off, either to the southward or northward as circumstances might dictate."[41]

Sergeant Lamb's diary was even more explicit:

> It was determined that he [de Choisy] should be attacked before break of day by the whole British force; and the success of the attack was not in the least doubted. The horses taken from him, (for he had a considerable corps of cavalry) would in part mount the infantry, and the rest might be supplied by others collected on the road.

Cornwallis selected the troops he would take with him, alerted them for the move, then, under cover of darkness at the eleven o'clock signal, started the first batch of men in small boats across the York River to Gloucester. More than 1,000 troops of light infantry made it safely. As the second wave prepared to cross, the earl sat and wrote a letter to George Washington asking him to take care of the sick and wounded he would leave behind. Then he watched the boats return for the next wave.

If everything worked on schedule, long before dawn, in three waves, the entire Yorktown corps would cross to combine with Tarleton's Gloucester dragoons, ready to explode through the allies' defensive lines and rampage up the peninsula to freedom.

Sometime after midnight a storm struck. Great sheets of rain carried by a violent squall burst from the west. Strong winds drove some of the returning boats back to Gloucester. It sent two boatloads of troops careening down the turbulent York into the hands of French sailors. Rain blew sideways, blinding the rowers, pouring torrents down until two A.M. The gale kept blowing until dawn. By then the plan was destroyed. Trying to complete the transfer in daylight was out of the question. The essential element of surprise was lost, and with dawn the allies could shell the river, shooting the redcoats like sitting ducks.

The next morning the first wave of troops was brought back to Yorktown under heavy fire from the French. It seemed now that even the weather was on the side of the allies. Washington's incredible run of luck remained unbroken.

With the dawn, Cornwallis discovered more bad news. While he was busy trying to cross the York, the Allies had been busy extending their second parallel. Hessian Johann Doehla noted: "Toward morning they brought a trench and a strong battery of 14 guns so close to our hornwork that one could nearly throw stones into it."[42] The cannonading now would be at almost point blank range. No place inside Yorktown would be safe.

Banastre Tarleton wrote in his diary: "Thus expired the last hope of the British Army."[43]

But there was still one faint spark of hope: the arrival of Clinton, all guns blazing.

On October 17 in New York, Clinton received the grimmest message of all from Cornwallis, telling him not to come. It was too late.

But at last, on that day, the fleet was ready to sail, waiting only for a fair wind, while Clinton paced on the quarterdeck. Finally the wind picked up on the 19th, and the forlorn-hope fleet sailed forth from Sandy Hook, with Graves using his signal flags to scold and prod his captains to make flank speed. Sir Henry Clinton was sailing onboard the flagship *London* with his fingers crossed.

Eight

Surrender

In Yorktown on October 17 at the break of day, the last of the British light infantry returned to Yorktown and remanned their posts on the crumbling fortifications.

Hessian Johann Doehla, watching them return as he stood on a firing step at the break of day, felt that the bombardment would never stop. "One saw nothing but bombs and balls raining on our whole line."[1]

The returning troops told Doehla that it was hopeless to try to break through Gloucester. The way was sealed completely.

Right after reveille, Cornwallis appeared on the hornwork, watched the pulverizing bombardment for a few minutes, then disappeared again.

At ten o'clock during the unending barrage, the allies were arrested by the appearance of a small drummer boy in a red coat who stepped up in clear view on the British hornwork. He seemed to be drumming a message, but in the deafening cannonade none could hear it. Slowly the barrage diminished, then stopped. Now the drumming message could be heard. In the first total silence in days, they could identify the international signal that the small boy was tapping out: "Parley." A moment later, a British officer stepped up beside the boy and waved his arm over his head. In his hand fluttered a white handkerchief.

"He might have beat away until Doomsday," Ensign Ebenezer Denny observed, "if he had not been sighted by the men of the front lines. The constant firing was too much for the sound of a single drum; but when the firing ceased, I thought I had never heard a drum to equal it—the most delightful music to us all."[2]

As the drummer and the officer walked toward the allies' lines, an American officer hurried forward to meet them. The youthful drummer was sent back to the British lines while the British officer was blindfolded, then led through both parallels to the rear of the allies' lines, then to General Washington's tent. All along the way, the wondering eyes of allied soldiers stared at that blindfolded figure. The firing had completely stopped.[3]

Was this it?

General Washington was dictating to Jonathan Trumbull, his paymaster general and aide-de-camp, when the British officer was led into his tent.

Lord Cornwallis, the officer said, wanted to parley about the terms of surrender. The siege had killed a large part of Cornwallis's army and the rest were dying from fever and disease. The officer handed Washington a letter from Cornwallis:

> York, Virginia, 17th Oct., 1781
> Sir
>
> I propose a cessation of hostilities for twenty four hours, and that two officers may be appointed by each side, to meet at Mr. Moore's house to settle terms for the surrender of the posts of York & Gloucester. I have the honor to be Sir Your most obedient and most humble Servant, Cornwallis.[4]

Surrender—the word, the event he had been striving for these six and a half years—was clearly written on the page before him. His hands must have trembled with emotion as he read that single word.

But he did not let himself savor those words long. Haste was important. He could not—would not—give Cornwallis twenty-four hours when at any moment Clinton could appear, bash his way through the French fleet, and free the earl.

"Every day's delay," the historian Henry P. Johnston wrote, "increased the danger."[5] As Washington started drafting a response, the allied barrage resumed.

Washington wrote:

> An Ardent Desire to spare the further Effusion of Blood, will readily incline me to listen to such Terms for the surrender of your Posts and Garrisons of York and Gloucester are admissible.
>
> I wish previously to the Meeting of Commissioners, that your Lordship's proposals in writing may be sent to the American Lines: for which Purpose a suspension of Hostilities during two hours from the Delivery of this Letter will be granted.[6]

When the British flag-of-truce officer made his way back with Washington's answer, the cannonading stopped again—and remained silent for two hours. Before the time had elapsed, Cornwallis answered.

Washington wrote in his personal journal, "He sent out a letter with such proposals (though some of them were inadmissible) as led me to believe that there would be no great difficulty in fixing the terms. Accordingly, hostilities were suspended for the night, and I proposed my own terms to which, if he agreed, commissioners were to meet to digest them into form."[7]

The great irony of the date was not lost on the allies. Exactly four years before—on October 17, 1777—at Saratoga, New York, Gentleman Johnny Burgoyne had also surrendered an entire British army.

And now, on a chilly Southern night, in a blessed quiet, St. George Tucker wrote happily to his wife:

> A solemn stillness prevailed. The night was remarkably clear, and the sky decorated with ten thousand stars. Numberless meteors gleaming through the atmosphere afforded a pleasing resemblance to the bombs which had exhibited a noble firework the night before, but happily divested of all their horror.
>
> At dawn of day the British gave us a serenade with the bagpipe, I believe, and were answered by the French with the band of the Regiment of Deux-Ponts. As soon as the sun rose, one of the most striking pictures of war was displayed. . . . From the Point of Rock battery on one side our lines completely manned and our works crowded with soldiers were exhibited to view. Opposite these at the distance of two hundred yards, you were presented with a sight of the British works, their parapets crowded with officers looking at those who were assembled at the top of our works. The Secretary's [Thomas Nelson's] house with one of the corners broke off and many large holes through the roof and walls, part of which seemed tottering . . . afforded a striking instance of the destruction occasioned by war. Many other houses in the vicinity contributed to accomplish the scene.[8]

The night was anything but poetic for the British troops, who busied themselves until dawn destroying equipment and stores. They opened the seacocks in the disarmed *Guadaloupe* and watched her sink. Carpenters drilled holes in the bottom of H.M.S. *Fowey* and so sank her. Her fate must have delighted many Virginians who remembered how Fowey had tormented the Tidewater going back to 1775, when Lord Dunmore, royal governor of Virginia, skipped onboard to take the royal government into exile with him, making mischief all up and down the Chesapeake and ultimately, foolishly, burning Loyalist Norfolk to the ground. French cannon fire had already some time ago burned *Charon*, which had brought Benedict Arnold's raiding party to the Chesapeake on New Year's Day. She now lay a charred hulk in shallow water.

Nor was the violence of warfare ended: That night thirteen British soldiers in Yorktown, just hours from prison camp, were blown to bits when a powder magazine exploded.[9]

Early the next morning, the 18th, after the first night of silence since the bombardment had begun, Washington replied to Cornwallis's second note. Having read Cornwallis's terms for surrender, Washington now presented his own.

Cornwallis had asked for full honors of war for his troops and their return—including the German mercenaries—on parole to England. This meant that Cornwallis and all his troops could march away, colors flying, military bands playing, still fully armed and equipped, free to embark for England. Washington countered by offering the same humiliating terms of surrender that Clinton had imposed on General Lincoln's army in Charleston. As for a return to England, Washington countered with his own demands: The entire British army was to be interred in an American prison camp—just as Burgoyne's was. Take it or leave it. And again he allowed Cornwallis a scant two hours to accept them or else the bombardment would resume.

Washington's flag-of-truce messenger hurried across the battlefield, now crowded with idle allied soldiers standing, talking, and gazing at the British fortifications. Cornwallis replied, asking now for just three items: terms of special honor for the Gloucester Point garrison, now under the command of Lt. Col. Banastre Tarleton; permission to send a ship to New York with private property; and immunity from punishment for the Loyalists and deserters in the two garrisons.

Washington accepted Cornwallis's note as a basis for negotiation. He named, not surprisingly, Lt. Col. John Laurens as his negotiation commissioner. General Rochambeau selected Viscount de Noailles, Lafayette's brother-in-law, to represent the French army. The meeting place was to be the one suggested by Cornwallis—Augustine Moore's farmhouse.

In the early afternoon, little more than twenty-four hours after the drummer boy appeared on the British fortifications, the two British peace commissioners, Col. Thomas Dundas and Maj. Alexander Ross, Cornwallis's aide, walked from Yorktown down along the riverbank, then trudged up on the bluff overlooking the river to the small frame farmhouse of Augustine Moore and there found Colonel Laurens and Viscount de Noailles waiting for them. After the introductions, the four men sat at a table where Colonel Laurens placed the articles of capitulation in front of Major Ross.

Major Ross observed, "This is a harsh article."

"Which article?" said Colonel Laurens.

"The troops shall march out with colors cased and drums beating a British or a German march."

"Yes, sir," replied Colonel Laurens, "it is a harsh article."

"Then, Colonel Laurens, if that is your opinion, why is it here?"

"Your question, Major Ross, compels an observation which I would have gladly suppressed. You seem to forget, sir, that I was a capitulant at

Charleston, where General Lincoln after a brave defense of six weeks [in] open trenches by a very inconsiderable garrison against the British army and fleet under Sir Henry Clinton and Admiral Arbuthnot, and when your lines of approach were within pistol shot of our field works, was refused any other terms for his gallant garrison, than marching out with colors cased and drums *not* beating a German or a British march."

"But," rejoined Major Ross, "my Lord Cornwallis did not command at Charleston."

"There, sir," said Colonel Laurens, "you extort another declaration. It is not the individual that is here considered; it is the nation. This remains an article, or I cease to be a commissioner."[10]

That was just the opening salvo in the negotiations. Despite their weak negotiating position, the two British peace commissions were tough bargainers.

Laurens even insisted on frisking the British army's wallet. There were only 1,800 pounds in silver there, Ross declared. The French officer, Noailles, agreed that it was a trifling sum.

"Only?" said Laurens. "A subject of one of the world's great monarchs may think eighteen hundred pounds inconsiderable, but in our new country with its poor currency, this means a great deal indeed."

Laurens promptly pauperized Cornwallis's army by putting the silver on the list to be surrendered.

Ross and Laurens both continued to be ungiving, tough negotiators. The talks, pugnacious and relentless, extended into the evening, then through the evening into the night until twelve A.M. when Laurens and Noailles turned the draft over to a staff to refine and have ready for Washington and Barras to sign. It was now the morning of the 19th.

Washington promptly read the agreement, wrote "granted" beside ten of the fourteen provisions, and disallowed four: He would grant no immunity to the Loyalists, he would grant no immunity to American deserters who had joined the British army, he insisted that British civilian merchants were prisoners of war, and he required Cornwallis to care for his own sick and wounded.

With those changes he sent the revised document to Cornwallis with the admonition "that I expected to have them signed at eleven o'clock and that the garrison would march out at two o'clock."[11]

Sometime after eleven, Cornwallis and Capt. Thomas Symonds, the senior British naval officer present, returned the articles with their signatures of approval. Symonds was the captain of the burned *Charon;* his disagreement with Benedict Arnold over the division of plunder was now in dispute.

Washington was waiting, appropriately enough, in redoubt ten, which Colonel Hamilton had captured just a few days before. Washington added to the document: "Done in the trenches before Yorktown, in Virginia, October 19, 1781," with his signature, "G. Washington." The document was then submitted to General Rochambeau for the French army and Admiral de Barras for the French navy in place of de Grasse, who was ill with asthma. Both signed. The Battle of Yorktown was over.

With the articles of capitulation fully executed, the British and German sentries stood down and left their posts as contingents of allied troops entered the town and took possession of it, magazines and storehouses included.

At noon, Ebenezer Denny, the youngest ensign in the Pennsylvania Line, was chosen to plant the regimental flag atop the captured fortifications.

"All is quiet," he wrote. "Articles of capitulation signed. Detachments of French and Americans take possession of British forts. Major [James] Hamilton commanded a battalion which took possession of a fort immediately opposite our right and on the bank of York River. I carried the standard of our regiment. . . . On entering the fort, Baron Steuben, who accompanied us, took the standard from me and planted it himself."[12]

General von Steuben did more than "take" the standard and plant it on top of the enemy's works. Although he was commander-in-chief of the division of which the 2nd Pennsylvania Battalion of Wayne's Brigade was a part, he grievously offended Col. Richard Butler, head of that battalion, by preempting the Pennsylvanians' honor in planting their own regimental flag. Only the intervention of Washington and Rochambeau together prevented a duel between the hot-tempered Irishman and the stubborn German.[13]

Hessian Johann Doehla summed up the feeling of many British and Hessian troops: "I for my part had indeed just cause to thank my God that He was my Protector, mighty Helper, and Deliverer, who had so graciously preserved my life throughout the siege, and had guarded my body and all its members from sickness, wounds and every enemy shot. Oh how many 1,000 cannon balls I have escaped, with danger of my life hanging before my eyes!"[14]

The allies prepared for the next event, at two P.M. The army of Cornwallis, colors furled, musicians playing only British or German marches, was to come trooping out of their ruined fortifications onto the field and there lay down their arms.

October 19, 1781, was a bright, warm day when the trees were beginning to turn to autumn colors. The British surrender in Yorktown and across the river, in Gloucester, took place simultaneously.

Onto the plain where the surrender was to occur, the allied army marched out first.

George Washington by James Peale,
after Charles Wilson Peale, 1787–1790.

On the left side of Hampton Road, the French, seemingly able to produce refulgence required for any occasion, were gorgeous in purples and greens, and roses and crimsons and yellows, piping scrubbed white, splendidly accoutered in spotless uniforms and black gaiters, marching precisely in crisp cadence to their jubilant regimental bands, glowing with glory and celebrating the quintessential battle that could not have been won without them. Soon in their grasp would be those British regimental banners, the true spoils of war, to be carried back to the throne room in Versailles and there cheered and crowed over. The antidote for all those past insults: delicious, incomparable, intoxicating, addictive revenge.

On the right side, the Americans, looking as miscellaneous as a clothing sale, clapped together all anyhow and whatnot, most of the militia in their everyday working rags, accompanied by their fife and drums, were more threadbare in every way, including their marching and their music, but these were the true heroes who, despite unforgivable treatment by the Congress and the state legislatures, had stayed the course all through the impossible days of the past six and a half years, stumbling from one defeat after another, losing thousands of comrades from battle wounds, from fever, from starvation, from freezing, to prevail finally over their oppressors. They had proved to be invincible, claiming the one reward they wanted: They could shed their identities as British subjects and now call themselves free American citizens.

The French officer von Closen openly admired them:

> for most of these unfortunate persons were clad in small jackets of white cloth, dirty and ragged, and a number of them were almost barefoot. The British had given them the *nickname* of Yankee-Doodle [Janckey-Dudle]. What does it matter! an intelligent man would say. These people are much more praise-worthy and brave to fight as they do, when they are so poorly supplied with everything.[15]

When the allied troops were lined up and ready for the surrender, their lines made a corridor more than a half-mile long, according to historian Flexner. Others said it was a mile long.[16]

Pushing onto the field were great crowds of spectators who had come—in numbers "equal to the military," according to Dr. Thacher—in carriages and wagons, on horseback, on foot, now seeking to put a famous face to the famous names of their heroes that they had learned by rote. Among the spectators were some of the most powerful leaders of the Tidewater aristocracy.

Von Closen studied the aloof, imperious, slave-owning planters. "The only wonder is how they were ever induced to accept a government founded on perfect equality of rights."[17]

At the head of the American column, patiently, sat George Washington on his white charger, Nelson.

Beside him along the roadway sat his entourage, a number of whom had served under him since the first months of the war, including urbane general of artillery Henry Knox, thirty-one, the 300-pound Bostonian bookseller, and Col. Alexander Hamilton, twenty-six.

Enjoying his day of vindication for the contemptuous surrender terms Clinton imposed on him at Charleston sat Gen. Benjamin Lincoln, fifty-eight. General Daniel Morgan, fifty-five, nearly crippled with arthritis, sat visibly uncomfortable on his horse. Not far away were the iron-willed, fulminating inspector general of the Continental Army, Baron Friedrich Wilhelm Augustus von Steuben, fifty-one, and the slender Gen. Marie Paul Joseph Roch Yves Gilbert du Motier, Marquis de Lafayette, twenty-four. General Mad Anthony Wayne, thirty-six, sat looking at his tattered Pennsylvania Line, proud once more. Audacious Light-Horse Harry Lee, twenty-five, had been sent by General Greene, on the pretext of bearing messages, to observe the historic event; sitting not far from him was Lt. Col. John Laurens, twenty-seven, negotiator of the Yorktown surrender.

Beside them waited many others whose important contributions are remembered only by the historians: chief of engineers Brig. Gen. Marquis Louis Le Bègue de Presle du Portail, sent by Louis XVI in 1777 to the American army in Valley Forge, who had devoted his military engineering skills to West Point and to various battles including Monmouth and culminating at the Yorktown siege; and Brig. Gen. Moses Hazen, forty-eight, Canadian veteran of the Battle of Quebec under Benedict Arnold, leader of the Second Canadian Regiment of Volunteers that fought at Long Island, Brandywine, and Germantown and, during Yorktown, commander of a brigade in Lafayette's Light Infantry Division.

Army doctor James Thacher confided to his diary: "Being on horseback, I anticipate a full share of satisfaction in viewing the various movements in the interesting scene . . . and that vindictive, haughty commander and that . . . army who, by their robberies and murders, have so long been a scourge to our brethren of the Southern states."[18]

Mounted and waiting on the opposite side of the road were the French, headed by Gen. Jean Baptiste Donatien de Vimeur, Comte de Rochambeau, fifty-six, "Papa" to his troops, proudly watching his smartly turned-out French legions form up at this glorious moment for France.

Next to him was charming, urbane Maj. Gen. François-Jean de Beauvoir, Chevalier de Chastellux, fifty-seven, celebrated writer and member of the august French Academy. Drawn up in a row beside them sat Maj. Gen. Antoine-Charles du Houx, Baron de Viomesnil, commander of the Brigade Bourbonnois; his brother, Maj. Gen. Vicomte de Viomesnil, commander of Brigade Soissonois; and Lt. Col. Count Guillaume de Deux-Ponts, commander of the Royal Deux-Ponts Regiment, who led the successful French charge on redoubt nine.

Also eagerly waiting were Chevalier de Menonville, who had planned and created the parallel trenches that pinned Cornwallis against the banks of the York; aide-de-camp to Rochambeau Count Hans Axel "Lars" von Fersen, the handsome Swedish nobleman, a court favorite rumored to be a lover of Marie Antoinette; and Baron Ludwig von Closen, a Bavarian in the Royal Deux-Ponts Regiment who was to leave a valuable journal of the Yorktown campaign.

Testy Adm. Jacques-Melchior Saint Laurent, Comte de Barras, bringer of the French siege guns, mounted on a horse probably for the first time in his life, was startled when the animal squatted and relieved itself, causing him to call out, "Good heavens! I believe my horse is sinking!"[19]

The British army was late.

And now it was evident that there was another insult awaiting the Americans. At the head of the surrendering army rode not General Cornwallis but instead his second in command, the very handsome, very soldierly Irishman, Brig. Gen. Charles O'Hara of the Guards. O'Hara, the illegitimate son of an Irish peer, second Lord Trawley, had compiled a fine military record, and had distinguished himself most recently in the pursuit of Greene to the Dan, and also at Guilford Courthouse, where, twice wounded, he rallied his second battalion of Guards to save the

British from defeat and cause Greene to withdraw, only to learn that his own son had fallen in battle. Here was a hero in every sense, but he was not Cornwallis.

Von Closen described Cornwallis's failure to appear as "the pretext of an indisposition."[20]

Thacher's journal also opined that Cornwallis was "pretending indisposition."

Light-Horse Harry Lee commented that "Cornwallis held himself back from the humiliating scene; obeying sensations which his great character ought to have stifled."[21]

Were Washington and Rochambeau to be denied the capstone of their victory—the sword from Charles Earl Cornwallis, Washington's adversary in so many of his battles, including Long Island and New York, Trenton-Princeton, Brandywine and Monmouth, and most famously here at Yorktown?

O'Hara was met by Count Mathew Dumas, deputized to direct the surrendering troops. General O'Hara asked him to point out General Rochambeau, but as O'Hara rode toward him, sword in hand, Dumas deflected him toward Washington just as Rochambeau himself was pointing Washington out to O'Hara.

It was clear to all that O'Hara was trying to surrender to the French. Dumas told him what he already knew and didn't want to acknowledge, that the commander in chief of the allied forces was General George Washington. O'Hara then turned to Washington and offered his sword, explaining that his commander in chief was indisposed. Washington would take the sword only from Cornwallis and directed O'Hara to his second in command, General Lincoln. Many must have appreciated the fine and unexpected irony of the general who had surrendered the Americans in Charleston now receiving the surrender of the British under the same terms of surrender that had humiliated him at that city.

General Lincoln reached out and touched the sword as a symbolic gesture of surrender received, then indicated that O'Hara was to retain it.

Now he informed O'Hara that the British and German troops were to enter the circle formed by French hussars, a single regiment at a time, and there ground their arms.

All eyes now looked to see the approach of the surrendering army marching out of Yorktown, the survivors of the siege in their British red and their German blue, marching badly to military music played badly, bannerless, sullen, humiliated, defiant to the last, defeated.

Ensign Ebenezer Denny thought the "drums beat as if they did not care how."

Lieutenant William McDowell of the First Pennsylvania thought, "The British prisoners appeared much in liquor."

Dr. Thacher concurred: "A disorderly and unsoldierly conduct, their step was irregular, and their ranks frequently broken."

General Philip Van Cortlandt, commander of the Second New York Regiment, who had distinguished himself for bravery during the siege, said of them: "They performed it with more order than I expected."

M. Claude Blanchard, chief commissary to Rochambeau, observing O'Hara's manipulations with the sword, was incensed by the British behavior: "Throughout the whole *triste cérémonie* the English exhibited morgue [arrogance] and not a little insolence. Above everything else they showed contempt for the Americans."[22]

According to tradition, one of the marches played was an English tune called "The World Turned Upside Down."

As the British soldiers marched between the two ranks, their officers ordered them to look right at the French, pointedly ignoring the Americans. Incensed, General Lafayette called out an order to the American band, which burst out with a spirited version of "Jankey Dudle" to impel the British and Hessian soldiers to turn and look at them.

An officer of the New Jersey Line observed: "The British officers in general behaved like boys who had been whipped at school. Some bit their lips, some pouted, others cried. Their round, brimmed hats were well adapted to the occasion, hiding those faces they were ashamed to show. The foreign regiments [Hessians] made a more military appearance and the conduct of their officers was far more becoming men of fortitude."[23]

The captured troops were astonished by the great size of the allied army. Hessian Johann Doehla gazed "with wonder at the great force of the enemy," while Corporal Popp noted that his people were "staggered by the multitude of those who had besieged us. We were just a guard mounting in comparison with them, and they could have eaten us up with their power."[24]

British Captain Graham, marching with his Highlanders, seethed with resentment:

Drums were beat, but the colors remained in their cases—an idle retaliation for a very idle slight which had been put by our people on the American garrison of Charleston, and the regiments having formed in columns at quarter distance the men laid down their arms.

It is a sorry reminiscence, this. Yet the scene made a deep impression at the moment, for the mortification and unfeigned sorrow of the soldiers will never fade from my memory. A corporal next to me shed tears, and, embracing his firelock, threw it down, saying, "May you never get such a good master."

Nevertheless, to do them justice, the Americans behaved with great delicacy and forbearance, while the French, by what motive actuated I will not pretend to say, were profuse in their protestations of sympathy. . . . When I visited their lines . . . immediately after our parade had been dismissed, I was overwhelmed with the civility of my late enemies.[25]

Johann Doehla said that most of the men in his Bayreuth Regiment were sobbing, as was Colonel Von Seybothen, who marched his troops to the circle where their arms were to be surrendered.

"'Present arms!' he called.

"'Lay down arms!

"'Put off swords and cartridge boxes!'

"As he watched them obey him, tears flowed from his eyes."[26]

The historian Davis commented: "The enemy, one German officer thought, could never understand the grief and rage that shook them—to be here on this field, surrendering to a pack of farmers and shopkeepers."[27]

Their anger came from another source. These men, from some of the best outfits in the British army and fiercely proud of their battle records, had not been defeated on a battlefield; forced to cower behind wooden walls by orders from New York, they had had to passively endure a murderous artillery assault. They came out now not believing they had been beaten, not given a chance to fight their enemy.

Many British soldiers slammed down their weapons, evidently with the intent of breaking the locks. General Lincoln issued a sharp command to stop it.

Sergeant Joseph Plumb Martin: "It was a noble sight to us, and the more so, as it seemed to promise a speedy conclusion to the contest. The British did not make so good an appearance as the German forces, but there was certainly some allowance to be made in their favor. The English felt their honor wounded, the Germans did not greatly care whose hands they were in. The British paid the Americans, seemingly, but little attention as they passed them, but they eyed the French with considerable malice in their countenances."[28]

Von Closen, observing from the French ranks, noted: "In passing between the two armies, [the British soldiers] showed the greatest scorn for the Americans, who, to tell the truth, were eclipsed by our army in splendor of appearance and dress."[29]

In all, O'Hara led some 3,500 men out of Yorktown, which was not the entire British army. A few had been left behind on post, while well over 1,500 lay sick, from wounds or disease, fever mainly.

When the last musket had been pitched onto the pile, the disarmed troops marched back between the same two lines of allied troops. The American soldiers, now fully aware of the insult that had been flung at them, were shouting angry threats, shaking their fists, brandishing their weapons. Both the British and the French officers grew visibly alarmed.

The American Revolution was on the verge of ending there in a nose-biting, groin-kicking brawl. American officers silenced their troops, and the surrendered troops marched back into town without incident.[30]

Washington did not stay through the entire ceremony. He sent a messenger to General O'Hara and other British officers with an invitation, according to European military custom, to dine with him that evening, the first of a series of such ceremonial meals. While the surrender was still in progress, he returned to his headquarters.

Dr. Thacher had the last word on the evasions of Cornwallis. Resenting still the British army's "exalted Opinion of their own military prowess" as they "affected to view the Americans as a contemptible undisciplined rabble," he turned his own contempt on Cornwallis's failure to take his medicine like a man. "But there is no display of magnanimity when a great commander shrinks from the inevitable misfortunes of war; and when it is considered that Lord Cornwallis has frequently appeared in splendid triumph at the head of his army, by which he is almost *adored,* we conceive it incumbent on him cheerfully to participate in their misfortunes and degradations, however humiliating; but it is said he gives himself up entirely to vexation and despair."[31]

Captain Welles of Gimat's Light Infantry in Lafayette's Division seconded Thacher. He wrote to his father: "The most pleasing sight I ever beheld, to see those haughty fellows march out of their strong fortifications and ground their arms."[32]

In Gloucester Point, in a smaller surrender ceremony, matters were much tenser. The commander in chief of that garrison, Lt. Col. Banastre Tarleton, knew that awaiting him lined up rank and file were the Virginia militia, whose tempers were still inflamed by his recent depredations in their state. He didn't have to guess at what would happen to him if they were allowed to get too close. Before coming out of the garrison, he asked French brigadier general Claude Gabriel de Choisy to move the militia unit back while he proffered his sword. Choisy complied; he brought to the ceremony only Colonel Mercer's Virginians and the Duc de Lauzun's French Legion. The surrender went off without incident.

Still not feeling safe, Colonel Tarleton asked General Rochambeau himself for protection, which, reluctantly, the French general gave while privately expressing his opinion of Tarleton: "Colonel Tarleton has no merit as an officer—only that bravery that every Grenadier has—but is a butcher and a barbarian."[33]

Tarleton had every reason to be fearful. There were many Americans nearby who would not have hesitated to kill him. According to the London publication *Ruddiman's Weekly Mercury* of January 30, 1782: "Next day it was evident that Tarleton's alarm had a very justifiable foundation. The bed upon which he was to have slept had been stabbed in several places."[34]

Along with the great pile of muskets flung on the surrender field harum-scarum like jackstraws, the allies also impounded the rest of the weapons that had made Cornwallis so dangerous: 244 field and siege guns. Washington had known many a day when he could have raised cain with such a treasure trove of equipment like that.

But most of all, in terms of humiliation, there among the muskets lay the greatest shame of all: furled inside their cases like captives, twenty-four battle standards, six British and eighteen German.

After the surrender ceremonies, the Americans were particularly astonished at the behavior of the British officers. Casually, as if it were a Sunday afternoon in the park, following European military custom, they strolled into the allied camps, into Rochambeau's and Washington's headquarters, and freely fraternized with their recent enemies in the most amiable manner. In that same European tradition, the victorious officers hosted the defeated officers at a series of dinners and fêtes before final separation.

Yet some American officers, unfamiliar with this European tradition of fraternity between armies, could not forget the past so readily; outraged, they remembered only the arrogance, atrocities, and plundering of the British army.

The Americans also almost came to angry confrontation with the French, who seemed much too sympathetic with the defeated British. Indeed, the Americans were discovering the same aristocratic snobbery that they had come to despise in their former countrymen.

Flexner notes: "According to Commissary Blanchard [Rochambeau's Chief Commissary Officer], the Americans officers were annoyed to the point of a quarrel by the 'civility' their allies showed the enemy and the 'attention' the enemy showed the French."[35] Both the Frenchman Cromdot du Bourg and the American Trumbull also observed this prickliness.

But whatever forgiveness they extended ultimately, the Americans pointedly, deliberately did not invite to any of the American fêtes Lt. Col. Banastre Tarleton.

Yet in all, on this occasion, this supreme moment of victory was too significant to warrant any curbing of joy. That night, an American colonel later recalled, "I noticed that the officers and soldiers could scarcely talk for laughing, and they could scarcely walk for jumping and dancing and singing as they went about."[36]

Sergeant Joseph Plumb Martin took his last $1,200 in nearly worthless paper money and bought himself his own joyful celebration—a pint of rum.[37]

Colonel Richard Butler, commander of the Second Pennsylvania Battalion, celebrated the true significance of the victory in a letter to his friend and fellow Pennsylvanian General William Irvine: "Not a principal officer wounded or killed," he wrote, "and but very few men, and I think I may with propriety now congratulate you, my friend, and the country in general with certain Independence and the pleasing approach of Peace."[38]

On October 21, two days after the surrender, General Sir Henry Clinton set sail from New York with Graves's twenty-seven ships of the line and 7,000 troops.

But, as Lafayette had written to a friend, "The play, sir, is over."[39]

After the surrender the allies entered Yorktown and with wondering eyes discovered what punishment they had poured onto the army inside. On the streets of the town lay cannonballs by the hundred amidst tons of debris. Hardly a single structure had emerged undamaged.

Of the British artillery emplacements, Sergeant Lamb had noted, "not a gun remained on that part of the works attacked by the enemy, scarcely a shell was left."[40]

Baron von Closen noted: "I will never forget how frightful and disturbing was the appearance of the city of York, from the fortifications on the crest to the strand below. One could not take three steps without running into some great holes made by bombs, some splinters, some balls, some half covered trenches, with scattered white or negro arms or legs, [and] some bits of uniforms. Most of the houses [were] riddled by cannon fire, and [there were] almost no window-panes in the houses. Most striking of all was the consternation among the few inhabitants."[41]

Dr. Thacher looked with wonder at the damage and carnage: "Rich furniture and books were scattered over the ground and the carcasses of men and horses half-covered the earth . . . it is difficult to point to a spot where a man could have resorted for safety."

Conditions inside had been near starvation. Even before the battle began there was a critical shortage of food. Then the French navy had blocked any more food coming in from the British navy; the allied armies stopped any food from arriving by land for men and horses. A British soldier noted that for provisions they got putrid ship's meat and wormy biscuits.

Disease had struck. Smallpox killed many troops and civilians; more became ill with the bloody flux and died. So many of his troops were sick that Cornwallis had pressed into service large numbers of slaves to help in the construction of his redoubts. For many of them their only pay was death by smallpox.[42]

Ensign Denny took note of the human suffering: "Negroes lie about, sick and dying, in every stage of the small pox." He also observed with disgust the number of unexploded American shells that "did not burst as expected."

The siege had inflicted more than 500 casualties, dead and wounded. In the British hospital over 1,500 men lay, down with wounds or disease or both. Each day more died.

Now the allies could also see why Cornwallis had abandoned those redoubts before the siege had begun. Expecting relief from Clinton daily, he spared his dwindling troops the job of dying in defense of redoubts that they were to abandon shortly anyway. Instead he had them huddling behind their wooden walls, waiting for relief that never came.

Stephen Popp, the twenty-two-year-old German mercenary from Bayreuth, described it all graphically in his diary:

> Their heavy fire forced us to throw our tents in the ditches. The enemy threw bombs, one hundred, one hundred fifty, two hundred pounders; their guns were eighteen, twenty-four and forty-eight pounders. We could find no refuge in or out of the town. The people fled to the waterside and hid in hastily contrived shelters on the banks, but many of them were killed by bursting bombs. More than eighty were thus lost, besides many wounded, and their houses utterly destroyed. Our ships suffered, too, under the heavy fire, for the enemy fired in one day thirty-six hundred shot from their heavy guns and batteries. Soldiers and sailors deserted in great numbers. The Hessian Regiment von Bose lost heavily, although it was in our rear in the second line, but in full range of the enemy's fire. Our two regiments lost very heavily too. The Light Infantry posted at an angle had the worst position and the heaviest loss. Sailors and marines all served in defending our lines on shore.[43]

Nearly crippled with gout, the elderly Thomas Nelson, onetime secretary of the Virginia council, had been in his handsome house "in the skirt of the town" when General Cornwallis commandeered it for his headquarters. Both men had been inside the house while cannonballs smashed large parts of it. As Cornwallis evacuated the building for the safety of a bunker, he permitted "Mr. Secretary" to hobble out of the rubbled town under a flag of truce to the allied lines. The next day, the Secretary dined with a fellow Virginian, St. George Tucker. Tucker recorded the elder Nelson's observations:

> Two officers were killed and one wounded by a bomb the evening we opened. Lord Chewton's cane was struck out of his hand by a cannon ball. Lord Cornwallis has built a kind of grotto at the foot of the Secretary's garden where he lives underground. A Negro of the Secretary's was killed in his house.[44]

The old secretary's nephew, Thomas Nelson Jr., then governor of Virginia and general of the Virginia militia as well as a signer of the Declaration, had solemnly watched from the allied side as his own splendid mansion had been ball-battered along with his uncle's.

The surviving storekeepers and businessmen, having been mercilessly looted by the British, now hastily boarded up their shops against the expected waves of American looters, while the American quartermasters and commissaries braced themselves against the price gouging of supplies by civilians.

Colonel Butler of the Pennsylvania Line said of the British, "They have completely plundered everything in their power and do not pay the least regard to any treaty." Allowing for bias, the statement must have had some merit. Dr. Thacher, uniformly reliable in his reportage, opined that the British army, during the six-month campaign in Virginia, had looted property worth three million pounds sterling. If he was includling the joyful smash-and-grab binge of Benedict Arnold, as well as those of Phillips and Cornwallis, there may have been much merit in his number.

As mandated by military custom, that night Washington fêted General Charles O'Hara of the Guards and some of his officers with a dinner.

M. Claude Blanchard, chief commissary to Rochambeau, noted icily in his journal that military etiquette required Cornwallis to attend, but he had declined to dine with Washington that evening because of an "indisposition." Yet he readily accepted a dinner invitation from M. de Viomesnil that same evening.[45]

General O'Hara seems to have participated with a benign dignity and perhaps something beyond that. General Rochambeau, who was present and used to such affairs, nonetheless was struck by the "sang froid and gaiety even" of O'Hara and fellow English officers at dinner.[46]

Washington, still beset with many duties, did what he had done during the surrender ceremonies: He withdrew early from the banquet and, with his aides, colonels Trumbull and Laurens, retired to his headquarters to write the official "Victory" report to the Congress.

On the next night, the 20th, General Rochambeau also gave a dinner for General O'Hara, who was fluent in French, and to his officers. And again allied officers were struck by O'Hara's cheerfulness, apparently indifferent to the defeat he had just suffered. Banastre Tarleton was invited despite Rochambeau's contempt for him.

And when on that same day Rochambeau visited General Cornwallis in his quarters, the earl seemed to have recovered from his indisposition, whatever it may have been, for he received Rochambeau cordially. Later, after Cornwallis explained that he and his army were impoverished, the French general sent Cornwallis a loan of £150,000 in silver. Evidently the British government was a better credit risk than the Congress. It had the power of taxation.

In fact, Cornwallis became so social that he attended many dinners in Yorktown given by the French, and with great charm and the poise of an aristocrat, he discussed his campaigns in America, recognizing that even the British victories in the Carolinas contributed little.

The British behaved throughout as though the French deserved all the credit for the victory at Yorktown. Rochambeau, in his posthumous memoirs, was to claim Yorktown as a total French victory.

At dinner one night, General O'Hara told the French in a whisper so loud the Americans clearly heard him that he was glad he had not been captured by the Americans, implying that it would have been a barbaric experience.

Lafayette, overhearing him, said that obviously O'Hara did not like encores, a clear reference to O'Hara's capture at Saratoga.

Three very sensitive points were at issue. First of all, O'Hara was saying that he did not recognize his surrender to General Washington, that he had in effect—and as he tried to do during the surrender ceremony—surrendered to the French.

The second sensitive point at issue was the "convention army" from Saratoga. General Gates had concluded a surrender "by convention" with General Burgoyne that permitted the entire British army to return home with the stipulation that they were never again to bear arms against the Americans. But Congress, on the grounds of frangibility, contended that the returning troops, while technically not bearing arms again against America, could, by returning to duty in Britain, free other troops to come fight in America. Congress also accused General Howe, who was insisting that captured troops be sent home through a port controlled by the British, of intending to actually keep them on duty in America. Burgyone also made some unfortunate remark about "the public faith is broke." On those grounds, Congress set the surrender aside; Burgoyne's convention army was put in an American prison camp, including General O'Hara and General Phillips. Both sides had been quarreling about the issue ever since.

The third issue was even more sensitive. This was the treatment of prisoners of war. The Americans had been protesting vehemently about the "barbaric British practice" of putting Americans on prison ships, where they literally died like flies. This was in marked contrast to the convention army and other British prisoners, who were alive and well in prisoner of war camps in Virginia and Maryland. In contrast, Lincoln's surrendered army in Charleston, captured more than a year earlier, had been put on prison hulks, and most of them were now long since dead.

Lafayette could also have pointed out that, speaking of barbaric experience, in contrast with the six-year binge of rape, rapine, looting, murder, and burning by both British troops and their officers of rebels and Loyalists alike, not one French solider or officer, in their long march from New York to Yorktown, made off with so much as a teaspoon, harmed not a hair on any woman's head, and used their matches for lighting their pipes only.

In all, an uneasy friendship existed between the French and Americans, which foreshadowed the complete division between them that occurred during the peace conferences in Paris. Had he been prescient, Lafayette could have foreseen that many of his titled countrymen seated so mirthfully around O'Hara and his staff were destined for the guillotine.

Washington's most pressing order of business was to write to the Congress. He had to feel some astonishment at penning this report of his victory over the British, for he knew that the events that led two navies and four armies to Yorktown had come about only by the wildest strokes of fate.

As he wrote his report, Washington was profoundly aware of how close the colonies had come to losing, how close his neck had come to feeling the hangman's noose, a thought to carry for the rest of his life. He knew also that America could not have won without the French—the French army, the French navy, and French gold. He also had no illusions about the autocratic Louis XVI, whose motive was not to create a new republic in America but to wreak revenge on his hated rival, George III.

This had to be the most joyful letter he had ever written.

"I have the Honor to inform Congress," Washington wrote, "that a Reduction of the British Army under the Command of Lord Cornwallis, is most happily effected. The unremitting Ardor which actuated every Officer and Soldier in the combined Army of this Occasion, has principally led to this Important Event, at an earlier period than my most sanguine Hope had induced me to expect." So went the first and most important paragraph of his detailed report.

Washington informed Congress that the total number of British officers and men surrendered on October 19 was 7,247 soldiers and 840 seamen. British casualties were nearly 500: 156 killed, 326 wounded, over 1,500 sick or unfit for duty. American losses were 20 killed and 56 wounded; French, 52 killed and 134 wounded. The number of allied sick was 1,430.[47]

To carry the victory dispatch to France, General Rochambeau chose not one but two honorees. Facing the uncertainties of the midwinter Atlantic—and the ubiquitousness of the British navy—he felt that at least one would make it all the way to Paris. His choices were the Duc de Lauzun, for his defeat of Tarleton, and the Comte des Deux-Ponts, for his capture of redoubt nine.

Lauzun disagreed with him. He felt that M. de Charlus should be given the honor of carrying the message. Rochambeau insisted. He told Lauzun that he had been chosen to carry the news to France because he had distinguished himself on the battlefield.

Lauzun still demurred. He again urged Rochambeau to send M. de Charlus, son of one of Rochambeau's detractors, M. Castries, the very powerful head of the French navy. "I advised him to send M. de Charlus, by which he would make his peace with M. Castries, and perhaps secure the better treatment for his army. I could not persuade him; he said to me that I had been first in action and to me it fell to carry the news; Count William de Deux-Ponts, the second, and should carry the details of it."[48]

Rochambeau explained to the French minister of war why he had chosen these two soldiers: "They are the two officers of rank who have most distinguished themselves."

Lauzun and Deux-Ponts sailed for France on separate vessels. "I embarked," the Duc de Lauzun recorded, "on the king's frigate *La Surveillante,* and after a passage of twenty-two days, arrived at Brest and went up to Versailles without loss of time."

A few days later, the Comte des Deux-Ponts embarked on *Andromaque* to carry the duplicates and the favors requested for the army. Several army officers seized the opportunity to return to France, "and we who remained wrote reams and sent extracts from the newspapers, among others the summary of M. de Grasse's campaign until the end of the siege of York."

As will be seen, the choice of the two messengers was to have political consequences that lasted more than ten years and ended only with the bloodletting of the French Revolution.

General Cornwallis wrote to his commanding officer, Sir Henry Clinton, the next day, and he adopted an accusatory tone from the start. It reads like an indictment of Clinton's failures:

York Town, Virginia, Oct. 20th, 1781.

Sir—I have the mortification to inform your Excellency that I have been forced to give up the posts of York and Gloucester, and to Surrender the troops under my command, by capitulation on the 19th instant, as prisoners of war to the combined forces of America and France.

I never saw this post in a very favorable light; but when I found I was to be attacked in it, in so unprepared a state, by so powerful an army and artillery, nothing but the hopes of relief would have induced me to attempt its defence; for I would either have endeavored to escape to New York by rapid marches from the Gloucester side, immediately on the arrival of General Washington's troops at Williamsburgh, or, I would, notwithstanding the disparity of numbers, have attacked them in the open field, where it might have been just possible that fortune would have favored the gallantry of the handful of troops under my command. But, being assured by your excellency's letters that every possible means would be tried by the navy and army to relieve us, I could not think myself at liberty to venture upon either of those desperate attempts; therefore, after remaining for two days in a strong position in front of this place, in hopes of being attacked, upon observing that the enemy were taking measures which could not fail of turning my left flank in a short time, and receiving on the second evening your letter of the 24th of September, that the relief would fall about the 5th of October, I withdrew within the works on the night of the 29th of September, hoping by the labor and firmness of the soldiers to protect the defence until you could arrive. Everything was to be expected from the spirit of the troops; but every disadvantage attended their labor, as the work was to be continued under the enemy's fire, and our stock of entrenching tools, which did not much exceed four hundred when we began to work in the latter end of August, was now much diminished.

The earl then wrote a number of pages detailing the operations of the allies as they built their parallels and attacked his fortifications to compel his surrender.

Under these circumstances, I thought it would have been wanton and inhuman to the last degree to sacrifice the lives of this small body of gallant soldiers, who had ever behaved with so much fidelity and courage, by exposing them to an assault which, from the numbers and precautions of the enemy, could not fail to succeed. I therefore proposed to capitulate.[49]

Cornwallis finished by praising the men under him and enclosed a copy of the Articles of Capitulation. His tone left no doubt about where he felt the blame belonged for the debacle at Yorktown.

On that same day, Col. Banastre Tarleton encountered yet another mis-adventure. A Virginia horse trainer by the name of Day with a sweet gum stick in his hand "as thick as a man's wrist" stopped Tarleton in the mid-dle of the roadway and demanded that he dismount and relinquish the horse he had stolen from Day's employer. Watched now by a jeering crowd, Tarleton, having galloped into American history with his dripping saber, would now have limped out of American history on foot, his name ever an anathema on American lips, had not a French officer loaned him his groom's horse.

Although most of the British officers were allowed to go home rather than to prison camp, the articles stipulated that one officer should go to prison camp for each fifty enlisted men. The choice was made by casting lots.

Captain Graham noted glumly in his diary: "It fell to my lot to be one of the captains of the 76th detailed to remain with the soldiers."[50]

The British troops were permitted a few days' rest, then, guarded by militia, marched off with a number of their officers to prison camps in Winchester, Virginia, and Frederick, Maryland.

Captain Graham related an incident that occurred along the way to camp: Accompanying their troops to prison camp through Ashby's Gap, several British officers found Mrs. Ashby's tavern and bespoke dinner.

She didn't recognize their uniforms.

"A militiaman, I guess?"

"No," said the officer.

"Continental, mayhap?"

Another negative.

"Oho!" she exclaimed. "I see; you are one of the sarpints—one of old 'Wallis's men. Well now, I have two sons; one was at the catching of Johnny Burgoyne, and the other at that of you, and next year they are both going to catch Clinton in New York. But you shall be treated kindly; my mother came from the old country."[51]

On October 24 the British fleet arrived off Cape Charles. Small craft were put over the side to seek out the news from Yorktown.

By early morning, three British soldiers had been found and brought onboard Graves's flagship. They reported that they had escaped from Yorktown on the 18th, the day after the earl called for surrender negotiations. They had not heard any firing since then.

Clinton and Graves spent the next five days cruising up and down through heavy seas. Small boats busily gathered more bad news. Many sources confirmed that Yorktown had surrendered. But by now they had more direct evidence. Lookouts could clearly see de Grasse's huge fleet at anchor in Lynnhaven Bay. On the 29th, after another council of war, the fleet turned away and sailed back to New York.

Sir Henry now had to write the most difficult letter of his life—and the most shocking letter of the war—to his superior in London, Lord George Germain, secretary of state for the American colonies. Hanging over his head like a baleful cloud was the memory of Gen. Thomas Gage's similar letter six and a half years before from Boston, in which he had to explain his incredible defeat at Lexington/Concord, losing in one day one-tenth of the king's army. General Clinton's assignment was even more difficult—he had to explain the probable loss of thirteen entire colonies.

After sending the letter, he had not much else to do but return to his endless planning of campaigns while hoping the king would send him another army. He must have sensed that wasn't likely. The Americans had won.

A young Lieutenant Revel, in de Grasse's fleet, put the British defeat in a French metaphor: "On October 27 the British Fleet appeared at the entrance of the Capes and thirty-one sail were counted on that day. Forty-four sail were counted on the next day; and then on the 29th they had all disappeared. . . . We learned later that Admiral Graves had brought with him from New York the Army under Clinton to succor Lord Cornwallis—*mais il était trop tard. La Poule était mangée.*"[52]

On the 29th, the chicken had indeed been eaten.

Nine

The World Reacts

Williamsburg

Williamsburg needed no post rider to announce the surrender. Many of the residents had ridden in carriages and wagons and on horseback the twelve miles to Yorktown to witness the actual ceremonies.

The town was in ruins and dying. Plundered and gutted by Benedict Arnold, then plucked to the bones by Cornwallis, it was too vulnerable to sea attacks. A few years before, Williamsburg had yielded its role as Virginia's capital to Richmond.

Williamsburg was now a city with a history and no future. Instead, for more than 150 years, it would crumble into genteel decay until it was restored as a historic site in the 1930s.

Still unsure, the residents were asking each other the same unanswerable question: Is it over—the war, the fighting? Are the British going home? Are we free?

The celebration meant little to the slaves other than the festivities themselves. Many suffered terribly during the Revolution, especially in the Carolinas, where want and poverty and fever shrank their numbers. Many more young black men, pressed by Cornwallis to build Yorktown's fortifications, died from festering wounds and fever, abuse and starvation.

In his first draft of the Declaration of Independence, in a paragraph that suggests the pot calling the kettle black, Thomas Jefferson put the blame for the flourishing slave trade squarely on George III's shoulders. Adams and Franklin removed it.

Patrick Henry, having owned slaves, deplored slavery, calling it a lamentable evil. So did George Mason, whose plantation was built by slaves. But they were in a tiny minority. When Jefferson introduced into the Virginia legislature a measure to permit manumission of slaves, he was surrounded by furious faces bellowing "Traitor!" at him while enraged hands flung the bill out of the legislative doors. The voice of humanity and high principle had collided with the grasping fist of economic gain. The results

214

were predictable. Jefferson summed up the slavery problem in words that were to haunt the South until the Civil War: "We have a wolf by the ears and dare not let go."

Despite the opposition, slavery continued because the Southern tobacco, rice, and indigo economy demanded it, while the invention of the cotton gin was to intensify it vastly. The South was to prove deaf to all remonstrance for another eighty years, while the slave population was to grow eightfold to four million by 1860.

Few seemed to notice the great irony of a free people dancing in the streets while slaves looked on like mute remonstrances.

Mount Vernon

At Mount Vernon, a post rider came galloping up the long drive bearing a letter from General Henry Knox to his wife, Lucy, pregnant with their fourth child, and a welcome guest of Martha Washington. They had been waiting for news ever since Washington and his French army guests had ridden off to besiege Yorktown.

Martha watched Lucy open the envelope, watched the great joy that spread across her face as she read the message aloud, shrilly, with mounting enthusiasm. General Knox announced that he was proud that "I might be the first to communicate good news to the charmer of my soul. A glorious moment for America! This day Lord Cornwallis and his army march out and pile their arms in the face of our victorious army."

In less than two months, on December 10, Lucy Knox was to celebrate the victorious year with the delivery of a son. George Washington was to be the godfather.[1]

Philadelphia

For the signal honor of carrying the historic victory dispatch to the Continental Congress in Philadelphia, General Washington selected Lt. Col. Tench Tilghman, his military secretary. He set off by sailboat from Yorktown for Philadelphia on what became a mini-odyssey that rivaled Paul Revere's alarm-spreading ride from Boston and Caesar Rodney's fever-racked overnight ride from Dover, Delaware, to Philadelphia to provide the key signature for the adoption of the Declaration of Independence.

Urged to make haste, Lt. Col. Tilghman, barely recovered from malaria, started out sick. He sailed down the York River, past the French flotilla, and turned north up the Chesapeake, where he encountered maddeningly weak winds. Then the inept skipper of the craft ran aground off Tangier Island, where they waited the entire night for the tide to float them free. He fumed at the continuing weak winds that puffed the craft so slowly northward. Thirty miles below Annapolis, still more than 100 miles from Philadelphia, the winds stopped entirely. They were becalmed.

The colonel finally broke out of the doldrums south of Annapolis and sailed to Rock Hall on the eastern shore of Maryland, only to have his fever flare up as he went looking for a horse.

At the nearest farmhouse he cried out, "A horse for the Congress! Cornwallis is taken!" They stared at him in disbelief. Some suspected him of being a madman. Only after impassioned pleadings did he get a mount from their stables. Refusing to rest, he started out for Philadelphia, making his way by swapping blown horses for fresh ones and all along the way causing many to regard him as a madman babbling the impossible as he shouted the same message over and over: "Cornwallis is taken. A horse for the Congress."

Sometime after three A.M. on October 22, he came pelting into Philadelphia, exhausted, every muscle aching and trembling with fever, riding a spent horse.

He cantered up to the front door of the home of the president of the Continental Congress, Thomas McKean.

At first Tilghman thought he was too late. Two days before, on October 20, sometime after midnight, an express rider from Baltimore had paced into Philadelphia and hurried to President McKean's home. Sent by Thomas Sim Lee, governor of Maryland, he had carried with him a copy of a letter Lee had received from Admiral de Grasse. On the cover were the words "To be forwarded by night and by day with the utmost dispatch—Lord Cornwallis surrendered the garrison of York to General Washington, the 17th October [the day Cornwallis offered to surrender; the official instrument of surrender was signed on October 19]."

The town watch had found that post rider pounding on a window shutter and shouting that Cornwallis had been taken. He decided the rider was drunk and was arresting him when McKean opened his shutter to hear the most joyful news of his life. As a signer of the Declaration, President McKean had spent the war years on the run with his eleven children, evading the British army.

Tradition says the town watch, in a heavy German accent, resumed his patrol of the streets crying: "Basht dree o'glock, und Cornwal-lis isht da-ken."[2]

So while Tilghman was not the first with the news, the first report was treated with such skepticism that the Congress had been waiting impatiently for irrefutable official word from Washington. And that, Tilghman held in his feverish hand.

* * *

The city was quickly roused to near-hysterical joy. Church bells through-out the city chimed. The great Liberty Bell in the State House—later Independence Hall—that had pealed daylong on July 8, 1775, to cele-brate the signing of the Declaration of Independence now tolled without stop until dawn. Crowds with candles and lanterns, shouting and sing-ing, beating on pots, firing muskets, and playing musical instruments, thronged onto the dark streets. Many ran to their churches, while Presi-dent McKean sent messengers to the residences and inns of the mem-bers of the Congress to rouse them from their beds to read Washington's official victory dispatch.

The *Journal of the Continental Congress* was typically terse:

> A letter, of 19, from General Washington, was read, giving information of the reduction of the British army under the command of the Earl of Cornwallis, on the 19th instant with a copy of the articles of capitulation.

Charles Thomson, secretary of the Continental Congress since its inception in 1774, with all eyes upon him, opened the letter and to a silent Congress read Washington's opening words that would be repeated for generations: "I have the Honor to inform Congress, that a Reduction of the British Army under the Command of Lord Cornwallis, is most happily effected. The unremitting Ardor which actuated every Officer and Soldier in the combined Army of this Occasion, has principally led to this Important Event, at an earlier period than my most sanguine Hope had induced me to expect."

The Congress sat attentively as they heard the full story of Cornwal-lis's fall. Now even the skeptics were convinced that the incredible was true: Cornwallis had indeed surrendered his entire army, more than 7,000 men.

The Congress completed their resolution:

> Whereupon, On motion of Mr. [Edmund] Randolph, seconded by [name not supplied by Congressional secretary Charles Thomson]:
>
> Resolved, That Congress will, at two o'clock this day, go in procession to the Dutch Lutheran Church, and return thanks to Almighty God, for crowning the allied arms of the United States and France, with success, by the surrender of the whole British army under the command of the Earl of Cornwallis.[3]

Lieutenant Colonel Tilghman had arrived penniless. To cover all his expenses—of hiring post horses, hiring a boat to sail the Chesapeake Bay, and more—Congress looked into the general coffers and found them empty.

Elias Boudinot, a wealthy congressman from New Jersey and a past president of the Continental Congress, recorded the ironic truth in his diary: "It was necessary to furnish him with hard money for his expenses. There was not a sufficiency in the treasury to do it, and the members of Congress, of which I was one, each paid a dollar to accomplish it."[4] The money was enough to pay room and board for the fever-ridden colonel during his recovery.

After sending the exhausted Tilghman off to bed, the Congress turned back to business; joy changed to a quivering rage—at Cornwallis, at Tarleton, at Wemyss, and at the Philadelphia native Christian Huck and the brutal savagery of the British army in the Carolinas.

Furious voices were raised, green baize tables pounded. Arthur Middleton of South Carolina, shaking with anger, his memory filled with the British butchering of his state, demanded that the Congress pass a resolution to order General Washington to hang Cornwallis at once, right there on a gibbet in Yorktown. There were other British officers he also had in mind.

A violent quarrel broke out. Cornwallis couldn't be hanged; he was protected by the terms of surrender that had been signed by three armies. Washington's reputation would be destroyed.

But Cornwallis could be detained, insisted Mr. Middleton, prevented from escaping on the next ship to London, his crimes unpunished.

Elias Boudinot, delegate from New Jersey, recorded the fury of the debate: "This motion was strongly advocated by a very large party in the House, and the prospect of its success greatly alarmed many moderate Members of Congress—Mr. Duane and Myself opposed it with all our powers, as contrary to all good faith, having entered into a Capitulation with him, after the facts committed, & having knowledge of them.—That it would Expose our Commander in Chief to the necessity of resigning his Command or forfeiting his Honor & Reputation etc etc etc."

The anger raged on without stop. "The debate," Boudinot observed, "continued several Day's."[5]

Several days. Not hours. Days. Catharsis—it had come at last. The anger after more than six years of British army depredations had finally boiled over into an ecstasy of hatred. Hour after hour, the delegates waited on line to stand and bellow their rage, as though their voices could carry 3,000 miles across the sea to the ears of the hated monarch.

These furious voices were driven by the memories of six years of rape and murder, pillaging and burning, of that sadistic scathing aristocratic British contempt for the "colonials," of the terrible pain the British had visited on hundreds of thousands—on men, women, and children alike—at the multitudinous graves throughout all the states that had been filled by the redcoated horror, of a country deliberately and systematically destroyed.

The time had come to let it all out—time for a recitation of British crimes, of broken hearts, raped women, smashed families, ruined lives, wrecked businesses, burnt barns and homes, slaughtered animals, millions upon millions of pounds of stolen and destroyed property. The names of Gage and Howe and Clinton, Burgoyne and O'Hara, Cornwallis, Tarleton—these were bellowed over and over until hoarseness claimed their voices.

Cornwallis couldn't simply be allowed to sign a piece of paper and sail home unscathed, beyond justice. He and his cohorts must be made to pay somehow. Victory, it was apparent, was not enough. Freedom by itself didn't compensate. Congress wanted vengeance. They wanted to ride down to Yorktown and watch the hangings, hear the snapping of necks—see the humiliators humiliated, see them pay with their own lives.

Despite the opposition of the moderate delegates, a vote was forced. The Congress's Journal recorded what happened next.

"A motion was made by Mr. [Arthur] Middleton seconded by Mr. [Isaac] Motte.

"That General Washington be directed to detain Earl Cornwallis, and the officers captured in the garrisons of York and Gloucester, till the further order of Congress."

Congress then voted on the motion.

Massachusetts, Rhode Island, Connecticut, New Jersey, Pennsylvania, Maryland, Virginia, and North Carolina all voted no. Georgia's vote was split.

Only South Carolina voted yes.

So it passed into the negative.
Adjourned to 10 o'clock tomorrow.

Nineteen congressmen had voted no; four, ay. Surprisingly, even North Carolina, which had good cause to hate Cornwallis, Tarleton, and his cohorts, voted no. With the exception of Mr. Jones of Georgia, South Carolina was alone. Despite the writhing anger of the South Carolina delegates, Earl Cornwallis would sail unpunished.[6]

The vote must have been much closer than the final count indicates. Evidently, a number of Congressmen who initially would have voted to hang Cornwallis were persuaded finally to vote against the bill out of respect for Washington. But for the moderate voices, "fighting with all our powers," who finally calmed many of the delegates down, Cornwallis would have ended his days dangling from a rope in Yorktown.

It is to be regretted that no one recorded those speeches, for they would give us a true, voice-top sense of the terrible price exacted and paid for the freedom they passed down to us. What reading they would make. What a warning.

* * *

At two o'clock in the afternoon, with the unceasing clamor of celebration ringing throughout the city, the Reverend Mr. George Duffield, a Presbyterian minister, led the Continental Congress, the Pennsylvania Supreme Executive Council, and the Pennsylvania Assembly in procession out of the State House onto Chestnut Street and through the city streets to the Dutch Lutheran Church.

Reverend Duffield, forty-nine, from the Old Pine Street Presbyterian Church, which the British had used for a stable, was an ideal choice to give thanks to God for the victory. A fiery preacher for American independence, in addition to being one of two chaplains of the Continental Congress, he was also chaplain of the Pennsylvania militia and for a time had served in the Continental Army. When he joined as a chaplain, he led into the army with him sixty men from his congregation, thirty-five of whom served as officers, including Gen. John Steele, who was Washington's aide-de-camp and also officer of the day at Yorktown when Cornwallis surrendered. Reverend Duffield had spent much of the war with a price on his head and had almost been captured during the Battle of Trenton.

Among the other notables who crowded into the church were the minister of France and his secretary and a great number of Philadelphia's most prominent citizens. Looking down on an acre of smiling faces, the Reverend Duffield, noted as a fervent extemporaneous preacher much praised by John Adams, conducted services to "return thanks to Almighty God for crowning the allied arms of the United States and France with success."

Later, Congress, back in its chambers and calmer now, passed resolutions of thanks to the army, authorized the erection of a monument at Yorktown, and voted Lieutenant Colonel Tilghman a horse, saddle, bridle, and sword. It also issued a resolution calling for a grand illumination of the city for that evening.

On this extraordinary day, the Congress could look back on its extraordinary—its improbable—history with both awe and self-respect. From September 5, 1774, the day the First Continental Congress met in Carpenter's Hall, to September 3, 1783, when the Treaty of Paris was signed, the Continental Congress had compiled a remarkable record, both good and bad. It had sat at various times in Baltimore, Lancaster, York, Princeton, Annapolis, and Trenton. But except for the two years of British occupation, 1777–1778, it met for most of those years in Independence Hall (originally the Pennsylvania State House) in Philadelphia.

During that time Congress was often guilty of the worst political jobbery, dereliction, skullduggery, bribery, self-service, and cowardice. There were some congressmen who committed treason by taking bribes from the French. Mixed in with the true patriots and statesmen were scalawags and intriguers, incompetents and liars. At their worst moments the congressmen could easily be likened to a crew on a leaking ship selling the bilge pumps.

In particular, the Congress compiled a dismal record handling the army. It practically starved its troops and failed them repeatedly in many other ways, cynically making promises and cynically breaking them. While derelict in its own duties, it intruded on Washington's authority and, over his stern objections, appointed favorites of the moment like Gen. Robert Howe, who lost Savannah, General Lincoln, who lost Charleston and an entire army, and General Gates, who lost Camden and another entire army before fleeing from the battlefield, making the American army the jest of Europe.

With good cause, Washington's generals had a scathing contempt for the gang in Philadelphia, particularly the perennial troublemakers like Sam Adams, Richard Henry Lee, and Thomas Mifflin—the incompetence of the latter, many commentators agree, causing the suffering during the starvation winter at Valley Forge. General Nathanael Greene regarded Congress as nothing short of a debating society: "The Congress have so many of those talking gentlemen among them that they tire themselves and everybody else with their long labored speeching that is calculated more to display their own talents than to promote the public interest."[7]

Yet without the Congress, the revolution would have sputtered and died. Its moments of courage, its remarkable deeds, more than offset its flaws. It courageously created itself in 1774; declared the thirteen colonies free and independent of Britain by issuing the Declaration of Independence; created the Articles of Confederation; created the United States Army, Navy, and Marine Corps; created the diplomatic service; negotiated with foreign governments; signed treaties such as the one with Louis XVI, without which the new nation could not have prevailed over George III; created a post office and a national bank; issued money; provided a mechanism for the intercourse between and among the former colonies, which were almost as hostile toward each other as they were toward England; and created many constitutional elements that were later to appear in the federal constitution of 1789 under which the United States lives today. And these are just some of its highlights.

Many of its flaws and shortcomings can be attributed to its lack of powers, especially taxation.

Serving in Congress was hardly the road to riches. Many, like President Thomas McKean, served without pay. Many, with their guiding hands absent from home, watched their businesses falter toward collapse and even fail. More than half lost property to looters or vandals. Others were thrown in prison; others fled for their lives; still others saw family members persecuted.[8]

Just simply serving in Congress was an act of courage, for it could easily have been the road to the rope. Every one of the 342 men who served at different times in the Continental Congress knew that if the army collapsed, they were gallows bait. And on more than one occasion the army did come close to collapsing. In fact, sheer gallows humor caused the Congress to term the desperate year of 1777 the "Year of the Hangman," because the sevens resembled men hanged from a gibbet.[9]

Over 130 Congressmen also served in the military. One was killed, twelve were wounded, and over twenty were captured in combat.

Withal, the greatest danger the Congress faced was this day—the day of Cornwallis's surrender at Yorktown, the longed-for day of victory. For with it came the real danger of dissolution: the separate colonies, forced together by the war, now would lose their interest in confederation. With true peace in sight, each state would want to be free of the others, to go its own way, to become in effect an independent nation, heedless of the danger of foreign attack they invited. The quarreling among them would now increase. With war's end a new enemy would appear—from within.

When he heard the sounds of celebration filling the night, Robert Morris, Congressional Superintendent of Finances, could draw a deep breath of relief. After seven years of personally playing the most dangerous financial game of his life with little more than sheer fiscal legerdemain, after having repeatedly pledged his own business and reputation to back the Congress's worthless credit, finally the game was over. Both he and the new nation had made it into peacetime. They had won.

Over those years, always just one step away from government ruin, he had pulled one fiscal rabbit after another out of the political hat, finally turning in his masterpiece just a few weeks before when the whole revolutionary effort was about to irrevocably collapse on the eve of Yorktown: he had helped finance the Yorktown campaign, had helped Washington borrow money from General Rochambeau, had covered other debts as they came due barely one half-step ahead of the creditors, and, taking the greatest risk of all, had issued Continental instruments of credit that were accepted only on his own personal credit.

But with victory at hand, the work was not over. Robert Morris was now working tirelessly to stop one of the worst consequences of the wartime fiscal gamesmanship—a steep-climbing inflation.

Signer of both the Declaration of Independence and of the Articles of Confederation and a deeply committed patriot, Morris, forty-seven on victory night, deserved his sobriquet of the "Financial Wizard of the American Revolution": without him, the revolution probably could not have succeeded. A jovial, shrewd, and supremely confident Philadelphian, he had shown financial brilliance early in life and by age twenty had become a full partner in the Philadelphia counting house of Willing, Morris & Co., which had extensive interests in ships, shipping, and foreign trade. As a member of the Congressional Council of Safety, Morris had arranged the flow of munitions and naval armament into the United States that had enabled Washington to field his armies.

Morris's commitments and workload had been staggering. In addition to his involvement with the Congress and with hectic shipping and diplomatic matters, he found the time and energy to serve as the first president of the Pennsylvania Assembly under its new constitution in 1776. In all these roles, he struggled long and hard to curb the unbridled printing of paper money issued by the blithe members of Congress, most of whom had not the tiniest understanding of fiscal policies and consequences.

He had stamped out one crisis after another, but by 1781, inflation was out of control. Congress had been cranking out paper money for too many years. The states, with far more power to tax and far less excuse, followed suit. When the paper became worthless and the consequences of reckless printing came home, the bankrupt Congress tried to force people to accept the paper with jail terms, boycotts, and mobs led by the Sons of Liberty. Making the situation worse, the states wouldn't accept one another's paper unless at a steep discount.

Then, to confound the situation, the British army in New York had dealt the American economy an almost fatal blow by flooding the states with counterfeit Continentals. Prices climbed. Farmers refused to send goods to market. Consumers hoarded. Working people and their families became threadbare and turned violent. Wartime profiteers and speculators took over the markets, making fortunes overnight while Washington's troops went barefoot. A bushel basket of paper Continentals couldn't buy a loaf of bread.

Drawing on his unfailing optimism, Robert Morris set out to establish a stable money system by creating the Bank of North America, a repository for specie—hard money. Prospects for the badly needed new bank improved significantly with the loan of more than $200,000 in specie by Louis XVI, thanks to the audacity of Colonel Laurens.

Now, with the noise of victory celebrations dinning in his ears, Morris could see that with his help the new nation had weathered the seven-year financial storm that should have sundered it. He was now just weeks away from opening the doors of the nation's first bank. He could celebrate his own personal victory.

The news from Yorktown must have caused Haym Solomon, a Jewish immigrant from Poland, to heave a sigh of great relief. Twice interned by the British in New York for suspected rebel support, he had acted, along with Robert Morris, as broker to the Congress's Office of Finance and as French financial agent in America to filter desperately needed French gold into the American economy.

As in the Congress, so on the streets of the city: Joy was mixed with rage. After dark, in the midst of the victory night's illumination, came violence. Congress had proclaimed that during the Grand Illumination the citizens should show a candle in every window. And most did, the affluent putting thirteen candles in at least one window. Mobs of self-appointed enforcers flowed through the streets checking windows, especially the windows of Quakers, accused of being pacifists and Loyalists. Homes were beset by howling mobs standing in the dark streets, shying stones at windows, shouting imprecations.

Quaker Elizabeth Sandwith Drinker, ill in her home, recorded the terrifying night in her diary: "the 17th of this month Octor. Genl Cornwallace was taken; for which we grievously suffer'd on the 24th. By way of rejoyceing—a mob assembled about 7 o'clock or before, and continud their insults until near 10; to those whose Houses were not illuminated scarcely one Friend's [Quaker's] house escaped we had nearly 70 panes of Glass broken the sash lights and two panels of the front parlor broke in pieces—the Door crack'd and Violently burst open, when they threw Stones into the House for some time but did not enter—some fared better and some worse—some Houses after braking the door, they enterd, and distroy'd the furniture etc—many women and Children were frightened into fitts, and 'tis a mercy no lives were lost."[10]

On the streets of Philadelphia, the Yorktown celebrations lasted days. Bells from many churches rang, military units paraded with their bands at full volume, topers in taverns shouted, laughed, sang. Artillery in Independence Hall roared a salute. Ships' cannon in the harbor boomed in reply. Still loomed the overriding question: Is this really the end? Is peace here? There was still a strong British army in New York and another in Charleston, still more redcoats in Canada. The answer could come only from London.

People returning to Philadelphia after a long absence were astonished with the changes. The city had taken a terrible six-year nonstop battering. With a population of 30,000 in 1774, the second-largest city in the British empire—London was first—Philadelphia had become the capitol of the new nation and thus became a magnet for a huge new population beyond count: legislators, soldiers, militia, sailors, merchants selling to the army, munitions salesmen, cannon makers, uniform makers, manufacturers, opportunists, and hordes of refugees, the latest from the Carolinas, arriving penniless and telling shocking stories of the British reign of terror. The streets were home to roving bands of criminals and plunderers. The crime rate soared. Many of the criminals were British army deserters, over 1,000 alone deserting when the British army left Philadelphia for New York, many more deserting during the Battle of Monmouth. Living on the run, they knew what would happen to them if the British army ever caught up with them.

Sanitary facilities were overcome, and the streets were deep with festering garbage. Overcrowding bred disease, disease spawned a series of wartime epidemics, epidemics filled cemeteries—the old grim cycle.

Philadelphia had willy-nilly become an important arsenal for the war. Manufacturing, long forbidden by restrictive British trade policies and now flourishing, greatly increased productive capacity and turned the city into a boomtown.

The city had been additionally disfigured by the Great Fire just before Christmas 1778. Fires were not uncommon, most of them caused by soot-caked chimney flues. But for the foresight of William Penn, that fire of 1778 could have burned the whole city down. Having witnessed the Great Fire of London in 1666, in which a great part of London, built of wood, did indeed burn to the ground, Penn had ordered the city of Brotherly Love to be built of brick. And those brick structures, acting like fire walls, had stopped the fire of 1778 from being much worse.

Yet by far the greatest destruction the city suffered had been inflicted by the hands of the British army. Administered by General Howe and later General Clinton, arbitrary British military law governed the city for two years, 1777–78. Abrogating the long-established British civil law they were sent to uphold, British officers, from the day they arrived, committed the one act that would instantly enrage the entire city population, rebel and Loyalist: They roughly pushed themselves into whatever private homes, rebel or Loyalist, that suited their fancy. The British generals seemed to have learned nothing about placating and winning back the estranged American population; unauthorized quartering of troops in private homes was one of the key issues that had ignited the Revolution.

Howe took over the mansion of Gov. Richard Penn. Hessian general Wilhelm Baron von Knyphausen occupied the city's showpiece, the Cadwalader mansion. Others of Howe's top-ranking officers quickly followed suit by taking over a number of the city's finest homes, including Mayor Samuel Powel's mansion.

Even lowly British captains like John André lived in captured luxury. With Gen. Sir Charles Grey, he shared the home of Ben Franklin, who was away in France. On the eve of departing, André took two storage trunks filled with Franklin's prized books, "impossible to replace," his musical instruments, his electrical apparatus, his account ledgers, a printing press and matrices, and even a portrait of Franklin by Benjamin Wilson, all of which was packed off to England. Probably he took some of this material to ship to General Grey's estate in England, for in 1906, Earl Grey, then governor of Canada and a descendant of Gen. Charles Grey, returned the Franklin portrait, which now hangs in the White House.

British officers also helped themselves to the use of horses and carriages, brought riotous parties into genteel homes, seduced young girls, crowded into taverns and then left the tavern bills unpaid, and tore up the demands of creditors—committing acts that, back in England, would have sent them to prison.

Army personnel, ignoring their own regulations for issuing reimbursement chits for all material purchased, made looting a way of life.

Lord Howe himself introduced an "anything goes" morality. He scandalized the straitlaced city by openly consorting with his mistress, Mrs. Elizabeth Loring, wife of his commissary general, Joshua Loring. Other officers soon took mistresses whom they paraded through the city streets and homes.

The British occupation had done almost unbelievable damage; as they departed, they left a once magnificent city in ruins.

On the catch-all plea "to prevent snipers," they had looted the valuable contents of many dozens of the finest mansions in the city, then torched them, including the widely admired Fair Hill, summer home of revolutionist Quaker John Dickinson.

For firewood, whole houses and their contents, even whole neighborhoods, had disappeared in chimney smoke. With no civil law to stop them, the British had taken miles of wooden fencing—regardless of ownership and despite protests—to warm British rumps. Almost all the churches in the city, except for established Churches of England, had been stripped of every stick of wood—handsome pews, beautifully carved pulpits, flooring, doors, shutters, roof rafters, supporting beams, all gone for firewood. Gone were many of the shade trees that the city was celebrated for.

When two British warships, *August* and *Merlin*, exploded on the riverfront, thousands of windows had been blown out and never replaced. Of incalculable value, now "eyeless" buildings and many others, empty, neglected, admitting all weathers, stripped of anything burnable, were used as dumps as they decayed into ruins.

Presbyterian cemeteries had been desecrated, their headstones uprooted and cast aside to allow for the exercise of horses that turned the churchyards into manure-filled cantering rings.

Three of the city's four lovely squares—now known as Franklin, Logan, and Rittenhouse—were stripped of their trees and churned to mud by exercising cavalry horses. The fourth square, nearest Independence Hall, now named Washington, was turned into a vast stench-ridden potter's field. Dumped into great trenches were the 2,000 American soldiers who had died under British confinement the previous winter, along with quantities of excrement and the corpses of horses.

Five companies of artillery had been quartered on the ground floor of Independence Hall, long admired as the largest public structure in America. In the rooms where the Congress had debated, where documents like the Articles of Confederation and the Declaration of Independence had been signed, they had burned everything, desks, chairs, wallboards, doors.

The second floor was used as a prison and hospital. Windows and shutters had been nailed shut to prevent escape, which must have turned the interiors into raging airless infernos during Philadelphia's notorious summers, greatly accelerating the mortality rate. Other American soldiers had been stuffed into the basements.

Trash, garbage, heaps of wood ash, slops, rotting bodies of animals, abandoned carts, and wagons were dumped anywhere, anyhow on all the streets. A plague of flies forced people to keep their windows shut even on the hottest days.

A disfiguring moat that ringed the city, built by the British army and filled with abatis, was simply abandoned as Clinton marched off.

As a parting gesture of undying malice, Clinton detoured a detail of soldiers sixty miles from their march to New York for the express purpose of burning Quaker George Clymer's mansion and its splendid contents down to the basement stones as his terrified family watched from the nearby woods. Clymer had signed the Declaration of Independence.

When the residents who had fled returned to the awesome damage done to their city, they found, in the midst of this ruination, a square mile of neatly cared-for, prosperous handsome brick townhouses, well-stocked shops, and covered markets offering fresh farm produce, untouched by marauding British hands. This was an enclave of wealthy Quakers and Loyalists.

Dismay turned to murderous rage. Only the strongest protection from the returning Continental Army could protect these two groups. And that job had gone to military governor Gen. Benedict Arnold.

British and Hessian vandalism was later set at a stunning £187,280. Departing British officers, including Banastre Tarleton, left behind an estimated £10,000 sterling in debts.

And when the army departed, more than 3,000 Loyalists, knowing the fate that would be meted out to them by the enraged rebels, hastily left with them, most of them sent to New York by Clinton onboard ship. As they crowded on the decks, ship's captains made room by seizing their possessions—much of them quite valuable pieces of furniture—and pitching them into the river.

Colonel Walter S. Stewart wrote to fellow Philadelphian Gen. Anthony Wayne that the devil himself "wou'd blush to be here." To him, the city looked "as if it had survived a fearful storm. Peeling paint and broken windows on houses and shops bespoke years of wartime neglect. The slightest rainfall turned broken pavements to mud. Public buildings that had housed soldiers and horses still reeked of human and animal waste."

James Wilson, a signer of the Declaration and later a justice of the Supreme Court of the United States, cautiously observed the celebrations while ready to dash back into the safety of his home. Galloping inflation, with a 45 percent price jump in just one month, had caused food riots. Working men attacked the wealthy on the streets. The State Executive Council had to call out the army. A murderous mob had chased Wilson and twenty others into his house and was bringing up a field piece to blow open his front door when Assembly president Joseph Reed and the city's light horse with drawn sabers arrived, killing five and wounding seventeen in the "Fort" Wilson Riot.

The news from Yorktown gave printer Robert Bell cause to recall the day he printed Thomas Paine's "Common Sense" in January 1776, the remarkable Philadelphia pamphlet that convinced a wavering populace to take up arms, after a number of other printers refused to touch it.

With the celebratory bells still tolling, Quaker leaders like the Pembertons, Drinkers, Bowens, and Shippens met to ask each other if the victory was good news or bad for the Society of Friends. Certainly one of the great consequences of the war was the destruction of Quaker political power in Pennsylvania. With its conflicting pulls, the Revolution had shattered the Quaker religion into schisms. Non-Quaker "new men" tossed out William Penn's original Quaker charter, wrote a new one in 1776, and enfranchised every male over twenty-two—propertied or not, Quaker or otherwise.

The most divisive wartime event in the city was the exiling to Virginia of thirty prominent Quakers under the leadership of the "King of the Quakers," Israel Pemberton, for refusing to sign a loyalty oath and for preaching nonviolence. As they departed in carriages, they could hear the booming of cannon from the Battle of Brandywine that would shortly give the city to the British. Before the turmoil was over, the thirty had managed to vindicate themselves and to turn public opinion against the Continental Congress and the Pennsylvania Executive Committee, both of which bodies realized lamely that they had not the authority nor the public support to do what they did.

Once released, Israel Pemberton carried on his campaign to the Continental congressmen, and called them out, demanding apologies and reimbursement. All he got was an embarrassed silence. Returning home to British-occupied Philadelphia, he found his two mansions in ruins, gutted, looted of substantial valuables, and his seventy-five-year-old wife exhausted from endless campaigning for his freedom. She died shortly after and Pemberton followed her to the Quaker churchyard a few months afterward, buried in one of the largest funerals in the city's history, attended by Quakers and non-Quakers in great numbers.

The Quakers' religious beliefs had long caused serious philosophic conflicts with other religions. Unlike all the other Protestant sects and the Catholics, the Society of Friends had abolished the observation of all the Christian sacraments, including baptism. They also had no ordained, paid clergy. Their sole religious guide was the "light within," which, critics said, deprecated the authority of the Holy Bible. Their rule of endogamy—requiring Quakers to marry only other Quakers—created great internal stress and caused many Quakers, including flagmaker Betsy Ross, to be ejected. By 1775, striving to enforce all its social mores, the Annual Meeting of the Society had expelled more than one Friend in five for deviancy in one form or another. Starting in that same year, 1775, they were also the first organization in history to actively ban slaveholding and to form organizations to work toward its abolition, especially by way of the Underground Railroad. But the greatest conflict was caused by their unyielding opposition to war. For many other Americans, Quaker pacifism was really a cover for secret loyalism.

The revolutionists' distrust—and dislike—of Quakers was profound. The Pennsylvania government hanged two Quakers for trafficking with the British, an extreme penalty—the Quakers labeled it murder—that shocked the whole community and left the city's spirit of brotherly love in tatters.

The news from Yorktown found Dr. Benjamin Rush, a signer of the Declaration of Independence and medical reformer, busy planning a social war of his own. With an admirable if controversial record in military medicine, despite the still unsettled conditions of the war, he was about to fire his very early opening salvo of the American Civil War of 1861 by founding an organization, possibly inspired by the Quakers, dedicated to the abolition of slavery.

In a rundown hotel room, Gen. Charles Lee knew that the news from Yorktown was not going to help his unhappy situation one bit. Chased off the battlefield at Monmouth Courthouse by an infuriated Washington and still trying to clear his reputation with the Congress that had dismissed him from the army, he had found little to celebrate in Philadelphia. Only a few months later, weary with rebuffs and solitude, this former British officer who had initially been appointed second in command after Washington would die impoverished in his Philadelphia hotel room, cursing that "puffed-up charlatan" Washington. He was attended only by two faithful dogs, who frequently attempted in vain to awaken their dead master.

Events at Yorktown gave cold comfort to Dr. William Shippen, of an old Quaker family, who had served as head of the American army medical corps, incompetently, and was involved in a bitter, never-healed quarrel over proper medical practice in the Continental Army with Dr. Benjamin Rush. Dr. Rush had accused him of allowing "the crowding of the sick [to] spread the communicable diseases like wildfire. The mortality was unbelievable." Brought before a court-martial on charges of "scandalous and infamous practices," he was exonerated, but barely—by a single vote. He brooded thereafter that his reputation had been irreparably damaged. The reputation of the entire Shippen family had also been damaged when Margaret (Peggy) Shippen, the granddaughter of his cousin Edward, married Benedict Arnold.

The ringing bells proclaimed no freedom for Dr. Shippen's daughter, Nancy, and other women in her situation. After she had fallen in love with the youthful secretary to the French minister to America—penniless but with "honorable expectations"—her father had forced her into a marriage with a wealthy New Yorker, Henry Beekman Livingston, a hero of the Battle of Monmouth and an insufferable snob detested by his fellow officers with an ungovernable temper, who had spawned and ignored "uncounted" illegitimate children all over New York by many different women. Nancy, while pregnant, was beaten repeatedly by Livingston, who was openly consorting with two mistresses. With her infant daughter, she fled from his mansion and moved back into her father's house.

Livingston accused her of infidelity, "a social death sentence" that destroyed her reputation in Quaker Philadelphia and cast a shadow over the paternity of their daughter, who had been named after Livingston's mother. At the same time, he made repeated overtures to have her return. By law, she could not sue him for divorce or gain a legal separation. Worse, her father and mother sided with Livingston. Philadelphia society shunned her.

She described herself as "a wretched slave—doom'd to be the wife of a Tyrant I hate." She was to win her freedom years later only after Livingston sued her for divorce on the grounds of desertion.[11]

The bells had a bitter sound to Elizabeth Graeme Fergusson, who, like Nancy Shippen Livingston, had learned that despite the newly gained freedom in America, women were still owned by their husbands.

Elizabeth was an avowed patriot married to an equally staunch Loyalist, Henry Hugh Fergusson, a penniless immigrant Scot fourteen years her junior, who by law took possession of all her wealth on their wedding day. When he fled with the British army, a patriot committee confiscated his property—which was primarily Elizabeth's inheritance. Despite her protests of patriotism, the property was deemed his, not hers. Elizabeth Fergusson was to spend years in the postwar courts before she got it back.

A wife could not sue or be sued, couldn't write a will, enter a contract, or buy and sell property. Any wages she earned became his property; any property before marriage became his on the wedding day. Usually she did not know the value of the property her husband held, even of the home they lived in, and few knew their husband's income. And she discovered—often with dismay—the extent of her husband's indebtedness only on his deathbed.[12]

Another woman sat and explored the consequences of leaving her husband, then wrote in her diary: "It is more than I can bear to have the one who occasions my unhappiness to enjoy . . . that property I have endured so many hardships to obtain, and I turned once more in to the wide World bereft of Interest and friends."[13]

Grace Growden Galloway, wife of the once powerful, now-exiled politician Joseph Galloway, resenting bitterly the chattel role of wives, gloried in her freedom from him and, born to great wealth, found poverty "more agreeable than any time I ever spent since I married." Overjoyed "not to be kept so like a slave," her happiest day would come when he would sail to England without her, along with shiploads of other Loyalists.

Benjamin Franklin's daughter, Deborah Franklin Bache, as passionate a patriot as her beloved father, had turned Franklin's home into a mini-factory in which women of the town made some 2,000 shirts for Washington's troops. Just months before victory, she had caused consternation in this conservative city when she and her friend Esther Reed had posted an impassioned broadside about the plight of Washington's army and then organized a house-to-house campaign by patriot women to raise money for Washington's soldiers. They encouraged patriot women in other cities to follow suit. Critics, both men and women, questioned their unladylike behavior. Anna Rawle, a Quaker Loyalist, accused them of extortion from people who feared reprisals. Franklin wrote from Paris to praise Deborah's efforts.

Bostonian Abigail Adams, wife of John Adams, shocked by the new low-cut gowns, observed that the style made women "look like nursing mothers."

One of the giddiest moments of the celebration in Philadelphia came on November 7. The *Freeman's Journal* reported:

> On Saturday afternoon last, between the hours of 3 and 4, arrived here
> 24 regimental Standards, taken with the British and German forces under

Lord Cornwallis. They were received by the volunteer cavalry and conducted into town, displayed in a long procession, preceded by the American and French colors—at a proper distance. They were paraded through the principal streets amid the joyful declamations of surrounding multitudes. At the State House, the hostile Standards were laid at the feet of Congress and His Excellency, the Ambassador of France—a noble and exalted Memorial of the Victory gained by the Allied forces over the Slaves of tyranny and oppression.[14]

This was the tangible evidence the country needed—those hated standards that had flown over city and nation and battlefield now brought low, lying at the feet of Congress, supine, defeated.

The firestorm of joy continued to spread north and west, reaching through New Jersey into New York State and up the Hudson River Valley, creating a pandemonium of noise everywhere.

The *New York Packet* reported: "At Fishkill . . . the glorious victory was observed with exuberant joy and festivity. A roasted ox and plenty of liquor formed the repast; a number of toasts were drunk. . . . French and American colors were displayed, cannon fired, and in the evening, illuminations, bonfires, rockets, and squibs gave agreeable amusement. . . .

"At Newburgh . . . to enliven the entertainment, they hanged and burnt in effigy the traitor Arnold."

The army on the Hudson Highlands celebrated with the traditional *feu de joie*—a rippling salvo of musketry—during an officers' dinner at a table spread in the field that featured an extra rum ration for the men. General William Heath recorded in his journal an account he had heard of one of the celebrations:

The company collected had determined to burn General Arnold in effigy. . . . [but] just as they were going to commit the effigy to the flames, one of the company observed that one of Arnold's legs was wounded when he was fighting bravely for America, that this leg ought not to be burnt, but amputated; in which the whole company agreed, and this leg was taken off and safely laid by.

New York

Sometime during Wednesday, October 24, the British in New York City surmised that Cornwallis might have surrendered. British soldiers on Staten Island reported hearing the noises of celebrations that were skipping like summer lightning through all the nearby rebel towns in New Jersey. They had clearly heard the pealing of church bells and the firing of cannon and muskets.

Major Mackenzie noted in his journal:

24th [October] There was a good deal of firing heard yesterday in Jersey, and some last night, from which it is supposed that the Enemy have taken Yorktown. Some people from Elisabeth town this morning say, that accounts have been received from the Southward of the surrender of Lord Cornwallis's army.

This Evening the following hand bill, published at Trenton the 22nd Inst was brought in.—

Trenton, 22nd Oct 1781—

This afternoon an Express from Philadelphia passed thro' this place on his way to the Eastward: by him the following letter was received.—

Philadelphia 22nd Oct 1781—

I have the pleasure of congratulating you on the capture of Cornwallis and his whole army, on the 17th Instant. The particulars are not come to hand.

The President of the Congress has just received a copy of Count de Grasse's letter to the Governor of Maryland, sent by water to Annapolis; so that there is not a doubt of the fact. The Count has taken his troops on board, and gone out to meet Mr. Digby. That they may meet, is the hearty prayer of,

S. Miles, Dep: Qt Mr

Colonel Neilson—

From a Philadelphia paper of this day.

With the most unbounded pleasure we can assure the public, that dispatches have this Moment arrived, giving an account of the unconditional surrender of Ld Cornwallis on the 17th Inst., to our great & magnanimous Genl Washington.

Major Mackenzie concluded: "Many people believe that the foregoing hand bill is fact: Others doubt it, and think it is very improbable such an event should have happened when the situation of Lord Cornwallis's Army on the 15th is considered."[15]

On October 27 the Major had become convinced: "The fate of the Army under Lord Cornwallis is now no longer doubted."[16]

The news, even without official confirmation, wrapped New York City in immediate mourning. Until the return of General Clinton and his flotilla, the troops had to wonder how many of their friends and comrades had fallen in battle and just how a vaunted British army was crushed in battle by these upstart amateur Americans who were so notorious for running away from British steel.

The pessimists among the huge population of Loyalists—the many thousands who had fled from Boston, Philadelphia, Virginia, and the Carolinas—recognized that this might be the end of the war and that they might never go home again. Many who had Loyalist sons in the British army now waited in agony for news of them.

At first glance New York City under British occupation seemed to be thriving. The shops along Hanover Square, Williams Street, and Wall Street were well stocked, much of it imported: house furnishings, linen, clothing, shoes and boots, food, rum, wine, baked goods and confections of all kinds. They were crowded with customers. On Queen Street the artisans were busy—carpenters, tinsmiths, shoemakers, tailors, pot and pan makers, saddlers, tack shops, trunk makers, clockmakers.

Perhaps the busiest places on the entire island were the numerous taverns, roughly sorting themselves out according to clientele from boozing sheds to the tony Navy Coffee House, known for its food, as were Lennox Tavern and Ashley's Tavern. The best-known and most sumptuous was Roubalet's City Tavern, where army officers danced with the city's belles while warming up for the acclaimed food and wines. By threatening to remove their licenses, the British commandant of New York City was trying to limit the number to 200 taverns.

The abundance of gallant young British officers, most of them wealthy and many titled, and the abundance of young ladies from wealthy Loyalist families produced a brilliant social life that included a calendar stuffed with teas and dinners, receptions and balls, even extravagant weddings. British officers, especially under the leadership of the popular John André, had created their own theater, dubbed the Garrison Dramatic Club.

The social diversions would have horrified Sam Adams's proper Congregationalist Boston: cricket games, heavily wagered horse races, bull baiting, boxing events, golf. With the British also came a noteworthy increase—shocking to many—in drinking and gambling.

André's execution the year before had had a dampening effect on British social life in New York, which was then deepened by the news from the Carolinas and finally Yorktown. A bunker mentality now dominated the social world, although the arrival of seventeen-year-old Prince William, later to be King William IV, elevated military morale significantly. This was easily the high water mark of the New York social calendar.

But from behind the merriment and gadding peered the real city.

With a prewar population of 20,000, New York, like Philadelphia, had become filled beyond capacity. The floating population of émigrés and exiles alone amounted to at least 50,000 including thousands of homeless Loyalists from the most influential colonial families. Penniless and desperate, praying for a British victory so they could return to their homes, these uprooted wanderers were living in tents, canvas lean-tos, and primitive huts. For them, life in Canvas Town—tents scattered amidst the burnt-out ruins—was appallingly difficult; food, extraordinarily, dismayingly expensive. A number among them had suffered the ultimate humiliation—they begged on the streets. Caught between the hatred of the revolutionists and the indifference of the British military garrison, they were facing another winter of freezing in their barely heated hovels. New York Harbor was again expected to freeze to a depth of fifteen feet. Epidemics were likely to flash out with terrifying speed—cholera, small-pox, yellow fever. Everyone commented on the terrible stench every-where in the city.

New York appeared to have been sacked. Like Philadelphia, it had suffered terribly from fires that left large burnt-out areas in the midst of the city. Two major fires in particular had carried away a huge number of buildings. The fire of September 21, 1776, starting at two A.M. under stiff winds, burned 493 buildings, a quarter of all the houses in the town. The tower of Trinity Church made such a pyre that watchers in Paulus Hook across the river clearly saw it fall in a great rush of flames and sparks. Arson, suspected, was never proved, although during the roundup of suspects, the British netted Nathan Hale and, a short time later, hanged him for a spy.[17] The British claimed that the second fire, in August 1778, was also deliberately set, also at night, also by rebel arsonists.

Yet even as thousands of new immigrants pushed into the city, the British army administration made no effort to construct replacement buildings.

Most of the damage, though, was manmade. To save the cost of fire-wood, British army personnel ripped the clapboards off the houses they had taken over, chopped up doors and stair rails, flooring and carved moldings—chopped down whole forests of trees. On one estate alone, Morrisania, British soldiers chopped down more than 450 acres of prime forest. Looking through his telescope in New Jersey, Washington himself was astonished to see that the great forest of central and upper Manhat-tan Island had been chopped down, chopped up, and pushed into army fireplaces and ovens or used in the extensive fortifications General Clin-ton had built. Over congregations' objections, many churches—except Anglican ones—from roof tree to footings were torn down by soldiers and sold for firewood. Among the city's poor, death by hypothermia was commonplace.[18]

Ruined beyond repair were more than 300 public buildings comman-deered by the British army without payment—churches, brewhouses, homes, college buildings, barns, and storehouses—and used for hospi-tals, warehouses, stables, barracks, and particularly prisons.

Lewis Morris, third lord of the vast Morrisania estate on the Hudson and a signer of the Declaration, would return home to find hundreds of acres of prime forest clear-cut by the British army, while the mansion was left in such a state that he never occupied it again. The New York City mansion of Phillip Livingston, another signer, after use as a British barracks, was left in ruins, while his other home on the Brooklyn Heights, after serving as a Royal Navy hospital, was uninhabitable.

The streets were crowded with criminals and drunken sailors and soldiers, especially at night, stumbling out of taverns and bars.[19] Prostitutes stood openly on corners and had converted some of the city's finest mansions into cribs. No sensible woman would dare venture onto the streets after dark. Few men dared it—navy press gangs roved freely, kidnapping civilians to man the warships. Bands of wandering thieves set upon the unwary to beat and rob them, often to murder them. The civil police were overwhelmed. British army officials could shrug at the scene and say things were no better on the streets of London, yet the biggest element in the criminal class was the British army regular.[20]

Hessian Lieutenant von Krafft, who would not go out of an evening without the company of two bodyguards, wrote in his journal, "I could narrate many and very frightful occurrences of theft, fraud, robbery and murder by the English soldiers which their love of drink excited."[21]

The law was hardly a deterrent. Despite severe sentences passed by courts-martial, rare was the officer or soldier who was punished, even for murder and rape. Ready to the lips of all residents were such horror stories. At eleven o'clock one night five men jumped Peter Ball as he strolled along Broadway, knocked him down, threatened to murder him if he cried out for help, and relieved him of "his cash, shoes, buckles, broach, Freemason's apron, keys, etc." In another case, a Scots officer and a woman he was escorting were both murdered by British soldiers.[22]

For a great part of the population, stealing or fencing was a way of life. Taverns were prime clearinghouses for a vast array of stolen objects where looting soldiers would let go items of substantial value "for a few drams."

Lieutenant von Krafft's fellow German, the Anspach musketeer Doehla Eelking, was an eager plunderer who recorded his thefts with the care of an accountant. His journal, which recorded among other events a raid across the river in New Jersey, reveals just what was sold in those pawnshop taverns: "We took considerable booty, both in money, silver watches, silver dishes and spoons, and in household goods, clothes, fine English linen, silk stockings, gloves, and neckerchiefs, with other precious silk goods, satin, and stuffs. My own booty, which I brought safely back, consisted of two silver watches, three sets of silver buckles, a pair of woman's cotton stockings, a pair of man's mixed summer stockings, two shirts and four chemises of fine English linen, two fine table-cloths, one silver tablespoon and one teaspoon, five Spanish dollars and six York shillings in money. The other part, viz., eleven pieces of fine linen and over two dozen silk handkerchiefs, with six silver plates and a silver drinking-mug, which were tied together in a bundle, I had to throw away on account of our hurried march [back to Manhattan], and leave them to the enemy that was pursuing us."[23]

Thomas Jones, a justice of the Supreme Court of the Province of New York, learned of Cornwallis's defeat with profound dismay. For years, with a basilisk's eye, he had been watching General Clinton's military administration of the city. Sir Henry had an absolute life-and-death power over the city of New York and its residents, unmatched even by George III's power over his entire kingdom.

The justice made an impeccable witness. Born into a prominent and very wealthy New York family, he had become even wealthier when he married Anne De Lancey, daughter of Chief Justice James De Lancey, from one of the most powerful families of New York State. A graduate of Yale, he became a successful attorney and built Mount Pitt in lower Manhattan, considered to be one of the finest residences in that city. An avowed enemy of the patriots agitating against the crown, he had become in 1773 a justice of the Supreme Court. In June 1776 he was arrested by the Provincial Congress, then released, then arrested again, and was imprisoned in Connecticut until December 1776. His crime: "disaffection."

He returned to New York and was present in June 1778 when Clinton's army reoccupied the city, imposed martial law, and suspended the civil court system, closing with it the Supreme Court itself. Thus idled, Justice Jones began a long labor of recording in minute detail the operations of Clinton's martial law courts in New York.

Despite repeated proddings by British and Loyalist authorities, Clinton refused to rescind martial law and restore the civil courts. And for good reason, Jones felt. He believed and documented that Clinton and his military cronies were engaged in a "systematic, brutal, years-long sacking of the city of New York for self enrichment" to the tune of millions of pounds. Jones regarded Clinton as not only little more than a criminal run amok, but also a military incompetent and a fool who, failing to win the war he should have easily won, caused the Yorktown debacle.

Laboriously, day by day, with a trained legal eye, he recorded Clinton's "criminal policies" that "alienated the people he had been sent to win over." He also maintained a running police blotter of Clinton's red-coated street criminals.

"The military," he wrote, "had abolished—arbitrarily and illegally abolished—the civil law, and shut up the Courts of Justice." Citizens were turned out of their homes and their furniture put out on the street on the whim of British officers. Ezekiel Robins, a mechanic, was dragged from his house and thrown in amongst "deserters, rebel prisoners, murderers, and robbers, for more than a month." He was then released without being confronted with any charges, without trial, without explanation.[24]

Jones watched angrily as Clinton created an instrument he called "The Police Court" that quickly became notorious for its corruption and elastic laws. It bestowed on itself the right to seize any property inside the city lines that belonged to rebels—and then defined rebels as anyone living outside the city, rebel or Loyalist. Proceeds from sales or rentals usually disappeared.

With the connivance of a man he despised, New York's royal governor (and major general) James Robertson, Clinton used the Police Court for another method of arbitrarily seizing private property: The Police Court was given authority to seize property without the presence or even the knowledge of the owners who were thus barred from the opportunity to defend their property in court. A "judgment in default" was issued against the owner who, with no warning, was collared by militia sent by the Police Court and summarily pitched out on the street. "From such a judgment no appeal could be brought. The subject was without redress. The legal owner lost his property. The lands were then either given to favourites who destroyed the timber, sold the wood, and ruined the estates, or hired out, and the rents, by the Governor's orders, paid quarterly into the city funds," which in turn were pocketed by the malefactors.[25]

Jones witnessed another gross violation of civil law—navy press gangs. "From time to time, when the ships of the line, frigates and other war vessels were undermanned because of sickness or desertion, armed groups of sailors and marines scoured the city to pick up every able-bodied man they could lay their hands on. Visiting every grog shop, every low tavern, every seaman's lodging, they dragged off sailors of the merchant marine, local boatmen, clerks in stores, perhaps even a few farm hands."

The *New Jersey Gazette* condemned pressing as "unexampled barbarity." In April 1781, "a very hot press took place by which several hundred men from the city were carried on board the fleet."[26]

Quartering troops in private homes was another inflammatory issue, and Clinton's army had also gone far beyond that. In New York City they didn't just occupy homes; they commandeered homes at will, putting the owners in the street and paying no rent.

General Clinton himself benefited from this system in another way: He appropriated the use of six mansions with rents paid to the general of about £2,000 a year, a fortune.[27]

Sir Harry's officers followed suit. Brigadier General Samuel Birch, the commandant of the city, "a rascal who plundered rebels and loyalists indiscriminately,"[28] cast his gaze on a house owned by a "documented incompetent lunatic Mr. Samuel Verplanck." The man was confined to an asylum outside the city limits and so under the rules set up by Clinton's Police Court was technically considered a rebel. General Birch ordered Mrs. Verplanck and the children ejected from the house forthwith. In a real estate market where houses were literally worth their weight in gold, he then rented the Verplanck house out for the considerable sum of £300 a year, which he of course pocketed. He also confiscated the rents from two other properties worth £750 a year combined.[29]

Jones's relentless pen listed many others, including such British officers as Brigadier General Skinner, "who commanded a Brigade with the pay of a General, with all the emoluments of a Battalion, of which he was the Colonel, had a rebel house and farm on Long Island worth £400 a year, and another on Staten Island worth about £200, and rations, besides, of all kinds for himself, and a large family."

In addition, many American Loyalists also cut themselves in on the pie. Jones notes: "Colonel Ludlow, of the 3d Battalion of De Lancey's Brigade, with all the perquisites thereto belonging, though he had a genteel country-seat and farm of his own in Queens County, had a rebel farm given him at Jamaica, which rented for £300 a year during the war; Lieutenant-Colonel Stephen De Lancey, was accommodated with a rebel estate at Newtown, upon Long Island, worth £400 a year.

"Philip John Livingston had a farm and house at the same place, worth annually as much. He had also a pension of £200 sterling a year, as 'Superintendent of Rebel Estates.' Charles McEvers had a tract of woodland given him worth £150 a year. From this land he got all his fuel. Besides this, Mr. McEvers had a salary of £200 sterling per annum as Treasurer of the Long Island Court of Police and rations of all kinds, for himself, his horses and his family."[30]

In page after page, Justice Jones gave many examples of these same crimes committed against Americans loyal to the crown. One case in particular became notorious, that of a wealthy Loyalist, John Thurman, a merchant who lived on a large tract of land in Albany. When he refused to take the oath of allegiance to the United States, the rebels seized his property and ordered him to go live in New York City.

When he got there he found other people living in several houses he owned.

> He applied for the possession. This was refused. He applied for the back rents. This was refused. He applied for the payment of the rents to him in future. This was also refused. His applications were made to the General, to the Governor, to the Commandant of the city, to the Mayor, to the Court of Police; they were all equally fruitless, no redress was to be had.[31]

In Albany, he was a Loyalist. In New York, he was a rebel. He was "insulted, abused, and cursed, by those very people whose duty it was to see justice done to his Majesty's loyal, persecuted, subjects."

Thurman found himself going mad in a Kafkaesque world.

> Finding that his mansion, an elegant building, was out of repair, [he] took a carpenter, went to the house, showed him what was wanting, and ordered the necessary repairs. This the possessor, one De Blois, a fiddling refugee from Boston, took in dudgeon. Some warm words arose. Thurman was ordered out of the house. He refused to go. De Blois complained to the Commandant of the city, who ordered an officer with a guard of soldiers to seize Thurman and lodge him in the prevost. This was done. Thurman was paraded through the streets like a felon, and confined for many days in prison among traitors, deserters, and rebels. No habeas corpus could be had. Law was gone, justice banished, and equity fled. Thus were his Majesty's loyal subjects, within the British lines at New York, treated by the military during the war.
>
> While Mr. Samuel Pintard Esq. was acting as a volunteer in the royal army, serving as a guide, and risking his life in the field, and in all the dangers incident to war; at this very time, I aver it as a fact, his house and farm were plundered of their most valuable effects by a party of that army in which he was exposing his life as a Loyalist, a volunteer, a conductor, and a guide. His household furniture was taken from him, he was robbed of his plate, they stole his horses, and they killed his cattle, hogs, and sheep, and carried off his poultry. He complained to the General of the robbery. He obtained no redress. Such were the steps taken by the military to conciliate the affections of his Majesty's deluded subjects, to "reclaim" the disaffected, and "bring in" the rebellious.[32]

These crimes that Justice Jones recorded were visited not just upon the rich. Destitute old men were targets also. Justice Jones owned a house at Fort Neck that he called "the Refugee House" because he permitted several Loyalist elderly men to live in it. They "maintained, supported, and diverted themselves by fishing and fowling." A company of dragoons under the command of a Colonel Birch "very deliberately entered the house, pillaged it of the little furniture the poor loyal wretches had, took out all the sash windows, and carried the whole off with the rest of their plunder. Mr. Jones [referring to himself in the third person] getting full evidence of this black transaction, wrote several letters to the Colonel upon the subject, but never received an answer. He also called a number of times at his house, but never was let in. As Hempstead was Mr. Jones's parish church, he had every Sunday the mortification to see the windows of his house fixed in a barn, which Birch had converted into a barrack."[33]

Just before the British evacuated the city, Colonel Birch pulled off one of the great swindles of the British occupation. He "sent out a party upon Hempstead Plains, an extensive common sixteen miles in length, and six in width, belonging to the towns of Oyster Bay and Hempstead, and drove in about 2,000 sheep. He ordered them into a field, and had all their ears cut off. This done, he gave notice to the farmers to come in, prove their property, and each man to take away his own. . . . but if any one took a sheep which he could not swear to, or prove to be his property, he should be severely punished. All the cattle and sheep in Hempstead and Oyster Bay were marked in the ears, and nowhere else. Every farmer has a mark of his own and each mark is upon the records of the town. Birch having taken the ears off of the sheep, not a single man was able to prove his property. Birch, therefore, sold the sheep and by this piece of wickedness pocketed above £2,000."[34]

General Clinton was not the first commanding officer to help himself to another's property. His predecessor General Howe took money meant to reimburse farmers for commandeered cattle. Addlepated Admiral Arbuthnot, fading into senility, still kept enough of his wits about him to sell blank warrants to merchants, which they used, in turn, for illegal business transactions.[35]

British treatment of individuals in New York was equally criminal. A case that caused scandal in the city and beyond took place when a young man got into a dispute with a British subaltern, "not difficult to do, given the notorious arrogance and contempt of the British Army for colonials." They traded punches. In civil court, the case, if it even got that far, could have led to a fine plus damages at most. This civilian was dragged out of his house and thrown in prison. In a British court-martial he was given the extraordinary sentence of 300 lashes. In England this extreme punishment—since it could be lethal—was given only to criminals. But General Clinton personally confirmed the sentence. The young man was given 300 lashes.[36]

Jones records more Clinton "jack-law": Three army privates broke into a house. The occupant shot one dead and had the two others arrested. General Clinton released the two, then had the dead soldier brought to trial and convicted and the body, held together with chains, hanged from a gallows.

The behavior of anyone attached to the British military was subject to few restraints. Isaac Lefferts, a farmer in Jamaica, Queens County, had just gathered his annual crop of apples into mounds to make cider. A British foraging party turned fifty horses loose in Leffert's orchard, where they soon consumed the farmer's £200 apple crop.[37]

Another farmer named Polhemus watched sixty horses completely destroy his corn crop, while yet another farmer, Israel Okely, watched a teamster put 100 horses in his barn to consume 300 bushels of oats. Asking for payment or at least a certificate that could be filed for pay, the teamsters damned the man as rebel, an absurd charge since Okely was a lieutenant in the Queens County Loyalist militia.

Nor did elevated status provide a defense against arbitrary confiscation, as Justice Jones himself discovered, although he was well-known as a judge of the Supreme Court of the province. The quartermaster of dragoons took Jones's horses from their ploughs in the middle of a field, attached them to his own wagons, then ordered Jones's servants to drive the wagons to Southampton 100 miles away. For three weeks, the servants and animals remained there. The quartermaster provided neither food nor quarters for the servants. They were turned loose at last without certificate or pay.

In the midst of winter twelve pair of oxen were taken from Jones's barns to drag wagonloads of building materials from a Quaker meeting-house the British soldiers had torn down. Jones's servants this time "were required to drive the animals to Jamaica, twenty miles away, then released without pay or certificate."[38]

And Clinton himself did more than just turn a blind eye to all of this. He himself participated. In the spring of 1779, he led a party 100 miles to Southampton for a review of the troops there. Along a stretch of twenty miles, every goose, turkey, poultry of all description, calves, lambs, and pigs within sight were taken. Several houses were broken into and plundered. Linen, stockings, hats, and other nonmilitary valuables disappeared into the pouches and pockets of the marauding army. When the farmers, following Clinton's train, tried to reach him for compensation, they were "turned away with curses."[39]

On top of all the looting of civilians, Clinton's army was also stealing another fortune from their own British government with hundreds of invented no-show sinecure jobs—"supernumerary barrack-masters, land commissaries, water commissaries, forage masters, cattle commissaries, cattle feeders, hay collectors, hay inspectors, hay weighers, wood inspectors, timber commissaries, board inspectors, refugee examiners, refugee provision providers, and refugee ration deliverers, commissaries of American, of French, of Dutch, and of Spanish, prisoners, naval commissaries, and military commissaries, with such a numerous train of clerks, deputy clerks, and other dependents upon the several offices aforesaid, with pensioners and placemen."

The scope of this payroll padding was not uncovered until Clinton was replaced by General Sir Guy Carlton, who "promptly abolished many hundreds of these jobs that had drained from the British treasury some two million pounds sterling each year.

"Had this gentleman [General Carleton] been appointed Commander-in-Chief at first, the rebellion would soon have been finished, with one third of the expense which the American war cost the nation, besides her disgrace, the loss of thirteen valuable colonies, and a scandalous dis-memberment of the British empire."[40]

Justice Jones estimated that corrupt British officers departed from New York with some five million pounds in stolen property and cash. Jones also slated Clinton for his failure to rein in the "Despicable Dead-beats" in his army, including the infamous Banastre Tarleton, whose slaughter of surrendered prisoners in the Carolinas helped raise the entire area against the British there.

The Huntingdon town records show other bills unpaid by "absconding" British army officers, amounting to £7,249.[41]

Clinton's worst record was his handling of war prisoners. He stuffed these prisoners into churches and other buildings that had been converted into prisons, especially the notorious Sugar House, and also into the sixteen rotting prison hulks that floated at anchor in Wallabout Bay, Brooklyn, where the morning salutation was "Rebels! Turn out your dead!"

In the New Bridewell prison, in the worst winters New York ever recorded, "There was not a pane of glass in the windows, and nothing to keep out the cold except the iron grates." The prisoners had rags for clothes and no blankets.

The man most responsible for the savage abuse of the American prisoners of war was the British army commissary of prisoners, Joshua Loring, thirty-seven, a Massachusetts Loyalist. He had served a hitch in the British army as a lieutenant and retired in 1768 at twenty-four with a bonus of 20,000 acres of land in New Hampshire. The following year, at age twenty-five, he was appointed the high sheriff of Massachusetts and married Elizabeth Lloyd of Boston, which was to have a profound effect on both their futures. The pair left Boston with the British army, and in 1777 Loring made a deal with General Howe. Loring got the very lucrative post as commissary of prisoners, and Howe got the very attractive Mrs. Loring as his mistress, a notorious liaison that scandalized the colonists.

Judge Jones excoriated "the notorious Joshua Loring" for "appropriating to his own use nearly two-thirds of the rations allowed to the prisoners . . . [and] actually starved to death about 300 of the poor wretches before an exchange took place." Loring, needless to say, departed New York a very wealthy man.

But no man ever handled—mishandled—prisoners with more malice than the British army's provost marshal, William Cunningham, a brutal bull-like Irishman of sixty-five years who had led a miscellaneous life as a horsebreaker, riding teacher, and wanderer. In 1775 in Boston, on the run from the Sons of Liberty, who apparently tarred and feathered him, he was named provost marshal by General Gage and took to his job with a joyful, vengeful malevolence.

In 1791, at age seventy-five, he made a deathbed confession: "I shudder at the murders I have been accessory to, both with and without orders from government, especially while in New York, during which time there were more than 2,000 prisoners starved in the different churches, by stopping their rations, which I sold." Even on his deathbed he could not bring himself to tell the whole truth, for he did much more than stop their rations; he killed many of them by lacing their flour with arsenic. His favorite activity seems to have been to drag through the streets late at night selected war prisoners, bound and gagged, to a makeshift gallows on Barrack Street and there hang them. During these midnight hangings, neighbors were admonished to keep their shutters and their mouths shut or else. In all, Cunningham, without charges and without trials, hanged more than 250 innocent prisoners. He apparently left no explanation about his selection process. In the end the rope seems to have gotten Billy Cunningham himself. Some accounts say he was convicted of forgery and hanged at Newgate.[42]

Captain Alexander Coffin Jr., an American naval officer who had been a prisoner on the prison hulk *Jersey*, limned a vivid portrait of the British who ran it. "If you were to rake the infernal regions, I doubt whether you could find such another set of demons as the officers and men who had charge of the old *Jersey* prison ship.

"Into just one small compartment on the *Jersey* below decks, British guards jammed 350 men, . . . walking skeletons . . . overrun with lice from head to foot. How many hundreds I have seen in all the bloom of health brought on board that ship and in a few days numbered with the dead."[43]

Another witness talked of the sounds of the dying: "Some swearing and blaspheming, some crying, praying and wringing their hands, others delirious, raving, groaning . . . panting for breath. Air so foul at times that a lamp could not be kept burning, by reason of which the boys were not missed till they had been dead ten days."

The merchant vessel hulk *John* had no portholes. At night when hatches were closed, the air was so foul it "was enough to destroy men of the most healthy and robust constitution . . . every morning a large boat from each of the . . . ships went loaded with dead bodies . . . all tumbled together into a hole dug for the purpose, on the hill [where the Brooklyn Navy Yard later was sited]."[44]

In Fort Greene Park, Brooklyn, stands the Prison Ship Martyr's Monument, done by Stanford White in 1908. Underneath the monument are buried the piles of bones of American prisoners that for many years after the Revolution were cast up by the tide on the shores of Wallabout Bay in Brooklyn.[45]

"And well into the next century, low tide regularly exposed the rotting timbers of the *Jersey*, the ship they called *Hell*."[46]

More Americans died in Clinton's prisons than did in all the battles of the American Revolution—4,435 American battle deaths versus more than 11,000 deaths from prison ships alone plus thousands more in the impromptu jails of the city, from untended wounds, yellow fever, smallpox, starvation, suffocation, beatings, and freezing.

Another 1,300 Americans died in the prison ships in Charleston, while another 500, to escape the certain death that awaited them belowdecks, reluctantly joined the hated British army to serve in the Caribbean.

Before year's end, Loyalist justice Thomas Jones, with his carefully journaled history of Clinton's New York, would sail into exile in England, where he would continue to stalk General Clinton by publicly retailing his New York depredations.

At about the same time, in mid-December, two months after Yorktown, the British general who started the Virginia campaign, American traitor Benedict Arnold, with his wife, Margaret Shippen Arnold, and their son, sailed for England in a stormy winter crossing. With his Virginia plunder, Arnold, now "rich as a Nabob," planned to set himself up in London as a wealthy gentleman and owner of a number of commercial sailing vessels.

Sailing with the Arnolds was Gen. Charles Cornwallis, who would find at court a ready listener in King George III.

In early March 1782, five months after Yorktown, Sir Henry Clinton himself was called home. He departed from New York in almost solitary silence. That relentless recorder, Thomas Jones, took a final verbal snapshot of Sir Harry standing on the dock ready to sail for England: With "his family only and attended by a few dependents, sycophants, and pensioned hirelings, thus departed Sir Henry Clinton, after four years command in America, laughed at by the rebels, despised by the British, and cursed by the Loyalists."[47]

Boston

Up the Connecticut River Valley on the Boston Post Road came the express rider, shouting at every town and hamlet the greatest news of the war: *Cornwallis is taken!* Wherever he went, the effect was just like setting off strings of firecrackers, for as he rode out of each village, he left behind a tumult: church bells ringing, muskets firing, and demonstrators cheering as they spilled into streets and roadways.

It was a reprise in reverse of April 19, 1775, when post rider Israel Bissel, riding in the opposition direction, from Boston to New York, set off explosions of action as the towns he passed through seized their muskets and hastened into the American Revolution.

That night in 1775, the farmers had swarmed from their villages and hamlets and attacked a British army contingent searching for Sam Adams and John Hancock and for illegal arms. When the shooting stopped, one-quarter of that contingent lay dead or wounded along twenty-one miles of roadway from Concord to Boston, the others having survived by running for their lives.

Ironically, after Washington put cannon up on Dorchester Heights to drive General Gage's army out of Boston, the focus of the war shifted south. Boston was relatively untouched for the entire Revolution. Yet during those years Massachusetts was to send 67,907 men to the Continental Army, more than twice the number from either of the next two states, Connecticut with 31,939 and Pennsylvania with 25,678.

And the scars were still evident: the graves on Bunker Hill, the debris-filled, stone-blackened cellars of Charlestown, the empty places at the dinner tables.

When the news of Yorktown reached John Hancock, he had been sitting in his first term as the first governor of the *state* of Massachusetts since September 1780. He and Sam Adams, who had helped cook up the confrontation with the British, had had an irreconcilable falling-out.

Hancock had never forgiven Sam Adams for endorsing Washington and passing him over as commander in chief of the army. In truth, Adams had chosen Washington for political expediency, to bind the South to the northern rebels' cause. He had no more affection for Washington than Hancock did. And Hancock had none.[48]

Nonetheless Hancock had paid Adams back. He had dropped out of Congress the year before, in 1780, and nipped back up the Boston Post Road to run for and, with his enormous wealth, win the Massachusetts governorship. He also began immediately to undermine Sam Adams's political power while the unsuspecting Adams stayed in Philadelphia to keep the Congress in line.

As the bells pealed all over Boston, no man could have been happier than Sam Adams. He had returned to Boston in April of 1781 to save his political neck. And when he had stepped down from his Philadelphia coach, he stepped into deep political trouble.

In a sense, the changes in Boston that he saw everywhere reflected the changes in Sam Adams's own reputation. Having started out as the

Father of the American Revolution, famous the world around, Adams, during his years of service in the Continental Congress, had gotten out of touch with America. His old techniques—beatings, burnings, faction, intrigue, propaganda, whispering campaigns—wore thin in the State House and taverns of Philadelphia. He had raised a host of enemies, many of them now as skilled in the Adams techniques as Adams was. Unlike others, who stepped up to the level of statesmanship, he never managed to get above gutter politics—and his remaining career suffered for it. As historian John C. Miller said, "Although Sam Adams was expert in overturning governments, he knew nothing of rebuilding them."[49] And he seemed to find himself, more and more, on the wrong side of every issue.

Back in Boston, he learned that Hancock's whispering campaign against him had done major damage. Hancock had condemned him for opposing long-term enlistments in the army even though everyone knew that short-term militia enlistments weren't working; he had—it was a matter of record. Hancock said that Adams was a Congressional meddler, a spreader of faction, the principal fomenter of the Deane-Lee imbroglio; also true. He accused him of being a secret enemy of the revered Washington; it wasn't even very secret. And his pushing the Conway Conspiracy against Washington was the subject of scandal throughout the country. Also, he had fought frantically against every attempt by Congress to extend its woefully inadequate powers, the lack of which was clearly bringing the Revolution near collapse. He was even disliked by many of the citizens in Philadelphia: as a passionate Congregationalist, he hated Quakers. He asserted publicly that their true religion was making money.

Sam Adams was not happy with the Boston he returned to, a scene he viewed with horror. Everywhere, it seemed to him, there was change for the worse. Rising up in wartime, "new men" now ran Boston, flush with money and eager to flaunt it with the very fripperies and fopperies that had driven Adams on the war path against the now-fled Loyalist adherents of George III. And the man who was leading the cavorting was the free-spending, very wealthy former crony, now-governor John Hancock. He had actually celebrated his election as the first governor of the *state* of Massachusetts in a series of balls and routs with "the Pomp and retinue of an Eastern Prince" that recalled the abandoned old days of Governor Hutchinson. Although Adams in his fury must have toyed with the idea of breaking out the old torch and firing Hancock's mansion, as he had done to Hutchinson's, even the brutal old Puritan had to recognize that by trying to lead the parade back to the austere days of early Massachusetts he was marching alone under a forlorn banner. For most in Massachusetts, Puritanism was a dead letter. People did not want to celebrate their newly won freedom with a prayer meeting.

Adams's cohort and fellow Hancock-hater James Warren, of the Mayflower Warrens, was as shocked as Adams as he watched these "new men," "who five years ago would have cleaned my shoes," now lording it over him, "the Scum of Creation Rideing in State."[50]

Warren, recalling the days when he had taken his life in his hands by plotting in secret to overthrow the British king, saw that the beneficiary of his risk-taking was John Hancock and his war-wealthy worldly compeers.

Both Warren and Sam Adams regarded the future darkly.

The news found Paul Revere back in Boston, military duty done, on his way to becoming enormously wealthy. Home from the army, he had spent the war years casting cannon and bells. He would go on to establish a foundry that in time turned out copper bolts and spikes, pumps, and other accessories for *Old Ironsides*. He would invent a process for rolling sheet copper that made the boilers for Robert Fulton's ferry. He did not forget his passion for politics; he campaigned vigorously for the ratification of the Constitution. And in his old age, still wearing the long-outmoded dress of Revolutionary days, he gathered around him his sixteen well-loved children and their abundance of grandchildren. Healthy, wealthy, and wise, he would die at the age of eighty-three.

The stocky and once powerfully built Gen. Israel Putnam, hero of Bunker Hill, heard the news on his farm in Pomfret, Connecticut. Paralyzed by a stroke in 1779 while serving as commander of troops on the Hudson, he was now retired at home. With the news of Lexington, he abandoned his plow in its furrow, unhitched the horse, and rode one hundred miles in eighteen hours to Cambridge. He shared with Col. William Prescott the disputed distinction of having said, "Don't fire 'til you see the whites of their eyes." Despite the stroke, he was to live long enough to see the ratification of the new Federal Constitution in 1790.

In Leicester, Massachusetts, the news was received with some misgiving by Phebe Henshaw, who, after six years of successfully running the family farm, wondered what her role would be after her husband William came home from the army. When he had first gone off to war, he had been so concerned about her inability to handle their affairs that he sent a steady stream of letters telling her in minute detail how to run the farm. The letters ceased when she sent back to him letters detailing the proper way to run the army. The first rule, she told him, was to teach the soldiers not to swear.[51]

London

In London, at noon on Sunday, November 25, a messenger arrived at the house on Pall Mall of Lord George Germain, cabinet secretary of the American Department. Germain read the message from General Clinton to his guest, Lord Walsingham. Then the two of them quickly took a hackney coach to Portland Place and entered the residence of Lord Stormont. After a quick conference, the three men continued in the carriage to the chancellor's house on Great Russell Street, Bloomsbury. Now there were four, and they rode to the home of the First Secretary (Prime Minister), Lord North. It was about one-thirty. To him they revealed the explosive contents of Clinton's message: On October 19, in Yorktown, Virginia, General Cornwallis had surrendered his entire army.

Germain watched as North reacted—exactly as though "he would have taken a ball in his breast. For he opened his arms exclaiming wildly as he paced up and down the apartment, during a few minutes, 'Oh God! It is all over!' Words which he repeated many times, under emotions of the deepest agitation and distress."[52]

From Lord North's chambers, after the five men consulted, Lord Germain, as secretary for the American Department, sent off a dispatch to King George, weekending with his family at the White House at Kew Gardens. The five men then parted. Germain went to his office in Whitehall and found a confirming message, this one the French version of events at Yorktown.

By late evening, Lord Germain, still waiting for a reply from the king, was entertaining several dinner guests, including Sir Nathanael Wraxhall. Before the dinner was finished, the messenger had returned from Kew Gardens. One of Germain's servants handed Germain the king's reply. While all watched, Lord George opened it, perused it, then gave Sir Nathanael permission to read it aloud to the table. The other guests listened in profound silence as Sir Nathanael read the king's words:

> I have rec'd with sentiments of the deepest concern the communication which Lord George Germain has made me, of the unfortunate result of the operations in Virginia. I particularly lament it on account of the consequences connected with it and the difficulties which it may produce in carrying on the public business, or in repairing such a misfortune. But I trust that neither Lord George Germain nor any Member of the Cabinet will suppose that it makes the smallest alteration in those principles of my conduct, which have directed me in past time, and which will always continue to animate me under every event, in the prosecution of the present contest.

Wraxhall wrote in his memoirs: "We then discussed its contents as affecting the Ministry, the Country, and the War. It must be confessed that they were calculated to diffuse a gloom over the most convivial society, and that they opened a wide field for political speculation.

"We must admit," Wraxhall concluded, "that no Sovereign could manifest more calmness, dignity, or self-command, than George the Third displayed in this reply."[53]

More significantly, he also displayed a will to continue the war.

In the White House in Kew Gardens, Fanny Burney, a friend of Queen Charlotte as well as her lady-in-waiting, and a popular novelist whose tales are still widely read and whose diaries vividly depict British society, was in the queen's court when the news of Yorktown was reported. The reaction, she noted, was uniformly mournful.

Consternation gripped the king's adherents in the House of Commons. Gloom and outrage settled on the king's cabinet. Rejoicing and celebration activated the king's opponents, the Whigs. Edmund Burke, the leading Whig parliamentarian, widely famous for his thundering orations in the House of Commons against the war in America, rejoiced at the news from Yorktown.

On Tuesday, November 27, 1781, the king officially opened the new session of Parliament. In his welcoming speech he announced his determination to continue the fight for the recovery of his thirteen colonies.[54]

Charles James Fox rose up to ferociously denounce the king. In a stunning, long-remembered speech that shocked all of England, Fox accused George III of squandering his subjects' blood and treasury in a mad lust for revenge. Then, with pointing finger to draw a bead on the terrified king's cabinet, he told them they were the curse of the country, the laughingstock of the world. They would pay for their crimes, he assured them, with a visit to the executioner's axe. No one had ever dared speak like this since Cromwell's Parliament.

And that was just the beginning.

The outcry against the king and his war was deafening, while his support was slipping away by the hour. Critics and enemies swarmed. Petitions against the war flooded the palace, from all over England, from the City of London, from the City of Westminster, from the merchants of the ruined West Indies trade.

Huge public meetings cropped up, most of them demanding an end to the war with America. Then even the backbone of the king's support—the peerage, the country gentlemen—realized that with an appalling seventy million pounds already spent and still no victory in sight, the fight must cease. Increasingly, the king was alone.

Little more than two weeks after Fox's speech to Parliament, on Wednesday, December 12, 1781, a historic debate shook the walls of the

House of Commons. A resolution was introduced to censure the Navy, which was richly merited. Only by gathering forces and vote-chasing in the lobbies was the king's party able to narrowly beat back their opponents. Then a second resolution was introduced; even more baleful, this one petitioned the king to stop the war. A desperate goal-line stand blocked passage by a single vote. Even the king could see that his support was evanescent.

The Committee on the Commons in Parliament fired the next salvo. It passed the shocking Dunning motion. This said, without the least effort to shilly-shally, that "the power of the Crown has increased, is increasing, and ought to be diminished."

Worse was to follow. Lord North was hounded and pounded day after day until, exhausted, he resigned. This was the worst of all nightmares for the king. It meant that the Tories were out and all his enemies in the Whig party were in. If the new Parliament and cabinet had its way, the king in the future would rule, not reign. And eventually that could lead to a king of primarily ceremonial functions and no powers at all.

It was becoming apparent—finally, even to the king—that the American army was getting better at the game with every battle and that Clinton had been outgeneraled and outfought. In the end even George III realized what he should have known from the beginning (there were plenty of critics in the Parliament who had been shouting the news into his ear for years)—he could not beat the Americans into submission, he could not win by force, he could not conquer a map. With French support, the Americans would go on humiliating the British army, and George had no fallback position from military defeat except surrender.

Lord North was right: it was over. In March even the king had to accept defeat. Sinking into a deep depression, he ordered the royal yacht on standby to transport him into exile in Hanover. As it waited, he drafted a letter of abdication. But in the end, he didn't abdicate. He didn't leave. A few years later, he went mad.

George III had mounted the throne at twenty-three in 1760 and for twenty-three years stubbornly pursued a colonial policy that raised up a revolutionary spirit where there had been none; divided his colonial subjects into a civil war that tore at each other with unspeakable butchery for six years; ruined, then exiled, then abandoned the one class that was most loyal to him; sent marauding armies, British and German, that sacked at least three cities as they looted and raped and destroyed and murdered their way from Boston to Georgia, led by bigoted incompetent generals who, sent to win over the minds and hearts of the colonists, consistently pursued policies that alienated them in ever-larger numbers while enriching themselves with the colonists' property; spent his government almost into bankruptcy; left thousands upon thousands of dead, soldiers and civilians; finished with a Götterdämmerung policy in the Carolinas that soaked that area in blood and that so completely destroyed the last vestiges of civilized behavior there that decades were required to recover it; berefted an entire generation of husbands and fathers, children, wives, sons, daughters, and loved ones; created armies of widows and orphans; imposed human misery beyond calculation; and in the end simply, almost casually, dropped the matter and turned his attention from war to problems of British agriculture until madness claimed him.

Paris

The Duc de Lauzun, whose ship had been chased by the British navy, "after a passage of twenty-two days, arrived at Brest and went up to Versailles without loss of time.

"My news delighted the King extremely; I found him in the Queen's apartments; he put me numerous questions and said many kind things to me. He asked me if I proposed to return to America; I answered yes; he added that I might assure his army that it would receive great favors, greater than any other had ever received."

The French victory over the English must have given the young king the greatest joy of his life, for he was sure he had permanently wrested George's thirteen golden geese from him.

On Saturday, November 24, one day before the news reached George III in London, Count Deux-Ponts, the backup messenger, "after a stormy voyage of nineteen days, having eluded a British cruiser, reached the French court." With him came the infuriated Comte de Charlus.

"I enjoyed the inexpressible joy of embracing at Versailles those who are to me the dearest," wrote Count Deux-Ponts. He was made a full colonel and given the coveted order of St. Louis. He was also promised the command of a regiment when the next vacancy occurred.

The Duc de Lauzun, however, had a different fate. Just as he had warned, Rochambeau had made a political blunder. De Castries, the powerful Minister of Marine, had expected that his son, the Comte de Charlus, would make that grand entrance from Yorktown before all the assembled titled lords of France, with trumpets sounding, to report the joyful news to Louis XVI on his throne, not de Lauzun.

Balch comments that when de Lauzun arrived in France with the news of Yorktown, "as de Maurepas, Lauzun's protector, had just died, Lauzun's regiment received scarcely any rewards."[55]

Lauzun himself noted: "M de Castries and M. de Segur treated me as badly as they could," while the Comte de Charlus, the son, "never forgave him [Rochambeau] or me either." The duke, except for his moment of glory in the throne room of Versailles, never received any of the rewards Louis had promised him.[56]

Rochambeau himself paid dearly for his gaffe. His reward was to have been France's highest honor—the baton of a marshal of France—immediately upon his return from America. But it was withheld for nearly a decade.

Louis also ordered a Te Deum to be sung in the Metropolitan church in Paris on November 27, ironically on the same day that George III opened Parliament and received Fox's stunning attack.

To celebrate the victory over the English, the *Bureau de la Ville* (the city council) ordered "all the *bourgeois* and inhabitants" of Paris to illuminate the fronts of their houses.

France—royal France—still brooding over its humbling in the Seven Years' War, felt that by humbling in turn the British king along with his defeated army and navy, it had recovered to the full its national pride.

Yet Louis XVI, far more despotic than George III ever dared be, had little reason to rejoice. He ruled a nation of incredible poverty smoldering with hatred, a powder keg looking for a match. "And one could hear, too," Henrich Heine was to write later, "in between, the low sobs of the destitute, and now and then a harsher sound, like a knife being sharpened."

Underneath the festivities crept the first hints of bankruptcy in the French exchequer. Louis XVI's extravagance, including gifts of money and military support to the Americans, had undermined the national economy. Its collapse would lead directly to the guillotines and the wholesale execution of the ruling class now celebrating victory.

Ten

Afterward

John Laurens

The exceedingly handsome, charming, wealthy bachelor John Laurens, who had already had enough romantic adventures to furnish a dozen war novels, after helping to capture redoubt ten and firmly negotiating the Articles of Capitulation at Yorktown, instead of returning to civilian life, headed south where, in a distinctly minor campaign against a British foraging party on August 17, 1782, he was trapped in an ambuscade at Combahee Ferry, South Carolina, and, attempting to fight his way out, was shot and killed. He was twenty-eight.

Duc de Lauzun

Armand Louis de Gontaut, Comte de Biron and Duc de Lauzun, a man of great mirth and dashing cavalry leader of the 600-man Lauzun's Legion, who bested Banastre Tarleton in the last skirmish of Gloucester during the Yorktown siege, returned to France, where, becoming Citizen Biron, he fought against the Vendée counterrevolution, was accused of lack of initiative, and, in 1793, was guillotined.

Loyalists

About 15,000 New Yorkers alone joined the British army, while another 8,000 joined the British militia. The historian Van Tyne, who in 1902 produced the first definitive study of the American Loyalists, estimated that about 50,000 Americans served in the British military during the revolution.[1]

Simcoe's and Tarleton's American Loyalist dragoons escaped on the *Boneta,* so Yorktown was spared the spectacle of mass hangings. Many of the names of these dragoons later reappeared on the rolls of residents of New Brunswick, Canada.

Probably over 100,000 American Loyalists went into exile. Some of the wealthiest and most successful Americans—eminent lawyers and judges, prominent doctors, gifted businessmen, highly educated clergymen, talented politicians, many representing the cream of culture and refinement—all reluctantly left, taking with them those skills and talents the new nation desperately needed while enriching Canada, the Caribbean, and England.

Repressive laws in most states forbade them to ever return.

George Washington

George Washington is credited by many historians with the most high-minded act of the entire Revolution. After the emotional leave-taking of his officers on December 4, 1783, at Fraunces Tavern in New York City, he journeyed to Annapolis, Maryland, where the Continental Congress was then sitting, and there, on December 23, 1783, eschewing the blandishments of kingship, which surely could have been his, he instead surrendered his sword. As a civilian with no political or military power, he went home to Martha and Mount Vernon.

The Hessians

Many of the Hessians who fought in the American Revolution were not Hessians. In 1775, when George III sent his agents into Europe to rent soldiers, his order was so large—ultimately some 29,000—that it had to be parceled out among the rulers of six German principalities: Hesse Cassel, Hesse Hanau, Brunswick, Waldeck, Anspach-Bayreuth, and Anhalt-Zerbst.

These German principalities, Hesse-Cassel in particular, were all in the business of renting out superbly trained but very reluctant armies to other European nations. The inevitable confrontation had taken place in 1743 when 6,000 Hessians in the army of George II of England found themselves confronting 6,000 Hessians in the army of Emperor Charles VII of Austria.

In America, during their seven years of service, these "Hessians" acquired a checkered reputation. The British troops scorned them; the Americans hated them. They were good fighters, but they were angry with their money-grubbing kings, fighting a war they had no stake in, and contemptuous of the American starvelings they faced. They consoled themselves in the best European military tradition: They sacked and pillaged and looted and raped their way through most of the thirteen colonies.

But it was hardly idyllic service. Nearly 1,200 of them were killed or died of wounds on American battlefields. More than five times that many—some 6,354—died of disease, accident, or drowning.

Yet many liked what they saw here. A large percentage of those captured during the Battle of Trenton were sent to work for the German farmers in Lancaster—Amish, Mennonite, Moravian—where they married German girls, cleared some of the richest farmland in the country, and became American farmers. As for the Hessians taken at Saratoga, so many had escaped that at the end of 1783, when New York was being evacuated, the historian Duncan observed that they had "vanished, no one knew where."[2] The final nose count revealed that all told, some 5,000 had deserted and settled in America.

Counting the dead and the deserters, more than 12,500 "Hessians" never returned home—well over 40 percent of the total 29,000.

But, returning or staying, they felt a resentment that was never assuaged. Colonel Von Donop, wounded at the Battle of Fort Mercer in Red Bank, New Jersey, died sighing these words: "It is an early end to a fair career but I die a victim of my ambition and the avarice of my sovereign."[3]

Thomas Sumter

Thomas Sumter, who was voted a gold medal by the South Carolina senate for his war service and who served a number of terms in the South Carolina house of representatives, was hounded by lawsuits for his bloody "Sumter's Law" campaign against Loyalists and harried by creditors until South Carolina declared a moratorium for his debts. In 1832, the oldest surviving general of the Revolution, he died at almost age ninety-eight in bed.

William Washington

Imposing, portly, fearless, native Virginian William Washington, probably a second cousin once removed of George Washington, a former divinity student and a ferocious cavalry leader, continued the fighting in the South into 1782. Having lost his heart to a Miss Elliott during his term of capture following the fall of Charleston, he married her after the war. Refusing to run for governor of South Carolina because he was unable to make a speech, he served in the legislature and died in 1810 at age fifty-eight.

Anthony Wayne

Mad Anthony Wayne, whose sobriquet is attributed to various sources, all probably apocryphal, went on to more military adventures after the Revolution. For nine years he struggled as a rice grower on 800 acres of land voted to him by the grateful Georgia legislature. Returning to the army as a brigadier general, he helped bring peace to the frontier through a series of battles with the Indians, culminating in the Battle of Fallen Timbers, Ohio, in 1794. He died in 1796 in Erie, Pennsylvania, at age fifty-one. Waynesville, Ohio, is named after him. Mark Boatner, the historian, says he was one of "America's great soldiers."

Francis Marion

The much-celebrated Swamp Fox, Francis Marion, fought his last battle in August 1783 at Fair Lawn, where he ambushed a British force under Frazer that was trying to ambush him; however, having lost his ammunition wagon, Marion had to withdraw for lack of gunpowder. After his final muster with his troops, he rode his horse, Ball, back to his beloved plantation at Pond Bluff, which had been repeatedly vandalized and destroyed. Ten of his people crept from the swamp to help restore it. He was voted £500 a year by the South Carolina legislature and was reelected to the state legislature in 1782. Still a bachelor at fifty-four in 1786, he married, happily, his wealthy spinster cousin, Mary Esther Videau. Marion lost some of his popularity when he defended a number of Loyalists whose property had been confiscated. In 1790 he participated in the state's convention to ratify the new Constitution. Never robust, tiny Francis Marion died childless at Pond Bluff in 1795 at age sixty-three.

Not far from Francis Marion National Forest lies Swamp Fox Lake, manmade to feed a hydroelectric plant. Under its waters lies his plantation, Pond Bluff.

Daniel Morgan

After Yorktown, Morgan returned to the frontier and engaged in numerous enterprises with great success. By the mid 1790s he owned more than a quarter-million acres of land. Although plagued by arthritis until he died, he twice ran for Congress, first in 1795 when he was defeated, and again in 1797 when he won. He led a militia unit against the Whiskey Rebellion in 1794. As the years gathered around him, he became a devout Presbyterian and, having exacted more tumultuous living from the human body than most of us, died in 1802 at age sixty-six. Some commentators assert that Daniel Morgan was Washington's finest general.

John Simcoe

In December 1781, weeks after Yorktown, John Simcoe was promoted to full colonel, sailed home, married in 1782, and led a civilian's life on his estate in Devon until 1790, when he entered Parliament. The following year he became the first lieutenant governor of Canada, serving under Governor General Carlton. He was a highly regarded administrator, although his hostility toward the United States colored his dealings with the new nation. His relations with Carlton were often strained and within two years, now a major general, he was sent to command San Domingo, which had been captured not long before. He was back in England by 1797, elevated to lieutenant general, and in 1806 was appointed commander in chief of India. Brought low by disease on the way there, he returned to England to die. He was fifty-four.

Marie Joseph Paul Yves Roch Gilbert du Motier, Marquis de Lafayette

Lafayette returned to France followed by crowds of adoring admirers. King Louis XVI made him a *maréchal de camp* (major general).

In addition to his considerable military services to the United States, he had spent $200,000 of his own money on the American Revolution, for which he sought no recompense.

Lafayette proved invaluable to Franklin, Adams, and Jay during the peace negotiations and later helped Jefferson promote increased trade between the United States and France.

During the French Revolution, Lafayette at first was regarded as its leader, but his moderate position was soon overrun by wild excesses, and he was clapped into prison for five years, between 1792 and 1797. Even the best efforts of President Washington couldn't free him. Finally Napoleon himself set him free.

He was nearly bankrupt; one of the greatest fortunes in France had gone glimmering. The United States Congress voted him almost $25,000, and later 11,500 acres of land in Louisiana. From 1818 to 1824 he sat as a liberal in the Chamber of Deputies.

In 1824, President Monroe invited him, now sixty-seven and widowed, for a stunning triumphal tour of parades, fireworks, and banquets that lasted almost a year. Congress voted him another $200,000. Some fifty-five towns and counties have been named after him.

He died on May 20, 1834, age sixty-seven. His grave in Paris was covered with soil from Bunker Hill, sent by the United States.

Friedrich Wilhelm Augustus von Steuben

Friedrich Wilhelm Augustus von Steuben, inspector general of the Continental Army, was honorably discharged on March 24, 1784, and stepped into civilian life chronically short of money. Pennsylvania made him an American citizen in 1783, New York in 1786. An outgoing, charming bachelor, he settled in the social circles of New York City, where he became known as a man who would spend his last penny hosting a sumptuous dinner for his friends or funding the needy. An atrocious manager of money, he was constantly shored up by his close friend Alexander Hamilton until, in 1790, the new federal government mercifully settled on him a lifetime annual pension of $2,500 rather than the single lump sum of $60,000 due him. In 1786, New York State had bestowed on him some 16,000 acres in the Mohawk Valley, aided by a "friendly" mortgage engineered by Hamilton. Thereafter, in relative financial peace, he spent his summers in his country home north of Utica and his winters in New York City, the object of public affection wherever he went until he died in 1794, age sixty-four.

The Peace Treaty

Winning the peace proved almost as arduous as winning the war. The negotiations, begun even before the fighting ended, extended over a period of four years from 1780 to 1784, ending with the ratification of the peace treaty by Congress on January 4, 1784.

The two historians Commager and Morris are unstinting in their praise of the three official peace negotiators, Benjamin Franklin, John Adams, and John Jay. They stated flatly: "The successful negotiation of the treaty of peace with Great Britain still stands as the greatest achievement in the history of American diplomacy."[4]

The American peace treaty was part of a much larger treaty between Britain and its three adversaries, France, Holland, and Spain.

Fearing American demands could cause divisions among the allies to Britain's advantage, the French openly bribed some members of the

American Congress in Philadelphia to require Adams and Franklin to accept the lesser terms propounded by the French court. But the American delegates in Paris, John Jay in particular, simply ignored those instructions.

During the laborious and long-drawn-out negotiations, had not John Adams been the stubborn, intransigent, bellicose table-pounding Bostonian that he was, along with the brilliance and infinitely shrewd patience of Benjamin Franklin and the furious dislike of the French by John Jay, descendant of French Huguenot exiles to America, the peace treaty might have given the British most of Maine, part of the old Northwest, all of New York City, Charleston, and Savannah. Spain would have controlled the Mississippi and cost the United States Kentucky, Tennessee, Mississippi, Alabama, and much of Louisiana.

Sir Henry Clinton

Sir Henry Clinton's latter years beg comparison with the Ancient Mariner, doomed to tell his tale obsessively to anyone he could collar.

He spent his final thirteen years trying to justify his handling of the American war. After he wrote his self-praising, self-defending history, *The American Rebellion,* which was rebutted by Cornwallis's *An Answer* and by Tarleton—who rebutted both of them—he spent much of his time traipsing after former friends, waiting on the influential and petitioning the court for redress, cajoling, expostulating, failing to convince.

He had quarreled with so many during his career, and befriended so few, that he found little but indifference or even hostility everywhere. Simply, no one cared. Finally he quarreled with his powerful cousin, his last connection at court. He was further dismayed to watch the king advance Cornwallis's career substantially.

In his private life, he spent his last years in relative happiness, surrounding himself with his two families, that of his late wife and that of his mistress, Mrs. Mary O'Callaghan Baddeley, whose husband, the commissary of barracks, had died of fever in Charleston.

As she did in New York, Mrs. Baddeley in Paddington, London, used her noteworthy management skills to create such a comfortable and peaceful home life that Sir Harry much preferred living there with her and their out-of-wedlock children than he did in his own London home, which was filled with "extravagant, presumptuous, and quarrelsome" servants.[5] Possibly the greatest pleasure for such a solitary man was his considerable talent as an amateur violinist.

After a penniless childhood and a penurious early life, he had returned from New York with a substantial estate. He provided handsomely for his legitimate family and comfortably for his illegitimate family. Both of his two legitimate sons advanced to lieutenant colonel before he died.

Both in time became full generals and both would be knighted. Sir Harry expected his illegitimate sons to go to sea and his daughters to marry tradesmen.

He died quietly, on December 23, 1795, at age sixty-five, from an abscess. Despite his untiring and tiresome efforts, on his death, public opinion had made him the scapegoat for the loss of the American colonies.

Charles, Lord Cornwallis

To the end of his life, Cornwallis blamed Sir Henry Clinton for forcing him into that fatal defensive position at Yorktown and for then failing to rescue him from the allied siege that followed. And one who listened to him was King George III, who gave him a Garter and sent him to India as viceroy. There he won some notable military campaigns and built a solid reputation for his administrative skills.

He wrote his *Answer* to Clinton's accusatory account of the American war. Clinton then wrote a rebuttal, at which stage Cornwallis dropped the polemic, which Clinton carried on as a life's work, and went on to other matters.

In 1793 he was made the 1st Marquess Cornwallis, and in 1797 he became governor general of Ireland.

Cornwallis continues to get mixed reviews for his campaigns in America. Acknowledged for his bravery and battlefield tactics, he is slated for his failure to rein in the brutal Tarleton and his lieutenants, is held responsible for the pest ships in Charleston Harbor on which at least one entire American army perished, and is given a share in the blame for losing the thirteen colonies.

Yet if anything he was also too humane for the brutal civil war he had uncorked in the Carolinas. Before the fighting began, he was one of a handful of men in Parliament who defended the rights of the Americans; a dedicated member of the Church of England, he was nonetheless an eloquent petitioner for the emancipation of Catholics in Ireland. He always showed the greatest concern for his troops, who replied with ferocious loyalty; although hardly rolling in money he gave his £42,000 prize money for defeating Tippoo Sultan, the "Tiger" of Mysore, India, to his troops. Returning to command in India, he died there in 1805. He was sixty-seven. In the end he garnered the reputation of being one of the greatest generals of British history.

George Sackville, Lord Germain

Lord George Sackville Germain, secretary of state for the American colonies, after his years of incompetently handling the prosecution of the

American revolution, was utterly horrified over the thought of giving the colonies their independence. Vote for it? "Never!" he cried. He didn't have to. He didn't get the chance.

On February 11, 1782, barely four months after Yorktown, the king clapped an unmerited peerage title of Viscount Sackville on him, then quietly eased him out of the back door of the cabinet by announcing for him his resignation. In frail health, he died a year and a half later, in August 1785, at age sixty-nine.

"In all fairness," says the historian Chidsey, "Congress should have awarded him a medal; for he did as much as any one man to help America win the war."

Banastre Tarleton

Banastre Tarleton went on to a successful career as a parliamentarian, writer, man about town, and military figure. Returning to England in 1782—he was still only twenty-eight—he set himself up as a gentleman and lived for some time with the famous actress Mary Robinson, who had been the mistress of the eighteen-year-old Prince of Wales, the future George IV. Enjoying to the full the lustrous reputation of a Custer or a Wild Bill Hitchcock, he published, after the fashion of the day in the third person, a book that, while scanting the truth when it suited his purposes and glorifying his deeds, was critical of Cornwallis and, to a lesser degree, of Clinton. He commissioned both Gainsborough and Reynolds to do his portrait in his cavalry regalia with the swirling mists of war and romance about him. For some years he was in and out of Parliament but was too much the bon vivant to be effective. He fared better pursuing his army career, and in 1794 became a major general and commissioner of the Cork district in Ireland. In 1812, he was raised to a full general and in 1815 was made a baronet. He married a duke's daughter, lived to be seventy-nine, and died, prosaically, in bed, issueless. Although his dashing portrait by Sir Joshua Reynolds hangs in the National Portrait Gallery in Trafalgar Square, ironically he is remembered only in America.

Jean-Baptiste-Donatien de Vimeur, Comte de Rochambeau

Because of his offense in choice of messengers from Yorktown, he did not receive the baton of a marshal of France upon his return to France as promised. Instead, it was finally awarded to him ten years later, in December 1791, not long before he was thrown in prison during the Terror of the French Revolution. He escaped the guillotine by a hair's breadth when Robespierre's sudden death abruptly ended the nonstop slaughter.

He died in 1807.

Horatio Gates

Horatio Gates, in order to exonerate himself after losing the Battle of Camden, demanded but never got a court of inquiry. In 1786, a widower, he married Mary Vallance, a woman with a fortune. In time he sold all his slaves, moved to New York City, and ran for Congress as a Jeffersonian Republican, serving one term, 1800–01. When he died in 1806, he had spent much of his fortune on the relief of Revolutionary War veterans.

François Joseph Paul, Comte de Grasse

Admiral François Joseph Paul, Comte de Grasse, did not fare well. In a battle off Saints Passage against the redoubtable Admiral Rodney, his beloved behemoth, *Ville de Paris,* was badly battered, and both the huge admiral and his huge ship were captured—which ever since has prompted speculation about the probable outcome of the Battle of the Virginia Capes preceding the siege of Yorktown if Rodney, not Graves, had been his adversary.

In 1788, in Paris, he died at age sixty-six, in circumstances that hinted of assassination. His children escaped to America, where descendants still live. The Château de Tilly, his pride and joy, was destroyed by a mob, and the four cannon captured at Yorktown, sent to him by a grateful American Congress, were melted down to make new coins of the revolution.

Sam Adams

Sam Adams's political power continued to wane. He was elected governor in 1794 only because Hancock had died, taking his opposition to the grave with him.

He and his cousin finally became opponents. When John Adams ran for president in 1796, Sam Adams campaigned furiously against him, claiming that John wanted to be a hereditary president—a king. John won.

Sam Adams lived out his days with his beloved Betsy in a moldering old frame house, showing little of its once bright yellow paint. His final days were described by John Adams: "a grief and distress to his family, a weeping, helpless object of compassion for years."[6]

Sam Adams died in 1803 at eighty-one, hating the American Constitution, still the South End rebel, half political genius, half political hoodlum, and largely discredited. He lies buried amidst his Puritan predecessors in the Old Granary Burying Ground in Boston. One wonders if his fists are still clenched.

Robert Morris

Robert Morris, the financial wizard of the American Revolution, who brought the new nation to safe financial haven, was not ultimately so successful with his own financial affairs.

Morris was able to place the United States on a firm financial footing when, with the $200,000 in seed money loaned by Louis XVI, he opened the doors of the Bank of North America in Philadelphia in January 1882, less than three months after the surrender at Yorktown.

In 1798 his enormous financial empire, based on credit and margin, centering on land speculation in the west, collapsed, taking down with him a number of other wealthy men. With his fortunes beyond repair, unable to raise the cash to cover his taxes and interest on loans, Morris himself spent three and a half years in debtors' prison. He lived his last few years in a small Philadelphia row house with his wife, whose small annuity was their only support. He died in 1806 at the age of seventy-three, "nearly forgotten and much pitied."[7]

Thomas Nelson

Thomas Nelson, admired by his friends as "a jovial fat man," a wealthy planter, educated in Cambridge, England, a signer of the Declaration of Independence, governor of Virginia after Jefferson, and the general who led Virginia's militia in the siege against Yorktown—where his home had been one of the allied artillery's targets—resigned in ill health weeks after Cornwallis surrendered. Owing $2,000,000 he had spent on the revolution, he retired, bankrupt, with his wife and eleven children to a small estate in Virginia, uncompensated by the state of Virginia and cursed by many fellow Virginians for having pressed "their horses, wagons and forage" for the siege. He died in poverty in 1789 at age fifty-one from asthma. To keep his creditors from holding his body as collateral, his family buried him in an unmarked grave in Yorktown.

Congressional Legacy

Sergeant Joseph Plumb Martin spoke for most veterans of the Continental Army when he made the following entry in his journal:

> They [the Continental soldiers] were promised a hundred acres of land, each, which was to be in their own or the adjoining states. When the country had drained the last drop of service it could screw out of the poor soldiers, they were turned adrift like old worn-out horses, and nothing said about land to pasture them upon. Congress, did, indeed

appropriate lands . . . but no care was taken that the soldiers should get them. . . . No one ever took the least care about it, except a pack of speculators, who were driving about the country like so many evil spirits, endeavoring to pluck the last feather from the soldiers. . . .

Had I been paid as I was promised to be at my engaging in the service, I needed not have suffered as I did . . . there was enough in the country and money would have procured it if I had it. It is provoking to think of it. The country was rigorous in exacting my compliance to my engagements to a punctilio, but equally careless in performing her contracts with me, and why so? One reason was because she had all the power in her own hands and I had none. Such things ought not to be.

Slaves in New York

More than 4,000 runaway slaves who had lived in freedom for years in New York City under British protection fled when their former masters, many of them coming from as far away as Virginia, journeyed to that city to reclaim their "property."

Yorktown

Yorktown died. At its peak in 1750, when it contained some 300 buildings, including many stately homes and a population of nearly 2,000 people, it was a crowded and busy port with wharves, docks, warehouses, taverns, rope walks, other types of shops that must have made it seem like a permanent institution. It had already fallen into desuetude by 1781. The siege destroyed a great part of the town. On the day of surrender only seventy buildings were still standing.

The census of 1790 lists only sixty-six people in the whole town. In 1814, a fire added the finishing touch, burning much of the waterfront and even the county courthouse. In 1862 the Civil War visited more destruction on the few remnants of the town with another siege. Much of the trenching was done on the same ground as the siege of 1781, and when the Union troops marched out, there wasn't much more damage that time could do. A modern town occupies the site.

Sergeant Major John Champe

American Sergeant Major John Champe, carried back to New York with Arnold and the American Legion, made his escape there and worked his way down through his native Virginia, in the gravest danger with every step, liable, if captured, to be shot as a traitor by either the Americans or the British. Living up to his reputation of having "inflexible perseverance," he finally located his old outfit, Lee's Legion, in the Carolinas under General Greene and was welcomed back into the fold with much ceremony, then released from duty for fear he might be captured in battle and executed by the British as a deserter.

In 1798, Washington searched for the sergeant major to promote him very belatedly to captain only to learn that he had just died in Kentucky, age forty-two.

Light-Horse Harry Lee

After the war, Henry Lee entered a second career, politics, with the same brilliance he had shown as a cavalry officer, but in the end his financial extravagance combined with an economic downturn led him to debtors' prison, ill health, and early death.

He married his cousin Matilda Lee, inheritor of Stratford, the Virginia seat of the Lees; entered politics as a Federalist; and, with a reputation as a gifted orator, was elected to Congress and in 1792 became governor of Virginia. He returned to Congress in 1793, then donned his cavalry uniform long enough to put down the Whiskey Rebellion in Pennsylvania in 1794—with great skill, and without the loss of a single life, adding still more luster to his reputation.

At this point, his financial problems swarmed. Land speculations failed. He plunged so deeply into debt that he was put in debtors' prison in 1808. Desperate for money, in 1809 he wrote his invaluable and brilliant *Memoirs of the War in the Southern Department.*

In 1812 in Baltimore he was badly injured during a mob riot. To recover his health—and, some said, to evade his creditors—he sailed the next year to the Caribbean; three years later, now clearly dying, he headed home but never made it. He got as far as the Georgia plantation of his old friend and comrade in arms Gen. Nathanael Greene, who had died in 1786. There he was nursed by Greene's daughter. Henry Lee died in 1818 at age sixty-two. Buried on Cumberland Island, Georgia, his remains were transferred in 1913 to Washington and Lee College, where Robert E. Lee, his son by his second wife, is also buried.

Benedict Arnold

Benedict Arnold did not manage the life and times of Benedict Arnold any better after Yorktown than he had before. Unable to penetrate cast-iron London society, unable to make a career in the British army, after being refused the governorship of the East India Company he took his family to the Loyalist colony in New Brunswick, Canada, where neither he nor his wife were accepted. Returning to London, he took to privateering against the French, but just about broke even. Finally, nearly penniless and aging, his great spirit faltered, he became despondent, failed, and died in 1801. Papers from the British archives in the 1920s revealed that Peggy Shippen, his wife, was much more involved in his treason than she had admitted or was previously believed. Although nineteen years younger than he, she died soon after, of cancer.[8]

Benjamin Cleveland

Benjamin Cleveland, who forced a Loyalist to cut off his own ears to escape hanging, continued his violent ways. When he captured the former Loyalist Henry Dinkins, a notorious horse thief and plunderer who lived among the Cherokee, he hanged him on the spot, which made Benjamin Cleveland quite popular in the district. He served for many years as a judge; a contemporary who knew him said that he spent most of his time on the bench snoozing while lawyers argued. He grew so large that he could no longer mount his horse. Buchanan noted that he was a most effective guerrilla leader and a fearful man to have as an enemy.[9] He ultimately reached 450 pounds, and although his weight decreased considerably in his last year, he was at the breakfast table when he died.

Going Home

Elijah Fisher was discharged on April 9, 1783, from the "old Jarsey prison-ship." For a week he knocked about New York. Then, on the 16th, as he writes:

> I com down by the markett and sits Down all alone, allmost Descouraged, and begun to think over how that I had ben in the army, what ill success I had met with there and all so how I was ronged by them I worked for at home, and lost all last winter, and now that I could not get into any besness and no home, which you may well think how I felt; but then Come into my mind that there ware thousands in worse circumstances then I was, and having food and rament [I ought to] be content, and that I had nothing to reflect on myself, and I [resolved] to do my endever and leave the avent to Provedance, and after that I felt as contented as need be.

Fisher, an army veteran of three years who had helped win American independence, was now almost a skeleton from the British prison ship *Jersey*. He found the strength somehow to walk from New York City to Boston in burgeoning springtime, stopping in taverns along the way to beg for food.

George III Says Farewell to His Colonies

King George III bade farewell to his former subjects as ungraciously as he could. Overlooking the knavery of his own government and his armies in America, he wrote to his new first minister, Lord Shelburne, about the new United States: "Knavery seems to be so much the striking feature of its inhabitants that it may not be in the end an evil that they become aliens to this Kingdom."

His former subjects must have regretted that he had not discovered this attitude in himself on April 19, 1775.

The Last Word

Two men—William Pitt the Elder and Benjamin Franklin—left the final words about the American Revolution for history to ponder.

Pitt, standing in the House of Commons, warned the Parliament and the British Army not to make war on the American Colonies.

"You cannot conquer a map," he said.

Benjamin Franklin, asked about the meaning of the American Revolution and of the Constitution that ensued, answered:

"A Republic . . . if you can keep it."

Timeline of the Revolution's Endgame

1780

- May 12, Clinton takes Charleston.
- August 16, Battle of Camden. Cornwallis destroys Gates.
- October 7, Battle of Kings Mountain. British defeated.
- December 2, Greene replaces Gates at Charlotte, North Carolina.
- December 30, Benedict Arnold lands in Virginia.

1781

- January 1, mutiny of Pennsylvania Line.
- January 17, Battle of Cowpens. Morgan defeats Tarleton.
- February 14, Greene crosses the Dan River.
- March 15, Battle of Guilford Courthouse.
- May 19, second mutiny of the Pennsylvania Line. Wayne executes its leaders.
- August 2, Cornwallis makes his base at Yorktown.
- September 5, de Grasse wins the Battle of the Capes.
- October 19, Yorktown surrender ceremony.

Notes

One Adversaries in a Cauldron

1. Willcox, 235.
2. Ibid.
3. Ibid., 482–3.
4. Ibid., 483.
5. Jones, 2:228.
6. Willcox, 325.
7. Ibid., 25.
8. Lee, 271.
9. Ibid., 275.
10. Boatner says he crossed at Tappan.
11. Van Doren, *Secret History*, 392–3.
12. Brandt, 237.
13. Fitzpatrick, *Writings of Washington*, 20: 223.
14. Ibid.
15. Bonsal, 56; Flexner, 398.
16. Flexner, 409.
17. Freeman, 5: 232n.
18. Bonsal, 19.
19. Flexner, 429.
20. Ibid., 430.
21. Burnett, *Edmund Cody*, 484–5; Montross, 31.
22. Burnett, *Edmund Cody*, 485.
23. Ford, *Journals of the Continental Congress*, XVI: 326.
24. Rutland, *Papers of George Mason*, II: 493; Selby, 229.
25. Smith, *Letters of Delegates*, 15: 572.
26. Flexner, 422n.
27. Montross, 306.
28. Ibid.
29. Clarke, 98.
30. Edgar, 40.
31. Lee, II: 160.
32. Ibid.
33. Montross, 273.
34. Randall, *Arnold*, 572.
35. Ibid., 573.
36. Boatner, 27.
37. Lee, II: 185.
38. Ibid.
39. Simcoe, Preface, vii.
40. Lee, II: 9.
41. Ibid., 8–10n.
42. Willcox, 484.
43. Randall, *Hamilton*, 214.
44. See Simcoe's *Journal.*
45. Van Doren, *Secret History*, 419.
46. Krafft, 128–9.

Two Arnold versus Jefferson

1. Burk, 4:452.
2. Randall, *Jefferson*, 329–30.
3. Randall, *Jefferson*, 329; GW to TJ, Dec. 9,1780; Fitzpatrick, *Writings of George Washington*, XX: 21, 51–2.
4. Fitzpatrick, *Writings*, XIX: 323, Letter, June 29, 1780.
5. Ward, 867.
6. Selby, 204.
7. Randall, *Jefferson*, 327.
8. Ibid., 314–5.
9. Selby, 213.
10. Randall, *Jefferson*, 326.
11. Ward, 866.
12. Wildes, 224–5.
13. Ibid., 225–7.
14. Brandt, 242.
15. Lancaster, 219.
16. Randall, *Jefferson*, 330.
17. Simcoe, 1196.
18. Selby, 124.
19. Randall, *Jefferson*, 332.
20. Ward, 869.
21. Randall, *Arnold*, 582.
22. Burk, 4: 454.

23. Lee, 2: 7.
24. Randall, *Jefferson*, 333.
25. Simcoe, 159–65.
26. Callahan, *Knox*, 176.
27. Simcoe, 164.
28. Randall, *Arnold*, 583.
29. Freeman, 5: 235.
30. Wildes, 229.
31. Ibid., 235.
32. Brandt, 245.
33. Ibid.
34. Sabine, 2: 177.
35. Rakove, 289–90.
36. Brandt, 246.
37. Ibid., 247.

Three   Cornwallis versus Greene

1. Boatner, 285.
2. Wickwire, 40.
3. Buchanan, 105.
4. Wickwire, 246.
5. Williams and Epstein, 62.
6. Buchanan, 310.
7. Wickwire, 183.
8. Ibid., 233.
9. Buchanan, 366.
10. Bass, *Swamp Fox,* 54.
11. Buchanan, 248.
12. *Pennsylvania Gazette,* Wednesday, July 19, 1780.
13. Edgar, 61. For a detailed and compelling account of the Carolinas' history, see his *Partisans & Redcoats.*
14. Edgar, 73–87. Absorbing reading.
15. Buchanan, 185.
16. Bass, *Green Dragoon,* 105.
17. Ibid.
18. Wilkinson letters, 28–30.
19. Edgar, 99–100.
20. Buchanan, 241.
21. Ibid., 95.
22. Ibid.
23. Edgar, 137.
24. Ibid., 60.
25. Lee, II: 409.
26. Edgar, 122.
27. Hallahan, *Misfire,* 9–12.
28. Edgar, 116.
29. Ibid., 119–23.
30. *Pennysylvania Gazette,* October 28, 1780.
31. Commager and Morris, 1134.
32. Hallahan, *The Day the American Revolution Began,* 80.
33. Duncan, Louis, 325.

34. Greene, III, 131–2.
35. Lee, 2, 49.
36. Bilias, 123.
37. Wickwire, 193.
38. Bass, *Swamp Fox,* 6.
39. Said of the late Sen. Barry Goldwater.
40. Bass, *Marion,* 82.
41. Lee, 2, 407.
42. Buchanan, 257.
43. Martin, 241.
44. Wickwire, 169.
45. Bass, *Green Dragoon,* 153.
46. Commager and Morris, 1156.
47. Buchanan, 326.
48. Wickwire, 264.
49. Boatner, 299.
50. Commager and Morris, 1157.
51. Wickwire, 264.
52. Commager and Morris, 1155.
53. Buchanan, 334.
54. Billias, 127.
55. Buchanan, 367.
56. Commager and Morris, 1162.
57. Ibid., 1160.
58. Ibid., 1021.
59. Lamb, 347.
60. Commager and Morris, 1160.
61. Buchanan, 381.
62. Commager and Morris, 1164.
63. Buchanan, 381.
64. Tucker, "The Southern Campaign," 43.
65. Buchanan, 382.
66. Walpole, in *Lancaster,* 342.
67. Fox, in *Wickwire,* 311.
68. Graham, 268.
69. Tucker, "The Southern Campaign," 201.
70. William Dickson to Robert Dixson, *Dickson Letters,* November 30, 1784; in Scheer, 452.
71. Greene Papers, Commager and Morris, 1167.
72. Wickwire, 240.

Four   Lafayette versus Arnold

1. Boatner, 1151, drawing upon Fisher.
2. Gottschalk, 189.
3. Ibid., 190.
4. Ibid., 214.
5. Ibid., 217–9.
6. Ibid., 222.
7. Ibid., 223.
8. Ibid., 225.

9. Stille, 264, Wayne letter of May 21, 1781.
10. Stille, 265.
11. Ibid., 265–6.
12. Wildes, 241–2.
13. Ibid.
14. Ibid., 242.
15. Ibid., 242–6.

Five Lafayette versus Cornwallis

1. Wickwire, 328.
2. Randall, *Arnold*, 585.
3. Gottschalk, 235; Lafayette letter to Noailles, May 22, 1781.
4. Gottschalk, 237; Lafayette to Washington, May 24, 1781, *Memoirs*.
5. Callahan, *Knox*, 176.
6. Gottschalk, 242; Lafayette to Greene, June 20, 1781.
7. Burk, 4: 502.
8. Wildes, 249.
9. Gottschalk, 246–7.
10. Gottschalk, 256.
11. Johnston, 40–9.
12. Willcox, 430.
13. Bonsal, 145.
14. Gottschalk, 274.
15. Ibid.
16. Commager and Morris, 1202.
17. Randall, *Arnold*, 585.
18. Doehla, *Journal*, 249.

Six Cornwallis versus Washington

1. Flexner, 429.
2. Casey, 327.
3. Ibid.
4. Freeman, 278.
5. Fitzpatrick, *GW Writings*, XXII: 450; Fitzpatrick, *Diaries of GW*, II: 240; Flexner, 436.
6. Chidsey, 115.
7. Flexner, 441.
8. Scheer, 473.
9. Freeman, V: 311.
10. Chidsey, 119.
11. Davis, *Burke*, 72.
12. Ibid.
13. Ibid.
14. Martin, 223.
15. Johnston, 95.
16. Scheer, 474.
17. Johnston, 174.
18. Martin, 223.
19. Lee, 467n, 469.

20. Lancaster 342.
21. Mackenzie, 673.
22. Freeman, 325.
23. Trumbull, 333.
24. Johnston, 100–1.
25. The French account came from an anonymous French officer reprinted in Shea, 154–158. The British account is from Larrabee and from Davis, *Burke*, 147–66.
26. Jones, 2: 67.
27. Mackenzie, 630.
28. Willcox, 429.
29. Mackenzie, 631.
30. Willcox, 430.
31. Ibid., 429–30.
32. Callahan, *Knox*, 180.
33. Mackenzie, 631.
34. Willcox, 431.
35. Mackenzie, 635–8.
36. Bonsal, 145.

Seven Siege at Yorktown

1. Tucker, *The Southern Campaign*, 212–3.
2. Commager and Morris, 1218.
3. National Park Service, Yorktown.
4. Martin, 228–9.
5. Mackenzie, 636.
6. Willcox, 436.
7. Denny, VII, 205.
8. A cannon was designated by the weight of the cannonball it fired.
9. Lauzun, 52.
10. Boatner, 1179.
11. Lauzun, 52–3.
12. Davis, 197.
13. Tucker, *Journal*, V: 380–1.
14. Balch, *Letters*, 162.
15. Lee, 332.
16. Willcox, 437.
17. Martin, 231.
18. Ibid., 232.
19. Ibid., 232–3.
20. Callahan, *Knox*, 184.
21. Van Cortlandt, II: 294.
22. Graham, 272.
23. Martin, 233.
24. Thacher. See Davis, *Burke*, 222.
25. Davis, *Burke*, 223.
26. Ibid., 223–4.
27. Scheer, 485.
28. Ibid., 486.
29. Johnston, 138.
30. Pension application. Her photograph is in the Virginia Visitor's Center in Yorktown.

31. Randall, *Hamilton*, 242.
32. Scheer, 487.
33. Ibid., and National Park Visitors Center, Yorktown, Yorktown website.
34. Yorktown website.
35. Martin, 235.
36. Johnston, 145–7; National Park Visitors Center, Yorktown.
37. Johnston, 143.
38. Ibid., 148.
39. Scheer, 399.
40. Graham, 272.
41. Ibid., 273.
42. Doehla, 254.
43. Bass, *Green Dragoon*, 127.

Eight Surrender

1. Doehla, 254.
2. Denny. Also see Davis, *Burke*, 256.
3. Denny, VII: 206.
4. Lee, 352.
5. Johnston, 152.
6. Lee, 353.
7. Scheer, 491.
8. Ibid., 492.
9. Davis, 258.
10. Balch, *Letters*, 285, from a manuscript of Major Jackson.
11. Scheer, 493.
12. Denny, VII: 14.
13. Butler, *Journal*, 384.
14. Doehla, 256.
15. Closen, 153.
16. Flexner, 462.
17. Closen, 155; Flexner, 462.
18. Thacher, 289. See also Commager and Morris, 1241.
19. Closen, 156.
20. Ibid., 153.
21. Lee, II: 361.
22. Bonsal, 165.
23. Davis, *Burke*, 267.
24. Ibid., 267.
25. Graham, 274.
26. Doehla, 259; also Johnston, 157.
27. Davis, *Burke*, 267.
28. Martin, 240–1.
29. Closen, 153.
30. Flexner, 462.
31. Thacher, 289, also Commager and Morris, 1243.
32. Johnston, 157.
33. Bass, *Green Dragoon*, 4–5.
34. Ibid.
35. Flexner, 464.

36. Scheer, 495.
37. Martin, 242.
38. Johnston, 202.
39. Scheer, 495.
40. Lamb, 377.
41. Closen, 156.
42. Callahan, *Knox*, 181.
43. Popp, XXVI: 25–41.
44. Tucker, *Journal*, 386–7.
45. Bonsal, 165.
46. Scheer, 495.
47. Johnston, 158.
48. Lauzun, 53.
49. Johnston, 181.
50. Graham, 273.
51. Ibid.
52. Bonsal, 11.

Nine The World Reacts

1. Callahan, *Knox*, 189.
2. Scheer, 495.
3. *Journals of the Continental Congress*, XXI: 1071.
4. Boudinot, *Journal*, 55.
5. Ibid., 59.
6. *Journals of the Continental Congress*, XXI: 1072.
7. Billias, 115.
8. Montross, 131.
9. *Encyclopedia of the American Revolution*, 266.
10. Drinker, 3: 393.
11. Norton, 49.
12. Ibid., 46.
13. Ibid., 48.
14. Bonsal, 174.
15. Mackenzie, 674–5.
16. Mackenzie, 679.
17. Burrows, 240.
18. Ibid., 255.
19. Abbott, 264–5.
20. Wertenbaker, 216.
21. Krafft; Schecter, 276.
22. Wertenbaker, 216.
23. Quoted in Lowell, 256.
24. Jones, 2: 85.
25. Ibid., 36.
26. Wertenbaker, 217.
27. Jones, 2: 67.
28. Fleming, 45.
29. Jones, 2: 67.
30. Ibid., 75–6.
31. Ibid., 64–5.
32. Ibid., 68–70.
33. Ibid., 73.

34. Ibid., 74–5.
35. Burrows, 252.
36. Jones, 2: 83–4.
37. Ibid., 87.
38. Ibid., 89.
39. Ibid., 90–1.
40. Ibid., 226.
41. Website, Long Island History, lihistory.com.
42. Boatner; Burrows; Lossing; *History*, Wilson.
43. Wertenbaker, 166.
44. Ibid.
45. Burrows, 254.
46. Website, Long Island History.
47. Jones, 2: 222–3.
48. Miller, 346–50.
49. Ibid., 344.
50. Ibid., 360.
51. Hoffman, 241.
52. Commager and Morris, 1243.
53. Ibid., 1245.
54. Clarke, 103.
55. Balch, *The French*, 162.
56. Lauzun, 53.

Ten Afterward

1. Montross, 295.
2. Duncan, Louis C., 365.
3. Lowell, 207.
4. Commager and Morris, 1249.
5. Willcox, 471.
6. Miller, 399–400.
7. Boatner, 745.
8. Chidsey, 160.
9. Buchanan, 216.

Bibliography

Abbott, Wilbur Cortez. *New York in the American Revolution*. New York: Charles Scribner's Sons, 1929.

Allinson, Edward P., and Boies Penrose. *Philadelphia, 1681–1887: A History of Municipal Development*. Philadelphia: Allen, Lane & Scott, 1887.

Anonymous. "Siege of Yorktown and Gloucester, Virginia." *Magazine of American History*, VIII, No. 3 (September 1881).

Atwood, Rodney. *The Hessians: Mercenaries from Hessen-Kassel in the American Revolution*. New York: Cambridge University Press, 1980.

Bakeless, John Edwin. *Turncoats, Traitors, Heroes*. Philadelphia: Lippincott, 1960.

Balch, Thomas. *The French in America during the War of Independence of the United States of America*. 2 vols. Philadelphia: Porter & Coates, 1891–1895.

——————. *Letters and Papers Relating Chiefly to the Provincial History of Pennsylvania*. Philadelphia: Crissy & Markley Printers, 1855.

Bass, Robert D. *Gamecock*. New York: Henry Holt and Company, 1961.

——————. *The Green Dragoon*. New York: Henry Holt and Company, 1957.

——————. *Swamp Fox*. New York: Henry Holt and Company, 1959.

Bergman, Peter M. *The Negro in the Continental Congress*. New York: Bergman Company, 1959.

Bernier, Olivier. *Lafayette: Hero of Two Worlds*. New York: E. P. Dutton Inc., 1963.

Billias, George Athan. *George Washington's Generals*. New York: William Morrow & Company, 1964.

Biographic Directory of the American Congress 1774–1927. House Document No. 783, 69th Congress, Washington, 1928.

Blanchard, Claude. *The Journal of Claude Blanchard, Commissary of the French Auxiliary Army Sent to the US During the American Revolution 1780–1783*. Translated from the French manuscript by William Duane and edited by Thomas Balch. Albany, N.Y.: J. Munsell, 1876.

Blumenthal, Walter Hart. *Women Camp Followers of the American Revolution*. New York: Arno Press, 1974.

Boatner, Mark M. III. *Encyclopedia of the American Revolution*. Mechanicsburg, Pa.: Stackpole Books, 1990.

Bonsal, Stephen. *When the French Were Here; a narrative of the sojourn of the French forces in America, and their contribution to the Yorktown campaign drawn from unpublished reports and letters of participants in the National Archives of France and the ms division of the Library of Congress*. New York: Doubleday Doran and Company, Inc., 1945.

Boudinot, Elias. *Journal: or Historical Recollections of American Events during the Revolutionary War*. Philadelphia: Bourquin, 1894.

Brandt, Clare. *The Man in the Mirror: A Life of Benedict Arnold*. New York: Random House, 1994.

Brown, Wallace. *The Good Americans, Loyalists in the American Revolution.* New York: Morrow, 1969.

Buchanan, John. *The Road to Guilford Courthouse: the American Revolution in the Carolinas.* New York: John Wiley & Sons, Inc., 1997.

Burk, John. *The History of Virginia from Its First Settlement to the Present Day,* 4 vols., Petersburg, Va.: Dickens & Pescuo, 1804–1816.

Burnett, Edmund Cody. *The Continental Congress.* New York: Macmillan and Company, 1941.

———, ed. *Letters of the Members of the Continental Congress,* 8 vols., Washington, D.C.: Carnegie Institution, 1921–1936.

Burrows, Edwin G., and Mike Wallace. *Gotham: A History of New York City to 1898.* New York: Oxford University Press, 1999.

Butler, Richard. "Continental Line. Fifth Pennsylvania, Jan. 1, 1777–Jan 1, 1783." *Pennsylvania Archives,* Fifth Series III (1906).

———. "Journal of the Siege of Yorktown." *Historical Magazine,* VIII (March 1864), p. 110.

Callahan, North. *Flight from the Republic: The Tories of the American Revolution.* Indianapolis: Bobbs Merrill, 1967.

———. *Henry Knox, General Washington's General.* New York: Rinehart, 1958.

———. *Royal Raiders: The Tories of the American Revolution.* Indianapolis: Bobbs Merrill, 1963.

Casey, William. *Where and How the War Was Fought.* New York: William Morrow, 1976.

Chastellux, François Jean, Marquis de. *Travels in North America in the Years 1780, 1781, 1782.* Chapel Hill: University of North Carolina Press, 1963.

Chidsey, Donald Barr. *Victory at Yorktown.* New York: Crown Publishers, 1962.

Christie, Ian R. *The End of North's Ministry 1780–1782.* New York: St. Martin's Press, 1958.

Clarke, John. *The Life and Times of George III.* London: Book Club Associates, 1972.

Clinton, Sir Henry. *The American Rebellion: Sir Henry Clinton's Narrative of His Campaigns, 1775–1782,* with an Appendix of Original Documents, edited by William B. Willcox. New Haven, Conn.: Yale University Press, 1954.

———. *Observations on some parts of the Answer of Earl Cornwallis to Sir Henry Clinton's Narrative. To which is added an appendix; containing extracts of letters and other papers, to which reference is necessary.* New York: Research Reprints, 1970.

Closen, Baron Ludwig von. *The Revolutionary Journal of Baron Ludwig Von Closen 1780–1783,* translated and edited with an Introduction by Evelyn M. Acomb. Chapel Hill: University of North Carolina Press, 1958.

Cobb, Lt. Col. David. "Before Yorktown, Virginia, October 1–November 30, 1781." *Proceedings of the Massachusetts Historical Society,* XIX (1881–1882).

Collins, Varnum Lansing. *Brief Narrative of the Ravages of British, Hessians at Princeton 1776–1777.* Princeton: The University Press, 1906.

Commager, Henry Steele, and Richard B. Morris, eds. *The Spirit of Seventy Six: The Story of the American Revolution as Told by the Participants.* New York: Da Capo Press, 1975.

Cumming, William P., and Hugh Rankin. *The Fate of a Nation: The American Revolution Through Contemporary Eyes.* London: Phaidon, 1975.

Dann, John C., ed. *The Revolution Remembered: Eyewitness Accounts of the War for Independence.* Chicago: University of Chicago Press, 1980.

Davis, Burke. *The Campaign That Won America: the Story of Yorktown.* New York: Dial Press, 1970.

Davis, Capt. John. "The Yorktown Campaign." *Pennsylvania Magazine of History & Biography,* V (1881).

Denny, Ebenezer. "A Military Journal . . ." *Memoirs of the Pennsylvania Historical Society,* vol. 7.

"Diary of a French Officer, 1781." *Magazine of American History,* IV (June 1880): 205–14 *et seq.*

Dictionary of American Biography, New York: Charles Scribner's Sons, 1961.

Dictionary of National Biography, 22 v., London: Oxford University Press [1963–65].

Doehla, Johann. "Journal." *William and Mary Quarterly,* Vol. 22, No. 3, pp. 229–74, July, 1942.

Drinker, Elizabeth Sandwith. *The Diary of Elizabeth Sandwith Drinker.* 3 vols. Boston: Northeast University Press, 1991.

Duncan, James. "Diary of Captain James Duncan of Colonel Moses Hazen's Regiment in the Yorktown Campaign, 1781." *Pennsylvania Archives,* 2nd Ser., XV: 743–52. Harrisburg, Pa.: E. K. Myers, 1890.

Duncan, Louis C. *Medical Men in the American Revolution 1775–1783.* Carlisle Barracks, Penn.: Medical Field Service School, Army Medical Service Bulletin No. 25, 1931. Reprint: New York: Augustus M. Kelley, Publishers, 1970.

Dupuy, R. Ernest & Dupuy, Trevor N. *An Outline History of the American Revolution.* New York: Harper & Row, 1975.

————. *Compact History of the Revolutionary War.* New York: Hawthorne Books, 1963.

————. *The Compact History of the U.S. Army.* New York: Harper & Row, 1973.

————. *Encyclopedia of Military History 3500 B.C.–Present.* New York: Harper & Row, 1974.

Dupuy, Trevor. *People and Events of the American Revolution.* New York: R.R. Bowker Co., 1974.

Edgar, Walter. *Partisans and Redcoats: The Southern Conflict That Turned the Tide of the American Revolution.* New York: William Morrow, 2001.

Engle, Paul. *Women in the American Revolution.* Chicago: Follett, 1976.

Evans, Elizabeth. *Weathering the Storm: Women of the American Revolution.* New York: Scribner's, 1975.

Ewald, Johann Von. *Diary of the American War. A Hessian Journal.* New Haven: Yale University Press, 1979.

Feltman, Lt. William. "The Journal of Lieut. William Feltman, of the First Pennsylvania Regiment, from May 26, 1781 to April 25, 1782, embracing the Siege of Yorktown and the Southern Campaign." *Pennsylvania Historical Society Collections,* I, No. 5 (May 1855).

Fenn, Elizabeth A. *Pox Americana: The Great Smallpox Epidemic of 1775–82.* New York: Hill and Wang, 2001.

Ferris, Robert G., and Richard E. Morris. *The Signers of the Declaration of Independence.* Flagstaff, Ariz.: Interpretive Publications, Inc., 1982.

Fisher, Sidney George. *The Struggle for American Independence,* 2 vols. Philadelphia: Lippincott, 1908.

————. *True History of the American Revolution,* 2 vols. Philadelphia: Lippincott, 1902.

Fitzpatrick, John C., ed. *The Diaries of George Washington,* 4 vols. Boston: Houghton Mifflin, 1925.

————. *The Writings of George Washington,* 39 vols. Washington, D.C.: U.S. Government Printing Office, 1931–1944.

Fleming, Thomas J. *Beat the Last Drum: The Siege of Yorktown, 1781.* New York: St. Martin's Press, 1966.

Flexner, James Thomas. *George Washington in the American Revolution 1775–1783.* Boston: Little, Brown and Company, 1968.

Ford, Worthington Chauncy, ed. *The Journals of the Continental Congress,* 34 vols., Washington, D.C.: Library of Congress, 1904–1937.

————. *The Writings of George Washington,* 14 vols. New York: G.P. Putnam's Sons, 1889–1893.

Freeman, Douglas Southall. *George Washington, A Biography,* 7 vols. New York: Scribner, 1948–57.

Gallatin, Gaspard Gabriel. *Journal of the Siege of Yorktown: Unpublished Journals of the Siege of Yorktown in 1781 Operated by the General Staff of the French Army.* Washington, D.C.: U.S. Government Printing Office, 1931.

Galloway, Grace Growden. *Diary.* Ed. R. C. Werner. New York: The New York Times, 1971.

Gottschalk, Louis. *Lafayette and the Close of the American Revolution.* Chicago: University of Chicago Press, 1942.

Graham, Captain Samuel. "An English Officer's Account of His Services in America, 1779–1781." *History Magazine,* IX (September 1865), 272.

Greene, George Washington. *Life of Nathanael Greene, Major General in the Army of the Revolution,* 3 vols. New York: G. P. Putnam's Sons, 1867–71.

Hall, Jonathan N. *Revolutionary War Quiz and Fact Book.* Dallas: Taylor Publishing, 1999.

Hallahan, William H. *The Day the American Revolution Began, 19 April 1775.* New York: William Morrow, 2000.

————. *Misfire: The Story of How America's Small Arms Have Failed Our Military.* New York: Charles Scribner's Sons, 1994.

Hatch, Charles E., & Thomas M. Pitkin. *Yorktown, Climax of the Revolution.* Washington, D.C.: U.S. Department of the Interior National Park Service, 1941. (1956 printing, Source Book Series No. 1).

Hibbert, Christopher. *Redcoats and Rebels: The American Revolution Through British Eyes.* New York: Norton, 1990.

Higginbotham, Don. *Daniel Morgan, Revolutionary Rifleman.* Chapel Hill: University of North Carolina Press, 1961.

Hoffman, Ronald, & Peter J. Albert, eds. *Women in the Age of the American Revolution.* Charlottesville: University Press of Virginia, 1989.

Jefferson, Thomas. *Papers,* edited by Julian Boyd et al. Princeton: Princeton University Press, 1950.

Johnston, Henry Phelps. *The Yorktown Campaign and the Surrender of Cornwallis, 1781.* New York: Eastern Acorn Press, 1997.

Jones, Thomas. *History of New York During the Revolutionary War and of the Leading Events in the Other Colonies at That Period,* 2 vols., ed. Edward Floyd DeLancey. New York: Printed for the New York Historical Society, 1879.

Ketchum, Richard M. *The Winter Soldiers: The Battles for Trenton and Princeton.* New York: Henry Holt & Co., 1973.

Krafft, John Charles Philip von. "Journal of Lieutenant John Charles Philip Von Krafft 1776–1784." *New York Historical Society Collections,* XV (1882).

Lamb, Roger. *An Authentic Journal of Occurrences During the Late American War.* New York: New York Times, 1968 [reprint of 1809 edition].

Lancaster, Bruce. *The History of the American Revolution.* New York: American Heritage Publishing Co. Inc., 1971.

Larabee, Harold Atkins. *Decision at the Chesapeake.* New York: C. N. Potter, 1964.

Lauzun, Duc de, Armand Louis. "Memoirs." *Magazine of American History,* VI (1881): 51–3.

Lee, Henry. *Memoirs of the War in the Southern Department of the United States,* 2 vols. New York: Burt Franklin, 1970 (reprint of 1812 edition).

Lossing, John Frederick. *History of New York City, embracing an outline of events from 1609 to 1830.* New York: G. E. Perrine, 1884.

————. *The Pictorial field-book of the Revolution; or, Illustrations, by Pen and Pencil of the History, Biography, Scenery, Relics and Traditions of the War for Independence.* Spartanburg, S.C.: Reprint Company, 1969.

Lowell, Edward J. *The Hessians and Other German Auxiliaries of Great Britain in the Revolutionary War.* New York: Harper & Brothers, 1884 (1965 reprint).

McDowell, William. "Journal of Lieut. William McDowell." *Pennsylvania Archives,* Second Series, XV (1893).

Mackenzie, Frederick. *The Diary of Frederick Mackenzie Giving a daily narrative of his military service as an officer in the regiment of Royal Welch Fusiliers during the years 1775–1781 in Massachusetts, Rhode Island and New York.* New York: Arno Press, 1930.

Magazine of American History, X (1883): 410–3.

Malone, Dumas. *Jefferson the Virginian.* Boston: Little, Brown and Company, 1948.

Martin, Joseph Plumb. *Private Yankee Doodle, Being a Narrative of Some of the Adventures, Dangers, and Sufferings of a Revolutionary Soldier.* Boston: Little, Brown and Company, 1962.

Meigs, Cornelia. *The Violent Men, A Study of Human Relations in the First Continental Congress.* New York: Macmillan, 1950.

Miller, John C. *Sam Adams, Pioneer in Propaganda.* Boston: Little Brown, 1936.

Montross, Lynn. *The Reluctant Rebels: The Story of the Continental Congress 1774–1789.* New York: Harper and Brothers, 1950.

Moore, Frank. *Diary of the American Revolution. From Newspapers and Original Documents.* New York: C. Scribner, 1860.

Morrissey, Brendan. *Yorktown 1781: The World Turned Upside Down.* Oxford: Osprey Publishing Ltd., 1997.

Norton, Mary Beth. *Liberty's Daughters: The Colonial Experience of American Women, 1750–1800.* Boston: Little Brown, 1980.

Oberholtzer, Ellis. *Robert Morris, Patriot and Financier.* New York: B. Franklin, 1903.

Paine, Thomas. *Common Sense.* Mineola, New York: Dover Publications, 1997.

Pavlovsky, Arnold M. "Between Hawk and Buzzard: Congress as Perceived by Its Members 1775–1783." *William & Mary Quarterly,* 3rd series, 349–64.

Pennsylvania Archives, Series 2, Vol. II: 631–74.

Pennsylvania Gazette and Weekly Advertiser, January 5, 1779–March, 1782; October 23–November 6, 1782.

Popp, Stephan. "Journal, 1777–1783." *Pennsylvania Magazine of History,* XXVI (1902): 25–41 *et seq.*

Prechtel, Johann Ernst. *A Hessian Officer's Diary of the American Revolution.* Bowie, Md.: Heritage Books, 1994.

Quarles, Benjamin. *The Negro in the American Revolution.* Chapel Hill: University of North Carolina Press, 1961.

Rakove, Jack N. *The Beginnings of National Politics: An Interpretive History of the Continental Congress.* New York: Alfred A. Knopf, 1979.

Randall, Willard Sterne. *Alexander Hamilton, A Life.* New York: HarperCollins, 2003.

——— . *Benedict Arnold, Patriot and Traitor.* New York: William Morrow & Company, 1990.

——— . *Thomas Jefferson: A Life.* New York: Henry Holt and Company Inc., 1993.

Reiss, Oscar. *Blacks in Colonial America.* Jefferson, N.C.: McFarland & Co., 1997.

Royster, Charles. *Light Horse Harry Lee and the Legacy of the American Revolution.* New York: Knopf, 1981.

Rutland, Robert A., ed. *The Papers of George Mason.* Chapel Hill: University of North Carolina Press, 1970. 3 vols.

Sabine, Lorenzo. *Biographic Sketches of Loyalists of the American Revolution,* 2 vols. Port Washington, N.Y.: Kennekat Press, Inc., 1966.

Scharf, J. Thomas, and Thompson Westcott. *History of Philadelphia (1609–1884),* 3 vols. Philadelphia: L. H. Everts & Co., 1884.

Schecter, Barnet. *The Battle for New York: The City at the Heart of the American Revolution.* New York: Walker & Company, 2002.

Scheer, George F., and Hugh F. Rankin. *Rebels and Redcoats: The American Revolution Through the Eyes of Those Who Fought and Lived It.* Cleveland: World Publishing Co., 1957.

Selby, John E. *The Revolution in Virginia, 1775–1783.* Williamsburg: The Colonial Williamsburg Foundation, 1988.

Selby, John Millin. *The Road to Yorktown.* New York: St. Martin's Press, 1976.

Shea, J. G., ed. *The Operations of the French Fleet under the Count de Grasse in 1781–2 as Described in two Contemporaneous Journals.* New York: The Bradford Club, 1864.

Simcoe, J. G. *Simcoe's Military Journal, A History of the Operations of a Partisan Corps, Called the Queen's Rangers, Commanded by Lieut. Col. J. G. Simcoe, During the War of the American Revolution: Illustrated by ten engraved plans of action, etc. Now first Published, with a Memoir of the Author and other Additions.* New York: Bartlett & Welford, 1844.

Smith, Paul H. *Letters of Delegates to Congress 1774–1789.* Washington, D.C.: Library of Congress, 1976.

Sparks, Jared, ed. *The Writings of George Washington,* 12 vols. Boston: American Stationers' Company, 1834–37.

Staloff, Darren. *The History of the United States.* Chantilly, Va.: The Teaching Company, 1996.

Stille, Charles Janeway. *Major General Anthony Wayne and the Pennsylvania Line of the Continental Army.* Port Washington, N.Y.: Kennikat Press, 1968.

Talmadge, Benjamin. *Memoir of Colonel Benjamin Talmadge.* New York: New York Times, 1968.

Thacher, James. *Military Journal of the American Revolution.* New York: Arno Press, 1969.

Thayer, Theodore. *Israel Pemberton, King of the Quakers.* Philadelphia: The Historical Society of Pennsylvania, 1943.

Tilden, John Bell. "Extracts from the Journal of Lieutenant John Bell Tilden." *Pennsylvania Magazine of History and Biography,* XIX, No. 1 (April 1895).

Tilghman, Tench. *Memoir of Lieut. Col. Tench Tilghman, Secretary and aide to Washington Together with an appendix containing Revolutionary Journals and Letters Hitherto Unpublished,* ed. by S. A. Harrison. Albany: J. Munsell, 1876.

Trumbull, Jonathan. "Minutes of Occurrences Respecting the Siege and Capture of York in Virginia, extracted from the Journal of Colonel Jonathan Trumbull, Secretary to the General, 1781." *Proceedings of the Massachusetts Historical Society,* IV (1876): 331–8.

Tucker, St. George. "Journal of the Siege of Yorktown, 1781." *William and Mary Quarterly,* 3rd Series, V (July 1948), 375–96.

———. "The Southern Campaign, 1781, From Guilford Courthouse to the Siege of York. Narrated in the Letters from Judge St. George Tucker to his Wife," ed. by George Washington Coleman Jr. *The Magazine of American History,* VII (July 1881), 36–46, 201–16.

Van Cortlandt, Philip. "Autobiography of Philip Van Cortlandt, Brigadier General in the Continental Army." *Magazine of American History,* II, No. 5 (May 1878): 294.

Van Doren, Carl. *Mutiny in January.* New York: The Viking Press, 1943.

———. *Secret History of the American Revolution.* New York: The Viking Press, 1968.

Walpole, Horace. *Journal of the Reign of King George the Third.* 2 vols. London: Bentley, 1859.

———. *Memoirs of the Reign of King George the Third,* 4 vols. New York: G. P. Putnam's Sons, 1894.

Ward, Christopher. *The War of the Revolution.* New York: Macmillan, 1952.

Weigley, Russell, ed. *Philadelphia, A Three Hundred Year History.* New York: W. W. Norton Company, 1982.

Wertenbaker, Thomas Jefferson. *Father Knickerbocker Rebels: New York City During the American Revolution.* New York: Charles Scriber's Sons, 1948.

Wheeler, Richard, ed., with Bruce Caton. *The Voices of 1776: The Story of the American Revolution in the Words of Those Who Were There.* New York: Crowell, 1972.

Wickwire, Franklin, and Mary Wickwire. *Cornwallis: the American Adventure.* Boston: Houghton Mifflin Company, 1970.

Wilbur, C. Keith. *Revolutionary Medicine 1700–1800.* Old Saybrook, Conn.: Globe Pequot Press, 1997.

Wild, Ebenezer. "Journal of Ebenezer Wild." *Proceedings of the Massachusetts Historical Society,* Second Series, VI (1800–01).

Wildes, Harry Emerson. *Anthony Wayne, Trouble Shooter of the American Revolution.* New York: Harcourt, Brace, 1941.

Wilkinson, Eliza. *Letters of Eliza Wilkinson during the Invasion and Possession of Charleston, S.C., by the British in the Revolutionary War,* ed., Carolina Gripman. New York: Samuel Coleman, 1839.

Willcox, William B. *Portrait of a General: Sir Henry Clinton in the War of Independence.* New York: Knopf, 1964.

Williams, Beryl, and Samuel Epstein. *Francis Marion, Swamp Fox of the Revolution.* New York: Julian Messner, Inc., 1956.

Wilson, James Grant, and John Fiske, eds. *Appleton's Cyclopaedia,* 7 vols. Detroit: Gale Research Co., 1968.

Wilson, Joseph T. *The Black Phalanx: African American Soldiers in the War of Independence, the War of 1812 and the Civil War.* New York: Arno Press, 1968.

Wolf, Edwin. *The History of the Jews in Philadelphia from Colonial Times to the Age of Jackson.* Philadelphia: Jewish Publication Society of America, 1957.

Index